The Tragedy of Philosophy

The Tragedy of Philosophy
(PHILOSOPHY AND DOGMA)

SERGIJ BULGAKOV

Translated by Stephen Churchyard
Foreword by John Milbank

Angelico Press

Copyright © Angelico Press 2020
Foreword © John Milbank 2020

All rights reserved:
No part of this book may be reproduced or transmitted,
in any form or by any means, without permission

For information, address:
Angelico Press, Ltd.
169 Monitor St.
Brooklyn, NY 11222
www.angelicopress.com

978-1-62138-558-5 pb
978-1-62138-559-2 cloth
978-1-62138-560-8 ebook

Book and cover design
by Michael Schrauzer
Cover image:
Kazimir Malevich, *Dynamic Suprematism* (1915)

TABLE OF CONTENTS

Foreword by John Milbank ix
Translator's Introduction xxxv
Abbreviations lix
Author's Preface lxi

I. TYPES OF PHILOSOPHICAL CONSTRUCTION
1 The Nature of Thought 3
2 Characteristics of the History of Modern Philosophy 23
    A. Idealist systems 24
    B. Panlogistic systems 51
    C. Systems of substantiality:
       the philosophy of identity and monism 65

II. PHILOSOPHY OF TRIADICITY
1 The Philosophical Meaning of Triadicity; Excursus on Kant . . . 91
2 From Image to Archetype 123
3 The Postulate of Triadicity and Its Dogma 131

EXCURSES
I Excursus on Kant 159
    On transcendental apperception in Kant 159
II Excursus on Hegel 171
    1. Hegel's logic is an ontology and a theology 171
    2. The construction of the *Logic* 183
III Excursus on Fichte 207
    I. Exposition of the idea of a science of knowledge;
       On reality 207
    II. Critique of Fichte's theory 223
       1. *Ich-Philosophie* 223
       2. The Not-I and nature 225
       3. Fichte and Hegel 234

Index of Authors Named 237

FOREWORD

From Grammar to Wisdom

IT IS A GREAT PLEASURE TO WRITE THIS FOREWORD to Stephen Churchyard's lucid and careful translation of a very important text. Increasingly, Sergij Bulgakov is regarded as one of the major voices of twentieth-century theology that sounds even more resonantly in the twenty-first than that of most of his contemporaries. So far, however, it has been hard for English readers to gauge the full measure of his achievement. The major theological texts are now translated, but not hitherto all of the earlier philosophical ones. Since, for Bulgakov, theology and philosophy were a more or less seamless whole, this prevents a full comprehension of his thought and its purposes.

However, the present volume offers us one of his most crucial philosophical works, alongside *Unfading Light* (already translated) and *The Philosophy of the Name* (still untranslated). It can be interpreted, as its title suggests, as a theological critique of all philosophy as such, but more specifically it is a critique of German Transcendental Idealism and its three greatest exponents: Fichte, Hegel, and Schelling, besides being a critique of the thinker who made this philosophy possible, Immanuel Kant.

As passages in *Unfading Light* indicate, Bulgakov also conceived this exercise as part of his specifically Russian response to German culture as a whole.[1] His attitude to this culture was thoroughly ambivalent. Negatively, he regarded it as half-barbaric, whereas Russia and the Eastern Church for him sustained a continuous link to the ultimate Greek sources of Western civilization. By contrast, the Latin West, and still more the Teutons, had half-mangled this legacy, which contained at its core an anthropocentric art and a Platonic philosophy which interpreted this art as epiphanic. The Teutonic mangling is connected in the Russian theologian's mind with the Arian heresy which had especially appealed to the northern barbaric tribes. Thus he accuses the German tradition of being marked by an "Arian monophysitism." A failure to grasp correctly the dogmas of the Trinity and the Incarnation has supposedly engendered opposite and yet complicit tendencies both to a Faustian exaltation of the human ego

---

1 Sergius Bulgakov, *Unfading Light: Contemplations and Speculations*, trans. Thomas Allan Smith (Grand Rapids MI: Eerdmans, 2012).

and yet at the same time to a pantheistic spiritualism, reducing God to nature. Moreover, this has too frequently taken pessimistic forms, which Bulgakov thinks is connected to a barbaric refusal of a refined sensuality, of sexuality and of the feminine—variously exemplified by Luther, Böhme, and Wagner. German civilization has either lured us into the echo-chamber of the self or has grimly celebrated blind forceful striving, unilluminated by the disclosures of the beautiful.

All this was surely thought and written not without awareness of the disasters into which Prussian nationalism had led Europe at the time of the First World War. On the other hand, Bulgakov was of course equally aware of the catastrophe engulfing his own country during the same period. The Russian tradition is mainly castigated by him for an overly Oriental world-refusal which had taken variously quietist and hysterically ecstatic forms over the centuries. In his own epoch, of course, this had dialectically encouraged an unprecedently appalling reversal: an immanentism that was sheerly arid, atheistic, and mechanical, reducing not only religion but also art to economics.

In the face of these Russian diseases, the West and even specifically the German tradition offered for Bulgakov after all, if not a remedy, then at least a salve. As *Unfading Light* relates, it had to some degree rightly celebrated life in this world: the beauty of nature, participation in politics, and the practice of art. Furthermore, it had seen all these things as suffused with the divine. Much of Bulgakov's work can be interpreted as an attempt to do justice to the German sense of immanence while avoiding what he saw as the German descent into a gloomy pantheism, for which the totality of everything discloses literally nothing. It is equally and inversely the case that he attempts to do positive justice to the Western and most of all the German sense of anthropocentrism and subjectivity. Faust was not just to be condemned by the Russian master, but also to be redeemed. It is by no means irrelevant here to think of the great novelistic gloss upon Goethe written by his distant relative Mikhail: *The Master and Margherita*.

This double attitude towards German culture contains considerable delusion besides great insight. Too much is projected backwards in terms of a supposed continuity of Teutonic character: thus, in *Unfading Light* Eckhart is read too much through the lens of Jacob Böhme, whose mode of mysticism specifically follows Luther (though one could suggest that too many German scholars have themselves made the same mistake). And a pantheistic tendency is traced ultimately and again debatably to the Irish theologian of Aachen: John Scotus Eriugena. Yet in both cases it can seem as if Bulgakov goes on to reproduce different Russian versions of doctrines that he has repudiated in their "German" guise.

For example, he condemns Eckhart's notion of a *gottheit* beyond the God/Creation contrast, but then speaks himself of a deeper "Absolute" that only becomes "God" in relation to the world. Or again, he denounces Eriugena's talk of Creation as "Created God," but then himself proposes *Sophia* for a not totally dissimilar and problematically liminal role. He notably situates the divine ideas within Sophia rather than within the original Trinitarian Godhead, just as Eriugena places them with the immanent *primalitates*.

One can also observe that Bulgakov somewhat disguises the way in which he is developing (albeit with brilliance) *German* Romantic critiques of German Idealism — especially the thoughts of Jacobi, Hamann, Herder, Novalis, Friedrich Schlegel, and Humboldt. To a degree, he wants to claim all the "romance" for the Russian steppes and birchwoods, rather than the Rhineland, *Schwarzwald*, and the Baltic coast.

This ambiguity towards German theology and philosophy is most strikingly apparent in terms of Bulgakov's attitude towards Johann Gottlieb Fichte in the current work. His appropriation and critique of this philosopher lies surely at its core. This can seem strange insofar as the thesis of the book, as Churchyard so clearly explains in his introduction, is that philosophy inevitably falls into error and contradiction by ignoring the dogmas of revelation and specifically the doctrine of the Trinity. It is well-known that both Hegel and Schelling try to incorporate this doctrine into their respective philosophies: indeed it is impossible to comprehend them unless one takes this into account. By comparison, Fichte does no such thing: he does not mention the Trinity at all, even when writing at length about religion. For this reason Bulgakov says that Fichte was in effect the philosopher of a Jewish God, of a pure monotheism. And yet, it is apparent in the following text, and in later ones towards the end of his career, that Bulgakov much more derives his proposed Trinitarian ontology from an engagement with Fichte than he does with Hegel or even with Schelling. Why should this somewhat surprising fact be the case?

First of all and very simply, it is because he can more think of Fichte as offering an "Old Testament" that is nearer to being acceptable so far as it goes. By comparison, Hegel and Schelling are seen as articulating highly heterodox versions of Trinitarian metaphysics. But in the second place, there is something much more crucial which takes us back to the issue of the Faustian. Certainly, for Bulgakov, Fichte is the "Luciferian" thinker *par excellence*, trying, like Jonathan Swift's spider in *The Battle of the Books* (as Churchyard well notes), to weave all of reality out of his own selfhood. Bulgakov observes that this endeavor in effect goes in the opposite direction from all of philosophy hitherto, including even that of Kant: instead of trying to situate the subject amongst objects or things, or to locate subjectivity in being, it tries to position all things and all of being within the scope of the knowing self, taken as the "truly existing." However, the Russian thinker does not *only* regard this attempt as demonically perverse (though he does that); he *also* thinks that in a way this attempt is in continuity with the specifically Christian cultural and conceptual revolution which newly elevated *personhood*. Thus any metaphysics true to the Bible and to credal faith ought indeed to place the personal subject at the ontological outset. For this reason Bulgakov *retains* the Fichtean understanding of the self as the "truly existing."

What is more, this understanding can be regarded as in keeping with the greater Eastern Christian insistence on the "monarchic" primacy of the hypostasis of the *Father*, which Bulgakov, like so many Orthodox theologians, thought has been too often obscured in the West by a primacy of essence in the Trinity and by the added *filioque* clause in the Western creed that was in danger of suggesting a secondary and equally potent hypostatic origin in the Godhead. Thus the West had been in peril *at once* of reducing God to an impersonal essence *and* of a tritheistic approach to the Trinitarian persons, compounded by a tendency (running counter to an emphasis on their co-relational definition which Bulgakov supports) to identify the persons with particular psychological faculties.[2]

It is against this background that Bulgakov was inclined to take Fichte very seriously. Other factors were involved also: in particular, his awareness of the proximity of neo-Kantian thought to the Fichtean legacy. In

---

2   In reality, Bulgakov ascribes to the whole of Western Trinitarian theology exaggerations which tended to appear only in the High to Later Middle Ages.

a contemporary philosophical landscape from which neo-Kantianism has long vanished, this can seem to be no longer of relevance and one can readily suppose that Bulgakov's philosophical concerns were already outdated. He makes scarcely any mention or shows very much awareness of either Analytic philosophy or Phenomenology. However, contemporary scholarship (in part based on more detailed textual research) sometimes suggests that Fichte is the most crucial of all modern Continental philosophers: his problematic not only anticipated phenomenology, but also foreshadowed its deconstruction and the more recent Continental turn back towards metaphysics.[3] It not only took Idealism to a new extreme, but also suggested how neither Idealism nor Realism seem to be entirely coherent. Moreover, Bulgakov's own simultaneous linguistic reworking and yet critique of Fichte is not without echo in some exponents of the Analytic philosophy of language.

For these reasons, it may be that perhaps only today, in the first quarter of the twenty-first century, can we newly appreciate the relevance of Bulgakov's philosophy. What is more, when we realize how Bulgakov was revisiting the problematics that Fichte was trying to resolve in the wake of the critique of Kant, then we can get a sharper sense of the degree to which Bulgakov proposed a novel and specifically theological philosophy of his own. Indeed, his degree of philosophical inventiveness is perhaps unsurpassed amongst other modern systematic theologians.

If Bulgakov now appears after all prodigious rather than belated in foregrounding Fichte, then that is above all because he was aware of all the ambiguities in Fichte's thought, long before they have been more regularly stressed. For a start, he grasped that Fichte's shift beyond Kant to a more absolute idealism was also and paradoxically a move back towards constitutive metaphysical realism. This concerns initially the role of the knowing "I" in philosophy.

Kant had spoken of a "transcendental apperception" on the part of the subject as accompanying all of his "judgements of experience" and Bulgakov commends Kant's awareness that in all our judging we are always dimly aware of ourselves as knower. However, he also agrees with

---

3 See, for example, Walter E. Wright, 'Introduction,' in J. G. Fichte, *The Science of Knowing: J. G. Fichte's 1804 Lectures on the* Wissenschaftslehre (New York: SUNY, 2005), 1–20 and Andrea Bellantone, *La métaphysique possible: Philosophies de l'esprit et modernité* (Paris: Hermann, 2012), 191–220.

Fichte that this insight does not go far enough. For it is not possible merely to say, with Kant, that we assume our own knowing reality as a logical condition of the possibility of knowing. This pretends to lock our awareness into a mutually referential circle of mere appearance, such that it is supposed that our real, ontological, and "noumenal" self is concealed from us. But in reality this is absurd; everything is the other way around. We only know anything besides ourselves because we are, as Descartes said, directly aware of our own existence as thinking beings. Everything else that is thought is thought "for us," "posited" by us as a mode of our own self-thinking, else we would not be able to think it at all.

Moreover, Bulgakov points out that Kant also falls suspiciously silent even about transcendental apperception at a crucial point in the *Critique of Pure Reason*: namely, with respect to his transcendental aesthetic, which argues that space and time are transcendental assumptions of sensory awareness which allow the "schematization" of sensory information through the application of rational categories of the understanding.[4] By not, in this specific context, pointing out that we are also apperceiving ourselves when we apprehend space and time, Kant is suppressing the degree to which the self only knows itself as something that actually transcends space and time, inevitably intuiting itself as eternal, since it is always able to imagine itself elsewhere and in another moment, while being unable to think of itself in its experiencing selfhood as dead.

By ignoring this, Kant can suggest that the theoretical self is "trapped" in spatial and temporal perspectives, even while contradictorily regarding them as "merely subjective." Bulgakov's subtle Fichtean point here is that if Kant had considered apperception also with relation to *aesthesis*, if he had more allowed that space and time are encountered experientially always in terms of our sense of selfhood, then he could *also* have seen that, since the self thereby transcends space and time, in consequence space and time more objectively and realistically confront the self as something somewhat alien and external to it. Instead of doing that, Kant tries to secure the merely phenomenal reach of our theoretical categories by the fact of their supposed schematic applicability only to finite and specifically Newtonian space and time which are already taken to be

---

4 See the current text, and also Père Serge Boulgakov, *La Philosophie du Verbe et du Nom*, trans. Constantin Andronikoff (Paris: L'Age d'Homme, 1991), 85–112.

sheerly subjective frameworks. Thereby, as Bulgakov argues, the comprehensible is arbitrarily restricted by Kant to the temporarily sequential and spatially relational, not allowing for the equal objectivity of holistic coherence (as with the belonging of accidents to substance—which Kant reduces to external relation) that can be readily imagined, as with selfhood, as extending to infinity.

Because he perceived the inadequacy of the doctrine of transcendental apperception, Fichte consciously and explicitly returned to Descartes behind Kant. He grounded knowledge not in an "as it were" subject that is only apparent through her knowing of this or that, but in a directly perceived and fully real subject that is "absolute" in the sense that it transcends any particular content.[5] This is not in any way to speak of an illusory Lockean "punctual" self outside and before social and linguistic instantiation, but merely to note that the subject can indeed "ironically" stand back from any particular content—imagine herself as born elsewhere, undergoing totally other experiences, learning completely different languages, etc., which sometimes she may indeed actually do. It is for this reason that we have a sense of the universality of our subjectivity which allows us readily to say "we" alongside other people who are the existential possessors of quite different contents of experience.

The paradox of Fichte's position is that this direct realism about the subject is also the basis for his attempted absolute idealism. He argued that we have direct insight into the noumenal realm in terms of our own subjectivity: what we are, we also immediately act and will. We are not just "given" to ourselves, but are given as self-posited and as "self-made" in the sense that we cannot stand back from ourselves, we cannot not "go" with ourselves or not play our own parts. We are never an object to ourselves because as soon as we try to look at ourselves we displace ourselves by being exhaustively the self who is doing this looking. Thus to be a self is ineluctably to perform the self—we can assume a role, tell a lie, but it is always "I" who is doing so. This is the self as *Thathandlung*, as Fichte puts it. By the very token of the subject's *real* transcendence of any objectivity, we can never exit the circle of the self: we can always go

---

5 J. G. Fichte, *The Science of Knowing; The Science of Knowledge*, trans. Peter Heath and John Lachs (Cambridge: Cambridge University Press, 1997); *Introductions to the Wissenschaftslehre and Other Writings*, trans. Daniel Breazeale (Indianapolis, IN: Hackett, 1994).

somewhere else, but only by being ourself somewhere else. Subjectivity is a permanent metaphysical sentence of absolute lockdown, as it were. For this reason it further follows that we cannot affirm or "posit" the reality of anything save as a mode of our own self-awareness, or as in some sense a derivation from our own self-understanding. I cannot know the clock as a clock outside the accompanying reflexive awareness of myself using it to tell the time.

Moreover, we have no reason, as with Kant, to suppose that hidden essences of "things in themselves" lurk behind phenomena. This is all the more true because in the instance of our self-awareness we now have a direct insight into the noumenal, which Fichte has extended from Kant's practical to his theoretical reason, while somewhat fusing the two — since to "be" oneself is also immediately to "enact" oneself.

These two theoretical shifts, in combination, give the basis for Fichte's absolute idealist project. While he returned from Kant to Descartes and so to a certain realism about the self, he still entertained and sought to extend Kant's "critical" project which would found certainty in knowledge and not being, and so in a subjective starting point, not in being in general as, for example, with Spinoza. It then follows that the "critical" knowledge possessed by the subject, if it is to be certain knowledge and to overcome skeptical doubt as to its import, must now be an absolute knowledge of things in their appearance as being how they really are.

Moreover, since pre-Kantian speculation is still refused, the only way to ground this knowledge with certainty is to see these things in their very manifestness as derived from the subject. It is not that Fichte denied their external reality (as Berkeley is supposed to have done on the usual mistaken reading), but rather that he affirmed that all of their knowability was derived from the knowing subject. This subject does not actually make them, but she does entirely posit them insofar as they can be known. There is a certain anticipation of both Husserlian bracketing and Husserlian intentionality involved here.

All the same, and as with the neo-Kantians and Husserl in some of his phases, the loss of the *Dinge an sich* seems to reduce things to our awareness of them. However, and again as with phenomenology, there is some ambiguity: just because there is no longer any skeptical gulf between phenomena and noumena, phenomena start to assume a greater at least quasi-ontological weight than is the case with Kant.

And in fact a reversion to realism after all goes further than this in the case of Fichte. From the very outset of his reflections, although the self as absolute must be assumed, and assumed as prior to the contrast of subject and object, I and Not-I—in order that it may be a final ground which is more or less the immanent presence of God—Fichte also considers that this self can never directly appear to us, but remains, as it were, unconscious. Thus for him *sum ergo sum* precedes even *cogito ergo sum*. For as soon as we have started to enact ourselves consciously we are involved with the objective "Not I" with which we are in a co-constitutive relation. The Not-I or the object is really just as fundamental as the I, even though it *prevents* there being any absolute foundation after all. And since the I only first knows itself in encountering the Not-I, and yet the Not-I is only there at all as grounded in the I, it follows (in a very proto-postmodern manner) that the self is from the outset divided from itself, unable because of a primordial fall into reflection ever fully to know itself or existentially to be at one with itself.

In this way realism eats deconstructively into the very heart of Fichte's idealism. But equally, even though he tries to "deduce" all the structures of our knowing of external things from the conditions of our self-awareness, he admits that this attempt is never complete, rather in the way that phenomenological description will later prove "an infinite task." At the core of what we posit is always something that is obstinately after all just "there," confronting us in all its irreducible density, including Being as such. The latter cannot after all be spun out of our *Dasein*, with a pre-echo of Heidegger's philosophical dilemmas. Since these given appearances are for Fichte no longer floating on a sea of noumena with which they may have no intrinsic connection, his position at this point becomes *evidently more realist than that of Kant*. And he says so. The Not-I is bafflingly posited as irreducible for the I, as just given for it in an alien mode. Also, in contrast to Hegel, there is no logical route from the I to the Not-I in Fichte, and this is part of why he appealed more to Bulgakov. Nor is this difference between the two poles, subjective and objective, engulfed in a vitalist sea of nature, as for Schelling. Again, this was attractive to the Russian thinker.

Therefore, we can see how the Fichtean *Anstoss* or "push-back" of objective appearances involves much more genuine practical exteriority that the Kantian *noumena*.

All the same, there is nothing straightforward here and nothing, from Bulgakov's perspective, that clearly overcomes Jacobi's charges of nihilism and atheism as consequent upon the Fichtean attempt (again anticipating Husserl) to turn philosophy into a strict science. Fichte was always trying to overcome these charges, while not surrendering to Jacobi's perceived "fideism."[6] Indeed, as scholarship has now shown, his work was driven as much by Jacobi's simultaneous critique of both Kant and Spinoza as by his attempt to deepen the Kantian critique itself. Jacobi had charged that any rational foundationalism, in trying to suppress pre-rational presuppositions, tends to deny reality altogether in favor of an empty self-reference or an infinite regress. In order to meet this challenge, Idealism was forced to try to show that the rational subject could indeed do justice to and encompass all of the actually real, including both the subject and the object, both freedom and necessity (beyond Spinoza), both culture and nature in a complete system.[7]

Bulgakov correctly perceived that Fichte's system remained nonetheless thoroughly aporetic, in part because the latter grasped the radicality of Jacobi's challenge. For Fichte, the knowing subject is self-grounded and absolute. In consequence, the drive of philosophy towards full comprehension of everything has to be idealist in character. The recognition of a realism that cannot be overcome is indeed the recognition of a blockage for philosophy as such, even though it intrudes from the very outset of philosophical investigation. The self must seek to overcome this obstacle even in order to achieve an unproblematic self-recognition, but it cannot do so. Fichte "resolves" this cognitive and existential conundrum by declaring, somewhat like Kant, though in an altered way, the primacy of practical reason over theoretical. The practical will involves an endless drive to assert its own all-encompassing self-willing and free all-comprehending or positing of all that it knows. Ethics is grounded

---

6 Friedrich Heinrich Jacobi, 'Jacobi to Fichte,' in *The Main Philosophical Writings and the Novel Allwill*, trans. George di Giovanni (Montreal-Kingston: McGill/Queen's University Press, 1994), 497–536. Bulgakov in places accuses Jacobi of producing a surrogate of religious faith as ontological trust, yet surely makes the same move himself. Jacobi is rarely given his due because he wrote in an amateurish, journalistic idiom that makes other more professional thinkers consistently reluctant to admit the devastating direct brilliance of his insights and their crucial role in the later unfolding of all modern philosophy.

7 See Paul W. Franks, *All or Nothing: Systematicity, Transcendental Arguments and Skepticism in German Idealism* (Cambridge, MA: Harvard University Press, 2005).

in this will to absolute and uninhibited self-assertion.

Nonetheless (and here Bulgakov is arguably not quite fair to Fichte and somewhat disguises his more surreptitious borrowings from him) the real barriers that this subjective drive constantly comes up against include our encounters with other selves, whose equal absoluteness we are able to acknowledge just because we experience our own subjectivity as something undetermined and so potentially shared in common: the always latent sense of the "we." It is for this reason that Fichte faintly sustained (after Jacobi) some sense of the interpersonal or of an "I-Thou" consciousness. Yet the need to mediate between equally absolute poles gives rise in Fichte to the advocacy of a politics at once extremely liberal and resolutely totalitarian, as the British Hegelian Gillian Rose was fond of pointing out. Nothing can mediate between such subjective poles save a doctrine of private rights and nothing can guarantee our non-interference with each other's liberties save the most continual state surveillance and policing.[8] Ultimately then, in practice, it would seem that for Fichte the shared "we" is the unlimited political state committed to what Bulgakov would have understood as a total "economizing" of all human life where practical regulation, and not art and culture, is what we thereby fundamentally share in common.

But it is already at the gnoseological and ontological level that Bulgakov finds Fichte to be unsatisfactory. He is not content with the theoretically unresolved *aporia*. It is in this respect that he notes that, while Fichte proposes something like a shadow of the human imaging of the Second Person of the Trinity in terms of the "Not-I," which can also be seen as the inescapable "predicate" required to establish any reflective and effective "subject," he lacks altogether (unlike Hegel and Schelling) any inkling of the Third Person or of the grammatical copula. The I and the Not-I are not conjoined by Being or by an existential judgement because they always just kick against each other, being caught up in an endless and always unresolved agonistic tussle.

Bulgakov refuses this agonism in its ontological import, rather than as a contingent mark of our fallen propensities. He does so essentially by re-instating against Fichte the proto-Romantic and Romantic critiques

---

[8] J.G. Fichte, *Foundations of Natural Right*, trans. Michael Baur (Cambridge: Cambridge University Press, 2000).

that were levelled against him and to which he was constantly seeking to respond.

These critiques were basically threefold. First, as we have seen, Friedrich Heinrich Jacobi had suggested in relation to both Fichte and Kant that philosophy always arrives too late to secure any rational foundation of thought in subjective self-awareness. By the time we start to reflect, we are already existentially and culturally situated, have already embarked on a thousand ungrounded assumptions which we nonetheless require in order to be able to think at all. Taking ourselves on trust, we equally take on trust and with an equal certainty the real world that surrounds us. Fichte, with great intellectual respect, half-concedes Jacobi's point, and as we have seen allows that we cannot really catch up with our absolute selfhood. Yet unlike Jacobi he continues to insist that our subjectivity, which we have to assume from the outset, must *in principle* be fully self-transparent and thinkable, even though our doomed failure to do so results in an irresolvable antinomy that we cannot just push to the margins, as with the antinomies of Kant.

Significant here is Fichte's attitude towards religion. Jacobi had suggested that since we inhabit the real world necessarily "by faith," actually religious and mythical pre-comprehensions of our subjectivity cannot be displaced and must, to some degree, be trusted. Fichte instead thought that the only revelation that could be accepted was one which did not violate our *a priori* criteria for what a true revelation would be: namely, one that did not contradict our absolutely given rational philosophical understanding.[9] In consequence, for Fichte, God is really the finite and unblocked realization of the Absolute ego: indeed a pure monotheism with no Trinitarian inflection. Arguably, a kind of acosmism seems to ensue, since if the independence of the Creation can in any way "count" for God, he would be himself caught up in the agonistic tussles of understanding that Fichte had disinterred. It is this Behmenist route that Hegel and Schelling were indeed variously to explore.

It is here apparent that Bulgakov sides once more with Jacobi. Before human beings ever get to philosophy they have already made elective existential choices which they express in terms of myths and dogmas.

---

9 J.G. Fichte, *Attempt at a Critique of All Revelation*, trans. Garrett Green (Cambridge: Cambridge University Press, 2012).

Just because we can never catch up with ourselves, these shared decisions are unavoidable. The Idealist claim to surmount them or surpass them is deluded: either, as with Fichte's honesty, one runs into a cognitive *impasse*, or one succumbs to alternative and heterodox religiosities, as with Hegel and Schelling: gnostic mythologies which hover between acosmism and pantheism or agonistically combine both at different moments.

For this reason, Bulgakov thinks that no philosophy really escapes from religion: in reality, every philosophy is an attempt to think more clearly through various different religious presuppositions. This is what he claims for his own Christian philosophy: it is a reflection on Christian "myths" and "dogmas"—in the sense of primordial written teachings or cognitive reflections that have liturgically acquired such a collective status. Given his statement that philosophy is the *ancilla* of dogma and not of theology, one can validly conclude that Bulgakov in reality abolished the entire distinction between philosophy and theology. He is arguably the very greatest modern theologian just because he realized, like the Church Fathers, both Greek and Latin, that the only real Christian theologian is one who directly assumes the philosophical task in the light of the Holy Scriptures.

In another vital and linked respect, also, Bulgakov in effect agrees with Jacobi against Fichte. If the knowing subject is fully real, as for Descartes, and not just "transcendental," as for Kant, then we no longer have any warrant for staying with Kant's "critical" subjectivism. To know ourselves as a real living and thinking self is to know ourselves as situated in a world alongside other things and other selves with the same immediacy of cognitive trust. For this reason we need not see the always already co-given "Not-I" as a contradictory blockage to our understanding, nor even our divided self-hood as entirely irresolvable. We can instead think in more originally relational terms of a natural if selective blending of self with other and of different moments of our own self-hood in terms of a narrative coherence (as for Paul Ricoeur or Alasdair MacIntyre), albeit one that is never finitely complete.

This means that we must engage with Fichte's neglected *copula*. At this point we can invoke the second crucial proto-Romantic critique of Idealism that Bulgakov explicitly appeals to in the *The Philosophy of the Name* and which he is equally developing in the current work. This is the charge that Kant had ignored the philosophical import of language. In relation to

Fichte, this means that Bulgakov suggests that all becomes much clearer if we replace the supposed existential primacy of *logic* with the real existential primacy of *grammar*. Again and again, the Russian theologian suggests that the over-extension of logic in German Idealism from Kant through to Hegel leads to all sorts of argumentative *legerdemain* of which he is as disdainful from the Eastern margins of Europe as the British tend to be from the Western.[10] One should not pretend to be able to deduce even the knowledge of objects from our subjectivity as Fichte seeks to do, nor imagine that any proposed "deduction" of ontological categories can be anything more than the Aristotelian "rhapsody" of classification which, from Kant onwards, the Idealists sought in turn to try to escape.

Yet this is now, for Bulgakov, for a more than Aristotelian reason: it is because prior to any classification of things into substance, accident, and relation (these being the crucial poles of Aristotle's ten categories) lies the already-lived grammatical arrangement of things into subject, predicate, and copula. Every predicate is, for Bulgakov, a kind of universal idea, and the hypostatic subject is still more universal and open in character. However, there exists for him no simple priority between the two, and so the subject does not play any straightforward role of substance to which things just accidentally attach. For there can be no real, living subject prior to received and selected attachments and therefore any unproblematic sifting between substance and attribute, or between external and constitutive relations, is grammatically disturbed from the outset. Thus this entire work concludes that "Substance is a *living proposition* consisting of a subject, a predicate, and a copula."

Bulgakov's case, explicitly following Hamann, Herder, and Humboldt, is that philosophy goes astray if it seeks to transcend or escape the cultural (because linguistic) mediation of nature. In a sense he reads Fichte as half-conceding this, because the German philosopher had rightly concluded that when we say, for example, "the table is in the dining room," we are really saying "I can see that the table is in the dining room," in such a way that only by imbuing the table in a certain sense with our own subjectivity are we able to see the table at all. However, Bulgakov adds to Fichte that this circumstance reveals that we inevitably subscribe

---

10 Though of course one must note that other central European traditions from Bolzano through Frege to Tarski have been equally disdainful.

From Grammar to Wisdom

to a *grammatical ontology* that we cannot seriously refuse without lapsing into incoherence. The subject-predicate-copula structure of all human language reveals indeed that we can only perceive the world at all by animating it—and for this reason Bulgakov, in *Unfading Light*, cautiously endorsed "occultist" and esoteric natural philosophies.

However, this ontological "propositionality" also for him tells against Idealism and against Fichte. In a kind of admitted exacerbation of Fichtean insights, which the third Romantic current, that of the self-named actual "Romantics" Novalis and Friedrich Schlegel, had already sketched, we need to see that the only available subjectivity that we can inhabit is, in later Lacanian terms, "the subject of the statement" and not the sublimely inaccessible, though always assumed, "subject of enunciation."[11] If we do admit this beginning always already with the linguistic subject as the only available "I," then more drastically than Fichte we will see that we have also to admit the equal co-reality from the outset of the "Not-I" now taken in the mode of the predicate. For it is not just that the predicate always blocks our advance, requiring our integral retreat into ironic subjective reserve, it is also the case (as Fichte already in effect admitted) that without adopting some attachment to predicates, without appropriating them as properties of our selfhood—without, as Bulgakov sees it, *naming* ourself—we will not enter into subjectivity at all. We surpass negative irony, as Schlegel taught, when we positively embrace flashes of linguistic "wit" that are fragments of revelatory and participatory disclosure. Then our lives and the reality we inhabit can turn into continuous symbolic allegories.[12]

From such a perspective, there is in fact no easy distinction to be made between the subject and predicate positions, either in grammar or in reality. Thus, in *The Philosophy of the Name* Bulgakov stresses that every word as an "idea" is transcendentally prior to its grammatical position as a part of speech. This also means for him that the inflection of a word is genetically prior to linguistic structure and that for this reason the older languages are the inflected ones. There is a wholesale fluidity between

---

11   Novalis [Friedrich von Hardenberg], *Fichte Studies* (Cambridge: Cambridge University Press, 2003); *Philosophical Writings*, trans. Margaret Mahony Stoljar (New York: SUNY, 1997).

12   Friedrich Schlegel, *Philosophical Fragments*, trans. Peter Firchow (Minneapolis MN: University of Minnesota Press, 1997).

absolutely individual substance and the universal qualities that attach to it — they can always confusingly change places because they so radically require each other, just as a noun may turn into a verb or vice-versa.

Indeed, Bulgakov maintains that the claimed identity between subject and predicate that allows us to make sense at all is nonetheless grounded in an apparent nonsense that transcends the Law of Non-Contradiction. In order to achieve *any* locatable identity in the first place, the human subject or the thing taken in the subject-position has to claim that something also *is* without reserve what it is not. The table is round and brown, etc.; it also is neither of those things, and yet without them it cannot really be there at all. Likewise, I am not my name, my history, my location, etc., and yet without these things I also simply vanish. In terms of such considerations, Bulgakov declares that *any* name is at once both proper and empty and yet descriptive and universal, with only a series of relative variations of respective emphasis. One could well wonder if this approach does not entirely outflank that of Saul Kripke and his successors.

In terms, therefore, of the three fundamental grammatical and ontological positions, Bulgakov considers that he has exceeded and corrected Fichte.

First, the mysteriously fundamental subject whose circle we can never exit is nonetheless a co-situated subject in a sense less inherently problematic than it was for the German philosopher. If it has absolute depths coinciding with the divine presence, then this is not a problematic implied identity with God that we must ceaselessly and hopelessly endeavor to realize, but a given participation in his infinity mediated to us by symbolic nature and by the inspired signs and allegories of revealed religions.

Secondly, predicated objects are radically external to us and yet even their resistance is a gift of shared community in being. Our ceaseless advance towards the perspective of the divine Father is therefore also a quest for the perfectly answering and supplementing other. The Christian revelation has astonishingly shown us that this need not imply a quandary, whereby we alternatively lose the world in the absolute divine subjectivity, or else abandon transcendence through an attempted pantheistic dilation. For now we realize that God himself is the infinitization of our grammatical circumstance: he is only an absolute Paternal hypostasis because he is also Filial and Spiritual subjectivity.

From Grammar to Wisdom

Thus, where philosophy seeks to overcome grammar by absolutizing one or other of the grammatical poles—either the Subject (Fichte), the logical predicate (Hegel), or yet again the vital being of their combination (Schelling, Spinoza, and the pre-Socratics)—Christian theology keeps them all in play. The truth is not a logical displacement of our ontological grammar, which already embodied a mode of faith: it is rather the doctrine revealed to religious faith that this grammar, and so finite reality, remains fully in triple play because it is a participation in an infinite triunity.

Thus thirdly, the spiritual moment in God infinitizes also the copula. For Bulgakov, the linkage between subject and predicate is neither aporetic (Fichte) nor governed by logical negation (Hegel) nor yet either fated or darkly willed by nature (Schelling). Instead, the linkage is one of natural creativity and of specific art in the case of human beings. In all of nature the immanent and actively receptive hypostasizing power of God as Sophia is at work to link subject and predicate together as ineffable beauty and to overcome the ugliness of extrinsic matter (as opposed to intrinsic body) that is the result of the Fall. In human beings, as described especially in *Unfading Light*, this is simultaneously the work of conscious self-creation and of the recreation of nature in anticipation and prospective enabling of the final resurrection.

Our selfhood is not entirely and tautologically self-made as with Fichte, as from the very outset we co-create ourselves alongside our environment, and all of this process is but a participated if active reception of the divine creative act. On the other hand, we do not just "posit" external things according to an intentionality that is just an "internal" imaginative creativity which half just accepts these things as resisting us and half tries to deduce them from pre-given *a priori* structures of subjectivity. The only external creativity involved here is a sheerly arbitrary attempt to reduce the impact of all external obstacles, to just will them away, economically to master and control them.

By contrast, Bulgakov's sophiological and more Romantic vision actually *increases*, beyond Fichte, and with Novalis and Schlegel, the sense of an external creativity over things which even, as with Novalis, is granted a kind of "magical" reach. Thus we do not just posit those things with which we identify: in re-shaping them and bringing them under our purposive and spiritual (not instrumental) control, we actually "bring them to birth" in participation of the eternal Paternal generation of the Son.

Thus the somewhat difficult point to grasp here is that the Romantic switch to a greater realism *also* allows a greater external reach for a human creativity which is neither the operation of a given logic, nor merely the assertion of will, but rather the realization along with things of a shared teleology only intuited in the very process of co-construction. In the very long term, one can somewhat simplifyingly venture that Idealism is the remote offspring of Plotinus, who stressed the internal creative action of the soul on the body (which is not to be denied), and of Romantic Realism, the remote offspring of the later neoplatonists after Iamblichus, who stressed also the creative action of soul-plus-body on the surrounding cosmos as a ritual action which allowed the synergic or "theurgic" working of the divine descent through ritual.

Bulgakov explicitly understood himself as lying within this legacy via the Christian mediation of Dionysius and Maximus, though he distinguished (however problematically) between the "sophiurgic" operation of art and the more humanly passive and solely divine theurgic operation of the liturgy or *Opus Dei*. The redeemed Faust is for him a much more effective if purely white *magus*, one might say.

It is indeed the theurgic dimension which serves to link Bulgakov's critique of philosophy to his specific mode of Christian piety. *The Philosophy of the Name* is a long and extremely sophisticated defense of the Russian "Name worshippers" in terms of a complete philosophy of language. It is legitimate, Bulgakov thinks, to say that "the Name of Jesus is God," though not, like the more extreme onomaphiles (Rasputin?), to say that "God is the name of Jesus," because this is to confuse Subject with predicate. We should not say that the absolute Paternal hypostasis is exhaustively the name any more than he is the incarnate God-Man or even the Second Person of the Trinity. Nevertheless, the predicate position is not subordinate to the subject position and can even be raised to co-hypostaticity as most perfectly achieved within God himself—since it is there paradoxically required to exist as a co-subject out of the existence of the primal subject itself. Similarly, I am not my name, and yet, without my name in the widest sense, I am not me at all. Unidentified, I am so lost that I do not really exist, for existence or "being" is not, as for Hegel, an empty starting point identical with nothing, but instead always arises as the third position of attachment.

From Grammar to Wisdom

To be is for something to be this or that in various modes or degrees. *Not*, for Bulgakov, in the Kantian sense that being is a mere existential copula that is not a predicate, but rather in the sense that the copula is always a judgement as to the real holding in place of the predicate or not—such that one could infer that, for the Russian thinker, "possible" or fictional Thalers (Kant's famous example) do in fact really exist in some measure or other. Thus, for Bulgakov, Being is indeed not directly a predicate, but it is never detached from the judgement of predication.

Because, as we have seen, a name for Bulgakov is indeterminately general or proper, descriptive or vacuously nominative, he insists after Plato's *Cratylus* that no word and no name is ever *purely* arbitrary. Language (following Hamann and explicitly disagreeing with Gregory of Nyssa) cannot have been simply invented by human beings, because everything human already presupposes its existence and we cannot really imagine a world outside our articulation of it. For Bulgakov, it is literally the world that speaks through us, and all language is originally poetic manifestation. Every word is really a disclosure of the "idea" behind things which things themselves cannot fail to proclaim. In consequence, a defense of the Platonic sense of the universal goes along with a defense of the primacy of language. A forest is not a manifold exemplification of an abstract idea of a tree, nor is it plausibly an accidental evolution. Instead, it is actually more rigorous to think of every tree as really striving to realize one single, absolutely named most proper tree with which it is somehow identical. For were trees only realizing a blueprint, one might ask why they so constantly vary and alter, or why they generate in time at all. Similarly, Bulgakov thinks that the Bible is right to speak of languages as fragments of one lost language *rather than* being various attempts to express a shared conceptuality. Outside language, such a conceptuality is meaningless, so the fact that translation is possible suggests a constant struggle to reunify language and recover a lost shared tongue, which attempt he thinks was initially realized on the day of Pentecost.

It follows that for him the name Jesus is the name of names and the word of words which unites us to the eternal Word and begins to usher in the eschatological and more final reversal of Babel. Just as the Incarnation is only an abstract affirmation unless Christ continues to be manifest to us through the shape of ritual and sacred images (which themselves bear named inscriptions), so also it must be conveyed through specific language. The name Jesus Christ, like all names, sustains a complex freight of association, including both acquired and buried onomatopoeic resonance. This is why in the Bible God names the world into being, and throughout its texts naming and re-naming are clearly regarded as ontological and revelatory events.

All this for Bulgakov suggests a Biblical metaphysics, pre-intimated by Plato, which in exalting naming or the proposition exceeds mere rational or logical classification. Reality as such, spoken into being by an infinite Subject, is itself linguistic or propositional. It is surely highly significant that, somewhat before Bulgakov, the Italian priest-philosopher Antonio Rosmini had come to a similar conclusion in his massive *Teosofia*, also in part through a reflection on Fichte and also in explicit connection with the elaboration of a Trinitarian ontology.[13]

In terms of such an ontology, however, one might conceivably detect ambiguities in Bulgakov. Is he not too Fichtean after all? In the later long article *Capita de Trinitate*, he even speaks of God as a single hypostasis appearing in three subjective moments.[14] Is there a lurking modalism here not so unlike that of the also Fichte-influenced Karl Barth? This, however, would be to fail to understand Bulgakov's radical purposes.

Throughout his *opus*, one of the intentions of his focus on the divine Wisdom is to undercut any too simplistic a duality of hypostasis and essence, whether in the case of the Trinity or of Christology. Yes, in either case the difference of the terms is trying to indicate two incommensurable and therefore non-competitive planes, but this must not be allowed to override their nonetheless paradoxical fusion, on pain of impairing the divine simplicity. Thus Bulgakov toys with a certain conceptual inversion: although it is less true than the reverse orthodox formula, it is not quite untrue that Christ is also two persons (as he is an "atomic" human individual, as Aquinas eventually allows) in one divine nature, since God cannot be divided. Likewise, though it is less true than orthodoxy, it is not quite untrue that God is one hypostasis in three natures. Here Bulgakov notably pleads the Cappadocian doctrine of *tropes* in his favor: in some ineffable way, the three divine persons possess three different though not divided "characters" which implies a certain incomprehensible

---

13 Antonio Rosmini, *Teosofia* (Milan: Bompiani, 2011).

14 Sergius Bulgakov, '*Capita de Trinitate*' [in three installments] in *Internationale Kirkliche Zeitschrift* 26.3 (1936): 144–67; 26.4 (1936): 210–30; 35.1–2 (1945): 24–55.

variation of "kind." Conversely, the unity of nature cannot be thought of as anything other than the original and absolute hypostaticity of the Father. In a sense, the Persons of the Son and the Spirit are not "new" persons, but necessary co-original manifestations of one and the same Personhood. To a degree, indeed, Bulgakov remains Fichtean here—the I itself requires the Not-I and its linkage to it. But as we have seen, he has abandoned Fichtean self-making of the I and mere positing of the Not-I in favor of a relational self-making through a creative giving birth to the other which still "surprises" in its upshot its originator—just as a human parent is always amazed by its new baby and it is as if he had always been there.

It is for this reason that in Bulgakov's theology the divine essence as Sophia is not exactly impersonal, even if it is not exactly a "fourth hypostasis," except when God reflects on his own essence as "loving love" in an action that is co-terminous with the external creation. The result of this initial reflection and initial ecstatic giving is the bringing into being of the Plotinian sphere of the intellect or *nous*, which for Bulgakov is identical with Sophia as the world-soul.

But what prevents, in Bulgakov, an unambiguous hypostatization of Wisdom, either within God or within the Creation, is his important grammatical *qualification* of any outright personalism which would despise the blind witness of *things* and so of sacramentality. It is in this respect very important that his primary *vestigium trinitatis* is *not* social and relational, even though he builds up to that, such that the ultimate "predicate" is the *Thou* and the ultimate copula is the "he" which then allows the sophiological shared essential but personal "we" to come into being. Rather, his consistently very high valuation of the bodily, the sensual, the sexual, the feminine (as he sees it) and the sacramental, requires him to insist that the personal cannot emerge at all without a sort of sublimated fetishistic attachment to things, which alone supplies us with any "character" or operable content. Adam, he declares, was lost in Eden, which lacked for him any charm till the arrival of the disclosive Eve. He did not require simply a companion, but rather an ultimate attachment to another freely self-expressive "thing" like himself, with which he could be corporeally united.

In a lesser way, all our speaking involves a continuous appropriation of things, including of those things that are spoken of in terms of their appropriation by other things, like the inclusion of the table in the dining-room. For this reason, Bulgakov declares that the whole of a human life is actually one long string of propositions, or alternatively one long continuous proposition. But this is not just a process of realization; it is also a further disclosure of the world through its further poetic re-creation. It is ontology as autobiography and shared history, because reality itself is both autobiographical and historical.

In consequence, the second, predicamental moment in the current book is first impersonal before it is personal and is even identified with *essence*, with which the primary hypostasis of the self must identify if it is to become a real person at all. This means that, perhaps rather surprisingly, Bulgakov consistently associates essence, both divine and created, with the Second Person of the Trinity, including its created echo. One might say that for him, and in very Johannine terms, we have to see that the Son is the complete Word and utterance *before* we can grasp the complete import of his personhood and eternal birth.

The essential rather than the purely personal also matters to Bulgakov insofar as, according to Trinitarian doctrine, it is essence, albeit a personifying sophianic essence, that is *one*, whereas hypostases are in principle plural. The lurking and somewhat disturbing emptiness of our self-hood witnesses to us that there can be other selves, in a way that the continuity of the earth, air, sea, sky, and light does not, nor inversely, the absolute specificity of *this* rock, beach, cottage or jug, and so forth.

The problem with philosophy, to reiterate, is that it tries to escape this solidarity of grammar with ontology, whereas the Incarnation of the Word in person reminds the Universal Adam, and so all of us, of the primacy of the propositional judgement. As Churchyard well says, the point here is not simply to rebuke philosophy, to say that it is all a terrible mistake, since even a philosophy that has tried impossibly to shake off its religious moorings still bears a negative and providential witness when it is foundering in the immanentist sea. If it is a *tragic* endeavor, then so too for Bulgakov are human art and human economy. The artist is always, like the great poet Pushkin, prey to melancholy, as he realizes that he cannot ever produce the work that is within him to bring forth. The economist is equally so prey, because he is always half-aware that what Bulgakov calls his "gray magic" is an often meaningless substitute for the white Adamic magic of powerful naming, while only half-avoiding the black magic of demonic control of natural forces for the mere sake of such control. As the "art of concepts," philosophy shares in both frustrations, but can begin to be redeemed insofar as it becomes also an exposition of Christian dogma.

As we have seen, and as the reader of this work can further verify for herself, Bulgakov's understanding of Fichte is pivotal for his work in both philosophy and theology. His attitude towards the German idealist is at once extremely positive and extremely negative. What does this double stance imply for Bulgakov's attitude towards the modern "critical" turn in philosophy as such? In my view, he does not really accept it and only finds it to be of value to the degree that he can subvert it and turn it metacritically against its own assumed intentions.

He finds it to be of value, to reiterate, to the degree that it exalts the human, the subjective, and so, the personal. But the Russian theologian *refuses* the post-Kantian assumption that to emphasize the subject is to turn critically away from metaphysics and towards the primacy of epistemology. To the contrary, he emphasizes here and in *Unfading Light* that metaphysics itself *first appeared* as a break with the "physics" and monism of pre-Socratic philosophy when Socrates started to enquire into himself and linked this inquiry to transcendent, theological origins. It would then follow that the later deepening of such enquiries from Augustine through to Kierkegaard to Bergson are naturally linked (as indeed these three thinkers variously supposed) to a renewed insistence on the metaphysical in an explicitly Platonic or neoplatonic sense. In this context, Descartes is a profoundly ambivalent thinker (as scholarship increasingly attests), who can be read either in terms of a deepening of the metaphysical or of a modern turn to the epistemological. As we have seen, Bulgakov construes Fichte's critique of Kant as a return to the metaphysical import of the Cartesian *cogito* which Kant had incoherently suppressed, while at the same time refusing Fichte's clinging to an absolute subjective foundationalism which absurdly tries to erect metaphysics within a purely epistemological space that has already been called into question.

That is to say, once I admit that I am as a knowing subject fully real and not just (as for the theoretical Kant) real as knowing, it is indeed a kind of Satanic delusion to then try to suppress, after all, the secondariness of knowing to existence (which Fichte actually admitted, beyond even Descartes, as we have seen) and to ignore the co-primacy in reality of all things and other people around me. For one now lacks even Kant's skeptical excuse to be a sad spider, spinning away in a dusty library corner.

Instead of claiming Bulgakov as a modern, post-critical thinker, one can rather situate him, alongside Augustine and the other named thinkers, as another great Christian theorist who, by re-emphasizing subjectivity, also insisted on the primacy of a constitutive metaphysics as a holistic speculation which our very existential perplexity cannot really evade.

However, he does this in a novel way which is metacritical as well as pre-critical, since he rounds upon critical thought by stressing the primacy of language beyond the remit of most pre-critical thought. Quite simply, the primacy of the modern knowing subject, or the subject of enunciation, is trumped by pointing out that this is always also the grammatical subject, or the subject of the statement. But with the primacy of the statement comes also the co-primacy of the predicated thing and its copulative link to the subject.

All the same, this Romantic and metacritical neo-realism is not just identical with pre-critical realism, to the extent that, first of all, it emphasizes that our only access to the external real is through expressive appropriation. And secondly, to the extent that it realizes (like the early G. E. Moore and Alfred North Whitehead)[15] that it cannot actually think any reality whatsoever outside the assumption that all of nature approaches in its structures the subjective and the propositional. This is not, however, a matter of our fated and self-deluded propensity to project. To the contrary, the fluidity of words as between subjects and predicates as identified by Bulgakov rather shows that we only begin to be as subjects at all by identifying with predicates already bearing within themselves some mode of subjectivity. A kind of totemism is at work here: I do not wrongly see the stream as a nymph; I only begin to have any sense of self in the first place by partly identifying with the stream, as with stone and tree and plant and bear and so forth.

All this amounts to an implicit claim in Bulgakov that a real linguistic turn *returns us* to metaphysical speculation rather than deepening the

---

15 See Fraser MacBride, *On the Genealogy of Universals: The Metaphysical Origins of Analytic Philosophy* (Oxford: Oxford University Press, 2018).

Kantian epistemological project. This then constitutes his challenge to Analytic philosophy at least in its Fregean and Wittgensteinian modes.

It is also clear that Bulgakov's preference for Fichte over Kant is because Fichte's hyper-critique of Kant in one dimension points back towards realism. And following Hamann and Herder, the Russian thinker also applied his linguistic critique to Kant himself. The latter is accused of falsely trying to distinguish "judgements of appearance" as merely subjective from "judgements of experience" taken as objective, in the sense that they fall under shared categories of understanding, especially of causality.[16] Thus "I feel sad" is subjective, but not "he has fallen over" or even "Mary has caused John to feel sad by spurning his love." Bulgakov argues that, to the contrary, the fact that we can take simply "he feels sad" as objective suggests that objectivity is already sufficiently secured by propositional grammar and not by a supposed placing of sensory or affective information under *a priori* conceptual categories. Because all of our understanding is linguistic, every appearance is already, if reflexively, judged as an experience, and nothing not already schematized or categorized by language ever appears to us at all. We have therefore no warrant for distinguishing the purely empirical from the purely rational, the *a posteriori* from the *a priori*, or the synthetic from the analytic. In consequence, a more "internal" event of feeling is just as objective as a more external event of falling over, and the latter is no more certain or purely factual in character.

It can therefore be concluded that Bulgakov's critique of modern, non-religiously-based philosophy by no means accepts its "critical" starting point, which for him is identical with this bracketing of religion. Instead, he offers us a Trinitarian ontology which newly accentuates the place of the subjective person only because it also newly accentuates the importance of things, of community, and of creativity with respect to all of nature, with Humanity at its crown. A still more Biblically-infused philosophy can in the future lead us through grammar to wisdom, since the lesson of both is that personhood and essence are to be distinguished, yet never divided.

John Milbank
The Feast of Pentecost, 2020

---

16 Bulgakov, *La Philosophie du Verbe et du Nom*, 85–112.

INTRODUCTION

On the Idea of a Christian Materialism

1

On 28 January 1919 the remains of St Tikhon of Zadonsk (1724–1783), one of the most important saints in the Orthodox Church, were opened up in the Monastery of the Mother of God in Zadonsk in Voronezh province. Tikhon had been canonized as recently as 1861. . . . The brochure published by the Holy Synod at the time of his canonization claimed: "Notwithstanding the fact that it has lain in the earth for seventy-eight years, the body of St Tikhon remains uncorrupted, thanks to divine grace." When his tomb was opened, however, it was said to contain a bandaged skull, various bones plus "a mountain of ordinary rags and wadding."[1]

IN THE YEARS AFTER THE RUSSIAN REVOLUTION, ONE significant cultural front opened up by the Bolsheviks was the desecration of Christian shrines and relics. Remains and relics of the saints would be uncovered and taken apart, in order to show that they had been as subject as any other human thing to time's work of decay—rather as, centuries earlier, in western European reformations, the putative "idols" of the church had been smashed or given to children to play with, in order to prove, demystifyingly, how powerless were these objects supposedly filled with sacred power. Repeatedly, the same story was told: the reliquary or coffin had been broken open to discover "nothing but" corrupted human remains or dry bones.[2]

Such cultural aspects of the Revolution may perhaps seem unremarkable or even unimportant when compared with, say, the Bolsheviks' capture of the machinery of state, appropriations of land and capital, and

---

1 S. A. Smith, "Bones of Contention: Bolsheviks and the Struggle against Relics, 1918–1930," *Past and Present* 204 (August 2009): 1–40.

2 On the Reformation practice of giving "idols" to children to play with, see Joe Moshenska, "Spenser at Play," *PMLA* 133.1 (January 2018): 19–35.

The Tragedy of Philosophy

the scale of the losses of life experienced in its first two decades. But for the Russian theologian, political economist, and critic Sergij Bulgakov, they formed what was clearly one of the most painful episodes of his life. Bulgakov had, after a childhood in a poor clerical family and a youth as a seminarian, become a convinced "legal" Marxist, a believer in crisis as a structural rather than an accidental feature of capitalism, and in the possibility of a different social order which would leave capitalism behind altogether. Without altogether abandoning *these* features, at least, of his early Marxism, he had, however, lost faith in what he considered to be Marxism's scientism, necessitarianism, and immanentism. He had moved, at first, as the title of a collection of his essays had announced, *From Marxism to Idealism*; and then, impelled partly by a vision, at his four-year-old son's funeral in 1909, of the opening of heaven itself, he had returned to the Orthodox church, and had, eventually, taken holy orders.[3] Bulgakov was ordained in January 1918, and was a significant actor in the historic Council of Moscow which had opened on 15 August 1917 in order to reconsider the Russian church's governance and mission in the world—a reconsideration which was, however, quickly overtaken by political events.[4]

Just at the moment when Bulgakov had decisively turned to the church, then, Russia itself seemed decisively to be bent upon destroying it; and it was at this juncture that the desecrations of relics made themselves felt. Part of Bulgakov's response was to write a moving essay about them which remained unpublished until after his death.[5] From it we can learn much about the orientation of Bulgakov's whole inter-war project in theology, a project whose philosophical medium or idiom (but not its "foundation") still awaits full elucidation.

The essay on desecrations is not simply an expression of pain or rage, but effects a subtle and implicit meditation on two terms central

---

3 For Ivan Bulgakov's funeral, see, amongst several other places in which Bulgakov recounts the story, "Iz intimnago pis'ma," in *Avtobiograficheskiya Zametki*, ed. L. A. Zander (Paris: YMCA-Press, 1946), 67–70.

4 Catherine Evtuhov, *The Cross and the Sickle: Sergei Bulgakov and the Fate of Russian Religious Philosophy* (Ithaca and London: Cornell University Press, 1997), 189–206. For the Council of Moscow, see Hyacinthe Destivelle, *Le Concile de Moscou (1917-1918): La création des institutions conciliaires de l'Église orthodoxe russe* (Paris: Éditions du Cerf, 2006).

5 "On Holy Relics (in response to their desecration)," in *Relics and Miracles: Two Theological Essays*, trans. Boris Jakim (Grand Rapids, MI and Cambridge, UK: Eerdmans, 2011), 1–40.

to Marxist theories of religion: "fetishism" and "materialism." Instead of denying that there is anything fetishistic about the veneration of relics, or providing sub-rationalist justifications for that veneration, Bulgakov admits the charge. God's kenosis in the incarnation, Bulgakov suggests, means that, in so far as "He lives in space and time," then "places and times are not a matter of indifference in this Being of God's."[6] God is not indifferently present everywhere, as though He were just an indifferent and univocal equivalent for "being." "[A]s the God-Man He lived in the Holy Land and sanctified by His presence only certain definite places."[7] Christianity will inevitably be "materialist" in this sense, at least: that the Word became flesh. For this reason, Bulgakov undertakes what he calls a "defense of fetishism," of a "righteous, pious fetishism" whose model is Jacob's, after his sleep, having anointed the top of the pillar and his having named it Bethel.[8] "When a savage worships some stone, associating it with the presence of some lover or evil spirit, the falsity of this worship consists not in worship of the stone but in worship of the spirit itself..."[9] In other words, animism is not materialism proper at all. It is a *spiritualistic* materialism—just as is, ultimately, any materialist metaphysics which superstitiously awards to mere matter those powers and freedoms which are possessed only by persons. Bulgakov thus believes deterministic or necessitarian or evolutionistic materialisms to be much more superstitious than they think themselves. For a contemporary equivalent, we might think of the way in which a scientistic writer such as Richard Dawkins superstitiously personified the gene as "selfish."

Bulgakov, in this essay and elsewhere, remains uncompromising in his opposition to any metaphysical materialism, to a materialism claiming that matter is what truly is. The term "materialism" remains, throughout his work, pejorative, except in this single context of a "religious" materialism, a "materialism" which could account for the way in which times and seasons, places and persons, can come to be invested with sacred meaning. (Without such investments, Bulgakov bluntly asserts, there is no religion, but at most "religious philosophy": "this fetishism

---

6 "On Holy Relics," 15.
7 Ibid.
8 Ibid., 14.
9 Ibid.

is an inalienable trait of religious phenomenology without which there could be no religion."[10]) Human beings are not spiritual beings, but "spiritual-corporeal" ones, and "[t]his ontological essence of man contains the reason why, in the divine liturgy, in the mysterious side of the Church, there is manifested that which is called—at times with censure, and at times defiantly—religious materialism."[11] Bulgakov had used this phrase, "religious materialism," eight years earlier, at a crucial juncture in his turn away from philosophical idealism and back towards the church. In his lecture on "Nature in the philosophy of Vladimir Solovyov," Bulgakov had attributed the idea to Solovyov, and had spoken of it as Solovyov's response to the bad choice between the two "nightmares" of contemporary thought, "mechanical materialism and idealistic subjectivism." "Religious materialism," it appears, affirms that human faith is spiritual-corporeal, is embodied as well as thought, willed, felt, believed. It refuses, as ultimately heretical, any philosophical idealism. Yet at the same time, "religious materialism" is the *opposite* of a mechanical, spiritualistic, or metaphysical materialism.

We can sense some of what was personally at stake for Bulgakov in this risky and only apparently heterodox phrase, "religious materialism," from a quotation from William James's *Pragmatism* which he introduces to help explain it:

> To anyone who has ever looked on the face of a dead child or parent the mere fact that matter *could* have taken for a time that precious form, ought to make matter sacred ever after. It makes no difference what the *principle* of life may be, material or immaterial, matter at any rate co-operates, lends itself to all life's purposes. That beloved incarnation was among matter's possibilities.[12]

---

10 Ibid., 16. Compare, on the same page, the following: "[o]utside of space and time, i.e., outside of holy places, acts, and objects, cult does not exist; and outside of cult, religion does not exist (the most we can have is religious philosophy)."
11 Ibid., 8–9.
12 William James, *Pragmatism: A New Name for Some Old Ways of Thinking* (New York: Longmans, Green, and Co., 1911), 95, quoted in Bulgakov, "Priroda v filosofii Vl. Solov'eva," in S.N. Bulgakov, *Sochineniya v Dvukh Tomakh*, ed. S.S. Khoruzhij, 2 vols. (Moscow: Nauka, 1993), 1:17–46; 18–19.

Bulgakov's own son had died the year before. The *face* of the dead beloved is the decisive evidence for "religious materialism" not only for this immediately powerful personal reason, however, but also because of the intimate connection of the face with personhood itself—especially for Russian devotional thought. *Litso* can mean either "face" or "person"; *lik* is both an archaic word for "face" or "countenance," and a term for the representation of a face on an icon. The face makes both philosophical idealism *and* metaphysical or mechanical materialism operable only with difficulty. It takes a complex act of willed self-alienation to look at a human face and to see it merely as a collection of meaningless atoms; and the more one loves the person, the more impossible such self-alienation will become. It takes a complex act of willed self-alienation to think of one's absent or deceased beloved as a perfectly disincarnated spirit, without mentally seeing their face, hearing their voice; and the more one loves the person, the more impossible such self-alienation will become. Precisely because human love cannot be made either purely material or perfectly disincarnate, the human face of the loved other person is the very figure of a "religious materialism." All Bulgakov's theology can be said to test itself, continually, against this image.

2

THE BOOK WHICH YOU HOLD IN YOUR HANDS WAS written at one of the most testing moments of Bulgakov's long expulsion from his homeland. Before the Great War, Bulgakov had been a celebrated public intellectual, an important member of the reform-minded *intelligentsiya* of pre-revolutionary Russia. Shortly after the revolution, he lost his post at Moscow University, and was obliged to move to the Crimea, where he briefly taught political economy and theology, before losing that work too when the city was captured by the Bolsheviks in 1920.[13] In the midst of these personal disasters, and without access to a research library, Bulgakov wrote two works still more difficult, more angular, and more original than any of his previous writings: the *Philosophy of the Name* (still untranslated into English), which remained

---

13   Evtuhov, *The Cross and the Sickle*, 230.

unpublished until after his death; and the present work, *The Tragedy of Philosophy, or Philosophy and Dogma*, which was published in 1927 in a German translation by Alexander Kresling, but in Russian only long after Bulgakov's death.[14] These works represented the beginning of Bulgakov's final transition to the mature works of theology which have now emerged as his most significant and lasting achievement: the "minor trilogy" of his angelology, Mariology, and his study of John the Baptist, and the "major trilogy" on God-manhood [*bogochelovechestvo*] of Christology, pneumatology, and ecclesiology, with its posthumously published epilogue in the commentary on Revelation which has very recently been translated into English.[15]

The historian Catherine Evtuhov has persuasively suggested that the catastrophe of Bulgakov's dismissal and exile may have been precisely the necessary shock which produced his mature theology:

> To be nobody can be immensely liberating. His "death" seems to have been an emancipation; his soul ceased to be tied to earthly political concerns and became free to repent and pray and be a passive observer of past life.[16]

Evtuhov also notes the distance from Vladimir Solovyov which the new life and work implied. She quotes from a telling letter to Pavel Florensky which Bulgakov wrote in 1926.

> In Soloviev I can see a certain religious immaturity, with its properties — dilettantism, experimentation, flights of fancy, and so on. *Tel quel* he is simply religiously unconvincing and unauthoritative, not an elder, but merely a writer (incidentally

---

14 Sergius Bulgakov, *Die Tragödie der Philosophie*, trans. Alexander Kresling (Darmstadt: O. Reichl, 1927); "Tragediya Filosofii (Filosofiya i Dogmat)," in S. Khoruzhij, ed., *Sochineniya v Dvukh Tomakh*, 2 vols. (Moscow: Nauka, 1991), 1:309–518. A French translation of *Filosofiya Imeni* has been made by Constantin Adronikof: *La Philosophie du Verbe et du Nom* (Lausanne: L'Age d'Homme, 1991); and its sixth chapter has been translated into English by Boris Jakim: "The Name of God" in Bulgakov, *Icons and the Name of God* (Grand Rapids, MI and Cambridge, UK: Eerdmans, 2012), 115–66.

15 Sergij Bulgakov, *The Apocalypse of John: An Essay in Dogmatic Interpretation*, trans. Mike Whitton, revised by Michael Miller (Münster: Aschendorff Verlag, 2019).

16 Evtuhov, *The Cross and the Sickle*, 237.

I think precisely the same of Dostoyevsky)... True life in the Church signifies not just overcoming, but becoming free of or outgrowing Soloviev; here he gives no nourishment.[17]

The paradox of Bulgakov's Parisian theology is that while it has taken a conscious distance from the whole tradition in which Bulgakov was nurtured and by which he was formed, it is precisely by its having been formed through Solovyov (and Florensky), and through his own independent study in the history of philosophy and especially in German idealism, that Bulgakov's becomes the singular and profoundly creative theology it is. His philosophical formation, in other words, has been internalized and put at the service of the church in such a way that it is not the "foundation" of his thinking but something like its second skin, the element or idiom in which it strives to interpret and to make intelligible the deep paradoxes of Christian dogma.

The present work can itself be seen as a protracted act within Bulgakov's long yet decisive self-submission to Christ and to the Church, and it bears within itself the marks of painful struggle. The critique of German idealism which is the book's central negative task is strangely split between protracted passages on Kant, Fichte, and Hegel in the main body of the book, and the separate "excurses" on each of these philosophers which follow at its conclusion. Bulgakov's articulation of the elements of what one must, really, regard as a Trinitarian ontology, drawing on the speculative philosophy of language which he had developed in the then unpublished *Philosophy of the Name*, comes before and between these passages of fierce polemic upon the idealists and other philosophers, and somewhat contrasts with those passages in its register and approach. The book is by no means an organic unity; yet at the same time it offers some of the most extensive and powerful passages of philosophical argument which Bulgakov ever wrote, as well as the fullest elaboration of philosophemes whose influential presence is quite clearly detectible, now fully subordinated to the attempt to interpret dogma, in Bulgakov's last theology. The now well-established Anglophone interest in Bulgakov's thought has, with one or two exceptions, naturally concentrated more on his theology proper than on its philosophical

---

17   Ibid., 238.

infrastructure.[18] Despite the book's inequalities, it may nevertheless be amongst the most important sources in his authorship for any current theology which wishes to learn from Bulgakov's example, and to continue to provide philosophical interpretation of dogma—for example, in the shape of a "Trinitarian ontology"—because it sets out with such sharpness, even with abruptness, ideas and assumptions which are more often left implicit in his later writings.[19]

Risky as it might be to offer a summary of the book's argument, the task cannot be shirked. Schematically put, Bulgakov posits that the nature of ultimate reality—"substance"—is constitutively triune. This triunity is, for him, imaged in the nature of language, in the structure of the proposition itself, which, Bulgakov thinks, whatever its particular external form, always at root consists of a subject, a predicate, and a copula which links the two. The proposition is three in one. "Substance is a

---

18 In addition to the books and articles cited elsewhere in this introduction, important studies in English include, but are by no means limited to, John Milbank, "Sophiology and Theurgy," in Adrian Pabst and Christoph Schneider, eds., *Encounter Between Eastern Orthodoxy and Radical Orthodoxy: Transfiguring the World through the Word* (London: Routledge, 2016), 45–85; Paul Gavrilyuk, "The Kenotic Theology of Sergius Bulgakov," *Scottish Journal of Theology* 58.3 (August 2005): 251–69; Paul Vallière, *Modern Russian Theology: Bukharev, Soloviev, Bulgakov. Orthodox Theology in a New Key* (Grand Rapids, MI and Cambridge, UK: Eerdmans, 2000); Robert Slesinski, *The Theology of Sergius Bulgakov* (Yonkers, NY: St Vladimir's Seminary Press, 2017); Aidan Nichols, *Wisdom from Above: A Primer in the Theology of Sergei Bulgakov* (Leominster: Gracewing, 2005); Andrew Louth, *Modern Orthodox Thinkers: From the Philokalia to the Present* (London: SPCK, 2015), chapter 4; Brandon Gallaher, *Freedom and Necessity in Modern Trinitarian Theology* (Oxford: Oxford University Press, 2016), Part I. For an excellent bibliography of primary and secondary works, see *Sergij Bulgakov: Bibliographie*, eds. Barbara Hallensleben and Regula Zwahlen (Münster: Aschendorff Verlag, 2017).

19 In addition to the influence which Bulgakov's theology has exerted on major anglophone theologians such as John Milbank, David Bentley Hart, and Rowan Williams, see also, for instance, Klaus Hemmerle, *Thesen zu einer Trinitarische Ontologie* (Einsiedeln: Johannes Verlag, 1976); Piero Coda, *Il logos e il nulla: trinità mistica religioni* (Rome: Città Nuova, 2003); and also the international conference on "New Trinitarian Ontologies" held in Cambridge in September 2019, recorded proceedings of which are readily available online, and at which, notably, Prof. Dr. Barbara Hallensleben of the University of Fribourg gave a presentation on *The Tragedy of Philosophy*. The book's significance for recent scholarly attention to Hans Urs von Balthasar's interest in Bulgakov and in Russian thought—as represented in particular by Jennifer Newsome Martin's *Hans Urs von Balthasar and the Critical Appropriation of Russian Religious Thought* (Notre Dame, Indiana: University of Notre Dame Press, 2015) and by Cyril O'Regan's *The Anatomy of Misremembering: von Balthasar's Response to Philosophical Modernity. Volume One: Hegel* (Chestnut Ridge, NY: Crossroad, 2014), especially 305-30—is also evident.

living proposition consisting of a subject, a predicate, and a copula," as the book's very last sentence claims.

Philosophy's "tragedy" consists in its inability, as it were, to tolerate the "tri-" in "triunity." Bulgakov understands an underlying drive towards unity and identity—what a later idiom might characterize as "identity thinking"—as essential to the practice of philosophy itself, whatever the particular ontology adhered to by individual philosophers. Philosophy therefore *selects* one pole of the primordial triunity as fundamental, and makes the others result or proceed from that selected pole. In Bulgakov's typology, philosophical authorships can be classified according to which limb of the proposition they seek to absolutize. Those which absolutize the subject are idealist; those which absolutize the predicate are panlogist; those which absolutize the copula are realist systems of various kinds. The triune nature of ultimate reality cannot be captured by philosophy, but is instead a matter of revealed religious truth.

As suggested, this map develops out of Bulgakov's notion that the triune structure of the proposition, and, therefore, of language itself, is a clue to the triunity of ultimate reality. In *The Philosophy of the Name*, published only in 1953, seven years after Bulgakov's death, most of which still awaits translation into English, Bulgakov develops what we might think of as a Chalcedonian poetics of language. He is sharply critical of any merely instrumental view of language, in which it would serve simply as a vehicle for the transmission of thoughts—the familiar "coal-truck" conception, in which thought would be packed up in words by a speaker or writer and then subsequently unloaded, identical, from those words by a listener or reader. Yet at the same time—and unlike many advocates of the "linguistic turn"—he also admits the necessity of a moment of *non*-identity between language and thought. In an extremely striking and suggestive way, it becomes clear that the model for Bulgakov's idea of the identity and non-identity of language and thought is none other than the Christological formula of Chalcedon, for which

> one and the same Lord Jesus Christ, the only begotten Son, must be acknowledged in two natures, without confusion or change, without division or separation [ἕνα καὶ τὸν αὐτὸν Χριστὸν υἱὸν κύριον μονογενῆ ἐν δύο φύσεσιν ἀσυγχύτως, ἀτρέπτως, ἀδιαιρέτως, ἀχωρίστως γνωριζόμενον] [*hena kai ton*

auton Khriston huion monogenē en duo phusesin asugkhutōs, atreptōs, adiairetōs, akhōristōs gnōrizomenon].[20]

"The Λόγος [*Logos*] has a *double* nature; in it word and thought, body and meaning are without separation and without confusion."[21] *Without separation and without confusion* specifies the paradoxical relationship which Bulgakov holds to obtain between thought and language, as between Christ's divinity and his humanity. Such identifications-with-differentiations cannot, of course, but remind us of Hegel's speculative propositions, of his identity of identity and non-identity—which Bulgakov, however, sees as an immanentized and therefore heretical secularization of the Chalcedonian and incarnational paradox. Bulgakov's incarnational theory of language has the striking result of extending the conception of "language" beyond words and right into embodiment. "Strictly speaking, our language is always realized not only with words, but also with gestures, which play an auxiliary role in speech: we do not speak with the tongue alone, but with the whole body."[22]

Of crucial importance here is the ecclesiastical context for *The Philosophy of the Name*'s speculations in the philosophy of language. On this occasion, Bulgakov's resistance was directed towards the violence not of Bolshevik commissars but of the pre-revolutionary Tsarist regime. "On 13 June 1913, 120 marines arrived from Imperial Russia and stormed the Panteleimon Monastery on Mount Athos, to enforce orthodoxy against those who believed that the invocation of the Name of Jesus in prayer makes him truly present."[23] *The Philosophy of the Name* can be understood as the deep indirect groundwork for an explanation of why the so-called *imyaslavtsy*, the "name-worshippers," ought not to be dismissed as heretical. Bulgakov, reviving an expression of Patriarch Nicephoros,

---

20 Heinrich Denzinger, *Compendium of Creeds, Definitions, and Declarations on Matters of Faith and Morals*, forty-third edition revised, enlarged, and, in collaboration with Helmut Hoping, edited by Peter Hünermann for the original bilingual edition, and edited by Robert Fastiggi and Anne Englund Nash for the English edition (San Francisco: Ignatius Press, 2010), 109.
21 Bulgakov, *Filosofiya Imeni* (Paris: YMCA-Press, 1953), 19. All translations mine except where otherwise stated.
22 Ibid., 230n.
23 See, on this topic, the article by Nicholas Turner in the *Church Times* for 14 June 2013.

calls the denouncers *onomatomakhoi*, "onomaclasts" [*imyabortsy*], name-smashers.²⁴ For Bulgakov, the proper name is a special instance of language. Names are by no means, he thinks, borne "arbitrarily" by the persons and places to which they attach; they are not invented by human beings, Bulgakov suggests, but discovered. If language is, in Bulgakov's conception, an "art," it is an art not in the sense that words are, fundamentally, simply made up, but that they are, rather, discovered. Running beneath all Bulgakov's thinking about language, as beneath his thinking about what it is to be human as such, is a refusal to side with reductively dogmatic anthropologies of the human, whether naturalistic or culturalistic: for Bulgakov, human life is irreducibly both natural and cultural, both biological and historical, both real and imagined, and, ultimately, both created yet indissolubly connected, in "divine-humanity," to the uncreated source of all life and being.

There is not space here for a full account of the speculative philosophy of language explored in Bulgakov's *Philosophy of the Name*. It seems unlikely, to say the least, that all the terms of Bulgakov's account could be found workable exactly as they stand for a contemporary theology of language, if only because so much has happened in the interim to the professional discipline of linguistics, on some of whose former results, in the work of now relatively or wholly neglected figures such as Alexander Potebnya (1835–1891) and Gustav Gerber, the author of *Die Sprache und das Erkennen* [Language and Cognition] (1885), even Bulgakov is partially reliant. Yet Bulgakov's insistence, partly informed by his acquaintance with developments amongst early twentieth-century Russian poeticians, on the continuity between language and those embodied elements of communication which are often sidelined as "paralinguistic" or even "quasiparalinguistic"—gesture, intonation, rhythm—offers an important stimulus for further thought in the theological poetics of language. Here too we can see a kind of "religious materialism" at work, in a twofold insistence on language's *embodied* or incarnate character, both in Bulgakov's attention to "the whole body" as involved in speech, and in his insistence on the importance of the phonetic and graphic body of the word. "The proper name...stands at the very limit of language; it is a

---

24   Bulgakov, *Filosofiya Imeni*, 181; "The Name of God," in Bulgakov, *Icons and the Name of God*, 120–21.

word only by virtue of its sonic envelope."[25] The proper name, like the relic of the saint, like the individual face, becomes a sort of test case for "religious materialism," for the thinking of incarnate divine-humanity.

3

RETURNING TO BULGAKOV'S HERESIOLOGICAL account of philosophy, meanwhile, there are several points to note. First, Bulgakov is not suggesting that the philosophers should have done something else. If they had, they would not, he thinks, have been philosophers. That is why the book diagnoses philosophy as a *tragedy*. Philosophy finds itself compelled to try to explain everything and also destined to fail. Human reason, in the philosophers, finds itself incapable of tolerating its own finitude and dependence; yet this refusal to acknowledge what must appear to it as an arbitrary or external limit is part of what makes reason reason. "[P]hilosophical aporias must come to be known in their full depth; the tragedy of reason must be lived through honestly and unflinchingly, and in suffering lies the special stamp of greatness in philosophy" (p. 51). *The Tragedy of Philosophy* is therefore not an argument for doing philosophy differently—as though Bulgakov were to offer to show philosophy, after millennia of its having got things wrong, how to get them right—but an argument that philosophy has to recognize and admit its own dependence in and origination from religious thought.

Second, there is a historiography at work here too. Philosophy is not merely a tragedy but a series of *heresies*. Bulgakov takes the root meaning of Greek *haeresis*, "choice," as his cue here. The philosophers, unable to tolerate tri-unity, *choose* some one limb of it to make into their absolute. Just which limb is chosen determines the nature of the heresy in question, because Bulgakov is working throughout with an analogy which sporadically comes to the surface between the three limbs of the proposition and the three persons of the Trinity: as though, in the eternal triune proposition, the Father were its subject, Christ its predicate, and the Holy Spirit its copula. Post-Christian philosophies always, for Bulgakov, have a profound if concealed heretical relationship to Christian dogma, because

25 *Filosofiya Imeni*, 155.

they can always ultimately be interpreted as philosophical transcriptions of Christian heresies; and the corollary implication of understanding philosophy itself as a tragedy, as inability to tolerate triunity, is that there has so far never been, and perhaps there can constitutively never be, a fully adequate and self-sufficiently philosophical transcription of Christian *orthodoxy*. Heretical selection of unity and refusal of triunity is part of what makes philosophy philosophy. Philosophy cannot and should not, for example, simply try to be a little less heretical, any more than Oedipus can manage to avoid family problems by trying to make sure not to kill his father and marry his mother. Bulgakov quotes St. Paul to the Corinthians: "there must also be heresies among you, that they which are approved may be made manifest among you" (1 Cor. 11:19). He suggests that "[t]he merit of a philosophical system, as a heresy which reveals one of the possibilities established by 'autonomous' reason, is the purity, precision, and determination with which it pursues its path and with which it reveals its motifs and its motives" (p. 50). Another way of putting this is to say that philosophy is *fallen*, but cannot bear to acknowledge its own fallenness. It is unable to unhear the promise which leads to the fall, that *ye shall be as gods* (Gen. 3:5). And Bulgakov's heresiology, for all its schematism, perhaps helps us to see why scarcely any of the most significant theologians of the twentieth century was able to remain wholly free from any aspersion whatever of heterodoxy. If philosophy is a sort of needful heresy, its relationship to theology can clearly never be a placidly administrative division of labours, but will instead be a continuous gift-exchange, a co-operative antagonism. Any orthodoxy too frightened even to look over the brink of all it hates demonstrates only its own debility.

Third, despite philosophy's tragic and inherent gravitation towards heresy, it continues to be indispensable. Bulgakov had already announced in his *Unfading Light*, a work published in the very year of revolution, 1917, the conception of the relationship between philosophy and dogma which would govern the remainder of his life's work:

> From our understanding of religious philosophy as a voluntary art based on religious motifs, it follows that there cannot and must not be one canonically obligatory type of religious philosophy or "theology": dogmas are immutable but their

philosophical apperception changes together with the development of philosophy.²⁶

This is an account not so much, at this point, of the "development of dogma"—though Bulgakov by no means excludes the possibility and necessity of such development—as of a strict separation between the status of dogma and that of theology.²⁷ Bulgakov reveres dogma and deplores dogmatism, which, for him, consists in misattributing to changing theological interpretations of dogma the fixity and reverence which is due only to dogma itself. It is impossible for dogma to tell philosophy what to think without instantly dissolving philosophy's philosophical character, which will then vanish together with its freedom. Dogma is given to religious philosophy, instead, as an enigma for interpretation. "*Philosophy is the art of concepts*," Bulgakov emphatically tells us—where "art" is understood not as a licence to make things up, but as a paradoxical requirement truly to testify to the non-made, truth, by a free act of making.²⁸ Anything done freely can always go wrong, of course; yet nothing on earth can free human beings from freedom. Only when freely received can dogma, the fixed, the apparently dead, apparently archaic formula, reveal itself as an inexhaustible source of life, reveal itself as, on this day, the imperishably new. Just as, in the indurated core of a tree—a thought I borrow from the pre-eminent living English poet of trees, Peter Larkin—an apparently "dead" element is as vital to the plant as its shoots and leaves, so what is most truly alive in the spirit requires a fixity too; freedom with no constraint whatever is mere flux. As John Milbank has commented in his essential essay, "Sophiology and Theurgy," "orthodoxy is an always unfinished task. This is not only because new heresies may negatively pose to the Church new questions, but also because existing

---

26 Sergius Bulgakov, *Unfading Light: Contemplations and Speculations*, trans. Thomas Allan Smith (Grand Rapids, Michigan, and Cambridge, Cambridgeshire: Eerdmans, 2012), 95.

27 Paul Gavrilyuk has demonstrated in illuminating detail the complexity of the relationship between Bulgakov's approach to the relation to dogma and theology and that of the "neo-patristic" school of Florovsky in his *Georges Florovsky and the Russian Religious Renaissance* (Oxford: Oxford University Press, 2013). Gavrilyuk concludes (p. 158) that "in the end, Bulgakov could lay almost as strong a claim to a 'return to the Fathers' as Florovsky," but notes that Bulgakov's emphasis lay on the authority of dogma rather than on that of any patristic consensus.

28 Bulgakov, *Unfading Light*, 82.

doctrinal formulations may enshrine unresolved problematics, as much as they successfully resolve old ones."[29] Dogmas continue to reveal their full significance as human history and theological interpretation develop; in his Christology, *The Lamb of God*, Bulgakov writes of the Chalcedonian definition as not only "theologically ahead of its time" but even "to a certain degree ahead of our time."[30] Bulgakov calls the Chalcedonian Christological formula a "dogmatic miracle."[31] Philosophy's task is not to "de-mystify," but continuously to renovate our wonder at such real wonders.

4

ROWAN WILLIAMS (HIMSELF AN INFLUENTIAL CHAMpion of Bulgakov's in the West) uses, in his *Christ the Heart of Creation*, an expression which is in only apparent contrast with Bulgakov's. Williams says that Chalcedon's is a formula "of settlement," and Bulgakov's approach can admit this insight too: that such dogmas should have been arrived at in painful strife through many ecclesiastical lifetimes does not, for a perspective like Bulgakov's, make them any less, but rather more, miraculous.[32] Those dogmas are *both* miraculous gifts *and* concentrated sedimentations of ecclesiastical and social labour; in interpreting them, we nourish ourselves from an inexhaustible supply of spiritual experience long ago packed down into these language-artefacts, as though "in case of emergency"—as definite, sweet, and refreshing as Kendal mint cake to a lost fell walker. A drastic compression alone permits, amid the ceaseless proliferation and living-out of Christian heresies which we find in the post-conciliar intellectual and social landscapes alike, the formulas' survival as closely folded involutes of the true, good, and beautiful, ever calling us to ex-plicate them.

---

29 John Milbank, "Sophiology and Theurgy: The New Theological Horizon" (http://www.theologyphilosophycentre.co.uk/papers/Milbank_SophiologyTheurgy.pdf, accessed November 14, 2019), 5.
30 *The Lamb of God*, trans. Boris Jakim (Grand Rapids, MI and Cambridge, UK: Eerdmans, 2008), 57.
31 *The Lamb of God*, 59.
32 Rowan Williams, *Christ the Heart of Creation* (London: Bloomsbury, 2018), 67, 88. For Williams on Bulgakov, see his anthology *Sergii Bulgakov: Towards a Russian Political Theology* (Edinburgh: T & T Clark, 1999).

The Tragedy of Philosophy

Philosophy and Dogma, to promote this book's subtitle, by no means, therefore, rests content with having apparently put philosophy in its place, but rather continues to attempt new formulations for the religious philosophy which might be most adequate, in its new thinking, to the attempt to interpret and unseal the recalcitrant "miracles" of dogma. One of the most significant of these comes at the end of the first part of the book. If philosophy is itself characterized by its refusal of triunity, and by its *selection* of one member of triunity in which to ground a monism, how is philosophy, Bulgakov asks himself, to think triunity?

> How can the three points, which have become separated from each other, be combined so as to obtain a triangle; can they, indeed, at all be so combined? There can evidently be only one honest answer to this question: either philosophy is impossible, and it will remain its lot repeatedly to walk along the same old paths which it has already traversed, like a squirrel on a wheel — *da capo* forever — or philosophy is possible, if it is grounded in the antinomies and is religiously, that is, dogmatically, conditional. And this is not a diminution of philosophy, but its higher calling — to be the *ancilla* not *theologiae*, but *religionis*, the handmaiden, not of theology, but of religion itself, to become a revealed and conscious (and in this sense, a critical) religious empiricism. (p. 88)

The last parenthesis is significant. It indicates that Bulgakov's extensive critique of Kant and of post-Kantian German idealism is by no means to be taken for a one-way ticket back to a lost pre-Kantian paradise of ancient metaphysics. True, Plato and Aristotle are always spoken of with respect in this book, whereas Kant, Fichte, and Hegel repeatedly receive Bulgakov's sardonically interpolated exclamation marks and interrogation points. But the respect paid to the ancient metaphysicians is not to be mistaken for an instruction to strain, impossibly, philosophically to retro-fit ourselves as replica Greeks — just as, in the end, Bulgakov's response to the Bolshevik desecrations of relics is informed by an awareness of that dialectic of enlightenment already set out as early as Hegel's account of the relations between superstition and enlightenment in his

Phenomenology of Spirit.³³ Even gleeful desecration is significant and must be looked at steadily, since it is part of what Bulgakov would later call—in the lamenting refrain sounded towards the end of his pneumatology, *The Comforter*—"the kenosis of the Father's love."³⁴ "Once God permitted light to shine into the mysterious half-darkness of the holy place, be this only the light from a prosaic kerosene or electrical lamp, we must not shut our eyes to this light, but must rather calmly and firmly look around."³⁵ For Bulgakov, even though intellectual history is by no means pure progress, it can nevertheless contain "irreversible" discoveries of aporia. "There have been many systems of idealism both before and after Fichte, yet Fichte's surpasses them all in the purity and sharpness of its metaphysical theme. [...] Fichteanism is a permanent monument in the history of thought, in the dialectic of reason, an irreversible act in the tragedy of philosophy." What makes Fichteanism particularly important for Bulgakov is what he takes to be its unyielding insistence on the absoluteness of hypostaticity—even as he also shows in detail how, in Fichte's hands, unable to think not only nature but also the other *I*, a *thou* or a *we*, Fichte's "I" becomes a "Luciferian" narcissism turned in upon itself. Bulgakov's personalism, instead, requires a perspective capable of hearing and seeing the *other* person, whether human, angelic or divine, not as data but as person: a solidarity or "conciliarity" [*sobornost'*] in which the irreducibile singularity of the hypostatic members is preserved rather than annulled.

Greek thought has interwoven itself inextricably with Christian revelation, in Bulgakov's view, in such a way that it is impossible to imagine the possibility of an event like the dogmatic "miracle" of Chalcedon without it. But the concept of personhood which is at the centre of Bulgakov's philosophically-informed personalist theology—in the expanded, hypostatic sense not merely of human but also of divine and angelic personhood—was precipitated, he thinks, precisely by the difficulty which ancient philosophical categories have in framing Christian revelation.

---

33 G.W.F. Hegel, *Phenomenology of Spirit*, trans. A.V. Miller (Oxford: Oxford University Press, 1977), 329-49.
34 Bulgakov, *The Comforter*, trans. Boris Jakim (Grand Rapids, MI and Cambridge, UK: Eerdmans, 2004), 385-86.
35 Bulgakov, "On Holy Relics," 40.

Plato's theory of ideas as a whole is without doubt characterized by its anhypostaticity, by its lacking an interest in the problem of personhood, and by its lacking, therefore, any account of personhood either. [...] Plato's thought here by no means has a militantly anti-hypostatic character; rather, it is helpless and naïve in regard to the question of personhood, like antiquity in general. Thanks to this, Plato's theory of ideas does not have the characteristics of a closed and free-standing metaphysics, and is able to enter Christian theology.... (p. 52–53)

In a passage like this, what clearly emerges is the eminently paradoxical character of Bulgakov's conception of the relationship between philosophy and theology. The largely "anhypostatic" character of Plato's thought is by no means a merit, so far as Bulgakov is concerned, from a philosophical point of view; yet it is precisely this anhypostatic character which makes Platonism directly available to a Christianity which first, in Bulgakov's view, properly reveals the concept of personhood and presents it to philosophy as a problem.[36] Religious philosophy does not need to be modelled on ancient metaphysics, in other words, precisely because ancient metaphysics has already incorporated itself authentically and inextricably (Bulgakov has no time for Harnackian purisms) into Christian theology itself.

5

IT IS NO ACCIDENT, THEN, THAT THE BOOK'S OWN written form is not without its difficulties. These reflect not merely the trying circumstances of its composition, to which Bulgakov himself alludes in his preface, but also a much less temporary problem—the problem of its own status as a text. Is it a work of theology, of philosophy, or of both and neither? This is not an external or abstract difficulty, but emerges throughout in the book's instabilities of tone. Bulgakov can

---

36 Elsewhere Bulgakov writes of "the philosophical birth of the hypostatic person in Socrates and Plato," but then qualifies the remark: "so far, at least, as this can be considered as having happened in their work" (p. 66 below).

On the Idea of a Christian Materialism

within a few pages pass from satirical invective upon Hegel as a hopeless case, a cooker of the philosophical books, to emphatic eulogy of Hegel's enduring significance, and back again. At some places long passages of quotation are thrown, like missiles, in the general direction of the reader, punctuated by Bulgakov's exasperated asides ("cubism!," he at one point darkly mutters, of Kant). The extensiveness of Bulgakov's quotations seems almost to suggest a fear on his part that, in the severity of the crisis, even the basic primary materials of European thought are at risk of disappearance. Yet the book's instabilities of tone and form, instead of being simply a compositional defect, point us to a lasting equivocity in its underlying genre. This becomes evident as soon as we ask ourselves a question such as this: what *kind* of claim is the book's final sentence, its apparent destination, that "[s]ubstance is a *living proposition* consisting of a subject, a predicate, and a copula"? If it were taken as a philosophical claim, the book would become a self-consuming artefact, turning the consciousness of heresy into a new alibi for and continuation of heresy. Yet in form and content it sounds much more like a philosophical than like a theological claim. It does not seem, strictly speaking, to be a theological claim, because Bulgakov does not, here at least, precisely ground it in scriptural or dogmatic revelation.

We cannot, then, regard Bulgakov's final theology as an attempt to support or demonstrate scripturally or dogmatically the claim with which *The Tragedy of Philosophy* ends—this would be precisely to repeat the tragedy of philosophy by putting dogma into the service of philosophy rather than vice versa. Yet we can think of this *super*-philosophical ontology of the triune nature of substance, this ontology which *The Tragedy of Philosophy* does articulate, as providing the internal and usually implicit musculature of Bulgakov's later theology, something like its spiritual body.[37] *The Tragedy of Philosophy*'s incomplete success as a self-sufficient work, its own awkward amphibiousness as a text which can be neither

---

[37] One example from Bulgakov's Christology will have to suffice here. In considering the opposition between the Antiochene and Alexandrian schools, he writes that "[b]oth schools remained in the plane in which Christology leads not to antinomy, which is inevitable, but to logical contradiction, which is unacceptable" (*The Lamb of God*, 49), and he suggests that "[t]he truth resides not in the middle but in the antinomic unity of the two; and we have this truth in the Chalcedonian dogma, in which the Alexandrian and Antiochene theologies are joined together like Siamese twins and live inseparably in the Church's dogmatic consciousness" (ibid., 34).

fully philosophical nor fully theological, is precisely its richness as a source of cogitative energies and idioms for Bulgakov's final theology. It is a kind of damaged masterpiece, intimately essential at every turn to his fully developed theology, yet not, at this juncture, always secure in that later, fully kenotic, voice. Might there, for this reason, have been a sense in which it suited Bulgakov to have the book, during his lifetime, ambiguously both published and unpublished—in print, but only in a foreign language, in an apparent partial separateness from his own theological authorship?

Certainly, the book's amphibious genre, its neither fully philosophical nor fully theological status, is essential to its power. Whereas one might have anticipated, that is, that a book which regards the history of philosophy as a Christian heresiology might simply abstain from offering fresh philosophemes of its own, this does not turn out to be the case. Bulgakov offers a number of slightly different formulas for the philosophical approach which he believes should now be taken. One of these, as we have already seen, and recalling our initial theme of "religious materialism," is "religious empiricism." Elsewhere, commenting on the impossibility of reason's grasping the All in Hegelian fashion, Bulgakov comments that "there is only one possible outcome—a singular [*svoeobradnie*] empiricism freed from the narrow and vulgar idea of empiricism, and capturing living and mystical experience in all its depth. Empiricism is the true epistemology of life." Bulgakov is imagining, effectively, an empiricism which would not be imprisoned in a metaphysical absolutization of matter, but which would instead admit a more capacious and richer conception of "experience" in which aesthetic, spiritual, and religious experience could be permissible objects for interpretation: what we might think of, in just the sense given to "religious materialism" by Bulgakov's early essay on Solovyov and by that on the desecration of relics, as a "Christian materialism."

Bulgakov offers other formulas too for the approach which he wants to take to what he can call "religious philosophy." Such a philosophy would be able to renounce the wish to generate, like Jonathan Swift's spider in *The Battle of the Books*, all its objects from out of itself. It might become able, exceptionally, to admit those "elements quite alien to thought and inadmissible by thought, elements which, nevertheless, turn out to be the basis of thought." For Bulgakov, such a thought must be openly aporetic,

On the Idea of a Christian Materialism

openly antinomical. "The antinomies by which reason is cloven are just those which build it up and which give it determinate form. Thus 'critical antinomism' in metaphysics and in epistemology replaces dogmatic rationalism" (p. 21).

Critical antinomism and *singular* or *religious empiricism* are not two different programs, we might consider, but one and the same, because both recognize and allow for the necessary finitude of human thought without taking this as a pretext for skepticism. And it is when we consider these ideas for the new religious philosophy that we can begin to see *The Tragedy of Philosophy* as a characteristic product of its historical moment—a perspective which may not diminish, but rather intensify, its potential significance for theology today. The single most important epistemological context against which Bulgakov is rebelling is early twentieth-century German neo-Kantianism. In this, of course, he joins a number of German-speaking philosophers who were also schooled in turn-of-the-century neo-Kantianism, and who also tried in a number of different ways to break out of what was felt to be the limited and impoverished conception of experience with which neo-Kantianism worked. We can think, first of all, of the proleptic ancestor of many of these break-out attempts, the late philosophical theology of Schelling; in this connection it is possible both to wonder whether there should not, in *The Tragedy of Philosophy*, have been provided a critical "Excursus on Schelling" to accompany those on Kant, Fichte, and Hegel, and, at the same time, to believe that Bulgakov's own final theology itself constitutes the practical purgation of Schelling which is largely missing from the present work—although Bulgakov does briefly remark that Schelling's "philosophical work retains to the end a certain aroma of rationalism," and states clearly (p. 83) that "Schelling's heresy and error (the reverse of Fichte's) lies in his putting the nature of the hypostasis *before* the hypostasis, and *deducing* the hypostasis from that nature."[38] We can think also, of course, of Edmund Husserl's phenomenology, and of Martin Heidegger's initial project of fundamental ontology. And Bulgakov himself mentions the work of Henri Bergson at one point. Yet there is also a way (no space to dilate on it here) in which those projects too

---

38 For sophiology as "purging" the legacy of Behmenism as transmitted through Schellingian ideas of an *Ungrund* and of a primordial conflict within the absolute, see Milbank, "Sophiology and Theurgy."

can be understood as having received a proleptic critique in Bulgakov's *Tragedy of Philosophy*, a work which sticks closer to the language of the idealism which it is in the process of shedding than do either Husserl or Heidegger—something which becomes clear when, towards the book's end, Bulgakov, startlingly, announces "*Fichte plus Spinoza*: this is the task"—since, in a certain sense, this is *already* the task for Schelling and even for Hegel. A closer affinity might be detected with, to take one example, the young Walter Benjamin's project of a reformulated critical thinking, a thinking not bound to the restricted and pre-scientized conception of "experience" as it is found in Kant's transcendental idealism, but instead capacious enough to include aesthetic, spiritual, and religious experience. Benjamin's "Program for the Coming Philosophy," as Howard Caygill has powerfully demonstrated in his study *The Colour of Experience*, wants to think what would happen to the rigid transcendental armor of the Kantian conceptual repertoire if we were to discern the colors inside the monochrome effigy of "experience" which is at its heart.[39] And Bulgakov's central emphasis on intersubjectivity, on the inadequacy of a subject-object model of cognition to the subjectivity of the other *I*, the *thou*, strongly recalls the thought of his Jewish contemporaries Martin Buber and Franz Rosenzweig. The precise extents and contours of such affinities and differences, however, remain to be explored.

Ineliminable from real apprehension of the least real thing is *wonder* at its being at all rather than being nothing. This is a wonder which does not have to be *added* to a matter which would otherwise be somehow indifferent and meaningless, as though to warm it and us up; it inheres in the colours, sounds, and textures of the real world, which is at one and the same time perfectly ordinary and inexplicably miraculous. Philosophy's necessary antinomies and aporias register an insight, that the inner substance of each real thing is a question. We fail to experience wonder just in so far as we cannot bear to look at reality. Sin is one name for this indifferent turn away from reality, which is *the same* turn as the turn away from wonder. After his son's death, Bulgakov wrote that all the corners of his "sinful soul" had been illuminated. "In general, in my, or rather our, life, an event of such immeasurable importance has taken place that

---

39   Howard Caygill, *Walter Benjamin: The Colour of Experience* (London: Routledge, 1997).

its results must, I think, affect everything: opinions, feelings, values, life. And I fear one thing, pray for one thing, that I may not forget, that the lighthearted, bustling, weak part of my soul, burdened with life's concerns, may not give in and harden itself once more."[40] In a collective life which is organized ever more gaplessly around just such busy "hardening," around a systematic turn away from reality and a systematic suppression of wonder, liturgical and dogmatic theology by no means offer a consoling illusion, but rather the possibility of our becoming, intermittently and fragmentarily, capable of "looking calmly and firmly" at the real.

* * *

Like all Bulgakov's works, *The Tragedy of Philosophy* presents acute difficulties to its translator. The work was first published in German in 1927 in a translation by Alexander Kresling: *Die Tragödie der Philosophie* (Darmstadt: O. Reichl, 1927). I thank the staff of the library of the University of Sheffield for enabling me to consult a copy of this translation. (It should be noted that occasionally one or two sentences present in the Russian text are omitted, whether with Bulgakov's agreement or not I do not know, from Kresling's translation.) I have also learnt much from the impressive achievements of my predecessors, especially Boris Jakim, in translating Bulgakov. I am grateful to Professor Vera Tolz, of the University of Manchester, for advice about one aspect of Russian usage; and to Mr. Nicholas Walker for help in locating one or two of the many quotations from and references to Hegel. Needless to say, I alone am responsible for errors.

The Russian text I have used is "Tragediya Filosofii (Filosofiya i Dogmat)," in Bulgakov, *Sochineniya v dvukh tomakh* (2 vols, Moskva: Nauka, 1993), ed. S.S. Khoruzhij, 1: 309–518. I have learnt much from Khoruzhij's scholarship.

It would require a further introduction of comparable length to the existing one to discuss fully all the particular hermeneutic and philological problems presented by an attempt to render Bulgakov in readable and intelligible English, and I must here pass over the only partly soluble difficulties presented by such terms as *sobornij* [conciliar; collective, solidary],

---

40   From a letter of 1909 to Grigorii Rachinskii quoted in Evtuhov, *The Cross and the Sickle*, 135–36.

sushchij [existing; authentic, real, true], and *obraz* [form; shape; image; icon]. Readers will see for themselves that it is undesirable always to render such polysemic terms with the same English word. It is worth being aware that there are in Russian two words for English "subject": *podlezhashchee*, which indicates a grammatical, propositional subject, and *sub"ekt*, which designates an epistemological or metaphysical subject. I have given the Russian word only where absence of apposition leaves unclear which is meant. I have in general tried to avoid too liberally peppering my text with Russian, but have made some exceptions, especially where there is a play on words in the Russian which cannot be fully communicated in translation.

I have reproduced Bulgakov's own varying letter heights and styles for the Russian pronoun *Ya* ("I") as follows. Emboldened capital **I** = **Я**; emboldened and italicized ***I*** = ***Я***; unemboldened and unitalicized capital I = я; unemboldened but italicized *I* = *я*. Bulgakov's use of these varying heights and styles for the pronoun is not perfectly consistent, yet some attempt to preserve them must be made in an English translation; readers need not become over-anxious about the distinctions involved, since, happily, these are usually clear from the context. (In quotations from existing published translations of others' philosophical texts, however, the word "I" appears as in the published text quoted from: it would have been too coercive to compel Kant, Fichte, and Hegel to appear in Bulgakovian dress.) Capitalizations of pronouns relating to the Divine Persons, etc., also follow Bulgakov's own lead, even where this might not seem perfectly consistent.

When translating Bulgakov's quotations from non-Russian authors, I have wherever possible either quoted from existing published translations of the original source into English, or translated from the original myself; in a very few cases, where Bulgakov has quoted from Russian editions unavailable to me, I have been obliged to translate these quotations directly from his Russian. I have elucidated Bulgakov's allusions and provided references for them wherever this seemed necessary and proved possible.

It would have been too complicated to try, as I once intended, to indicate patterns of emphasis *both* in the original texts from which Bulgakov is quoting *and* in his Russian quotations; accordingly italicizations are, throughout, those to be found in Bulgakov's Russian text. All footnotes are Bulgakov's own except where expressly attributed to the translator. All Biblical quotations are given from the King James Version.

ABBREVIATIONS

CPR = Immanuel Kant, *Critique of Pure Reason*, trans. Norman Kemp Smith (London: Macmillan, 1933)

E = Spinoza, *Ethics proved in geometrical order*, trans. Michael Silverthorne and Mathew J. Kisner (Cambridge: Cambridge University Press, 2018)

SK = *The Science of Knowledge*, trans. Peter Heath and John Lachs (Cambridge: Cambridge University Press, 1982)

SL = G.W.F. Hegel, *Science of Logic*, trans. A.V. Miller (London: George Allen and Unwin, 1969)

FROM THE AUTHOR
(*Preface to the German edition of 1927*)

THE WORK WHICH IS NOW PLACED BEFORE THE reader was written about five years ago (in 1920–21) in the Russian South. Although its contents represent a kind of culmination of my work in the field of philosophy, it may be proper to mention that its execution is marked by the external conditions under which it was written, and that it was particularly affected by my having only limited access to the relevant literature. Nevertheless, I retain it in its original form, with only minor corrections. Its real theme—which it shares with many of my earlier works, and, in particular, with *Unfading Light*—is the nature of the relationship between philosophy and religion, or the religious and intuitive basis of *any* philosophizing. This connection, which was, for me, already immutably fixed in its general outlines, is set out more concretely here; the history of modern philosophy is presented in its fully religious nature as a Christian heresiology. Modern philosophy is a tragedy of thought which cannot find a way out of its difficulties. The present work differs from Irenaeus's *Against the Heretics*, Athanasius's *Against the Pagans*, and so on, in its material and in its form, and it pertains to a different historical epoch, but it belongs in the same line as they, and is dedicated to what is essentially the same topic. Christian dogmatics as both criterion and *measure* of the veracity of philosophical constructions—such is the immanent judgement upon philosophy passed by philosophy's own history, and in the light of which, as Hegel writes, *die Weltgeschichte ist Weltgericht* [world-history is the world's court of judgement].[1]

The Author.
Prague, March 1925.

---

1 "Die Weltgeschichte ist das Weltgericht" is a line from Friedrich Schiller's poem "Resignation. Eine Fantasie" (1786), and the remark was later quoted and commented on in Hegel's *Lectures on the Philosophy of History*. — Trans.

I

Types of Philosophical Construction

1
The Nature of Thought

THERE EXISTS A COMPLEX OF PROBLEMS NATURAL to philosophical thought, together with aporias which are inescapable for philosophy, or from which it can exit only at great cost, by falling into the one-sidedness of "abstract principles," into philosophical heresy—if by "heresy," αἵρησις [*hairēsis*], we mean the arbitrary election, the choice, of some single thing or part instead of the whole: that is, precisely, a one-sidedness.[1] This election, this heresy, determines the theme and the characteristics of a philosophical system; it makes a system into both a thesis and an antithesis with respect to other systems, and incorporates it into the chain of dialectical thought, just as Hegel attempted, not without reason, to incorporate the whole history of philosophy into his own work. All philosophical systems known to the history of philosophy constitute such "heresies," such conscious and deliberate one-sidednesses, in that in all of them one side wishes to be everything, to extend to everything. A preliminary answer can be given to the question of what gives rise to this sort of one-sidedness or monothematism, from which the variety of the whole is then derived and developed. It is not difficult to suggest the reason, which lies readily to hand. It is the spirit of *system* and the pathos of system; and a system is nothing other than the reduction of many and all into one, and, conversely, the deduction of all and many out of one. Logical continuity, or, what amounts to the same thing, the continuous logical deduction of all from one, making the whole system circle around a single centre which can be passed through in any direction, and which admits of no hiatus or discontinuity of any kind: this is the task which human thought naturally and inevitably strives to complete, not stopping short of violence and self-deception, of evasions and illusions. Logical monism, which is a natural requirement of reason—*ratio*—and which already presupposes the possibility of an accurate and non-contradictory conception of the world, forms an ineliminable feature of every philosophical system, each of which claims, dimly or

---

1 The phrase "abstract principles" alludes to V.S. Solovyov's work *Critique of Abstract Principles* (1880) — Trans.

distinctly, instinctively or consciously, timidly or militantly, to be the absolute philosophy, and each of which regards its own sketch of what is as the system of the world.

The crucial question is this: is such a monistic system of the world at all possible? Is an absolute philosophy possible? And what is the foundation for such a faith in reason, in the power of reason, and in the correctness of reason's own way of understanding its role? This question is usually answered in a spirit of scepticism, of relativism, or of shameless repartee, *à la* Pontius Pilate: "what is truth?" Quite apart from the fact that scepticism too is, in its way, an absolute philosophy which lays claim to a very great deal, scepticism runs counter to reason's self-consciousness, to its seriousness, its persistence, its relentlessness, or, to speak more precisely, to reason's inescapable problematic. Reason cannot be corrupted by scepticism, for it is conscious of its own strength and of what it wishes to achieve. So great is reason's seriousness that it cannot be affected by sceptical frivolity, and authentic and deliberate scepticism has, historically speaking, been a rare phenomenon. Usually scepticism is mixed with various shades of relativism, that is, of a primitive, crude, scientific dogmatism, which can never be far removed from scepticism (such, for example, is contemporary scientific positivism). Reason attempts, and cannot not attempt, new flights; but each such flight is attended by a fall, and the history of philosophy is not only the story of these flights, but is also a melancholy tale of inevitable descents and of destined misfortunes—even if the creators of philosophical systems themselves do not notice these misfortunes, having exhausted themselves by their exertions, and remaining, like Schopenhauer, in love with their systems, or imagining, like Hegel, that they have comprehended Truth itself. So much the worse for them, since history dispels their illusions all the more thoroughly, and brands them as blind twice over. How, indeed, is it possible to keep going in the face of the plurality of systems, whilst establishing the absolute value of one's own? By branding one's rivals as idiots and charlatans, like Schopenhauer? This comes too cheap, and just reveals poor taste and a bad character. Or by interpreting them, like Hegel, as one's dialectically necessary predecessors, who are completely absorbed into the absolute system, so that the whole history of philosophy essentially turns out to be the history of Hegel's own philosophy in its dialectical self-unfolding? This signifies, without a doubt, the suppression of the very question, and this claim too is rendered comical by the subsequent history of philosophy. Each such system wants to be the end of the world and the culmination of history; for all this, though, history continues. Like Chronos devouring his own children, the history of philosophy judges all the efforts of reason to be either nonsensical or premature. A bleak prospect—unless we are saved from it by scholarly antiquarianism, with its predilection for collecting the history of philosophy and turning it into a museum housing uncommon articles of superior intellectual elegance. If we reflect, though, that it is not shells and trinkets that are collected in this *Kunstkammer* [cabinet of curiosities], but the results of the highest efforts of human reason, we can see that a museological approach is quite inappropriate, and even blasphemous.

The history of philosophy is a tragedy. It is a tale of the repeated falls of Icarus, and of his further flights. This tragic aspect of philosophy, which is also the fate of each individual thinker, was keenly felt by certain minds, such as Heraclitus and Plato. Kant arrived at the brink of the same abyss in his doctrine of antinomies, and came to a halt. The essence of tragedy consists in a person's suffering through no fault of his own, and in the fact that even though he is in the right individually, and submits his own needs to dictates from above, he at the same time inevitably comes to grief. The philosopher cannot not fly; he must ascend into the ether; but his wings inevitably melt in the heat of the sun, and he falls and breaks into fragments. On this flight, however, he sees something, and his philosophy speaks of this vision. The true philosopher, like the true poet (who, in the end, are one and the same), never lies; he does not make anything up, and he is completely sincere and truthful. Nevertheless, his fate is to fall. For he *has desired a system*. In other words, he has wished to create a (logical) world out of himself, out of his own principle—"you shall be as gods"—but such a logical deduction of the world is not possible for a human being.[2] It is impossible, first and foremost, because of something which lies beyond the human will and the powers of reason: the world is not rational, as "deductive" philosophy, philosophical system as such, a philosophy which found its classic and most extreme expression in Hegel, wants to take it as being. More precisely, although reason governs the

---

2 Bulgakov quotes the words of the serpent to Adam and Eve in the garden: "For God doth know that in the day ye eat thereof, then your eyes shall be opened, and ye shall be as gods, knowing good and evil" (Gen. 3:5)—*Trans.*

world, it is not possible to say that everything which is actual is rational, as Hegel believed. This does not mean that the actual is non-rational, much less irrational: the actual is not only rational, but also extra-rational, and reason is by no means the single, exhaustive, and all-powerful constructor of the world for which it is involuntarily taken by any philosophical system, whenever the latter might be setting about constructing the world. Reason, in a certain sense, is only a reflection on the world, not its origin. In comprehending the world, therefore, reason is dependent on the testimony of being, on some mystical and metaphysical experience which philosophy never really renounces, since philosophy always seeks to find the origin by contemplating, beholding, and disclosing it. This disclosure is by no means an act of thought. It does not yield to intellectual exertion, nor to a chain of deductions; it is a revelation of the world itself in human consciousness, a kind of knowledge.

Another question arises at once. Knowledge of that which is, the self-revelation of that which is, is ignited within reason, but can reason master and assimilate what is being revealed? Can reason bind it into a unity, a system? It is self-evident that reason does this, and cannot not do it. Such is reason's nature; "its ideal is architectonic," to use Kant's language.[3] Yet if reason itself is empty, and incapable of creating by itself or out of itself, how can it be strong enough to bring together into a unity—that is, into a system—everything which is revealed to it? It is evident that if the world, actuality, is not a single, purely rational being, it cannot be exhaustively disclosed, even if it is revealed to reason. The world always only discloses itself, since it is in essence a mystery which contains within itself the source of new cognition and revelation. It is impossible to shine the light of reason into all the hidden corners of the universe, to abolish all mysteries, and to make them all transparent to reason, as Hegel—and, in his person, all philosophy—supposed. Hence there is only one possible outcome—a singular empiricism, freed from the narrow and vulgar idea of empiricism, and capturing living and mystical experience in all its depth. Empiricism is the true epistemology of life. It is a revelation

---

3 "Human reason is by nature architectonic." Immanuel Kant, *Critique of Pure Reason*, trans. Norman Kemp Smith (London: Macmillan, 1933), 429 (A 474/B 502). References to this work will hereafter be given as CPR, followed by the page number and references to the page numbers of the first ("A") and/or second ("B") German editions of the text, as appropriate. —*Trans.*

of mysteries, as knowledge of reality and reflection upon reality always are. At the same time, philosophy cannot by any means remain mere empiricism—which, however, is in any case impossible, because reason, which makes what is plural one, and *vice versa*, understands everything as connected to everything else. Therefore reason cannot begin itself from itself, nor generate thought out of itself, for thought is born of what truly exists, and in relation to what truly exists. Thought is born in the self-revelation of that which truly exists; reason, meanwhile, reports to itself and legislates for itself on its path and in its work.

If reason is not a First Thing, but a Second, if reason is not primordial or self-engendering, but arises from and is born of something ontologically prior to reason, then its power is also relative to that from which it was born, and which serves as the object of its knowledge. The condition of reason, like the condition of the thinking human being, is capable of varying, and possesses differing levels. After all, if we can distinguish, within philosophy, between common sense or ordinary practical thinking, understanding, and, finally, reason (a distinction made with particular clarity by Hegel), then this shows that there are degrees of reason, and that reason can be more reasonable or less reasonable. The understanding is an unreasonable reason, whose wisdom, when compared to reason, is narrow-minded. Yet understanding is at the same time, nevertheless, a power of thought, of mind; one and the same rational element is at work in reason and in the understanding. Why not postulate, then, going further still, an ascent into super-rational [*zaumnye*] realms, realms which, although they are not yet accessible to reason, are attainable in principle, and are by no means inaccessible, according to the testimony of Christian ascetics?[4] Sickness, corruption, the perversion of all human existence which presented itself in original sin, also, in other words, afflicts reason, and makes it impossible for reason to gain access to the tree of heavenly knowledge, since access is denied by the fiery sword of the cherubim—the antinomies. And wisdom in any case itself requires

---

4 Bulgakov's adjective also recalls *zaum* or "trans-sense," a term associated with the slogans of the Russian futurists, whom Bulgakov briefly discusses in his *Philosophy of the Name*: see "Filosofiya Imeni," in Bulgakov, *Pervoobraz i obraz: sochineniya v dvukh tomakh*, 2 vols. (Moscow: Iskusstvo and St. Petersburg: Inapress, 1999), 5–241; 40–41. Compare *La philosophie du verbe et du nom*, trans. Constantin Andronikov (Lausanne: L'Age d'Homme, 1991), 43–44—*Trans.*

reason to have self-knowledge, not only in the Kantian sense of the dismantling of a machine so that it can be cleaned and then put back together again, but in the sense of a comprehension of the real limits of reason, which have to be acknowledged, even if they bring reason up against antinomies. Hence it follows that the fundamental aspiration of reason itself, the aspiration to logical monism, that is, to a logically coherent and consequent interpretation of the world from a single beginning, turns out to be impracticable, and an absolute system of philosophy impossible. This, of course, does not change the fact that, if philosophy is impossible, philosophizing is both possible and necessary, and that reason's work of reflection and comprehension is therefore every bit as significant even as reason's own mistaken and inflated self-appraisal believes it to be.

Reason, in striving towards monism, towards a logical construction of the world out of itself, executes, in fact, an act of arbitrary will. It chooses this or that beginning from those available to it and experienced by it, and so enters upon the path of philosophical heresy, in the sense explained above. The revelation of the world is God's revelation of himself. Religious dogmas — "myths," in an epistemological sense — are also at the same time problems for reason, which reason assimilates and interprets.[5] The religious foundation of philosophizing is an indisputable fact, whether or not it is acknowledged. The history of philosophy can, in this sense, be set forth and interpreted as religious heresiology. In the history of Christian theology, what distinguishes heresy, philosophically, is precisely the fact that a complex, many-faceted, and antinomical doctrine is simplified so that reason can understand it; the doctrine is rationalized, and is thereby distorted. All fundamental heresies embody such a rationalism in their approach to dogmas. Rationalism, as such an abuse of reason, has its source in a pride in reason: pride understood not in a personal sense, as if individual philosopher-heresiologues, say, were proud, but in an objective sense, as a failure to know one's own proper nature, limits, and condition. Consequently one may say, in the language of contemporary philosophy, that philosophical heresiologues are guilty of dogmatism. They lack a critical awareness of the limits of reason.

There are three fundamental self-determinations of thought which shape thought's outcome and determine its orientation. All philosophical

---

5 Compare the introduction to *Unfading Light*.

systems arrange their basic principles with reference to these three frontiers: (1) hypostasis, or personhood; (2) the latter's idea or ideal form, logos, thought; (3) substantial being as the unity of all moments or states of being, as the self-actualizing whole. *I am Something* (potentially, everything): this formula, expressing a judgement, not only provides in abbreviated form a schema of what truly exists, but thereby provides a schema of the history of philosophy too. This tripartite formula, which contains within itself a logical triunity and triplicity of moments which are indisseverably connected, is incessantly cut apart in different directions by whoever is philosophizing. Philosophizing thought produces heresies through the arbitrariness of these disseverations, and through its choices of discrete beginnings; and the style of philosophizing is determined by the way in which this dissection is made. This triplicity of moments forms the basis of self-consciousness, as of every act of thought, and is imprinted upon it; it is a triunity which finds expression in the simple proposition *I is A*. If we state this in universal logico-grammatical terms—subject, predicate, and copula—it can be said that at the basis of self-consciousness lies a proposition. The spirit is a living proposition which realizes itself without ceasing. Every subject [*podlezhashchee*], whether it is a "substantive" or a word which substitutes for one, exists in the image and likeness of the first person pronoun, the subject *par excellence*, both grammatical and philosophical: the first person splinters and multiplies into innumerable mirroring repetitions.[6] The first person pronoun, a mystical verbal gesture, has a completely unique nature, and is the basis on which any given thing can be a substantive. Every proposition can be traced back to the model of the combination of the **I** with its predicate; it can even be said that the real subject of the sentence is the **I**, since the sentence in its entirety is a predicate of the **I**—for in relation to the **I** everything, all meaning as such, is a predicate, and every new judgement is, in its substance if not in its form, a new self-determination of the **I**. Every judgement derives, ontologically, from the universal relation of subject to object, which are no other than the **I**, the hypostasis, and its nature, which reveals the content of the hypostasis, its predicate; the judgement connects the predicate with the subject through the copula of

---

6   The basic thesis about the word which is referred to here is developed in my study "On the philosophy of the name" (in manuscript). (This was later published as *Filosofiya Imeni.*—*Trans.*)

being. The judgement-form contains the mystery of thought, the nature of thought; this form is the key to the comprehension of philosophical constructions. The self-enclosed **I** finds itself on an island inaccessible to any kind of thinking or being, but discovers within itself a certain image of being, which it expresses [*vyskazyvaetsya*] using the "predicate" [*skazuemom*], and which it recognizes as born of itself, as a revelation of itself, as is the copula too. In this sense our whole life, and therefore all of our thinking too, is a continuously self-realizing proposition, a proposition which consists of a subject, a predicate, and a copula. This, however, is precisely why philosophy concerns itself least of all with the proposition or the judgement as the universal form of thought, the form which is implied by thought in and of itself; and even logic and grammar address it only in their own way, through a narrow framing of the question. Not even Kantian critique remarks on the universal significance of the judgement or proposition. The proposition contains the essence and the image of being, and bears the mystery of being within itself, for there it keeps hidden the image of triadicity. The proposition bears witness that this essential relation resists any monism or philosophy of identity which would try to disintegrate these three members by reducing them to one, by reducing them to a subject or a predicate or a copula. Every philosophical system, in so far as it is a philosophy of identity, is governed by an attempt of this kind: the subject, or the copula, or the predicate is announced as the single beginning, and everything is made to derive from it or to lead towards it. Such a "deduction," whether of the subject from the predicate, of the predicate from the subject, or of both from the copula, in fact presents philosophy with its principal task, and, thereby presents an insoluble difficulty to philosophical thought, which strives towards monism, strives to reduce everything to a first unity, no matter what. To take as its point of departure a primordial unity which denies the triadic nature of the proposition: such is the root of every philosophical system, and of its tragedy. This unity is not merely something which thought postulates, but is also the axiom from which thought begins, and this axiom underlies the whole history of philosophy.

Nevertheless, *this axiom is untrue*, which is why all the efforts of philosophy are in vain, and cannot but represent a series of tragic failures, characterized by the following model: the heat of the sun inevitably melts the wax which holds Icarus's wings together, whichever direction he might

The Nature of Thought

be flying in. For as the subject-predicate form testifies, reflecting, in this, the structure of the real itself, the basis of reality is not unitary, but triune, and the false monism to which the philosophy of identity pretends is a delusion, the πρῶτον ψεῦδος [primary falsehood] of philosophy. Substance is one, yet three, and this interconnected unity and multiplicity of the moments of substance can never be surmounted, which is why such an overcoming ought not to be attempted. The hypostasis, the person, the I, exists in so far as it has a nature of its own, that is, an unceasing predication, a revelation of its own which it can never exhaustively utter. "Substance" exists not only "in itself," as a subject, but also "for itself," as a predicate, and, moreover, "in and for itself," in the copula, as existence. And these three beginnings are by no means merely dialectical moments of a unity, negating each other and being sublated into a synthesis; no, they are, simultaneously and with equal dignity, three, like three roots of being which in their joint result make up the life of substance.

The hypostatic I is, in and of itself, essentially indefinable. Everyone is an I, and knows what is being referred to, even if this cannot be spoken (but only implied). The essence of the hypostasis consists precisely in the fact that it is indefinable and indescribable; it stands beyond the limits of the word and of the concept, which is why it cannot be expressed by word or concept, even though it continually reveals itself in them. Face to face with the Hypostasis, it is most becoming to be silent; only a mute mystical gesture is possible, a gesture which does not have a name, but which is marked, "instead of a name" [*vmesto imeni*] by the "pro-noun" [*mestoimeniye*], I.[7] This indefinability is not, however, a void, a logical nullity; on the contrary, the hypostasis is the precondition of logic, the subject of thought. It is a mistake to think that thought stands on its own two feet, that it supports itself. Thought arises from and consists in that which is not thought, but which at the same time is not foreign to thought's nature or alien to it, something out of which thought arises, and around which thought continuously entwines itself. If anywhere, the Kantian separation of noumenon from phenomenon is appropriate just here, to characterize the mutual relationship between the hypostasis and its nature, between subject [*sub"ekt*] and object, between subject [*podlezhashchee*] and predicate. For the *I*, the hypostasis, is indeed a thing in

---

7   More on this can be found in the work on the name mentioned above.

itself (a noumenon), and, as spirit itself, remains by its nature forever transcendent to thought, transcendent to any attitude or relation which thought might have towards it. But the transcendent is always also inseparably linked to the immanent; the transcendent becomes immanent. The subject, the hypostasis, is always revealed, always expresses itself, in the predicate. It goes without saying that the hypostasis in this sense is not the psychological I, psychological subjectivity, which already defines the hypostasis as a predicate, not as a subject: spirit is not psychological, nor is the hypostasis in any way a psychologism. Nor is the hypostasis the epistemological *I*, which Kant thinks of as the unity of transcendental apperception. This too is merely a placeholder "I," its "transcendental" predicate, and it is a mistake to think that the immeasurable depth of the hypostatic spirit could be reduced to this point of light, to a torch of cognizing consciousness. This is testified to, for one thing, by the fact that Kant in all his critiques takes notice of the fact that the hypostatic and noumenal I is an indissoluble unity, a unity which is realized not only in cognition, but also in the will, in feeling, in action, and in the whole of life. It connects "pure," "practical" and "aesthetic" (evaluative) reason. The hypostatic I is a living spirit — but "living" and "spirit" are in any case synonyms — and its life force cannot be exhausted by any definition. It reveals itself in time, but is itself not only above time, but above temporality itself. For the hypostasis there is neither origin nor demise, neither beginning nor end. Atemporal, the hypostasis is at the same time supra-temporal. Eternity belongs to the hypostasis; it is eternal in the same sense as eternal God, who Himself breathed His own Spirit into humanity at the latter's creation. The human being is the son of God and a created god; the image of eternity is an inalienable and indelible part of him. Therefore man can neither think nor desire his own annihilation, the extinguishing of the I (suicide attempts represent a kind of philosophical misunderstanding, and are directed not at the I itself, but only at the way in which it exists, directed not at the subject, but at the predicate). The hypostatic **I** is the philosophical and grammatical Subject of all predicates; its life is this predicate, endless in its breadth and depth.

But are we not, here, introducing into metaphysics as a founding principle something which cannot be defined in any way, since it is something which is in principle transcendent to thought? Are there not misunderstandings, mistakes, absurdities here? How can the unthinkable

The Nature of Thought

be thought? How can the unutterable be expressed? Is the verbal and mystical gesture of the pronoun really a word? Or is the I really a concept, when, by virtue of its own uniqueness and singularity, it destroys every concept, destroys, that is, the universal, the idea? Do we not, in sum, come up against a critical *veto* so strict that only those who are completely philosophically naive are not afraid of it?[8]

Such fears are the result of a timorous epistemological imagination. They are linked to the prejudice which holds that thought possesses the power to give birth to itself, that it has for its object something immanent to itself, that is, itself: a thinking that thinks itself, at once subject [*podlezhashchee*] and predicate. In reality, thought originates in a subject [*sub"ekt*]; thought is thought by a hypostasis, which continually reveals itself in thought. But this hypostasis is beyond the bounds of thought, and, as fully transcendent to thought, is a zero for it; whatever is perfectly and completely transcendent to thought, that is, simply does not exist for thought. Yet such transcendence is nothing other than a mathematical limit, which it is never possible for thought to make real, and the *Ding an sich*, the thing in itself, is still τὸ νοούμενον [*to nooumenon*], the intelligible. That which thought conceives of as transcendent to thought is, precisely, *non-thought*, and is in this sense alien to the nature of thought; it is, however, at the same time akin to thought, accessible to thought, revealed in thought. Transcendence is, by definition, a concept correlated with immanence, and in this sense it is possible to regard as transcendent that object of thought which is at the same time thought's philosophical subject, its hypostasis, or its grammatical subject. What is transcendent to thought is not that which is unthinkable, because it contradicts, destroys, and tears thought apart (besides, such a thing does not exist for thought; it is for thought an "outer darkness," a pure zero), but non-thought — or, more precisely, that which is not *only* thought, yet which is realized by means of thought. The whole problem of the conceivability of an object of thought consists, as we can see, in this problem of transcendence. One can expand the field of categorial synthesis at will, and can at will see, in things, categories of thought; but this fundamental question, of the conceivability of that which is not thought, or which is not only thought, retains all its force, and is thereby only transposed to another place.

---

8 "Veto" is in Latin in the original text. — *Trans.*

It is clear that thought cannot, from its own resources alone, give an answer to the question of how something transcendent is to be thought, how that which is *non-thought* can enter thought, can become thinkable, how the light of the *logos* can be diffused over a realm hitherto unknown to light, or how the matter of thought could be captured using the net of logic or categorial syntheses. Some sort of pre-logical constatation takes place here; a boundary separates thought from that which is non-thought. In this way, at the basis of thought lies a living act, testified to by the living image of thought, i.e., the proposition; and this act has three moments, which are linked, but not reducible, to each other. These moments are the pure hypostasis, the *I*, which is the philosophical and grammatical subject; the nature of the I, which reveals itself in and to the hypostasis, which is the predicate; and self-knowledge, self-ascription of one's own proper nature to oneself, the act of realizing oneself in one's proper nature, which is being or the copula, the *I* as living self-knowledge and self-affirmation. The eternal *I* has (potentially) everything, or the world, as its predicate, and in the act of this consciousness, it lives and recognizes its own being. Hypostasis, intellectual form, being (nature) — such is the triunity of substance, its statics and dynamics; but thought, in this triunity, is the predicate and only the predicate. All three members are inseparable from each other, for the hypostasis is not thinkable in isolation from its nature, just as no substantial nature exists without the hypostasis whose nature it is, and the hypostasis's taking-possession of its nature, the disclosure of this nature, is an act of being, is being as such, is life, and this is why it is by no means a concept or a logical definition, even though it is closely contiguous with the logical. For this reason, what truly exists [*sushchee*] is a *prius*, and stands before being or existence; existence is a continual enacting of the hypostasis's synthesis with its own nature, a self-revelation in the act of being. Philosophical thought has always looked for a definition of substance without finding one, for the reason that (if we except Christian dogmatics, with its doctrine of triadicity) it was seeking a bad, abstract unity, a simple and single substantiality. All the efforts of logical monism, which determines the task to be performed by philosophical systems, and which is an axiom universally implied by these systems, amount to reducing the triadicity of moments, the triunity of substance, to a unity; thought strives to assimilate to itself that which lies at the basis of thought but which is, however, unthinkable—or which, in logical language, is "irrational," is a kind of $\sqrt{2}$.[9] The "law" of identity, whose inverse counterpart is the law of contradiction, is fundamental; it is thought's self-definition and self-cognizance, which secures thought's continuity and keeps its immanent course free from leaps and hiatuses. Yet this law—or, more accurately, this postulate—of identity, which is applicable to everything which falls within the boundaries of thought, is nevertheless completely inapplicable to the origin of thought. It founders upon the basic form of thought, the judgement or proposition. Kant set up an entirely arbitrary and untrue distinction between analytic and synthetic judgements, a distinction which possesses a very great significance for his system. In reality (as Hegel remarks in the *Science of Logic*) all judgements are both synthetic and analytic in their form; under the guise of what is familiar and self-evident (analytic) they constitute a leap over an impassable gulf, and unite what that gulf divides (synthesis).[10] "I am A": this cell of thought signifies a fundamental denial of the very principle of the law of identity. The latter could only at best lead to mere iteration: I—I—I—I...—I, and so on, a fruitlessly self-repeating or self-consuming I. However, it is necessary to point out that the second I in the proposition "I—I," the predicate, is not the same as the unutterable, hypostatic I which is the philosophical or grammatical subject; this second I, as a predicate, already contains an idea within itself (and in this sense it is already a *not-I* in relation to the hypostatic I of the subject).

Subject and predicate—and this is the whole point—by no means constitute a logical analysis, a deduction, a syllogism, or a demonstration

---

9   The square root of 2 is a so-called "irrational" number. Cf. *OED*, 3. "*Math*. Of a number, quantity, or magnitude: Not rational; not commensurable with ordinary quantities such as the natural numbers; not expressible by an ordinary (finite) fraction, proper or improper (but only by an infinite continued fraction, or an infinite series, *e.g.*, an interminate decimal). Usually applied to roots (denoted by the radical sign $\sqrt{\ }$, or in *Algebra* by fractional indices) whose value cannot be exactly found in finite terms of the unit, or to expressions involving such roots; the same as *surd*." —*Trans*.

10 On the non-absoluteness of the analytic-synthetic distinction, see, for example, the section on "The absolute idea" in G.W.F. Hegel, *Science of Logic*, trans. A.V. Miller (London: George Allen and Unwin, 1969), 838: "though the method of truth which comprehends the subject matter is, as we have shown, itself analytic, for it remains entirely within the concept, yet it is equally synthetic, for through the concept the subject matter is determined dialectically and as an other." From this point onwards this work will be referred to as "SL." In all translations from this work, "concept" has been substituted for Miller's "Notion" as a translation of *Begriff*. —*Trans*.

(which are possible only in relation to a combination of propositions already present) but a completely non-logical, or, more exactly, an *extra*-logical synthesis. **I** is not-**I**, **I** = not-**I**, I is revealed in the not-I and through the not-I, which thereby becomes the I. The proposition always contains a synthesis of *I* and *not-I*. How can the subject be defined by the predicate, I by not-I? There cannot be a logical answer to this question, even though this definition possesses the force of a fundamental logical fact by virtue of which thought is possible as such. Conscious, self-legitimating thought, which is immanent and continuous in its movement and development, cannot comprehend itself in its own birth, in its very first cell. The relationship between the subject and the predicate cannot be defined as necessary and continuous thinking, but only as a self-generation: just as the word is born out of that which is not yet a word, so thought, too, is born in a place where there is not yet any logical connection, where such a connection is only just coming into being. This relationship is expressed in the naive chatter of philosophical empiricism and positivism, which quite rightly feel both the inexpressibility of the real, and logic's powerlessness to ground concrete knowledge. Here, of course, there arises the question whether all judgements of the type *A is B*, in all its modalities, can fairly be reduced to the type *I am A*. Are these not two completely different kinds of judgement? Although they are of course different in their content, they are identical in their structure. The epistemologically (and anthropologically) prior and typical form is, without doubt, *I am A*. From the I emerge the second and third person pronouns, and all forms of judgement spring from the latter by way of a personification of the concept. At the same time, it can be said that every judgement about an object can itself be regarded as a predicate of the I, as the I's self-definition: even if the independent grammatical subject ("this table is black") provides such a proposition with a likeness of hypostaticity, a likeness which is incessantly created by our I in innumerable mirroring repetitions, every proposition of this type is essentially (epistemologically and metaphysically) only a predicate of the I: I see, I think, I sense this black table. This judgement succinctly expresses the being of the table in itself and, *like the I*, for itself: this table is black. The original source of the thought, in each case, is not here, is not in these object-like grammatical subjects, but is in the initial formula: I am something, I am not-I (as Fichte, with exceptional perspicacity, noticed).

The I, as a hypostasis, is self-enclosed and inaccessible; it must bring about its own revelation of itself within itself, within its own depths and its own nature—a revelation which would already be an other with respect to the I, and which in this sense would be a not-I, but which would at the same time also be a revelation of the I. The copula, *is*—an "auxiliary verb" so familiar and so innocent in grammar, and so enigmatic and so significant in philosophy—testifies to and announces this. This IS, which is the chief instrument of the operations of thought, is also, logically, completely impossible, since it combines as equal and identical what is different and other. *A is A* is either a nonsensical, redundant expression, devoid of definite content and of effective significance alike, or it is a synthesis of the same with the different, of the other with the identical. Every *is* has originally not a grammatical or a logical, but an ontological, meaning. The hypostasis's self-revelation takes place in the *is*. *Is* is a bridge over the abyss, unifying what truly exists [*sushchee*] with being, subject with predicate, confirming their reality and existence. It is by means of the *is* that the image of what truly exists [*sushchego*] can be posited in being, that this image is brought to life and lives. The copula, IS, is the life of that which is. Therefore, substance—that is, spirit—is that triunity of the subject, the object, and the link between them which exists *in actu*, is their being; all three moments belong to this movement without separation and without confusion. No hypostasis exists without a nature which is the basis of its objectivity, and there is no being without a subject [*podlezhashchee*], without that which truly exists [*suschego*], or without its predicate, its nature. That which truly exists [*sushchee*] posits existence; being is the actual presence of that which truly exists [*sushchego*], which remains, in its self-sufficiency, higher than being. The inseparability of these moments is of itself, it would seem, clear; yet their inconfusibility must be equally so. Philosophy errs in both respects when it renounces triunity for the sake of unity. Each of these three moments, moreover, contains and preserves both of the others as actually present in itself. Pure hypostaticity cannot become an object of thought without being defined in respect of its being, that is, without having a predicate or a context in being. Bare hypostaticity, natureless and beyond being, is a pure zero, which can be arrived at only as a remainder, after every possible content of thought has been removed by an operation of intellectual abstraction. The copula, *to be*, which binds the hypostasis, the subject, to the predicate, is so durable that no power whatever, whether in heaven, on earth, or in the nether world, is able to rend it asunder. And this copula combines the hypostasis with its nature in the act of living, the act of being. Each sees itself in the other; they are correlated so that each, with the help of the copula, leads to the other. The hypostasis is not even a hypostasis without an object [*ob"ekt*] or without a predicate; it is necessarily a hypostasis of someone and for someone, just as no determination or predicate can be a *res nullius* [nobody's], can lack a hypostatic face. And it is self-evident that being, or the copula, necessarily has members which it links, the subject and the predicate, that the copula is someone's and something's being. In this way, substance is like an equilateral triangle

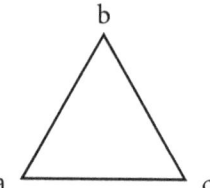

whose angles may be placed in any order, but in which each of the three necessarily presupposes both of the others.

Substance is thus a metaphysical triunity which finds expression in the proposition. This triunity must be strictly distinguished from Hegel's (putatively) dialectical triad, whose moments constitute either the simple analysis of a synthetic thought, or the moments of a single simple thought, in which each predecessor moment is absorbed or annulled by its successor, and in which, in the last analysis, thesis and antithesis lose their independent meaning and existence, and live on in the synthesis. Despite the intentional and hyperbolic sharpening of dialectic, its contradictions are completely sublated and cleared up in its relativity; these contradictions prove either to be moments in the development of the concept or to be misunderstandings. The triunity of substance which is under discussion here, by contrast, is completely non-dialectical; no kind of development of any concept whatever is brought about in it; in it there is no thesis, antithesis, or synthesis. True, there is a sequence, an order, and a connection between its moments, which results from the correlation intrinsic to them. The subject, the hypostasis, is the first; the predicate, the εἶδος [*eidos*], the second; the copula, existence, φύσις [*phusis*], the

The Nature of Thought

third. Yet it is impossible to say that the third element is thereby in any sense the synthesis of the first and the second, or that the first is the thesis to the second's antithesis. In general, these three moments are by no means of a logical nature, of the kind which necessarily characterizes dialectical contradictions. On the contrary, they stand for ontological relationships, which are givens for logic, and which may not be overcome by logic even if they cause serious difficulties for the latter. To resolve the triunity of substance into a dialectical triunity would mean to overcome it through logic, and to award victory to logical monism, that is, to a system of absolute philosophy possessing a single center. But this is impossible. It is impossible to break off or to blunt the corners of the triunity of substance, which lies at the basis of every thought, and which constitutes thought's outcome. This logical triunity is already unacceptable for thought, because thought searches for a single beginning and wishes to build only upon what is single. To start out from three beginnings is impossible for thought if it wishes to remain self-sufficient and immanent, and if, following ancient Parmenides, its creed is that "[t]hought and what it thinks about are one and the same,— no thought can be discovered without existence, since thought is spoken in existence. There is nothing other than being [that is, in this case, nothing apart from a logical first principle—S.B.] and there never will be."[11] The supra- or non-logical outcome of thought turns out to be anti-logical, too; or, to put it differently, it can be said that the object of thought—substance, that which is—is not immanent to thought, as philosophy invariably wishes and here claims in the person of Parmenides; thought's object is

---

11 This is a translation of part of Parmenides' fragment 8; I have translated it directly from Bulgakov's Russian. I give the text from G.S. Kirk, J.E. Raven and M. Schofield, *The Presocratic Philosophers*, second edition (Cambridge: Cambridge University Press, 2007), 252.
ταὐτὸν δ' ἐστι νοεῖν, καὶ οὕνεκεν ἐστι νόημα.
οὐ γὰρ ἄνευ τοῦ ἐόντος, ἐν ὧι πεφατισμένον ἐστίν,
εὑρήσεις τὸ νοεῖν· οὐδὲν γὰρ <ἢ> ἔστιν ἢ ἔσται
ἄλλο πάρεξ τοῦ ἐόντος,....
[tauton d'esti noein, kai houneken esti noēma.
ou gar aneu tou eontos, en hoi pephatismenon estin,
eurēseis to noein: ouden gar [ē] estin ē estai
allo parex tou eontos,....]
Kirk, Raven and Schofield translate thus: "The same thing is there to be thought and is why there is thought. For you will not find thinking without what is, in all that has been said. For there neither is nor will be anything besides what is..."—*Trans.*

instead transcendent to thought, and presents an extra-rational [*zaumnij*] mystery in relation to thought, a mystery which reason can only grope for, having oriented itself according to its own bases. Reason naturally falls into antinomies which determine its own structure and tasks. This does not deprive reason of the possibility of contemplating that which is, nor of that of philosophizing about the meaning and significance of these contemplations. Reason is, instead, bound up with these contemplations: thought has empirical roots. But this means that reason does not start out from an empty place; it does not, like a spider, spin its thread out of itself, but begins from mystical facts and metaphysical givens.[12] In other words, every philosophy is a philosophy of revelation—the revelation of Divinity in the world. The axioms of philosophy cannot be deduced, but only formulated; and autonomous, pure philosophy is either impossible or must with inescapable fatality meet its end in aporia, resulting in a tragedy from which there is no way out. These words should in no way be heard as skeptical. Altogether to the contrary: faith in a truth which is deeper than reason, and which lies beyond reason, by no means impairs or paralyzes our flights towards this truth. Nor can we see in this an abolition of philosophy. Philosophy, having freed itself from false claims, affirms instead that place which properly belongs to it. What is disputed and rejected here is only rationalism's claim to be able to build a single, absolute, transparent system of the world—that is, just that claim which, now in militant and self-confident, now in muted and melancholy tones, is the soul of modern philosophy since Descartes, and which finds its classic and most extreme expression in Hegel. The latter quite openly and consistently placed philosophy above religion, whilst simultaneously admitting that the object of philosophy and religion was identical, yet distinguishing between the methods by which they mastered it. We hold the contrary: religion, as revelation, as

---

12 For the image of self-sufficient rationalism as a spider spinning a web out of itself, see the bee's rhetorical question to the spider in Jonathan Swift's "Battle of the Books," in *A Tale of a Tub and Other Works*, ed. Marcus Walsh (Cambridge: Cambridge University Press, 2010), 151: "the Question comes all to this; Whether is the nobler Being of the two, that which by a lazy Contemplation of four Inches round; by an over-weening Pride, which feeding and engendering on itself, turns all into Excrement and Venom; producing nothing at last, but Fly-bane and a Cobweb, Or That which, by an universal Range, with long Search, much Study, true Judgment, and Distinction of Things, brings home Honey and Wax." —*Trans*.

a doctrine which is not rationalistic but dogmatic and mythopoeic, precedes philosophy, and, to this extent, stands higher than it. In this sense every philosophy, as a doctrine of the world, of everything, inevitably also theologizes. If man were able to generate the world *logically*, that is, to comprehend it through reason alone, he would, in such a case, be a god himself, or be completely merged with the God who creates the world (and this is what Hegel, essentially, claimed). Then his philosophy would of course also be theology, having attained to the highest degree of consciousness. But even that philosophy accessible to human beings is naturally theological, in view of the fact that the mysteries of God and the world are here disclosed logically, through the development of thought. Yet we do not mean, here, the self-consciousness of an immanent thought which, since it generates its own content itself, lacks for nothing. We mean elements quite alien to thought and inadmissible by thought, elements which, nevertheless, turn out to be the basis of thought. The antinomies by which reason is cloven are just those which build it up and which give it determinate form.

Thus "critical antinomism" in metaphysics and in epistemology replaces dogmatic rationalism. The latter is a self-intoxication of reason, reason's ecstasy over its own powers, and a desire to stake everything on reason to the very end, to pursue the experiment of a rational interpretation of the entire world. Such an experiment was pursued in its most grandiose form, of course, by Hegel. Criticism consists precisely in clarifying reason's grounds and structure—not in order to dethrone reason, but, on the contrary, so as to strengthen it. And it is precisely in the light of this critique that the history of philosophy can be seen to be a tragic heresiology.

2
Characteristics of the History of Modern Philosophy

THREE INSEPARABLE AND INCONFUSIBLE MOMENTS of substance and of substantial relation—(1) the hypostasis, the subject; (2) the determination or nature, the predicate; and (3) being or reality, the copula—in the history of philosophy, these moments which, in their singular combination, exhaust and determine substantiality, have always and invariably been either separated from, or amalgamated with, each other; or, rather, separation has usually been accompanied by amalgamation. Systems of philosophy started out from any of these moments, after which they deduced the others from it—yielding a peculiar philosophical modalism or Sabellianism.[1] In this sense, philosophical systems, instead of being philosophical transcriptions, or, if you like, schematic elaborations of the motifs of triunity, prove to be variants of the philosophy of identity, or, what amounts to the same thing, variants of monism, in which it is of only secondary and supplementary significance which of these three moments is taken as the point of departure. There are thus three possible forms of philosophical heresiology or modalistic monism, and systems of philosophy can accordingly be naturally divided into three broad groups: (a) *idealist* systems, which start out from the grammatical or philosophical subject, from the I; (b) *panlogistic* systems, which start from the predicate; (c) *realist systems*, which start from the copula, that is, from impersonal being, and whose realism may be of various characters: mystical-contemplative, empirical or mathematical. Let us examine these types more closely.

---

1 Modalism, usually known, after the doctrine of Sabellius, as Sabellianism, confessed three divine persons only as differing appearances (modes) of one and the same God, Who, in his substance, was uni-hypostatic (in the second century, Praxeas; in the third, Noetus, Berillus, Sabellius, and Paul of Samosata).

A.

IDEALIST SYSTEMS

HERE PHILOSOPHICAL THOUGHT IS ABOVE ALL STRUCK with philosophical "wonder" at the indisputable evidence of our self-consciousness that whatever is exists in, through, and for the I: the world is a spectacle for someone's contemplation, or is a certain subject's representation. The world is subjective, a subjective representation; without the subject, nothing exists. Let us take the words of Schopenhauer, who, as is well known, made this thought the basis of his doctrine of the world as representation:

> Therefore no truth is more certain, more independent of all others, and less in need of proof than this, namely that everything that exists for knowledge, and hence the whole of the world, is only object in relation to the subject, perception of the perceiver, in a word, representation [?! — S. B.]. Naturally this holds good of the present as well as of the past and future, of what is remotest as well of what is nearest, for it holds good of time and space themselves, in which alone all these distinctions arise. Everything that in any way belongs and can belong to the world is inevitably associated with this being-conditioned by the subject, and it exists only for the subject. The world is representation [?! — S. B.]. [...] That which knows all things and is known by none is the *subject*. It is accordingly the supporter of the world, the universal condition of all that appears, of all objects, and it is always pre-supposed; for whatever exists, exists only for the subject. Every one finds himself as this subject, yet only in so far as he knows, not in so far as he is object of knowledge. But his body is already object, and therefore from this point of view we call it representation. For the body is object among objects and is subordinated to the laws of objects.... Like all objects of perception, it lies within the forms of all knowledge, in time and space, through which there is plurality. But the subject, the knower never the known, does not lie within these forms; on the contrary, it is always presupposed by those forms themselves, and hence neither

plurality nor its opposite, namely unity, belongs to it. We never know it, but it is precisely that which knows wherever there is knowledge. Therefore the world as representation... has two essential, necessary, and inseparable halves. The one half is the *object*, whose forms are space and time, and through these plurality. But the other half, the subject, does not lie in space and time, for it is whole and undivided in every representing being. Hence a single one of these beings with the object completes the world as representation just as fully as do the millions that exist. And if that single one were to disappear, then the world as representation would no longer exist.[2]

This *subjectity* [*sub"ektnost'*] of the world, the fact that the world is a predicate for a subject, or that being in itself is also being for itself, is very often interpreted as the *subjectivity* [*sub"ektivnost'*] of the world, and this, in its turn, is then interpreted as illusoriness, spectrality, deceptiveness. This is a motif very widely found in Indian philosophy, in which the world is considered as a dream dreamt by a spectator, by the *atman*. For reasons which cannot be discussed in detail here, this subjective illusionism filtered out from the East into Europe. In Greece, it made itself felt in the epoch of individualistic disintegration, in the skepticism of the sophists, with their subjectivistic relativism (the Protagorean "man is the measure of all things").[3] If, in India, it possesses a mystical and contemplative character, and signifies an appeal to and a deepening of the dark, unconscious, invisible, and unutterable roots of being, a creative *stirb und werde* ["die and become"], a hopeful immersion in the universal nothing—*in deinem Nichts hoffe ich alles finden* ["I hope to find all in thy nothing"]—in Greece it is a symptom of decadence, of a superficial relationship to life which has become a rule.[4] Christianity

---

2 Arthur Schopenhauer, *The World As Will and Representation*, trans. E. F. J. Payne, 2 vols. (New York: Dover, 1969), 1:3, 5.
3 Hermann Diels and Walther Kranz, eds., *Fragmente der Vorsokratiker*, 3 vols. (Zürich: Weidmann, 1996), 2:263.—*Trans.*
4 "[S]tirb und werde" is a phrase from Goethe's poem, "Selige Sehnsucht" ("Blessed Longing"), included in his *West-östlicher Diwan: Gedichte* (Stuttgart: Philipp Reclam, Jr., 1980), 171–72; 172). The second quotation is from the second part of *Faust*, in J. W. von Goethe, *Faust: Die Tragödie erster und zweiter Teil*, ed. Erich Trunz (München: C. H. Beck, 1987), 192, l. 6256. The line is "In deinem Nichts hoff' ich, das All zu finden."—*Trans.*

overcame this subjectivism not just in theory but in a living way, for, of themselves, the new life in God and the deepening of the feeling of reality brought by Christianity deprived decadent subjectivism of its strength, and extinguished it. Out of Christianity was born, after the vigorous upsurge of thought brought by the epoch of the ecumenical councils, the Christian theology of the East and West (scholasticism) in which there was no place for subjective idealism; on the contrary, a religious realism held undivided sway, differing only in its philosophical expressions. True, in the light of later historical developments it is possible to find seams of rationalism even amid the massifs of patristic theology (and still more so in those of scholastic theology), seams which, later on, threaten to become a channel for subjective idealism. However, for this to happen, the underlying rock needed to be significantly exposed to the action of the weather. A spiritual earthquake was brought about in Christianity itself: in Protestantism, the principle of individualism raised its head, and quickly manifested itself in philosophical thought as well. It appeared first of all in England, in the teachings of Collier and Berkeley, who attempted to make the I, the hypostasis, cut off from real being, into the one and only universal principle of philosophy.[5] With this, the abyss of solipsism lying in wait for idealism was also immediately revealed. If the world is the act of the I, is posited by the I, or is a representation of the I, does anything exist outside the I, beyond its limits? Is there a way out of and beyond the I, or does it remain in the singular number, a *solus ipse* [self alone] held in an unbreakable ring? Is there any other sort of I — is there a *we?* — and is there anything which exists in itself, separate from the I's power of representation? In order to complete the heretical dissevering of the triunity of spirit, it is sufficient to isolate the hypostasis, in thought, from the other moments of the life of spirit and to treat it as a singular, mono-hypostatic moment which posits the others from out of itself — and at once it is discovered that an I which has been torn away from reality or nature, as its predicate, turns out to be cut off from all the sources of life, that it dwindles to a desert island, that it simply does not exist. Titanic pretension then gives way to bewilderment and alarm. The I tries to rescue and to draw to itself whatever it can of the lost fullness of life, and lays over the gulf

---

5   Bulgakov is referring to Arthur Collier, the author of *Clavis Universalis* (1713). — *Trans.*

the idealist bridge of *esse-percipi* [to be—to be perceived], the principle of immanent philosophy, in accordance with which being is wholly immanent to the consciousness of the I, that is, being's existence in itself merges with its existence for itself or for the subject.⁶ The subject is no longer separated from all reality; it is no longer empty; it is no longer an abstract point which occupies no place in spatial reality, since it has ascribed to its reverie, to its thinking, an immediate power of creation: the power to found reality, to create being. Yet the specter of solipsism has not gone away, but has only moved to another place. Instead of the question of how to overcome solipsism, there has arisen the question of how to overcome subjectivism, the question of nature and of reality, a question which the principle of *esse-percipi*—the fundamental proposition of idealist epistemology, for which being and consciousness or thought are equivalents, and the distinction between them only a logical one—cannot reach. Everyone familiar with the fortunes of philosophy knows what a curse this question of objectivity, of the "object" [*predmet*] of consciousness, of reality, and so on, has been to all idealist philosophy. The devout Berkeley recognized that this question was quite insoluble, and called frankly for the aid of a continuous miracle of divine intervention which would, as if by some hypnotic power, make our thoughts correspond to our needs, and instill in us the link between ideas and things. Berkeley in his idealism destroyed the world, converting it into ideas, and placed humanity immediately face to face with God, so as to restore, in this way, the reality of the world to humanity. Yet even God can reveal His being to humanity only through humanity's nature. How can a humanity which has been dis-humanized, and which consists only of an I, of a monad, receive such divine influence? It is in any case clear that Berkeley's answer to the philosophical question which he poses is not itself a philosophical one, for which reason it could not be convincing and remained unregarded, whereas Berkeley's idea of radical philosophical idealism was noticed and created an enormous impression. It is enough to remember that Kant is continually fighting against and guarding against this perilous ally, and that he is always in every way possible defending himself from, and acquitting himself of, the suspicion of Berkeleianism.

---

6 *Esse est percipi*, "to be is to be perceived," was a maxim of Bishop Berkeley's.—*Trans.*

The Tragedy of Philosophy

Descartes, the founder of modern philosophy, is also a representative of subjective idealism in the starting-point for his theory, if not in its subsequent development. Through his methodological doubt, in particular, a doubt which stops at nothing,[7] he considers it possible to suppose that there is "no God, no heaven," that there are "no bodies," and so on. He pauses only before the *cogito ergo sum* or *sum cogitans*. In Descartes this is, as can be shown, neither a deduction,[8] nor a syllogism, but only the constatation of a fact—the fact of the presence of self-consciousness. The I, hypostaticity, is taken for the sole point of orientation, a torch of consciousness which illuminates the impenetrable night of doubt. Rationalistic doubt, which demands logical demonstrations where logic is powerless to provide them—demonstrations, that is, not only of the particular forms of being, but also of being as such—bows its head before the fact of the I's being in consciousness, even though, at bottom, the being of this I is not in and of itself any more, though also not any less, self-evident than its attributes: predicatedness and being. Its

---

7 The following are Descartes' formulations in the *Principles of Philosophy*: "In rejecting—and even imagining to be false—everything which we can in any way doubt, it is easy for us to suppose that there is no God and no heaven, that there are no bodies, and even that we ourselves have no hands or feet, or indeed any body at all. But we cannot for all that suppose that we, who are having such thoughts, are nothing. For it is a contradiction to suppose that what thinks does not, at the very time when it is thinking, exist. Accordingly, this piece of knowledge—*I am thinking, therefore I exist*—is the first and most certain of all to occur to anyone who philosophizes in an orderly way.... This is the best way to discover the nature of the mind and the distinction between the mind and the body. For if we, who are supposing that everything which is distinct from us is false, examine what we are, we see very clearly that neither extension nor shape nor local motion, not anything of this kind which is attributable to a body, belongs to our nature, but that thought alone belongs to it. So our knowledge of thought is prior to, and more certain than, our knowledge of any corporeal thing; for we have already perceived it, although we are still in doubt about other things." René Descartes, *Philosophical Writings*, trans. John Cottingham, Robert Stoothoff and Dugald Murdoch, 3 vols. (Cambridge: Cambridge University Press, 1985), 1:194–95.

8 "Descartes himself distinctly declares that the maxim *cogito, ergo sum* is no syllogism. The passages are *Respons. ad II object.*; *De methodo* IV; *Ep.* 1, 118. From the first passage I quote the words more immediately to the point. Descartes says: 'That we are thinking beings is *prima quaedam notio quae ex nullo syllogismo concluditur*' (a certain primary notion, which is deduced from no syllogism); and goes on: '*neque cum quis dicit: Ego cogito, ergo sum sive existo, existentiam ex cogitatione per syllogismum deducit*' (nor, when one says, I think, therefore I am or I exist, does he deduce existence from thought by means of a syllogism)." From *Hegel's Logic, being part one of the Encyclopaedia of the Philosophical Sciences (1830)*, trans. William Wallace (Oxford: Clarendon Press, 1975), 100 (§ 64).

peculiarity and its advantage is its hypostatic form, in consequence of which it appears only as a subject and can never be a predicate. However, Descartes's theory is so ambiguous and unclear that its interest to us is primarily historical, deriving from the strength of the shock which it gave to European thought, impelling that thought more or less decisively into an idealist and immanentist course.

The true father, however, of philosophical idealism, which is both the most fully elaborated and the favorite philosophical heresy of our day, is, of course, Kant. Like Descartes, Kant starts out from skepticism, which was suggested to him by Hume, who thus exerts a continual indirect influence on Kant, whose final position is an anti-Humean doctrine; and Kant was of course right to campaign against this poisonous and fruitless skepticism. The motive which impelled him was a defense of the rule of reason, as whose advocate against skepticism he wished to come forward. Kant was under the sway of the pathos of the Enlightenment; he too was ruled by the Cartesian search for a solid place where one might confidently stand in the quagmire of doubt. It is well known how complex, ambiguous, and contradictory is Kant's thought, which is why every exposition of it is at the same time a commentary upon it and a stylized simplification of it. The history of philosophy for the most part recognized and singled out in Kant one main current, idealism, and that within an epistemological framework. For the majority of Kant's readers his thought as a whole can be reduced to this framework, but for us it is important to single out the central nerve of his philosophical activity, even if this central nerve was concealed from, and insufficiently singled out by, Kant himself. A schematic sketch of the *Critique of Pure Reason* would run thus. In his attempt to outline the objective conditions of knowledge, or, which comes to the same thing, the formal features of truth, Kant conducts, in a "transcendental aesthetic," an exploration of those forms, starting with the forms of sensuous perception.[9] Time and space are thus shown to be the universal forms through which the object

---

9 Translating Bulgakov's Russian vocabulary for Kant into English entails particular difficulties because of the need to triangulate with Kant's German. I have prioritized capturing Bulgakov's sense and tone over any attempt to produce a minutely faithful account of Kant. Time and space are in Kant the pure forms of intuition (*Anschauung*); Bulgakov uses the word *vosprinyatie*, "perception." N.O. Lossky's Russian translation of the *Critique of Pure Reason* renders *Anschauung* as *sozertsanie*, "contemplation" (I. Kant, *Kritika chistogo razuma*, trans. N.O. Lossky [St. Petersburg: Azbuka, 2017]). — *Trans.*

[*predmet*] or "appearance" is apprehended. The next stage is to set out the forms not merely of sensuous appearances, but of the logical concepts which, on the basis of these appearances, are developed into particular forms or categories—a "transcendental logic," divided into a "transcendental analytic" and then a "transcendental dialectic" which reveals the skeleton of reason itself. Kant here proceeds as follows. He takes the objective [*predmetnij*] world to be completely static, as it appears to an observer. By turning the world into a logical preparation, he separates it from its forms, unpacks them, reviews them, and then packs the world and reason back up again from these forms and the materials of sensuous perception—and where anything remains left over, he clears it up in the dialectic, with the help of the antinomies. Thus it seems at first as if pure objectivity governs Kant's thought, and as though there were no place at all in it for idealism, still less for the abstract hypostaticity of the *Ich-Philosophie* [philosophy of the I]. In Kant everything is organized according to the measure of the object—whether empirical or transcendental—even the subject itself. This is why, when he is considered as an epistemologist, Kant can easily be classified amongst the representatives of the philosophy of the predicate, that is, as coming close to Hegel on one hand, but also, like certain contemporary neo-Kantians, to the positivists and empiricists on the other. We do not deny that there is a sufficient basis for all this. However, if one looks for the ontological roots of Kant's system, which were laid bare by his immediate successors, and especially by Fichte, they must be found in a moment of hypostaticity which has been abstracted from and deprived of its nature. The forms of cognition—first time and space, and then the various categories—lie disassembled in Kant, and are oppressive in their plurality. Who will collect them up and give them life? It is evident that although these forms define the object, only a subject, an I, a hypostasis can do this. All these forms are the innervations of this I, are its self-determinations. The I connects the forms and leads them to move; it can be said that they are the I in its epistemological form, the epistemological subject—a concept which originated in the very depths of the Kantian philosophy and which plays an equally important part in neo-Kantianism. In Kant himself this point finds expression in a significant, and, it can be said, central doctrine of his, that of "transcendental apperception." The "synthesis" of separate features into an object, and objectivity itself, presuppose, for Kant, the presence of the unifying function of an *I* which is itself the synthesizing principle. This I is, if one can put it like this, the all-seeing eye which looks through cognitive forms and sees with them. Without this I, there is no synthesis, no object, and no cognition. Kant makes extreme efforts to reduce this I to a purely logical function, to make of it merely an epistemological subject, and in that static condition for which he takes cognition, this is still possible; but he gives himself away as soon as he crosses over to the domain of practical reason, where the I is already will, "practical reason," personhood. The missing center of Kant's epistemology, a lack which Kant's continuators so keenly felt, lies just here. "Transcendental apperception," the unity of the I, lies at the basis of all acts of cognition, and applies equally to the transcendental aesthetic and to the logic, to sensibility and to thought. (Cf. section 1 on the doctrine of transcendental apperception in the excursus on Kant below.) Kant did not succeed in demonstrating that the I may be taken merely as the "unity of transcendental apperception," as a logical function, without relation to an ontological center, be it only in the Cartesian *cogito ergo sum = sum cogitans = sum*. He becomes entangled in obscurities and contradictions. Kant's thinking about what the I, the subject, is, has a merely epistemological significance, and lacks any other; but this idea is for practical purposes abandoned in the *Critique of Practical Reason* and the other critiques. We ourselves need by no means be bound by this division of thought into departments, without any means of crossing from one to the other. A large and important question arises: does the epistemological I, the "unity of transcendental apperception," express the true nature of the I, or, what is the same thing, can that purely epistemological I, upon which Kant so much insists, at all exist? He maintains that the contents of consciousness contain nothing which would provide knowledge of the I (this goes without saying, of course, if he is not talking here of the domain of inner experience, the psychological I, which is concerned with empirical reality). But are knowledge or its separate acts possible as such without the presence of the I? In the act of knowing, the ontological I turns itself into the epistemological I too, but through this transparent film can be seen the fathomless depths of being. And if epistemology is only a transparent film, why can Kant see nothing in it or through it apart from this transparency itself?

The Tragedy of Philosophy

This doctrine of the "transcendental unity of apperception" nevertheless contains what can be called one of Kant's central illuminations. Kant persistently underlines the purely logical significance of this I and in this respect opposes to it the psychological I, which is known only on the basis of "appearances" and which concerns only the domain of internal experience. "It must be possible for the 'I think' to accompany all my representations," which representation ("I think") "cannot be regarded as belonging to sensibility," and must be identical in every consciousness (CPR 152–53 [B 131–32]). This representation confers unity on all the original representations, and without it they would not be my representations.[10] It is, it might be said, the general, universal, and unconditional subject [*podlezhashchee*] of all the contents of consciousness and of any act of cognition, irrespective of whether such an act is expressed in the first or in the third person. It can be said of the judgements in which cognition is accomplished that "a judgement is nothing but the manner in which given modes of knowledge are brought to the objective unity of apperception," that is, to the I (CPR 159 [B 141]). "This is what is intended by the copula 'is.' It is employed to distinguish the objective unity of given representations from the subjective. It indicates their relation to original apperception, and its *necessary unity*. It holds good even if the judgement is itself empirical, and therefore contingent, as, for example, in the judgment, 'Bodies are heavy.' I do not here assert that these representations *necessarily* belong *to one another* in the empirical intuition, but that they necessarily belong to one another *in virtue of the necessary unity* of apperception in the synthesis of intuitions, that is, according to principles of the objective determination of all representations, in so far as knowledge can be acquired by means of these representations—principles which are all derived from the fundamental principles of the transcendental

---

10 From this fact Kant arrives at a completely arbitrary and incorrect conclusion, according to which "[c]ombination does not, however, lie in the objects, and cannot be borrowed from them, and so, through perception, first taken up into the understanding. On the contrary, it is an affair of the understanding alone, which itself is nothing but the faculty of combining *a priori*, and of bringing the manifold of given representations under the unity of apperception." For Kant "this principle... is the highest principle in the whole sphere of human knowledge" (CPR, 154 [B 134–35]). This position is linked to Kant's subjective-cubistic epistemology, but it does not by any means follow from the recognition of a "transcendental unity of apperception," for it is entirely possible that "objects" (ideas) might possess their own existence, which could only be announced by thought or by the understanding to the knowing I.

unity of apperception" (ibid. [B142]). In other words, in the cognition which transforms a bare association of representations (in the example given, a body and heaviness) into a judgement, Kant arranges for each moment of objectivity to coincide with the unity of consciousness. This thought, however, may be interpreted not only in this epistemological, specifically Kantian, and highly questionable sense, but also in the wider sense that the content of any cognition is a predicate of the I: that is, that in addition to its particular subject—the object hypostatized in the image and likeness of the I ("bodies are heavy")—it also possesses another, universal subject, namely, the first person, I. I think: "bodies are heavy"; I reveal myself, I realize myself in the judgement "A is B." If we do not limit ourselves, as Kant did, to epistemology (and he himself only does so within the *Critique of Pure Reason*, without attempting, in any case, precisely to connect this theory of the unity of transcendental apperception with the theories of the other critiques); if we take the concrete I, which realizes itself not merely in thinking, but also in willing, and in creative intuition, it is possible to say in principle that every living act, every living substance is related to the "unity of transcendental apperception." All life is directed by an I, all life is predicated of an I, and the whole world is such a living proposition, is the self-revelation of an I, is its predicate.

And at the same time this I, as Kant quite correctly pointed out, is not our emotionally changeable I which can be known through our own experience, is not the psyche, the soul, the "bundle of representations," the "psychological subject," which lives in the body, and which is a corporeal organism, and so on. In relation to the "transcendental unity of apperception" represented by this absolute I, the psychological I is found in the same domain as the whole world of appearances, on the other side of apperception, and it is just as much a predicate as those appearances are. The absolute I is pure subject and never predicate, a subject which never becomes an object. Rather in contrast to his usual practice, Kant always expresses the peculiar nature of this I as an absolute subject imprecisely, without further explanation or definition, as "thinking": "On the other hand, in the transcendental synthesis of the manifold of representations in general, and therefore in the synthetic original unity of apperception, I am conscious of myself not as I appear to myself, nor as I am in myself, but only that I am. This representation is a *thinking*, not an *intuiting*"

(CPR, 168 [B 157]).[11] So that "[a]ccordingly I have no *knowledge* of myself as I am but merely as I appear to myself.... I exist as an intelligence which is conscious solely of its power of combination...." (CPR, 382 [B 429]). The following sort of expression is also found in Kant: "in the consciousness of myself in mere thought I am the *being itself,* although nothing in myself is thereby given for thought" (ibid.). At the same time, Kant regards even the Cartesian *cogito ergo sum = sum cogitans* as being either a contentless identity (an "analytic judgement") or a false conclusion, as he puts it on another occasion, arrived at by "subreption of the hypostatized consciousness."[12]

In one sense, therefore, Kant's transcendental unity of apperception, the *I* as a logical function, is by no means a pure zero, but must itself in some undefined sense have existence ascribed to it—and no wonder, since this *I* is indeed the world's sun, around which moves the whole universe of this new Copernicus, holding in place all the categories by which he creates and secures the world; and if this *I* were taken away, everything would be turned upside down, and would whirl around in a mad dance. Yet at the same time the strict law of the categories does not permit anything to be said or known about this I. It may know everything else (including its own perishable psychological I) yet may not peer into its own self, may not turn its head towards itself. This is "the simple, and in itself completely empty, representation 'I'; and we cannot even say that this is a concept, but only that it is a bare consciousness which accompanies all concepts. Through this I or he or it (the thing) which thinks, nothing further is represented than a transcendental subject of the thoughts = X. It is known only through the thoughts which are its predicates, and of it, apart from them, we cannot have any conception whatsoever..." (CPR, 331 [A 346/B 404]). This thought is continually and tiresomely repeated, even though it is in no way clarified, in Kant's analysis of the "psychological paralogisms," where the same question of the transcendental unity of the I is explored from the point of view of the doctrines of rational psychology as to the soul's substantiality, simplicity, and so on. And here Kant's main prop is a peculiar agnosticism, according to which there can be no act of cognition of any kind concerning the

---

11 I have amended the very end of the quotation to replace Kemp Smith's *thought* and *intuition* for *Denken* and *Anschauen* with *thinking* and *intuiting.—Trans.*
12 "[A]nalytic judgement": CPR, 337 (A 355); "subreption": CPR, 365 (A 402).

I. Moreover, in the first, less guarded, edition, Kant sometimes resorts to an extremely strange argument of this kind: "The 'I' is indeed in all thoughts"; none the less, we would not, "in resting it upon experience, be able, by any sure observation, to demonstrate its permanence." "[W]e can indeed perceive that this representation is invariably present in all thoughts, but not that it is an abiding and continuing intuition, wherein the thoughts, as being transitory, give place to one another" (CPR, 334 [A 350]). Whether seriously or ironically, Kant agrees here to acknowledge a "constant logical subject of thought," whose substance is "only in idea, not in reality" (ibid.) This whole heap of misunderstandings does not get us any nearer to answering this question: how we are really to understand this epistemological lever, upon which the whole Kantian universe—that is, "the world of appearances"—rests? It is not a zero, yet neither does it exist. It is not the individual I, since it is decisively opposed to the I of inner experience which possesses its *Anschauungen*; yet nor is it the supra-individual I, *the* **I**, for such an I is not mentioned either. Is it the one and only I of its kind, or is it merely a single I? There is self-evidently no way in which the logical function could be *repeated*, no way, that is, in which one could see, from one's own I, with one's own "unity of transcendental apperception," the logical function at work in another consciousness, since this would already be *Anschauung* [intuition], already "experience." Consequently, there is apparently no way of overcoming epistemological solipsism or of exiting from its *splendid isolation*.[13] True, Kant does, in passing, and most infelicitously, speak of transcendental consciousness from the standpoint of another (CPR, 342 [A 363]), but he does this without having any grounds for it, and it can be said that here and in the "paralogisms" of rational psychology he shatters that epistemological possibility of knowing or of recognizing other epistemological subjects which he himself nevertheless takes for a criterion of objective knowledge. The multi-hypostaticity of the epistemological **I** is incompatible with the mono-hypostaticity of the I as a logical function, to which the ideas of plurality or of repetition are in no way applicable. There is no epistemological bridge from I to thou, since epistemology does not permit a psychological handling of the question. The Thou—that is, the other I, other and at the same time

---

13 "Splendid isolation" is in English in the original.—*Trans.*

identical, an epistemological point of view outside me yet at the same time within me — is impossible here. This, of course, is not of itself an objection, but it does confirm the contradiction in Kant's theory and the clear insufficiency of his principles.

Kant becomes entangled in his own web here, and falls victim to the dogmatic prejudice that there is no cognition without "sensibility" — a sensibility which is, moreover, narrowly and incorrectly understood here — even as he himself speaks of "thinking" as an activity of the "epistemological I." But if this I sees, thinks, and knows everything, can it really be impossible for it to look at itself? And what, if not the I's consciousness of the I, is represented by Kant's own reasoning when, like the ancient sage who began to walk forward so as to refute the idea of the impossibility of motion, his very doctrine of the unknowability of the I in fact demonstrates that it can be known? In other words, he both poses the problem of the I and solves it after all. Against such hyper-criticism, which leads only to self-deception and illusion, Hegel's suggestion that learning to swim should be done by getting into the water, rather than by trying to work things out on the bank, retains its force.[14] In fact, our thought possesses a powerful and inalienable instrument for self-knowledge: reflection, or, more precisely, self-reflection, which Fichte and Hegel put to just this purpose. The I, the epistemological I, even if it be merely a "function" (granting for a minute that there can be a function without anyone who or anything which functions), can itself reflect upon itself, can itself become the object of thought, of ideation, of intuition. In this consists, too, the logical meaning of the tautology "I is I," which, in reality, is neither a tautology nor a meaningless assertion. The second I is a predicate: the I becomes its own predicate. Of course, the I (or any other subject which occupies its place) cannot simultaneously be both subject and predicate; this is ruled out, and that is that. But Kant wants, on this basis, to maintain the unknowability of every propositional subject, that is, of all concepts. In a certain way this is true, if it is borne in mind that a subject can in general be disclosed only by a predicate. The propositional subject is transcendent

---

14 "But the examination of knowledge can only be carried out by an act of knowledge. To examine this so-called instrument is the same thing as to know it. But to seek to know before we know is as absurd as the wise resolution of Scholasticus, not to get into the water until he had learnt how to swim." *Hegel's Logic*, trans. Wallace, 14 (§10). — *Trans.*

to thought; it is a question to which the predicate is the answer. Is the question contained in the answer? Yes and no, because the answer would not be an answer if it did not presuppose the question, if it did not contain the question in itself; but it would also not be an answer if it simply repeated the question. The I in Kant's thought is of course distinguished from any propositional subject, from any concrete I or object, by the fact that it is as "transcendental apperception" the universal subject *par excellence*, the subject of subjects, in relation to which every subject is in a certain sense already a predicate, and thus transcendentally impure. Yet this does not mean that transcendental apperception is empty and abstract, like a logical function, but that it has a universal and metaphysical, an ontological, significance; that is, that transcendental apperception necessarily leads through the gateway of epistemology into metaphysics as the domain of the theory of being as such. For from a Kantian point of view, any living I, which speaks of itself as this or that, and which feels itself to be a concrete person, is still not a "transcendental" I: I want, I love, I am hungry, I consider that, I see, and so on. Such an I is not an epistemological I at all: the latter is, in this I, only a certain non-spatial point which funnels down into the opaque and earthly psychological I; it is a super-I within the I, which latter is merely the countenance, the predicate of that super-I. The enigmatic and chimerical character of such an **I** constitutes, of course, a riddle for thinking which Fichte faces head-on and which even in Kant leads to many opacities and contradictions, as previously remarked. The chief of these is that Kant has to ascribe both existence and non-existence to it. And this is correct, in the sense in which it can be applied to the distinction between phenomena and noumena. The noumenon does not possess being in the world of phenomena, yet, at the same time, it is not a zero, since the noumenon is the truly existent, and so existence, if not being, must be ascribed to it, and this is the noumenon's phenomenal manifestation, which is also *being*, the being of noumena and phenomena. In this way, the *Ding an sich* turns out to be not merely a "limit concept," a *Grenzbegriff* which marks the limit of experience itself, which demarcates non-experience from experience, and which does not wholly belong either to the former or to the latter, since it participates in both. The *Ding an sich* is what truly exists; it posits what exists and possesses being in what exists. It is not possible to say of it that it *is*, but being belongs to it; it is the true subject of any given predicate. Substance is also defined by this relationship between the noumenon and phenomenality, by this concrete proposition, and in this sense the only true noumenon in the Kantian sense is the "transcendental I," that is, the hypostasis. Kant does not, in essence, provide a theory of personhood in the *Critique of Pure Reason*, and although, as becomes clear in the remaining critiques, especially in the *Critique of Practical Reason*, his theory is through and through anthropological, perhaps even anthropomorphic, he does not, here, supply any kind of anthropology, nor, in particular, does he provide any theory of the person. Without realizing it, he walks past a crater which has unexpectedly opened up, and which leads into the depths of the earth, walks past, that is, his own theory of personhood—although he does stumble into this crater in his account of freedom and the intelligible character. Here it turns out that "in its intelligible character," the subject, which, empirically, is bound by all the laws of the chain of causal determination, is nevertheless free from that chain "[i]nasmuch as it is *noumenon*." In the intelligible character of the subject, "nothing happens in it; there can be no change"; "the active being of itself begins its effects in the sensible world.... In this way freedom and nature, in the full sense of these terms, can exist together, without any conflict, in the same actions, according as the actions are referred to their intelligible or to their sensible cause" (CPR, 469 [A 541/B 569]). It would seem that in order to see knowledge as the act of the subject [*sub"ekt*], as the self-revelation of the subject, it would be enough to take a single further step, by extending this account so as to characterize the relation between the "transcendental subject" of knowledge and knowledge itself. After Kant, Fichte took this step; but Kantians usually hold fast to the transcendental subject and take great care to avoid any account of the noumena. More will be said about this below, but here it is necessary to emphasize that Kant's theoretical philosophy and his anthropology also lack, in particular, any account of personhood. As was already remarked, there is no *other* person; each exists only in the singular number. For the psychological I which is accessible to experience is not a transcendental person, whilst the latter, in so far as it is merely a logical function, cannot form an object of experience. Therefore, according to Kant's theoretical philosophy, human persons are not persons, but constitute aggregates of properties, "objects," established by epistemological consciousness. True, from time to time Kant feels the want of them, and then he conjures them up (as we already saw in the discussion of the question of the I, when it is suddenly asked how the matter would appear to an external observer); the existence of another, alien and specifically epistemological consciousness also turns out to be necessary when it comes to defining the objectivity of judgements as having a universal significance for every consciousness (particularly in the *Prolegomena*). This dogmatic contraband is already at work in Kant's practical philosophy, where the concept of the person is central: "Rational beings... are called persons because their nature already marks them out as ends in themselves, that is, as something which ought not to be used merely as a means."[15] The whole edifice of the *Critique of Practical Reason* also stands on this foundation. A clear tension exists between theoretical and practical philosophy in Kant, a tension which is not made any less acute by the declaration of the primacy of practical reason. The doctrine of the transcendental I is of the very essence; it forms the heart of Kantian idealism or Kantian epistemologism, as was revealed and underlined in the subsequent history of thought. The real state of affairs, however, was obscured by the fact that the whole Kantian construction is governed by a different plan and from a different center. In the foreground are found epistemological obstacles and parts of the dismantled epistemological apparatus; these conceal the pilot himself. Fichte and Hegel believed that one of the inadequacies of Kant's epistemology was that he did not provide a deduction of the forms of cognition, but allocated them to a "rhapsody of categories," according to external, scholastic, and sometimes arbitrary schemas.[16] These categories relate both to the predicate and to the copula, and constitute the forms of thinking and the forms of cognition as such, but they are organically unified not by the predicate but by the subject; they make up the epistemological I, which casts its net over the material of cognition, over this something. Of this *something* it is either impossible to speak, as Kant himself

---

15 Kant, *Groundwork of the Metaphysics of Morals*, trans. H.J. Paton (New York: Harper and Row, 1964), 96.
16 In his *Prolegomena to Any Future Metaphysics*, Kant had distinguished his own deduction of the categories from "that ancient rhapsody (which proceeded without any principle)." *Prolegomena to Any Future Metaphysics*, ed. Gary Hatfield, rev. ed. (Cambridge: Cambridge University Press, 2004), 76 (§39). — *Trans.*

thought,[17] or, more precisely, a hiatus in cognition is found here, a tear between the subject and the object, a mutual separateness in the face of which every act of cognition becomes a riddle: how can anything at all be caught in the epistemological net, and what would do the catching? The question which Kant addresses, how cognition is possible, that is, precisely, how objective cognition is possible, becomes even more enigmatic after this, since it is merely deferred to another place, and gets connected to the link between the form and content of cognition. This is why "epistemology" emerged as the result of Kant's work, and why questions either about the nature of consciousness, on the one hand, or about the "object of cognition," on the other, are not on Kantianism's agenda. The question of "epistemological consciousness" is generally treated on the level of immanentism, in the sense that the whole content of cognition is taken to be immanent to the subject. The πρῶτον ψεῦδος [prōton pseudos, original error] of Kant's philosophy, and its main distinguishing characteristic, is his abstract subjectivism or egocentrism. He forcibly dissolves (only into abstractions, of course) the living unity of substance, the inseparability of subject and object as subject and predicate, noumenon and phenomenon, and there proves to be a disunity between, and perhaps even an impossibility of uniting, the subject, on the one hand, with the forms and categories which have been torn away from real experience, and into which have been inserted the alien material of "*Empfindungen*," *affizierende Dinge* [sensations, things which affect us] and, on the other, that formless, senseless and unthinkable material which is accessible, if at all, only to "pseudo-thinking" (Plato). How can this broken bond be mended? And how are knowledge itself, and consciousness, to be understood in the face of this split in experience, in which our feet give way with every step taken by thought? And what, finally, is known; what is such an object of cognition? The reader familiar with the latest Kantian literature will recall its basic lines of thought

---

17 "The much-discussed question of the communion between the thinking and the extended, if we leave aside all that is merely fictitious, comes then simply to this: how in a thinking subject outer intuition, namely, that of space, with its filling-in of shape and motion, is possible. And this is a question which no man can possibly answer. This gap in our knowledge can never be filled; all that can be done is to indicate it through the ascription of outer appearances to that transcendental object which is the cause of this species of representations, but of which we can have no knowledge whatsoever and of which we shall never acquire any concept" (CPR, 359–60 ["Paralogisms of Pure Reason (A), 393"]).

and its various answers to the fateful question of the object of cognition. Desperate attempts are made to break out from the enchanted circle of solipsism while at the same time remaining within it, to rescue and secure the "object of cognition" whilst remaining on the ground of epistemological subjectivism. Metaphysically, all this can be diagnosed as one of the complaints most characteristic of epistemologism: the separation of the hypostasis from substance, of the subject from the object. The epistemological expression of this sickness takes many forms, some of them unexpected. On one hand, of course, arguments continue about settling the content of the Kantian subject, i.e., the categories and the forms of cognition, about "pure logic" and "pure consciousness," about *a priori* cognition. On the other, attempts are made to define the "object of cognition" itself, cognition's *a posteriori*. With this, a pure and consistent immanentism proves possible, an immanentism which inevitably degenerates into a subjective panlogism: *esse = percipi*. Here the world and the object of cognition inevitably turn into a mist of daydreams, in which there is a vain struggle to secure the firm ground of objectivity in a despairing attempt to overcome solipsism (Schuppe and his school).[18] Yet equally desperate efforts are made to overcome any "givenness," and to dissolve the object of cognition into a logical category, to leave only *a priori* cognition remaining, having expelled *affizierende Dinge* [things which affect us] into the "outer darkness" of psychologism, whilst of course all the while continuing to draw nourishment from them. This is what Cohen does; he wishes to conquer the world by representing the "object of cognition" as a matter of "pure," "scientific cognition."[19] Hence for such a (Cohenite) neo-Kantianism the decisive and fateful question is the deduction of the fundamental elements of thought, which correspond to the sensations and, as it were, the stimuli given by things in themselves in Kant's thought. By means of cunning intricacies, including the application of the mathematical concept of infinitesimals, Cohen succeeds in eliding and perhaps in doing away altogether with the

---

18   The philosopher Wilhelm Schuppe (1836–1913), who edited a *Zeitschrift für immanente Philosophie* [Journal for immanent philosophy] towards the end of the nineteenth century. — *Trans.*

19   Hermann Cohen (1842–1918), the leader of the so-called "Marburg School" of neo-Kantian thought and the author of a *Logik der reinen Erkenntnis* [Logic of pure knowledge] (1914), amongst other works. — *Trans.*

distinction between God's earth — and zero (which is what evolutionism always tries to do). The *reiner Ursprung* [pure origin] of Cohen's "pure logic" exemplifies a sophistical dialectic whose goal is to erode and completely to dissolve irrational "givenness," and thoroughly to rationalize and to apriorize — that is, in the last analysis, to subjectivize — reality.

Another path towards attaining the same goal — to make an objectless subject and thereby to secure the triumph of "idealism" — is taken by the Freiburg school of Windelband and Rickert, whose fulcrum is not pan-categorism and pan-methodologism, but the exploitation of the *copula*.[20] The copula is interpreted subjectively [*sub"ektivno*], or, more precisely, subjectally [*sub"ektno*], as defined at will by the subject: it is taken in the imperative mood instead of in the indicative, is transformed into a demand, whilst a teleological character and a value (*Wert*) are ascribed to that act of the self-revelation of substance which is accomplished in the copula; the "object of cognition" turns out to be an absolute *ought*. Here, of course, all empirical cognition of the world is understood only as material for the exercise of a moral demand. The idea of "practical" consciousness, to which Fichte attributed primacy over theoretical consciousness, returns, but it lacks the audacity and foundational significance of Fichte's conception. Only the weaker aspect of Fichte's treatment is adopted, without his metaphysical doctrine. To turn the world into a fruitless and insatiable demand for knowledge, whilst at the same time retaining it as useful empirical material — this is a tedious and pointless idea, which is of more interest as one of the outcomes of Kantianism characteristic of Kantianism's blind alleys than it is in itself.

A Kantian idealism of the most decided kind is supported by Schopenhauer, who considered Kant's deepest teaching to be the separation between the phenomenality of the world and things in themselves. For Schopenhauer, the latter, as is well known, are made up of alogical, blind, unconscious, and anhypostatic will, which requires the whole world to consist of the "representation" of a dreaming consciousness. However chimerical this doctrine, the clarity and resolution which Schopenhauer

---

20   Wilhelm Windelband (1848–1915), the inventor of the distinction between "nomothetic" and "idiographic" approaches to knowledge, the former concerned with positing general laws and the latter with specifying singular instances; and Heinrich Rickert (1863–1935), the author of *The Limits of Concept-Formation in the Natural Sciences* (1896–1902). — *Trans.*

Characteristics of the History of Modern Philosophy

brings to his account of "the world as representation" deserve recognition. Schopenhauer comes close to the truth in his theory of the philosophical subject [*sub"ekt*] as the propositional subject [*podlezhashchee*] of all predicates, which subject, therefore, never itself enters the realm of experience; the subject is transcendent to experience, yet at the same time is immanently intuited in experience. "That which knows all things and is known by none is the subject. It is accordingly the supporter of the world, the universal condition of all that appears, of all objects, and it is always presupposed; for whatever exists, exists only for the subject. Everyone finds himself as this subject, yet only in so far as he knows, not in so far as he is object of knowledge. But his body is already object, and therefore from this point of view we call it representation. For the body is object among objects, and is subordinated to the laws of objects, although it is immediate object. Like all objects of perception, it lies within the forms of all knowledge, in time and space through which there is plurality. But the subject, the knower never the known, does not lie within these forms; on the contrary, it is always presupposed by those forms themselves, and hence neither plurality nor its opposite, unity, belongs to it. We never know it, but it is always that which knows whenever there is knowledge."[21] In particular, Schopenhauer considers arguments about the reality of the external world to rest on a misunderstanding, in so far as no causal interaction takes place between subject and object; such interaction pertains only to the world of objects.[22] However, on the whole this correct and precise distinction does not lead to any worthwhile results in the theory of hypostaticity, since it is completely lost in the nonsensical, or, more precisely, the anti-sensical doctrine of the will

---

21 *The World as Will and Representation*, trans. Payne, vol. 1, chap. 2, 5. Cf. vol. 2, chap. 1, 16–18. "Unser erkennendes Bewusstseyn, als äussere und innere Sinnlichkeit (Rezeptivität), Verstand und Vernunft auftretend, zerfällt in Subject und Object und enthält nichts ausserdem. Object für ein Subject seyn und unsere Vorstellung seyn ist dasselbe. Alle unsere Vorstellungen sind Objecte des Subjects und all Objecte des Subjects sind Vorstellungen." (*Über die vierfache Wurzel des Satzes vom zureichenden Grunde* [On the Fourfold Root of the Principle of Sufficient Reason] chap. 3, §16.) (The quotation is given in German in Bulgakov's text. "Our cognizing consciousness, which appears as external and inner sensibility [receptivity], understanding, and reason, divides into subject and object and contains nothing beyond these. To be an object for a subject, and to be our representation, is one and the same thing. All our representations are objects of the subject, and all objects of the subject are representations." — *Trans.*)

22 *The World as Will and Representation*, trans. Payne, 1:14–15.

as first principle, which first produces all the individual special effects and then gets rid of them when they are no longer needed. Despite all Schopenhauer's gifts, as well as the aesthetic merits of his work, his thought when taken as a whole too clearly bears the stamp of morbidity and of misanthropy, as well as of contradiction: having started out along one line of thought, a subjective-idealist one, he abruptly shifts to the philosophy of identity in his theory of the will.

The true monarch of the realm of idealistic subjectivism is, without doubt, J. G. Fichte, especially in the first period of his philosophical activity (around 1800: here we are concerned with the introductions to the science of knowledge, *Concerning the Concept of the Science of Knowledge*, *Foundations of the Entire Science of Knowledge*, and the *Outline of the Distinctive Character of the Science of Knowledge*). The aspects of Fichte's theory which are of interest to us here will be considered in detail in a dedicated excursus; for the moment, only a brief indication of its general significance will be given. Fichte's theory, as it is developed in his science of knowledge, is a unique phenomenon in the history of the philosophy. It is the most radical attempt to think through to its end a philosophy of pure and abstract hypostaticity, an attempt which does not stop short even of absurdity. It is the same as a philosophy of identity, but reversed. Usually, the philosophy of identity understands substance as nature (φύσις [*phusis*]), predicate, object, a he or it from which in one way or another the subject and the whole world of consciousness then originate. In Fichte it is the **I** which takes on this significance of being the sole substance; the **I** posits a not-**I** by means of its own resources and for the sake of its own needs. This is a philosophy of identity of absolute clarity and absolute subjectivity, from which the whole universe must be "deduced," and throughout the early treatises Fichte exhausts himself in these fruitless efforts at a forcible deduction (here too belongs the young Schelling's early and able exposition of Fichte in his essay on the *Ich-Philosophie*).[23]

The foundational significance of Fichte's system is enormous, and the philosophical experiment represented by this system, maniacal in its principled one-sidedness, is indispensable. Its meaning lies in the fact that in order to comprehend the true nature of the **I**, thought must test

---

23 F. W. J. Schelling, "Of the I as Principle in Philosophy or on the Unconditional in Human Knowledge," in *The Unconditional in Human Knowledge: Four Early Essays 1794–96*, trans. F. Marti (Lewisburg: Bucknell University Press, 1980). — *Trans.*

and explore its limits; and for this it is really necessary to transgress and cross these borders, to carry out a sort of philosophical vivisection, which is what Fichte's system also is. In Fichte there appeared, in all its dazzling vividness and incontrovertibility, a truth: that it is impossible to eliminate the I from everything which exists—not, however, in that false and slanderous sense which Schopenhauer gave to this idea in his theory of "the world as representation," where the subject turns out in the last analysis to be merely a temporal and illusory center, to be one of the reflexes of a blind and capricious will. No, Fichte grasped the substantial nature of the I in its indissolubility and ineliminability. The I is itself what is closest at hand, what is most trustworthy, what is first. Everything must be thought in and through the I, must be thought in terms of I-ness: this is the task. The I, the philosophical and propositional subject, like a spider in its web, must weave a world, must bring the predicate into being, must posit being. Never, either before or afterwards, has such a full attempt been made to reckon with the I, to display and to measure its force. Here Fichte stands on Kant's shoulders, and expounds the true meaning of Kant's theory to its conclusion, thereby illuminating and deciphering it—or expounds the meaning, at least, of one of the fundamental motifs of that unwieldy and many-motifed structure. The Fichtean system is nothing other than a development of the Kantian theory of the "transcendental unity of apperception" or the epistemological I. In Kant, this theory appears as if against Kant's own will, issuing from his account of the forms of cognition, as the missing link between the categories; the categories are not deduced from the I, but, on the contrary, the categories of themselves presuppose the necessity of the I as what unifies them. In Fichte, by contrast, the I is put in charge at once, and all the categories, as well as the pure forms of intuition, time and space, derive from it. To display the nature of the I as a logical centre, as a focal point for the epistemological forms, to display epistemological idealism in its strength and glory is the first and most fundamental task of the *Ich-Philosophie*. Although Kant famously bristled at his commentator's eagerness, it is doubtless true, historically, that Fichte did indeed reveal the truth about Kant.

Even more significant, however, were Fichte's projects of a metaphysical, rather than an epistemological, kind. Fichte ascribes to the I not merely the significance of an epistemological subject—as, insistently, do all the neo-Kantians—but also that of a metaphysical substance. Hypostaticity is awarded all its plenitude; substance is directly equated with hypostaticity, and this metaphysical daring is both the most paradoxical and the most interesting thing about Fichte's doctrine. Everything falls under the category of I-ness; everything is the I, and the I is everything; there is nothing without the I, nothing which is beyond the limits of the I, or which could be not-I or transcendent to the I. Such is the metaphysical postulate of Fichte's theory, and such its fundamental task. Here Fichte touches upon a problem of extraordinary significance: the problem of the role of the hypostasis in substance, of the bond between the I and that which is not I. This bond is something mysterious and unsoundable; in it lies the mystery of substance, that is, of that something which it is necessary to assume, and which can be grasped in its self-revelations, but which it is impossible to comprehend with the intellect and impossible to deduce—either by deducing the I from nature, or by deducing nature from the I. Usually, the philosophy of identity takes the first path, but Fichte, who has in this neither equals nor imitators, took, in his *Science of Knowledge*, the second path: the attempt to deduce everything from the I, to see in everything a state of the I or a positing by the I. (It should be admitted that Fichte did not himself stand fast for long at the summit of his own philosophy, and soon descended from it along the path of popular philosophical edification.) How and where does the I make contact with that which is not I, the subject with the predicate? Is it possible to grasp everything using the category of I-ness? Fichte tried to do so, and his *Science of Knowledge* is his answer. It is well known how this deduction is carried out: in the absolute and, obviously, unitary, I, which plays the same role as substance in Spinoza, or, if you prefer, the same role as the One in Plotinus, there emerges an opposition between the I, and the not-I as a reflection of the I (the logical conjuring tricks of the deduction possess no fundamental significance and are essentially of no interest, since they are merely auxiliary instruments). The greater, absolute I plays the role of a transcendent, self-identical beginning, in which there is neither I nor not-I, which are bound to each other by their mutual entailment and by their mutual inseparability. The absolute I is substance as it exists before the emergence of I and not-I, of hypostasis and nature. One of Fichte's many obvious ambiguities and unclarities, then, is that, starting out from a transcendental I, he converts this into an absolute

I, which he then exchanges for an empirical I inalterably bound to the not-I. Essentially, there is no more proximity or resemblance between the I and I [*mezhdu Ya i ya*] than between Spinoza's substance and the self-consciousness of its *modus*, the individual human person, or between the One in Plotinus and the self-consciousness of the individual human soul in this world. There is not, in essence, any kind of "deduction" here, nor can there be. Yet Fichte, with all his might, deduces; and, by means of a series of intermediate links, he fashions a chain which unites the centre with the periphery. Except that it turns out that there is nothing to which the chain can be fastened: however far the chain is stretched out, it still cannot come to an end, because there always remains a "stimulus" to the I, an *äussere Anstoss* [external stimulus], which cannot be explained, but only registered. In order to explain the "stimuli" it turns out to be necessary to presuppose, together with the theoretical I, a practical I which requires "limits" and "obstacles" to its continual movement. The practical I turns out already to be an absolute *ought*, and what leads to this impotent and unquenchable thirst, to this restlessly burrowing worm, an eternal revolution upon the burning wheel of the *ought*, is the Luciferian project of constructing the world in one's own image and likeness, out of a bare, abstract hypostasis. Fichte constructs, of course, not the world, but, at most, an abstract, I-shaped schema of the world, of its transcendental form. And the "practical exercises," the seminaries of practical reason to which all this construction leads, add nothing, since here too what is required is only some obstacle or some limit in general, and not a single step is taken in the direction of the concrete world, of our despised and—alas!—lovable "sensibility." This is not a world, since it is not yet even the schema of a world. And the Fichtean I, whether writ large or writ small, can never, however hard it tries, engender from itself so much as a real fly or a living cockroach, not a single blade of grass nor even a thistle. It dwells, dead and empty, in the wilderness of Luciferian self-isolation. The disappearance of nature, that is, a desert: such is the result of Fichte's venture, and it was only natural, perhaps even inevitable, that there should appear as the antithesis to this thesis that philosophy of nature which, from Schelling to Hegel, tries to deduce the I from the not-I, a venture just as hopeless as Fichte's.

A further peculiarity of the philosophy of abstract hypostaticity is that it is doomed to a fateful *solipsism*. We have already indicated that the concept of the absolute **I** wavers between the concrete and empirically plural I and the unitary **I**—which latter is already not a human **I**, but a divine **I**—so that the positing in this divine **I** of an I and a not-I, the primordial "deduction" of the not-I, is, properly speaking, the act of the creation of the world. It is obvious, however, that to create the world is by no means to "deduce" it, and is even quite the opposite of any such "deduction." Passing over these ambiguities and polysemies, let us pause only over the fact that, from the point of view of the **I** which, having posited a not-I, is already no longer absolute, no other **I** can be perceived, since there exists no means of "deducing" the other **I**, nor any epistemological organ for it. "I" remains, inevitably, in the singular. The other **I** is for it—if indeed it is anything at all for it—only a not-I, and there exists no sort of "introjection" whatever which could invest the not-I, as if through certain pores, with the image and likeness of its own **I**. In other words, Fichte is still somehow able to postulate the not-I as a predicate, but he does not even once pose himself the problem of how to postulate an other I, or a *thou*, a co-subject, nor does he even try to defend himself on this most perilous and ill-protected front. Kant in his theoretical philosophy no doubt finds himself in no better a situation than Fichte, since there is also no transition from the bundle of categories and schemata, or the "transcendental unity of apperception," to transcendental unity of apperception numbers two, three, four, and so on, to a *thou* or a *you plural*. But Kant disposes of this difficulty through the postulates of practical philosophy. A theoretical solution of this kind will not do at all, of course; apart from anything else, it would, if taken seriously, inevitably lead to the revision and re-organization of the whole theory. (What, indeed, would Kant's thought have looked like if practical philosophy had really occupied first place, in accordance with the "primacy" of practical reason, and if that primacy had really influenced his account of the basic presuppositions of the system?) For Fichte, who so often and so readily descants upon "human dignity," there is no such thing as a human being, nor a "thou," nor anything at all like them. The **I**, the abstract hypostasis, is capable in its Luciferian ecstasy of begetting only its own shadow, the not-I, and of reigning over this empire of shadows, this metaphysical *sheol*.

Fichte's philosophy is not only a theory of abstract hypostaticity, of a subject without an object, but also a theory of mono-hypostaticity. In

Fichte's work, substance is characterized as having a single and unitary countenance, that of the all-engendering subject, which, in truth, can beget nothing, but is able only to "posit," and which posits everything from out of itself. It is not difficult to see in this a distorted philosophical transcription of the image of the *first* hypostasis, the Father, which, however, when taken in isolation from the other hypostases and from the divine *pleroma*, Sophia, is neither a father, since it lacks a son, nor a creator, since it remains without a creation, even though it lays claim precisely to this. The deduction from the *I* not only of the not-I, but also of all the categories and forms of consciousness, together with the ideal (transcendental) form of the world, is, without doubt, an attempt to beget the Word; it is an intimation, from the depths of the I, from the first hypostasis, of the divine Logos. Since, however, only a completely empty transcendental schema of the world, devoid of content and of colour, can, by following the logical path of a "deduction," be deduced by such intimations from out of the I, such a mono-hypostatic philosophy is in fact doomed to acosmism, however much it struggles against it. For a transcendental schema is, in and of itself, only the possibility of a world, but not the world itself—which Fichte is therefore unable to deduce. This is just why there is no place whatsoever in Fichte's system for the third hypostasis, for the Spirit which creates life and brings it to fulfilment, and which confers sensible concretion upon the ideas of the world, as the world's possibilities. The surge of Fichte's thought does not extend to the third hypostasis; its power is exhausted before that hypostasis can be reached. The pitiful surrogate for life-creating spirit in Fichte's architectonic turns out to be "practical reason," which, in pursuit of the unattainable, performs a kind of running on the spot in order to keep theoretical reason supplied with matter, whilst the word "reason" amalgamates both domains, the theoretical and the practical, the world-positing and the world-creating, into a putative unity.

In the language of Christian heresiology, Fichte's doctrine represents, without doubt, a Sabellian variety of Unitarianism. To Fichte's theory belongs the honor, if it is one, of being a brilliant and resolute deduction of a philosophical heresy, and in this sense, because of its religious and metaphysical precision, it stands *higher* than Kant's theory, which it thinks through to its conclusion. At the source of this heresy, as of all heresies, is rationalism, reason's defiant refusal to submit to that mystery which finds a philosophical transcription only in those antinomies which tear apart the unified fabric of monistic philosophy. In Fichte this monism finds expression in his universal "deductions," but above all, and here more decidedly than anywhere else, in his deduction of the *not-I* from the **I**, whereas in fact no subject can be deduced from a predicate, nor can a predicate be deduced from a subject, nor a *not-I* from an **I**, nor an **I** from a *not-I*: there is no logical bridge here, for this is not a deduction, but a production, not the unfolding of a single thing, but the disclosure of one thing in and through another. Here is the tragedy of rationalistic philosophy, whose deductions condemn it to heresy. The merit of a philosophical system, as a heresy which reveals one of the possibilities established by "autonomous" reason, is the purity, precision, and determination with which it pursues its path and with which it reveals its motifs and its motives. Just as, in Kant, the foundations of "pure" reason's antinomies and transcendental illusions and self-deceptions—which turn out to be at the same time its ideas and ideals—are already laid in reason's very structure, so, in the same way, "the critique of philosophical (that is, of metaphysical) reason" is able to lay bare the logic of heresies, illusions, and aporias. Reason inevitably falls into these if it does not wish to remain skewered by those antinomies towards which it is led by the content of the dogmas of the faith, and by reason's own metaphysical self-reflection. A sphere located at the apex of a conical form will, provided that it move at all, choose for itself a definite direction, and having taken one slope, will inevitably fall down it until it reaches a limit, rolling down to the bottom. If it can only manage to, it may not move at all, remaining superior to all "directions." It proceeds, however, from this single point alone, a single point which, although it does not itself lie along any of these paths, nevertheless, by beginning all of them, belongs to each of them, without itself occupying any logical space whatever. The sphere goes further in the direction selected and in the path already determined, and cannot come to a halt until it has travelled along the whole path. To stop half-way, in indecision, is, here as elsewhere, a grievous, irreparable, and unforgivable sin. Philosophy is the tragedy of reason, which has its own catharsis. It is possible not to give way to passions, but if one is already fated to fall under their power, great passions stand higher than petty caprices, and folly stands higher than reasonableness. "For there must also be heresies amongst you, that they which are approved may be made manifest among you" (1 Cor. 11:19). And philosophical aporias must come to be known in their full depth; the tragedy of reason must be lived through honestly and unflinchingly, and in suffering lies the special stamp of greatness in philosophy. Intrepidity and madness, self-crucifixion on the cross of paradox, absurdity not only in the face of common sense, but also in the face of impartial philosophical thought, Dionysiac frenzy, a Khlystism of thought: such are the characteristics of tragic philosophizing.[24] It can embody itself in differing temperaments and in various forms, from Nietzsche's hysteria to the granitic imperturbability of Hegel, but such is its nature. And the stamp of such greatness is also imprinted upon the work of Fichte, who does not shrink from wild absurdity, despite his conversion of this great world of God's into a pocket edition under the title "not-I." There have been many systems of idealism both before and after Fichte, yet Fichte's surpasses them all in the purity and sharpness of its leading metaphysical motif. Fichte reveals the truth about idealism, and he, if anyone, can say of himself that "idealism is I, is my doctrine, and ought not to be otherwise." The idealist heresy has appeared fully and exhaustively, and Fichteanism is a permanent monument in the history of thought, in the dialectic of reason, an irreversible act in the tragedy of philosophy.

B.

PANLOGISTIC SYSTEMS

PANLOGISM IS USUALLY, WITHOUT FURTHER DISCUSsion, ascribed to idealist systems as such and considered as the type to which they belong—Fichte *and* Hegel. Such is the usual idea. In fact, there is, on the contrary, a fundamental opposition between them, an opposition only obscured by the general denominator "idealism," which is unimportant here. So far we have been dealing with the philosophy of

---

24 The Khlysty ("whips") were an ascetic Russian sect originating in the seventeenth century, originally known as the *khristoveroi*, or "Christ-believers," who believed in the possibility of direct communication with the Holy Spirit and in the Spirit's embodiment in living individuals; it is presumably this belief, rather than the sect's asceticism, that Bulgakov has in mind in describing philosophy as *khlystovshchina*. The sect's name was corrupted to "Khlysty" by its critics, who considered members of the sect to be flagellants. — *Trans.*

abstract hypostaticity, for which there exists only the subject, I. But it is no less tempting and no less possible for philosophical thought to proceed from the object, and to orientate itself solely from that. The object can be taken in one of two ways: either as a certain content, meaning, word, or idea—as a predicate, in the precise sense—or as being, *res*, which is expressed by the copula. Both these sides, the ideal and the real, are united in the I. The "I" is a dimensionless and indeterminate point; it is outside being and above being. The predicate, the object, by contrast, necessarily possesses content and thus leads into the domain of being. This ideal content is "the world as representation," the sum total of ideas, the organism of ideas. These ideas of an intellectual world, of an intelligible and eternally essential realm of pure being, are regarded by panlogism as substance itself. For panlogism the word, the *logos*, was not only *in the beginning*, but the word also *was* the beginning, and not only was "it" "all," but everything also originated from it: this is panlogism's fundamental thesis, its principal thought.

It is possible, in a certain sense, to regard Plato, in his theory of ideas, as having been the forefather of the philosophy of abstract predication. Plato's theory of ideas as a whole is without doubt characterized by its anhypostaticity, by its lacking an interest in the problem of personhood, and by its lacking, therefore, any account of personhood either. He fastens his gaze upon an intellectual place, a τόπος νοητός [*topos noētos*], where the "mother" of being resides, the eternal, divine ideas. It is these that he wishes to see and to hear; he wishes, in his dialectic, to hold still the sempiternal birth of the ideas and the conflicts inherent to them. Nor is Plato unfamiliar, moreover, with the problem of laying bare the very logical bases of this conflict, of this dialectic of ideas; so that he proceeds from the science of ideas to a "science of logic" (in the Hegelian sense) especially in dialogues such as the *Parmenides*, the *Sophist*, the *Philebus*, and in certain parts of the other dialogues. The moment of hypostaticity is either completely absent in Plato, or it is considered only as an aspect of the relativity, transience, formation, and confusion of authentic being—the ideas mingled with the inauthentic, material world. Nevertheless, Plato's thought here by no means has a militantly anti-hypostatic character; rather, it is helpless and naïve in regard to the question of personhood, like antiquity in general. Thanks to this, Plato's theory of ideas does not have the characteristics of a closed and free-standing metaphysics, and is able to enter Christian theology as a theory of Sophia and of the sophianicity of the world (compare my *Unfading Light*). Plato's thought must not without qualification be interpreted as panlogistic, despite the fact that, needless to say, Hegel, the "German Plato"—who, in fact, in no way resembles his putative forerunner—understands Plato precisely in this way, together with many of his compatriots (rather as, more recently, the Cohenites Natorp and Hartmann have tortured Plato so as to turn him into a forerunner of Cohen). If, for the reasons stated, Plato is not to be counted amongst the panlogists, we need to go straight on to Hegel, who is the only radical panlogist of his kind. The philosophy of Hegel, like the philosophy of Fichte, constitutes a classic and fully consummated panlogism, a panlogism of pure predication, of thought thinking itself. Hegel's panlogism represents the Herculean pillars of philosophical audacity, to which thought can attain when delirious in, and intoxicated by, its own strength; this is the ecstasy of thought, and, at the same time, it is a human frenzy, an idealist Khlystism. Just as Fichte, in his Luciferian madness, had the audacity to write his little *I* with a capital letter, and to equate his own spark with the divine Flame itself—to unify and to identify the creaturely I with the absolute I, so as to make of his putatively absolute I not only the creator of the world, but also the creator of the I itself and of its creaturely, human form—so Hegel, standing at the opposite pole, and starting out not from the philosophical or propositional subject but from the predicate, faced the same difficulty, to deduce and posit everything out of pure thought, out of the absolute predicate, to deduce not only the subject, the I, but also the world and nature. If, for Fichte, substance is I and I alone, for Hegel substance is self-engendering thought. The first-order significance and importance of such a project is evident. A more detailed account of it will be given in a dedicated excursus; here we will pause only over some features which are of fundamental interest in this connection. In Hegel's thought the subject, or the I, does not posit the *not-I* out of itself, together with the thought of the I and of the *not-I*, that is, thinking as such; instead it is thinking as such which posits the I, which becomes subjective, or even, at a certain moment of its own dialectical development, becomes the subject. Thinking begins and starts out neither from subjectivity nor from objectivity but from indifferent, self-thinking thought, which, in its own dialectical self-unfolding, becomes the concept and then the concept of the concept, the subject. "The concept, when it has developed into a *concrete existence* that is itself free, is none other than the I or pure self-consciousness."[25]

[25] SL, 583. In the introduction to the *Encyclopedia Logic*, 30 (§20), we find a remark made in passing: "Thought, regarded as an activity, may be accordingly described as the active universal, and, since the deed, its product, is the universal once more, may be called a self-actualizing universal. Thought conceived as a subject (agent) is a thinker, and the subject existing as a thinker is simply denoted by the term 'I'." *Hegel's Logic*, trans. Wallace (Oxford: Clarendon Press, 1975), 29. And that is all. But in the third part of the *Science of Logic*, at the zenith of speculation, where the twists of the dialectical transitions are followed patiently and acutely, this theme is given only the following definition: speaking of the nature of the concept, Hegel goes on to say that "I will confine myself here to a remark which may help one to grasp the concepts here developed and may make it easier to find one's bearings in them. The concept, when it has developed into a concrete existence that is itself free, is none other than the I or pure self-consciousness. True, I have concepts, that is to say, determinate concepts; but the I is the pure concept itself which, as concept, has come into existence. When, therefore, reference is made to the fundamental determinations which constitute the nature of the I, we may presuppose that the reference is to something familiar, that is, a commonplace of our ordinary thinking. But the I is first, this pure self-related unity; and it is so not immediately but only as making abstraction from all determinateness and content and withdrawing into the freedom of unrestricted equality with itself. As such it is universality; a unity that is unity with itself only through its negative attitude, which appears as a process of abstraction, and that consequently contains all determinedness dissolved in it. Secondly, the I as self-related negativity is no less immediately *individuality* or is *absolutely determined*, opposing itself to all that is other and excluding it—individual personality. This absolute universality which is also immediately an absolute individualization, and an absolutely determined being, which is a pure positedness and is this absolutely determined being only through its unity with the positedness, this constitutes the nature of the I as well as of the concept; neither the one nor the other can be truly comprehended unless the two indicated moments are grasped at the same time both in their abstraction and also in their perfect unity" (SL, 583). On p. 84, we find another remark made in passing: "The richest is therefore the most concrete and most subjective, and that which withdraws itself into the simplest depth is the mightiest and most all-embracing. The highest, most concentrated point is the pure personality which, solely through the absolute dialectic which is its nature, no less embraces and holds everything within itself, because it makes itself the supremely free—the simplicity which is the first immediacy and universality" (SL, 841). "The absolute idea, as the rational concept that in its reality meets only with itself, is by virtue of this immediacy of its objective identity, on the one hand the return to *life*; but it has no less sublated this form of its immediacy, and contains within itself the highest degree of opposition. The concept is not merely soul, but free subjective concept that is for itself and therefore possesses personality—the practical, objective concept determined in and for itself which, as person, is impenetrable atomic subjectivity—but which, none the less, is not exclusive individuality, but explicitly universality and cognition, and in its other has its own objectivity for its object. All else is error, confusion, opinion, endeavour, caprice and transitoriness; the absolute Idea alone is being, imperishable life, self-knowing truth, and is all truth" (SL, 824).

Characteristics of the History of Modern Philosophy

It goes without saying that we find only fleeting and inadequate judgements about the nature of the I. For Hegel, the **I** exists as a concept, as a generality, which in his view is always expressed by a word, by every word, and consequently also by the word **I**. There is, for Hegel, no such thing as the particular nature of the pronoun as a demonstrative, mystical gesture, namely, towards an individual, nor is there, accordingly, any such thing as the nature of any given substantive. This mistaken and one-sided appeal to the nature of the word as universal and universal alone is one of the main arguments which, as early as the *Phenomenology of Spirit*, leads Hegel to panlogism. Hegel treats the **I** from the same standpoint, simply as a general concept.[26]

---

26 "The object of sense-certainty is *Einzelnes, Dieses, ein Jetzt, ein Hier, dieses Jetzt, dieses Hier* [an individual, this, a now, a here, this now, this here], yet this immediate 'here' is already *schlechthin allgemeines* [directly universal]." (Despite the presence of German text, this is—at least so far as I have been able to discover—not a quotation but a paraphrase of the sense of Hegel's discussion of sense-certainty in the *Phenomenology*. See G. W. F. Hegel, *Phänomenologie des Geistes*, ed. Johannes Hoffmeister [Hamburg: Felix Meiner, 1952], 79–89; *Hegel's Phenomenology of Spirit*, trans. Miller, 58–66. — *Trans.*) To predicate an object means to generalize it; this expresses "die göttliche Natur der Sprache" [the divine nature of speech] (which is why one might perhaps pay closer attention to it). It is possible to indicate an object with one's hand; an individual is inexpressible, irrational; the definition of an object itself is, by contrast, already *allgemeines* [universal]; that is why what is spontaneous and intuitive is immediately ejected from the luminous kingdom of the logos into outer darkness, and panlogism's later path of abstraction is already predetermined.

This turn of thought is reproduced in the *Logic* and in the *Encyclopaedia*, and now it is applied to the I. Here we read: "Sensible existence has been characterized by the attributes of individuality and mutual exclusion of the members. It is well to remember that these very attributes of sense are thoughts and general terms.... *Now language is the work of thought: and hence all that is expressed in language must be universal*. What I only mean or suppose is mine: it belongs to me—this particular individual. But language expresses nothing but universality; and so I cannot say what I merely mean. And the unutterable—feeling or sensation—far from being the highest truth, is the most unimportant and untrue. If I say 'the individual', 'this individual', 'here', 'now', all these are universal terms. Everything and anything is an individual, a 'this', and if it be sensible, is here and now. Similarly when I say 'I', I mean my single self to the exclusion of all others; but what I say, viz. 'I', is just every 'I', which in like manner excludes all others from itself. In an awkward expression which Kant used, he said that I accompany all my conceptions—sensations, too, desires, actions, etc. 'I' is in essence and act the universal: and such partnership is a form, though an external form, of universality. All other men have it in common with me to be 'I'; just as it is common to all my sensations and conceptions to be mine. But 'I', in the abstract, as such, is the mere act of self-concentration or self-relation, in which we make abstraction from all conception and feeling, from every state of mind and every peculiarity of nature, talent and experience. To this extent, 'I' is the existence of a wholly abstract universality, a principle of abstract freedom. Hence thought, viewed as a subject,

The Tragedy of Philosophy

Every *here* or *now*, although it is immediate, is also *schlechthin allgemeines* [directly universal], something logical; this is ensured by *die göttliche Natur der Sprache* [the divine nature of language] (which divine nature, by the way, is why language deserves much more focused attention and concentrated scrutiny than it in fact gets in Hegel). Thus the **I**, too, when it is expressed, is "every I," "the universal in its abstract and free

---

is what is expressed by the word 'I'; and since I am at the same time in all my sensations, conceptions, and states of consciousness, thought is everywhere present, and is a category that runs through all these modifications." (*Hegel's Logic*, trans. Wallace, 31 [§20].) The lack of clarity in Hegel's arguments about words and thoughts, and in particular about pronouns, is characteristic of his reasoning, as is the fact that in his work hypostaticity vanishes, in panlogistic fashion, into the general *concept* of the I.

In another passage of the *Encyclopaedia* we find the following account: "Nature does not bring its νοῦς into consciousness: it is man who first makes himself double so as to be a universal for a universal. This first happens when man knows that he is 'I'. By the term 'I' I mean myself, a single and altogether determinate person. And yet I really utter nothing peculiar to myself, for everyone else is an 'I' or 'Ego', and when I call myself 'I', though I indubitably mean the single person myself, I express a thorough universal. 'I', therefore, is mere being-for-self, in which everything peculiar or marked is renounced and buried out of sight; it is as it were the ultimate and unanalysable point of consciousness. We may say 'I' and thought are the same, or, more definitely, 'I' is thought as a thinker. What I have in my consciousness is for me. 'I' is the vacuum [!?—S.B.] or receptacle for anything and everything: for which everything is and which stores up everything in itself. Every man is a whole world of conceptions, that lie buried in the night of the 'Ego'. It follows that the 'Ego' is the universal in which we leave aside all that is particular, and in which at the same time all the particulars have a latent existence [*Hegel has to get himself out of a tight spot here*—S.B.]. In other words, it is not a mere universality and nothing more, but the universality which includes in it everything. Commonly we use the word 'I' without attaching much importance to it, nor is it an object of study except to philosophical analysis. In the 'Ego', we have thought before us in its utter purity [?—S.B.]. While the brute cannot say 'I', man can, because it is his nature to think. [*Not because of this, of course, or, rather, not only because of this, but because the human being is spirit, which, for Hegel, is identical with thinking, is only thinking.*—S.B.] Now in the 'Ego' there are a variety of contents, derived both from within and without, and according to the nature of these contents our state may be described as perception, or conception, or reminiscence. But in all of these the 'I' is found: or in them all thought is present." (*Hegel's Logic*, trans. Wallace, 38 [§24, Zusatz].) A similar conclusion about the I is reached in the theory of quality, in the section on being-for-self: "The readiest instance of Being-for-self is found in the 'I'. We know ourselves as existents, distinguished in the first place from other existents, and with certain relations thereto. But we also come to know this expansion of existence (in these relations) reduced, as it were, to a point in the form of simple being-for-self. When we say 'I', we express the reference-to-self which is infinite, and at the same time negative. Man, it may be said, is distinguished from the animal world, and in that way from nature altogether, by knowing himself as 'I': which amounts to saying that natural things never attain a free Being-for-self, but as limited to Being-there-and-then, are always and only Being for an other." (*Hegel's Logic*, trans. Wallace, 141 [§96, Zusatz].)

existence. The **I** is, consequently, thinking as subject"; "I is pure thought." And since thinking distinguishes a person from an animal, the pure I can belong only to a person.[27]

It is natural that Hegel should, with carelessness and prejudice, pass over the problem of judgement.[28]

---

27   From time to time Hegel unexpectedly speaks of the I in strange accents which recall Fichte: "'I' is the vacuum or receptacle for anything and everything: for which everything is and which stores up everything in itself. Every man is a whole world of conceptions, that lie buried in the night of the 'Ego'. It follows that the 'Ego' is the universal in which we leave aside all that is particular, and in which at the same time all the particulars have a latent existence." (*Hegel's Logic*, trans. Wallace, 38 [§ 24].) (The reader will notice that Bulgakov has already quoted this passage in the previous note. — *Trans.*)

28   "[T]he propositional form ... is not suited to express the concrete (and the true is always concrete) or the speculative. Every judgement is by its form one-sided and, to that extent, false." (*Hegel's Logic*, trans. Wallace, 51 [§ 31].) "The chief feature of the method [of pre-critical metaphysics — *Translator*] lay in 'assigning' or 'attributing' predicates to the object that was to be recognized, for example, to God. But attribution is no more than an external reflection about the object: the predicates by which the object is to be determined are supplied from the resources of picture-thought, and applied in a mechanical way. Whereas, if we are to have genuine cognition, the object must characterize its own self and not derive its predicates from without [? — S. B.]. Even supposing we follow the method of predicating, the mind cannot help feeling that predicates of this sort fail to exhaust the object. From the same point of view the Orientals are correct in calling God the many-named or the myriad-named One. One after another of these finite categories leaves the soul unsatisfied, and the Oriental sage is compelled unceasingly to seek for more and more of such predicates. In finite things it is no doubt the case that they have to be characterized through finite predicates: and with these things the understanding finds proper scope for its special action. Itself finite, it knows only the nature of the finite. Thus, when I call some action a theft, I have characterized the action in its essential facts; and such a knowledge is sufficient for the judge. Similarly, finite things stand to each other as cause and effect, force and exercise, and when they are apprehended in these categories, they are known in their finitude. But the objects of reason cannot be defined by these finite predicates. To try to do so was the defect of the old metaphysic." (*Hegel's Logic*, trans. Wallace, 50 [§ 28].) Here, quite wrongly, predication is linked to the understanding and opposed to reason; the relation between a subject and a predicate is one of simultaneous identity and non-identity (for Hegel justly remarks that *omnis determinatio est negatio* and that every judgement contains a contradiction within itself). This is repeated in the *Science of Logic*: "[t]he proposition in the *form of a judgement* is not suited to express speculative truths; a familiarity with this fact is likely to remove many misunderstandings of speculative truths. Judgment is an *identical* relation between subject and predicate; in it we abstract from the fact that the subject has a number of determinatenesses other than that of the predicate, and also that the predicate is more extensive than the subject. Now if the content is speculative, the *non-identical* aspect of subject and predicate is also an essential moment, but in the judgment this is not expressed" (SL, 91). Then again, Hegel lets fall the following witty aphorism: "in death, as we ordinarily say, body and soul part, i.e. subject and predicate

The Tragedy of Philosophy

The plan of Hegel's system was that it should show how thought, starting from its simplest, barest, and most abstract determinations, comes to itself through its dialectical development; how, increasing in strength, it becomes in the end both an all-encompassing concept and the concept of concepts, becomes the subject, becomes the living idea, spirit, so that panlogism issues in spiritualism. So we have here a complete antithesis to Fichte. In the latter, the subject in all its own power and glory generates the object together with all its categories. Here, on the other hand, it is, if not the object, then the predicate—that is, thought—which reveals itself also to be the subject; thought is here, moreover, understood not in its concrete fullness but in terms of logical schemas and categories. It can be said in advance that this deduction of the non-deducible can be accomplished only by means of a series of forced interpretations and sophisms, and that Hegel in any case nowhere carries out any such deduction, but instead simply announces it in the third part of his *Science of Logic*, in accordance with the plan of that work, in which this part was to contain the "subjective" logic, and, consequently, the requisite subject. To announce, quite abruptly and dogmatically, that "[t]he concept, when it has developed into a *concrete existence* that is itself free, is none other than the *I* or pure self-consciousness," or that "the *I* is the pure concept itself which, as concept, has come into existence" (SL, 583) does not mean that one has deduced the **I**, even though this general task—to exhibit thinking not only as substance, but also as subject—is presented as the common aim of all Hegel's philosophical work as early as the "Preface" to the *Phenomenology of Spirit*.[29]

---

utterly diverge." (*Hegel's Logic*, trans. Wallace, 238 [§ 173, Zusatz].) (True, O king!) This is connected to Hegel's aforementioned failure to understand the nature of the word, which he in general so greatly misuses. The error about *Dies* [this] and *Hier* [here] which underlies the *Phenomenology* is also repeated in the *Science of Logic*: "By 'this' we *mean* to express something completely determined; it is overlooked that speech, as a work of the understanding, gives expression only to universals, except [*how can there be an 'exception' here!*—S.B.] in the *name* of a single object; but the individual name is meaningless, in the sense that it does not express a universal, and for the same reason appears as something merely posited and arbitrary; just as proper names, too, can be arbitrarily assumed, given, or also altered" (SL, 117; an astonishingly frivolous judgement about the word to have come from the philosopher of panlogism!).

29 "In my view, which can be justified only by the exposition of the system itself, everything turns on grasping the True, not only as *Substance*, but equally as *Subject*." Hegel, *Phenomenology of Spirit*, trans. Miller, 9–10.—*Trans.*

Characteristics of the History of Modern Philosophy

The transition from thought to the subject [*sub"ekt*], from the predicate to the subject [*podlezhashchee*], or, what amounts to the same thing, from a panlogistic schema to spiritualism, is both the most difficult and the most impracticable transition in Hegel's project. To posit an **I** from the *not-I*, or at least from the *non-I*, is much less manageable than Fichte's undertaking in the opposite direction—to deduce a *not-I* from the **I**. For in a certain sense the world, or predicate, is actually a *not-I*, to the extent that it can be defined in terms of categories of I-ness, and the **I** is really the starting point (the first hypostasis in the triune shape of substance). But this movement is irreversible: if it is possible to accomplish a leap (but by no means a transition) from the **I** to the *not-I*, there is no sort of path from the *non-I*—which had not previously even contained the *not-I*—to the **I**. Hegel's undertaking is, ontologically, perfectly absurd, and shows with how little intensity he experienced Fichte's philosophical discoveries (there are almost no traces of any attention on Hegel's part to Fichte's problem). It goes without saying that in fact there could not be a *non-I* which would not at the same time be a *not-I*, which would not, that is, conceal within itself an **I**; and this **I** must also duly come to light. In other words, the kind of thinking which Hegel wished to demonstrate, a thinking of a predicate without a subject, does not exist, and here one can say, to adapt a Russian proverb, that if you chase Nature (or the subject) in through the door, it escapes out of the window, and that Hegel, having begun as a panlogist, ends as a spiritualist—that is, either his system must in fact from its very beginning be understood as a gradually unfolding spiritualism, or spiritualism signifies the inevitable collapse of panlogism and itself stands for a completely new doctrine. In reality, Hegel's whole worldview wrestles together, in a fantastical way, two different systems, idealistic panlogism and monistic spiritualism, which is why it is also possible to understand him in the latter sense (Caird).[30] Despite this, Hegel's most original, significant, and interesting productions—i.e., almost all of the *Science of Logic*, as well as the *Phenomenology* and the *Encyclopaedia Logic*—are panlogistic. The remaining works have such a pronouncedly spiritualistic character that they in no way require either panlogism or the works just mentioned

---

30   Edward Caird's *Hegel* (1888), as Khoruzhij, ed. cit. (575) points out, appeared in a Russian translation in 1898, with a foreword by S. N. Trubetskoj and a prefatory essay on "The Philosophy of Hegel" by Vladimir Solovyov.—*Trans.*

in order to be understood. (As an external reminder of those works, the externally applied triadic form persists, metamorphosed into a particular kind of evolutionism; this is how it was possible for a Hegelian evolutionism, such as we find in Marxism, to come about). Nevertheless, Hegel's main efforts aim to bring panlogism and pan-spiritualism closer together, or even to identify the two—to pass from the schema to concretion, from abstraction to reality. He was not able, of course, to fulfil this requirement, since it was an impossible one, or, more precisely, a false one. However deep the separate analyses of the *Logic*, however dazzlingly brilliant certain moves of the dialectic, however astounding Hegel's industry and persistence in overcoming difficulties, in erecting a system of cast iron and granite, the project of an absolute philosophy nevertheless did not succeed, otherwise this system would in actual fact have been the system of the world, its reason a divine reason, and the rationality of everything existing transparent to thought. Hegel met with two fundamental and decisive misfortunes. The first was the impossibility of deducing the subject from the predicate, and the second, no less serious, the impossibility of deducing being or reality from thought, or, more precisely, from conceivability, from abstract possibility alone. This latter difficulty is the question of nature. In order to obtain reality, the world, and nature, Hegel—stopping his ears and screwing up his eyes so as to forget everything which he has argued up to that point—famously announces the "being-other" of the concept, which "releases" nature from itself in no less irrational and incomprehensible fashion than does the Schopenhauerian Will when it arbitrarily posits the world.[31]

31 Nature is depicted along these lines in relation to the concept: "This is the impotence of nature, that it cannot adhere to and exhibit the strictness of the concept and runs wild in this blind irrational [*begrifflos*] multiplicity. We can *wonder* at nature's manifold genera and species and the endless diversity of her formations, for *wonderment* is unreasoning and its object the irrational. Nature, because it is the self-externality of the concept, is free to indulge itself in this variety, just as spirit, too, even though it possesses the concept in the shape of the concept, indulges in pictorial thinking and runs riot in its endless variety. The manifold natural genera or species must not be esteemed as anything more than the capricious fancies of spirit in its representations [*indeed so!*—S. B.]. Both indeed show traces and inklings of the concept on all sides, but do not present a faithful copy of it because they are the side of its free self-externality. The concept is absolute power just because it can freely abandon its difference to the shape of self-subsistent diversity, outer necessity, contingency, caprice, opinion, which however must not be taken for more than the abstract aspect of nothingness" (SL, 607–8). (A pitiful hypostatization on the part of the haughty panlogist!) The following thought sounds even more absurd:

Characteristics of the History of Modern Philosophy

This irrational collapse affords the concept the further possibility (in the philosophy of nature and the philosophy of history) of overcoming this irrationality—an irrationality which, however, possesses the priceless quality of being real. The system is given a wholly spiritualistic meaning, and "spirit" or substance obviously takes the place of the idea and the concept; Hegel's philosophy turns into a metaphysical evolutionism. The "being-other" of the idea—that is, reality—becomes a springboard for spirit, an inert mass, in overcoming which spirit reveals its own nature and strength. Unfortunately, this "being-other" not only is not properly grounded in Hegel's panlogism, but does not admit of any sort of dialectical grounding either. For, of course, the external simplification into a dialectical "contradiction" of something which has nothing universal or dialectical about it—namely, the idea's relinquishing itself, at its point of fullest maturity and self-consciousness, into nature, into the darkness and meaninglessness of "being-other"—is unconvincing, and constitutes of itself a *petitio principii*. Equally unconvincing is the transformation of the faceless and anhypostatic idea into the subject, a transformation accomplished by an unexpected bare assertion that "the free subjective concept is not merely soul [!!!—S.B.] but also possesses personhood," that it is "a person...impenetrable atomic subjectivity."[32] This sort of leap of thought, these sorts of logical gaps and hiatuses, will stand for ever as a historic example not only of logical arbitrariness, but also of philosophical despair; they are Hegel's attempt to escape from the nets of his own system. And Hegel's position concerning the fundamental

---

"Life, or organic nature, is the stage of nature at which the concept emerges, but as blind, as unaware of itself [*what nonsense!*—S.B.] and unthinking [*!!!*—S.B.]; the concept that is self-conscious and thinks pertains solely to spirit" (SL, 586). Here panlogism is clearly making a transition to spiritualism (Hartman/Schopenhauer). The transition to nature is solemnly announced in the same way: "the idea *freely releases* [*entläßt*] itself in its absolute self-assurance and inner poise. By reason of this freedom, the form of its determinateness is also utterly free—the *externality of space and time* existing absolutely on its own account without the moment of subjectivity" (SL, 843).

32 I have rephrased Miller's translation (SL, 824) to reflect the different ordering in the Russian quotation given by Bulgakov. Miller's version of the passage quoted in part by Bulgakov runs thus (with his "Notion" for *Begriff* as usual replaced by "concept"): "The concept is not merely *soul*, but free subjective concept that is for itself and therefore possesses *personality*—the practical, objective concept determined in and for itself, which, as person, is impenetrable atomic subjectivity—but which, none the less, is not exclusive individuality, but explicitly *universality* and *cognition*, and in its other has *its own* objectivity for its object."—*Trans.*

The Tragedy of Philosophy

task of his philosophical work indeed remains, from a logical point of view, entirely aporetic. With his initial plan—a militant, abstract panlogism—Hegel confines himself to an airless cave, where, certainly, there are found the "mothers" glimpsed by Faust, but which neither sound nor light can penetrate.[33] Self-excommunicated from the hypostasis and from reality alike, there remain to Hegel only convulsive attempts to break down the door of the crypt which he has himself constructed. Without such a break-out, he would have had to put a full stop at the end of his *Logic* and rest from his labors, whereas in fact he continues his philosophical voyage to the ends of the cosmos, pronouncing *de omnibus rebus scibilibus atque quibusdam aliis* [about everything that can be known, and one or two other things too].

Hegel's philosophical undertaking is nevertheless, like Fichte's, significant, as a philosophical experiment of dizzying audacity and incredible force, which ends in inevitable and tragic failure. For all Hegel's pride in his own dialectic as fearless of contradiction and as throwing down the gauntlet to rationality, Hegel's system is a rationalism at breaking point. By means of innocent and in no way terrifying contradictions, it develops from its initial antinomies (insoluble by reason) and wishes to explain and to deduce everything by reducing the triunity of substance—the hypostasis, the word or idea, and reality or being—to a simple rational unity. In this attempt it founders. In theological terms, it can be said that Hegel's doctrine, like Fichte's, is a monohypostatic system, with the difference between them that in Fichte this hypostasis is the first hypostasis, the person, the philosophical and propositional subject, **I**, whereas, in Hegel, the hypostasis is the second, the Logos, the idea, the concept. Hegel's position is thus far more difficult and aporetic even than that of Fichte. For the first person is the beginning, from which, evidently, the movement commences, even though it does not stop there. By contrast, the conversion of the second person into the first and, consequently, only person is accompanied by absolutely fundamental distortions and difficulties. Here, to use Hegel's own expression, it is as though someone had had the idea of walking on his head for fun, and as if all objects

---

33   Bulgakov alludes to the mysterious goddesses with whom Mephistopheles terrifies Faust in Part Two of Goethe's play. See "Finstere Galerie" in Goethe, *Faust*, ed. Trunz, 190–94 (191), esp. ll. 6216ff.—*Trans.*

were to appear to him distorted and upside-down.[34] For to proceed from the idea to the hypostasis (from "objective" to "subjective" logic), from phenomenal revelation to the original noumenal source, from the predicate to the subject, is simply impossible; no such path exists, just as it is impossible to count from the second to the first. For Fichte, as we saw above, there was such a path. He was mistaken in his mono-hypostatic "deduction," but he did not distort the order of succession: the first hypostasis, the Father, really is the beginning, the originator of any movement within substantiality, and in a certain respect the world, the predicate, really can be defined as a *not-I*, in terms of the categories of I-ness. The I cannot, on the other hand, in any sense or under any circumstances be defined in terms of the categories of *not-I*, deduced from the *not-I*, exhibited as a development of the predicate, as the ripening of a concept which has become subjective—but this is just what Hegel attempted to do. This is why we do not see even an attempt at a deduction here, but only a metaphysical evasion of the logical difficulties involved by means of a hypostatization or spiritualization of the concept. Hypostaticity is attributed to the concept by means of a verbal somersault of unfathomable naïveté and crudity, a somersault which merely illustrates the full hopelessness of Hegel's position. Less hopeless is the deduction of reality or being from the idea, for here the path is leading from the second to the third hypostasis, and the natural order of succession between these two moments is at least not broken, but merely hampered by the absence of a hypostasis, of a philosophical or propositional subject of being. The latter (being) continues involuntarily to lack a subject; it exists for no one. In this sense, it is as though being loses consciousness. This transition from ideality to reality also expresses the celebrated "being-other" of the idea which becomes reality, which releases nature from itself, which, in other words, itself becomes a "living soul." Here yet another characteristic misinterpretation is added, namely the idea that knowledge of the third hypostasis, of being, is acquired by means of the second, whereas in fact it comes from the first. Particular difficulties follow from this. Since the

---

34 "When natural consciousness entrusts itself straightway to Science, it makes an attempt, induced by it knows not what, to walk on its head, just this once; the compulsion to assume this unwonted posture and to go about in it is a violence it is expected to do to itself, all unprepared and seemingly without necessity." Hegel, *Phenomenology of Spirit*, trans. Miller, 15 (§ 26).— *Trans.*

idea is merely an image of being, it obviously cannot in and of itself give rise to being as such; being exists for a hypostasis, and a putative deduction of being from the idea merely underlines the impossibility of beginning anywhere other than at the beginning. "Logic" (supposedly) "exhibits the elevation of the idea to that level from which it becomes the creator of nature and passes over to the form of a concrete immediacy whose concept, however, breaks up this shape again in order to realize itself as concrete spirit" (SL, 592).

Such is the metaphysical character of Hegel's thought. It is a typical philosophical heresy in this sense, that it is grounded in an arbitrary and self-willed *choice* of one of the moments of triune substance—the logical moment—and the subordination of both the other moments to it. What results from this is a philosophical Sabellianism, a mono-hypostaticity which dialectically converts itself into a triunity. (It is well known that, in theology too, Hegel elaborates a Sabellian doctrine in his account of the Holy Trinity: see the excursus on Hegel below.) This heresy brings Hegel's philosophy to a tragic collapse; the system, which is not secured from within, splinters apart because its philosophical principles are inadequate. Seen with the eyes of common sense, Hegelianism is absurd, a pipe-dream; but even when compared with "critical" reason, it is a metaphysical delirium, is possessed. Despite this, its significance and even in its own way its greatness lie precisely in its audacity, in the very fact that it is so bold and so singular, a one-sidedness or heresy which is one of a kind. If the words of the apostle Paul—"[f]or there must also be heresies among you, that they which are approved may be made manifest among you" (1 Cor. 11:19)—are applicable anywhere in the history of philosophy, they are applicable here. For here a philosophical experiment is conducted with astonishing persistence and with colossal strength; here the tragedy of heretical philosophizing is lived through to the depths and convincingly articulated, and the lessons of this experiment are stamped indelibly on the memory. If such an experiment could ever, in the history of philosophy, be repeated—*non bis in idem* [never the same thing twice]—then, apart from anything else, it would not, after Hegel, have either the freshness or the naivety which forms part of its strength. It was reserved to Hegel alone to test and to define the true limits of logicism and thus, in reality, to deprive the false claims of panlogism of their power.

C.

SYSTEMS OF SUBSTANTIALITY: THE PHILOSOPHY OF IDENTITY AND MONISM

THE PREDICATE CONSISTS OF AN IDEA AND THE COPula. The latter is not merely a grammatical part of the sentence, but is also a mystical gesture, full of the deepest ontological significance. The copula imparts significance to the predicate; it brings into being the meaning of the predicate as a revelation of the nature of the subject. The copula leads from the ideal into the real. Just as the **I** does not in itself contain any sort of thought, but is merely a philosophical or grammatical subject, so too the copula contains nothing but a *relation* between the subject and the predicate; it testifies to the reality of the predicate in the subject, and places the being of the subject in the predicate. The copula expresses an ontological moment, testifying to being, and making the predicate participate in the being of the subject. The copula is itself this being in its most universal and comprehensive form. It is the nature of substance, not in a special or particular, but in a universal and comprehensive, form. In a similar way to that in which the **I** expresses the hypostaticity of substance, the copula, the ontological bond, points symbolically to the nature of substance, φύσις [*phusis*]; the predicate is only one of its innumerable revelations. It signifies substance—not in its hypostatic face, but in its nature, not as subject, but as object, the unity of sheer being, its oceanic depth. It is the upfurled and incessantly self-unfurling *All* (not for nothing does Hegel begin his deduction of the *All* with the category of being—see the "excursus on Hegel"). It can be well captured by saying that in and through the copula's translucence shines substance in its ontological [*bytijnoj*] nature, permitting its reality to be sensed, and by means of the copula's power the word becomes flesh, becomes a living soul. By means of this role of the copula, in which the nature of substance and the reality of the predicate are revealed, the possibility is established of a type of philosophizing not thus far examined: the philosophy of ontological monism, of substantial all-unity, of metaphysical naturalism. If, in idealism, the all-consuming and definitive principle was the hypostasis, and if, in panlogism, it was thought, here this principle is substance as nature (anhypostatic, non-hypostatic, or pre-hypostatic). A philosophy

The Tragedy of Philosophy

of this type is, evidently, always a naturalism, but such naturalism can take many different shapes and forms, from the crudest to the most refined. Systems of naturalism are both extraordinarily numerous and extraordinarily widespread. This is understandable, when one takes into consideration that idealism and panlogism are the fruit of a refined speculation, and arise only on the basis of a highly-developed philosophical culture, whereas naturalism may be equally proper either to the lowest stages of culture or to the highest, and accompanies thought in every age as one of its possibilities. Thought seeks an explanation for the **I** in the *it*, just as it seeks the definite and particular in universality and all-unity; the demand made by the philosophy of identity sounds to thought almost like the voice of philosophy itself. In so far as it is possible to abstract from the moment of hypostaticity and of logical form, thought is right—in so far as it seeks to trace that which has originated to its origin, to trace phenomena to the nature which gives rise to them, to trace *natura naturata* in *natura naturans*. All ancient philosophy is this kind of naturalism, until the philosophical birth of the hypostatic person in Socrates and Plato (so far, at least, as this can be considered as having happened in their work). If we leave to one side the Milesian school, with its primitivism, two figures above all—Parmenides and Heraclitus—come to mind, even though they are in disagreement with each other. To them we can in a certain sense add Pythagoras; Empedocles and the atomists; and, later, the stoics.

It was given to Parmenides, in his verse fragment, to assert the principle of the all-unity of substance and of the philosophy of identity with such force and with such classical clarity and simplicity that it resounded unceasingly through the ages.

> ταυτῃ δ᾽ἐπι σήματ᾽ ἔασι
> πολλὰ μάλ᾽, ὡσ ἀγένητον ἐὸν καὶ ἀνώλεθρόν ἐστιν,
> οὖλον μουνογενές τε καὶ ἀτρεμὲς ἠδὲ τέλειον. [...]
> οὐδέ ποτ᾽ ἦν οὐδ᾽ἔσται, ἐπεὶ νῦν ἐστιν ὁμοῦ πᾶν,
> ἐν, συνεχές.

> [*tautēi d'epi sēmat' easi | polla mal', hōs agenēton eon kai anōlethron estin,| houlon mounogenes te kai atremes ēde teleion.* [...] | *oude pot' ēn oud' estai, epei nun estin homou pan,* | *en,*

sunekhes.] (On this way there are very many signs, that being uncreated and imperishable it is, whole and of a single kind and unshaken and perfect. [...] It never was nor will be, since it is now, all together, one, continuous.)[35]

οὐδὲ διαιρετόν ἐστιν, ἐπεὶ πᾶν ἐστιν ὁμοῖον.
οὐδέ τι τῇ μᾶλλον, τό κεν εἴργοι μιν συνέχεσθαι,
οὐδέ το χειρότερον, πᾶν δ'ἔμπλεόν ἐστιν ἐόντος.
τῷ ξυνεχὲς πᾶν ἐστιν. ἐὸν γὰρ ἐόντι πελάζει. [...]
αὐτὰρ ἀκίνητον μεγάλων ἐν πείρασι δεσμῶν
ἔστιν ἄναρχον ἄπαυστον, ἐπεὶ γένεσις καὶ ὄλεθρος
τῆλε μάλ' ἐπλάχθησαν, ἀπῶσε δὲ πίστις ἀληθής.

[*oude diaireton estin, epei pan estin homoion: | oude ti tēi mallon, to ken eirgoi min sunekhesthai, | oude ti kheiroteron, pan d'empleon estin eontos. | tōi xunekhes pan estin: heon gar eonti pelazei. | [...] autar akinēton megalōn en peirasi desmōn | estin anarkhon apauston, epei genesis kai olethros | tēle mal' eplakhthēsan, apōse de pistis alēthēs.*] (Nor is it divided, since it all exists alike; nor is it more here and less there, which would prevent it from holding together, but it is all full of being. So it is all continuous: for what is draws near to what is.... But changeless within the limit of great bonds it exists without beginning or ceasing, since coming to be and perishing have wandered very far away, and true conviction has thrust them off.)[36]

"Remaining the same and in the same place it lies on its own and thus fixed it will remain. For strong Necessity holds it within the bonds of a limit, which keeps it in on every side. Therefore it is right that what is should not be imperfect; for it is not deficient—if it were it would be deficient in everything. The same thing is there to be thought and is why there is thought. For you will not find thinking without what is, in

---

35 Text and translation are given here from Kirk, Raven, and Schofield, *Presocratic Philosophers*, 248–49.—*Trans.*
36 Text and translation from ibid., 250–51.—*Trans.*

all that has been said. For there neither is nor will be anything else beside what is, since Fate fettered it to be whole and changeless. Therefore it has been named all the names which mortals have laid down believing them to be true—coming to be and perishing, being and not being, changing place and altering in bright colour. But since there is a furthest limit, it is perfected, like the bulk of a ball well-rounded on every side, equally balanced in every direction from the centre. For it must needs not be somewhat more or somewhat less here or there. For neither is it non-existent, which would stop it from reaching its like, nor is it existent in such a way that there would be more being here, less there, since it is all inviolate: for being equal to itself on every side, it lies uniformly within its limits."[37]

Parmenides's doctrine of the one and immovable being laid the foundations of the future systems of the philosophy of identity and of the pan-unity of substance. Everything that is, "coming to be and perishing, being and not being, changing place and altering in bright colour," is immersed in this ocean of identical being, is merely one of its shapes, one of its changing faces. How is this unity revealed? By means of mystical contemplation, self-immersion, or by means of metaphysical speculation. The former takes place in Indian idealism, but also in post-antique European metaphysical idealism (Eckhart, Böhme, and others); the latter, in speculative-metaphysical idealism, a current to which Parmenides, who holds to an epistemological immanentism, also belongs: "Thought and the object [*predmet*] of thought are one."[38] Parmenides's doctrine of being is a philosophy of substantiality, in which the moment of oneness, of immovability, and of supra-temporality is emphasized. But this substantial unity can also be taken from the side of its dynamics, of its incessant

---

37 Translation from ibid., 252–53. Bulgakov does not supply the Greek text for this quotation, which, accordingly, has been omitted here too; Bulgakov himself quotes the present passage from Sergij Trubetskoj's quotation from the historian of philosophy Paul Tannery, in Trubetskoj's *Metafizika v drevnej Gretsii* [Metaphysics in Ancient Greece] (Moscow, 1890), 273–77.—*Trans.*

38 I have translated directly from Bulgakov's Russian here. Kirk, Raven, and Schofield translate the same proposition thus: "The same thing is there to be thought and is why there is thought" (see above).—*Trans.*

coming-into-being, of process, of temporality, and then, without any alteration of its philosophical principle, the doctrine takes on the characteristics of an evolutionism and a relativistic pluralism. We possess the prototype of the former, in ancient philosophy, in the figure of Heraclitus, and of the latter in those of the atomists. On one hand, Heraclitus, in agreement with Parmenides, holds that "[t]his world-order did none of gods or men make, but it always was and is and shall be: an everliving fire, kindling in measures and going out in measures."[39] "All things are an equal exchange for fire and fire for all things, as goods are for gold and gold for goods."[40] "They do not apprehend how being at variance it agrees with itself [*lit.* how being brought apart it is brought together with itself]: there is a back-stretched connexion, as in the bow and the lyre."[41] "It is necessary to know that war is common and right is strife and that all things happen by strife and necessity."[42] "The beginning and the end are the same (in the circumference of a circle)."[43] "And as the same thing there exists in us living and dead and the waking and the sleeping and young and old; for these things having changed round are those, and those having changed round are these."[44] Heraclitus speaks of identity in "opposites," in movement: "[u]pon those that step into the same rivers different and different waters flow...."[45] "The sun... is new each day."[46] "Everything flows": πάντα ῥεῖ, πάντα κινεῖται [*panta rhei, panta kineitai*, everything flows, everything is moving]. Through this universal movement and alteration, the immovable oneness of substance, from which everything issues and into which everything is immersed, is still more strongly emphasized. The ancient attitude is still vividly colored by religious cosmism ("everything is full of gods and demons"[47]), but the metaphysical basis of the philosophy of identity is already clearly laid out.

39 Kirk, Raven, and Schofield, *Presocratic Philosophers*, 198.
40 Ibid.
41 Ibid., 192.
42 Ibid., 193.
43 This fragment appears to be absent from Kirk, Raven, and Schofield, but is present in Diels-Kranz, 1:174. I have translated it from the Russian given by Bulgakov. — *Trans.*
44 Kirk, Raven, and Schofield, *Presocratic Philosophers*, 189.
45 Ibid., 195.
46 Ibid., 225.
47 Thales of Miletus, sometimes described as the first philosopher, is reported by Aristotle to have thought "that all things are full of gods." Kirk, Raven, and Schofield, *Presocratic Philosophers*, 95. — *Trans.*

Here too, however, belongs the doctrine of ancient atomism, as it appeared in Leucippus and Democritus. Here the one substance is no longer thought of as a continuous mass of being, but as something porous, interspersed with layers of emptiness within which move the atoms; these atoms are completely inaccessible to the human senses because of their insignificant size (διὰ σμικρότητα τῶν ὄγκων [*dia smikrotēta tōn ogkōn*]). This porosity of substance, or this multiplicity of centres of being lying within non-being, essentially changes nothing in the philosophy of identity; that philosophy is instead only complicated by the introduction of new problems. Being is imagined as an aggregated multiplicity of atoms linked to each other, which create the universe by means of the influence which they exert upon each other. Atoms are the plural substance of the world, making up the being of everything. Ancient atomism possesses materialistic overtones, anticipating the most recent materialism of our era.

The ancient monism of Parmenides, Heraclitus, and Democritus has prototypical significance for us, since in it is clearly laid down this path of thought, together with the possibilities contained in it. Yet at the same time these doctrines are, here, given in the form of a sort of sacred hieroglyph, which it is the task of modern philosophy fully to lay bare and unriddle.

There are two senses of the philosophy of pan-unity, two possibilities for it: mysticism and rationalism. The first occurs when pan-unity is understood as transcending reason; reason puts out its torch, and, confessing its limitations, enters the darkness of sacred ignorance. The One is Transcendent, lying beyond thought and cognition, subject and object, world and knowledge; it is the NOT of "negative theology" (cf. *Unfading Light*, part 1). Such is the One in, for example, Plato's doctrine, in many a representative of Christian theology, in Nicholas of Cusa, and in the Christian mystics, with Eckhart and Böhme at their head. In essence this is not a philosophy of identity, but rather supra-philosophy or non-philosophy, a renunciation of philosophy, and philosophy proper begins only where a return is carried out, a transition from the realm of reason to that of understanding, from transcendence to immanence. The manner of this transition and of its philosophical meaning determine the philosophical coefficients, so to speak, of a given system; hence reason, by this point, begins to be in its own domain. Our attention here, however, is addressed not to these mystical speculations, but to systems which are rationalistic in a properly philosophical sense, which do not desire to know the sacred darkness of ignorance, but which, on the contrary, test the power of reason to comprehend the world as a pan-unity and multiplicity as immovable being. And on this path towards modern philosophy, our attention is inevitably caught by the first move towards a doctrine in which rationalistic form—*more geometrico*—is combined with the rationalistic task of constructing a system of the world as a pan-unity, in order that, in this way, the correct manner of human conduct may also be worked out. We are speaking, of course, of Spinoza's *Ethics*. Spinozism is, it can be said, the fate of modern European cosmism; numerous theories of identity flow into it, issue from it, pass through it, and are transformed by it.

Spinoza's goal is a Parmenidean pan-unity, which he seeks in a concept of substance or God whose distinctive feature is self-causality (*causa sui*), such that essence includes existence within itself: *essentia involvit existentiam* (definition 1). Substance exists in itself, and is conceived through itself (definition 3). This distinction between existence and conception at once introduces a concealed Cartesian dualism (between thought and extension) in the concept of substance. To this is at once added a further concept—that of the attribute, that is, of that which mind (but what kind of mind, whose mind?) conceives of in a substance as constituting its "essence"—where God is defined as a substance which possesses infinitely many attributes (definition 6). The very difficult question, for the philosophy of identity or of pan-unity, of how plurality is engendered within unity, is not solved at all here, since the answer to it is given "axiomatically" (I. 1): all things that are, are either in themselves or in another thing. Having thus, in completely dogmatic fashion, recognized the plurality of substances, with their attributes, Spinoza establishes the principle of their hierarchical co-ordination, in which all substances are derived from the one absolute substance or God. According to theorems 14 and 15 of section 1, "[n]o substance can be or can be conceived without God" and "[w]hatever is, is in God, and nothing can be, or can be conceived, without God."[48] "The essence of things produced by God does

---

48 Spinoza, *Ethics Proved in Geometrical Order*, trans. Michael Silverthorne and Mathew J. Kisner (Cambridge: Cambridge University Press, 2018), 14 (§§ 14, 15). References to this work hereafter are given as "E," followed by the page number.

not involve existence," for "God is not only the efficient cause [*causa efficiens*] of the existence of things but also of their essence" (E 25, I. 14 and 15). "Nothing in nature is contingent but everything is determined to exist and to operate in a specific way by the necessity of the divine nature" (E 28, I. 29), so that "[t]hings could not have been produced by God in any other way or in any other order than they have been produced" (E 31, I. 33).

In this way, Spinoza immerses all shapes of being in the ocean of the one absolute substance, having declared them to be a state or product of it. Although this outcome cannot be considered as having been rationally proved or justified, the chief difficulty with Spinozism does not lie here, but in his anthropology, and, in particular, in his theory of consciousness or of the hypostasis. Why so? Because in order to make room for consciousness, Spinoza, from the infinite number of attributes of God — infinite in principle, of course, not for us — selects two, thought and extension, and both of these furnish a foundation to human self-consciousness, the former to its thinking and the latter to its embodiedness. Substantiality is not conferred on human beings, but only "[t]he idea of an actually existing particular thing" (E 53, II. 11) Human existence is only a *modus* of the absolute, an instant among the states of the absolute; but the human being can attain cognition of his own idea in God, and this can be true or false, adequate or inadequate, in accordance with the distinction between the three modes of cognition: first, opinion or imagination, cognition through a confused experience or communication; second, cognition by means of reason; third, intuitive cognition. The first mode is the only cause of error; the second and third are necessarily true (II. 40–41). Cognition of the third kind, that is, cognition by means of mystical self-immersion, *amor Dei intellectualis* [the intellectual love of God], leads to knowledge of all things, including consciousness of humanity itself, *sub specie aeternitatis* [from the standpoint of eternity], that is, in God. Ultimately, God, in and through humanity, loves himself, and "[t]he intellectual love of the mind for God is the very love of God with which God loves himself, not insofar as he is infinite but insofar as he can be explained through the essence of the human mind considered from the vantage of eternity, i.e., the intellectual love of the mind for God is a part of the infinite love with which God loves himself" (E 244, v. 36). The *modus* of humanity proves to be an eye through which God contemplates himself, and a mind by means of which he loves himself—by knowing himself. In its naivety, simplicity, and closedness, Spinoza's system is a classic expression of the philosophy of identity, and, for this reason, it represents a sort of model to which other monistic systems can be traced back. In it also appear all the insoluble difficulties and aporias which make monism to a considerable extent spectral and illusory. Spinoza proposes a pantheism, or, more precisely, a theocosmism: *natura sive Deus* [nature or God]. Bringing together God and the world to such an extent that God is the substance of the world, in the capacity of the sole absolute substance, Spinoza also wishes to delimit him, in order, by this means, to escape the inevitable amalgamation and identification of God with the world. That would entail, on the one hand, the negation of God in favor of the world—atheism, a charge frequently leveled at Spinozism—or, on the other, the denial of the world in favor of God—acosmism, as suggested by Hegel, amongst others.[49] In the work of some monists there prevails a more or less militant atheism, whilst others prefer a naive pantheism of a hylozoistic kind (Haeckel).[50] To draw a borderline between substance or God and its necessary manifestation, "the world," is indeed no easy matter. Spinoza seeks to solve the problem by means of his doctrine of *modes*, a doctrine which oscillates between interpreting the modes either as eternal and necessary, and, consequently, as flowing from the Divinity as his emanation, or as temporal and contingent—but then they are deprived of any solid roots and become the absolute's play of light and shade. The doctrine of modes is one of the principal specific difficulties with Spinozism, but it will not be examined in detail here. The greatest difficulty of Spinozism concerns the problem of hypostaticity. Substance, or God, is anhypostatic. Spinoza painstakingly protects the anhypostatic substance or God from hypostaticity, seeing in hypostaticity a definition and a limitation of the undefinable (*omnis definitio est negatio*). Although Spinoza recognizes God as a free causality, that is, as a

---

49 "Spinozism might really just as well or even better have been termed Acosmism, since according to its teaching it is not to the world, finite existence, the universe that reality and permanency are to be ascribed, but rather to God alone as the substantial." G. W. F. Hegel, *Lectures on the History of Philosophy*, trans. E. S. B. Haldane and Frances H. Simson, 3 vols. (London: Routledge and Kegan Paul, 1955-68), 1:281.—*Trans.*

50 Ernst Haeckel (1834-1919), the biologist and author of *Die Welträthsel* (1895-99) ("The Riddle of the World").—*Trans.*

self-causality, he nevertheless understands this self-causality as operating only according to the laws of nature, and determinedly avoids the doctrine of a free creation. Not only does Spinoza, in order to remove any trace of anthropomorphism from the concept of God, even deny him a mind and a will, but, in addition, even if mind and will did exist in the supreme being, they would so far differ from our own as to retain only the name ("no more in fact than the heavenly sign of the dog agrees with the barking animal which is a dog" [E 20, i. 17, scholium]). However, whilst advocating the safeguarding of the Divinity, in complete transcendental purity, from any definition, Spinoza, in a roundabout way, does attribute a vestigial consciousness and hypostaticity to his unconscious or supra-conscious substance, thanks to the modes. The modes possess, or at least can possess, an eternal and immutable nature, if they flow from the absolute nature of one or another of God's attributes (E 24, i. 23). And, in particular, such a nature is inherent in man, since "[t]he human mind has adequate cognition of the eternal and infinite essence of God" (E 84, ii. 47). Man's nature is capable of an "intellectual love of God... with which God loves himself, not insofar as he is infinite but insofar as he can be explained through the essence of the human mind considered from the vantage of eternity" (E 244, v. 36). However, knowledge is not conceivable without a subject of knowledge, without someone who knows, any more than there can be love without someone who loves, without a kernel of personhood, and to speak of God's loving himself in man's love for God, that is, in the self-consciousness of a mode, is simply to avoid the difficulty. To repeat Spinoza's own comparison, the mode's love of God and God's love for himself will have no more in common than the constellation of the Dog, *Canis Maior*, does with the barking animal. For the sake of monism, Spinoza sacrificed the real plurality of hypostases, and even hypostaticity itself, yet retained all those acts which are inseparable from hypostaticity: cognition and will—love. The abstract *it* which Spinoza makes of his "substance" must be conceived either as completely transcendent (as in Plato)—and then it can by no means be understood as a substance which grounds the *all* of the world and makes a place for it within itself—or else it stands face to face with the concreteness of the world and the hypostaticity of the human spirit, and then the fundamental principle of Spinozism clearly becomes inadequate to its own task. Spinoza's substance resembles a statue whose head, hands, and feet have been chopped off, leaving only a trunk; this torso is nevertheless passed off as a complete and perfect specimen of the human body.

All Spinozism is a decisive and worthy attempt, deriving from religious motives, to build a vision of the world on the sole basis of the idea of substance, that is, being, on to which are grafted definitions ("ideas") taken from the predicate and the subject. This is, in other words, a *philosophy of the copula*, in which the copula expresses the being of the subject [*podlezhashchee*] in the predicate, the reality of the world for the subject [*sub"ekt*], the existence of things for that which is, that is, for the spirit. Without what it binds together the copula does not exist, just as there can be no existence without something that exists, nor without the way in which it exists. To attend exclusively to the copula, to being, and to make of this the chosen object of philosophy, the theme of a philosophical heresy, has the effect of putting the whole system in an extremely unnatural and even perverse position, since here the first and only beginning is made not with what comes first, nor even with what comes second, but with what comes *third*, which, all the time, both presupposes and contains within itself both what comes first and what comes second. This is why Spinoza's philosophy also takes upon itself the burden of all these unintentional inventions and fatal borrowings, and exhausts itself beneath this burden. The only way left in which to camouflage these speculations, and to avoid the question of spirit and of consciousness here, is to drown, in the abstract origin of reality or being, everything which cannot be reduced to that origin, using the method of negative theology. On the pretext of absolute transcendence, it is asserted that the absolute eludes any sort of definition—definitions which, however, are later brought forward and allocated to their places wherever needed. Despite differences in its expression, the task remains the same: to comprehend both the hypostasis and the real plurality of the world, that is, both the subject and the predicate, while starting from a faceless, indistinct, abstract being. Despite a certain external resemblance to negative theology, which by its very nature disclaims any metaphysics, disclaims even the possibility of metaphysics, we have here a most decided dogmatic metaphysics, but one which is, however, worked out on the basis of such inadequate foundations that whenever necessary it can still have recourse to the *not* of "negative theology" as though to a deductive method, and can imitate that theology while in reality adulterating it. The most naive, the crudest contradictions and inconsistencies of the monistic philosophy of being emerge in that vulgar and very widespread natural-scientific materialism which returns to the primitivism of the Milesian school (whilst, of course, lacking the religious richness of the latter). Given a certain material substance, one will conceive of it materialistically, as a heap of atoms, another mechanistically, as energy, a third biologically, as living or at least as a life-creating essence, without qualities, without a face, without sentience; substance as such is characterized from the very first steps only by this "without" — by a negative (another unexpected enough borrowing from "negative theology"). From this substance are also deduced, and by this substance are explained, not only the whole of God's world with its wealth of forms and its ladder of living beings, but also consciousness, thought itself, and even this materialistic philosophy itself. All this ontological hocus-pocus is set up with the help of the idea of evolution, the idea of a gradual emergence and transition from one set of forms of life to the others. Ontologically speaking, though, it is self-evident that nothing can grow in the field of life which was not sown there, and the times and manners of its growing tell us nothing about the nature of the seeds. This is why gradualness, the principle of infinitely small changes, gets us essentially nowhere. The idea of evolution is our present *asylum ignorantiae* [refuge of ignorance], a twilight in which all cats are grey and in which it is impossible to make anything out.[51] Spinoza's static[52] monism, that geometrical diagram of the world, which directs all its attention to ontological coherence alone, is only preferable to the evolutionary varieties because it does not mask the problems by shifting them to another place without any attempt at solving them and having left them completely unaddressed.

It is usual to devalue Spinozism by referring to its "dogmatism," and by greatly exaggerating, as is fashionable today, the applicability of the distinction between "dogmatism" and "criticism" to serious research in

---

51 Bulgakov is alluding to Spinoza's criticism of the idea that everything which takes place in nature has a purpose, in which appears the following passage: "they will not stop asking for causes of causes until you take refuge in the will of God, which is the refuge of ignorance" [E 38]. — *Trans.*

52 The Russian text gives *statisticheskij*, "statistical," which is treated here as an error for *staticheskij*, "static." — *Trans.*

thought. Modern philosophy has seen attempts at a fully "critical" Spinozism, such as the post-Kantian systems of Schopenhauer and Hartmann.[53] For what else is Schopenhauer's will but Spinoza's substance, since it precisely possesses both the attributes of substance—thinking and extension in the "world as representation"—yet lacks hypostaticity, and so also lacks consciousness? This anti-hypostatic tendency is seen especially strikingly in Hartmann's philosophy, which already frankly professes the "unconscious" substance of the world in which we live and move and have our being.[54] Moreover, unconsciousness is interpreted as a super-consciousness, in relation to which consciousness is derivative and stands lower, like Spinoza's "attribute." This whole lengthy and colorful parade of philosophical doctrines—empiricist, positivist, materialist, and evolutionist, but also including among their number the "pessimistic"—is a series of variations on Spinozism as the philosophy of being, the philosophy of the one substance; and this doctrine, apart from its intrinsic interest, therefore has a prototypical significance too, since it determines the course of the most widespread and influential current of European thought in the nineteenth and twentieth centuries. In the translucent waters of Spinoza's philosophy can be observed all and any sorts of monistic thinkers. Spinozism is a kind of general and abstract schema of substantialist monism, an algebraic formula to which each monism can apply a number of its own choosing.

Leibniz's system, whose theological meaning is divided between pantheism and theism, is a singular one. In the first, pantheistic, sense it is a sort of pluralistic parallel to Spinoza's doctrine. What Spinoza's theory understands as an indifferent and undivided unity is thought of by Leibniz as composed of many metaphysical atoms or monads, which are linked in cosmic unity by a pre-established harmony. Both of the attributes—thinking and extension—which Spinoza awards to the single absolute substance are here, by contrast, regarded as properties intrinsic to every monad, as appetition and representation, from the first of which arises extension, and, from the second, thinking. Thus although the doctrines of Spinoza and Leibniz take up opposite positions concerning

---

53   Bulgakov is referring to Eduard von Hartmann (1842–1906), the author of *Philosophy of the Unconscious* (1869).—*Trans.*

54   Alluding to Acts 17:28: "For in him we live, and move, and have our being; as certain also of your poets have said, For we are also his offspring."—*Trans.*

The Tragedy of Philosophy

the definition of the unity of substance, when it comes to the principle of substantiality which is posited at the basis of both systems, they are related in their metaphysical structure. Each monad individually, as well as the whole world of monads combined, which is tuned in a "pre-established harmony," repeats, each in its own way, Spinoza's *substantia sive Deus*. Both are philosophies of being, of the copula understood as substantiality, and the whole life of substance is developed from this basis. Leibniz's monads also recall Plato's ideas, but with this difference, that the latter possess an ideal and logical character and are logically correlated and co-ordinated with each other, whereas Leibniz's monads are mutually impenetrable; the monads essentially repeat each other, and can constitute a universe only thanks to universal harmony. In Leibniz's monadology, for this reason, the principle of being, substantiality, is the determining principle (and here Leibniz is a continuator of Spinoza), whereas Plato's ideas are, above all, ideal archetypes, and Leibniz's monads and Plato's ideas are therefore related to different metaphysical moments: the former to the copula, to substantiality, the latter to the predicate, to the *logos*. It is characteristic of Leibniz's whole system not only that the monads are linked in a continuous unity, but also that change is always continuous and is brought about by way of imperceptible and infinitely small quantities, by way of obscure and unconscious representations. With the help of this idea, Leibniz establishes a hierarchical scale of monads. This hierarchy consists of the lowest monads, which have the most confused representations; of souls, whose representations attain clarity of perception; and, finally, of spirits, which possess reason and a likeness to God: "although each substance expresses the entire universe, spirits express God rather than the world, whereas other substances express the world rather than God."55 But the distinction between the soul and the spirit is merely quantitative, a transition accomplished by way of infinitely small alterations. What is more, Leibniz sometimes puts matters in such a way that there exists only a quantitative distinction between

---

55 Leibniz, *Discourse on Metaphysics*, trans. Jonathan Bennett, 25, §36. http://www.earlymoderntexts.com/assets/pdfs/leibniz1686d.pdf (accessed 8. viii. 2019). "Minds" for Leibniz's *esprits* has been replaced here by "spirits" only in order to reflect the Russian word *dukhi*, which is best translated as "spirits" when used in Bulgakov's own work, and which is used in the Russian translation from which Bulgakov is quoting. — *Trans*.

God and the spirit,⁵⁶ even though this is not consistent, from another point of view, with Leibniz's own understanding of God as the Creator of the world and of all the monads. Souls and spirits are distinguished from each other not by the nature of their substantiality, but only by its degree, since they are equally eternal, and, consequently, equally immortal. The human soul is defined only as a step on the ladder of monads. If there are animal souls lower than it, there are also beings higher than it,⁵⁷ "genii," otherwise there would be a gap in the kingdom of things, a *vacuum formarum*.⁵⁸ The difference between a spirit and a soul lies in the spirit's capacity for apperception: "perception is the internal state of a monad that represents external things, and apperception is consciousness, or the reflective knowledge of that internal state."⁵⁹ "These souls [i.e., the class of souls which Leibniz calls 'spirits'] are capable of reflective acts... so that they can think about what we call 'myself', substance, soul or mind: in a word, things and truths that are immaterial."⁶⁰ In this way, monads, at a certain stage, possess self-consciousness and become persons.⁶¹ If

---

56 "On sait aussi qu'il y a des degrés en toutes choses. Il y a une infinité de degrés entre un mouvement tel qu'on voudra et le parfait repos, entre la dureté et la parfaite fluidité qui soit sans résistance aucune, entre Dieu et le néant" [we also know that there are degrees in all things. There is an infinity of degrees between any given movement and perfect rest, between hardness and perfect fluidity without any resistance, between God and nothingness]. Leibniz, *Considérations sur le doctrine d'un esprit universel*, in *Œuvres philosophiques*, ed. Paul Janet (Paris: Felix Alcan, 1900), 1:681–90, 689.

57 "It is also reasonable that there should be substances capable of perceptions *below us as well as above us*." Bulgakov quotes this text from Kuno Fischer, *Geschichte der neuern Philosophie*, vol. 3, *Gottfried Wilhelm Leibniz, Leben, Werke, und Lehre* (Heidelberg: Carl Winters Universitätsbuchhandlung, 1920), but I have been unable to locate it. — *Trans.*

58 A *vacuum formarum* is a void in the chain of being. *Historisches Wörterbuch der Philosophie*, ed. Joachim Ritter, Karlfried Gründer, Gottfried Gabriel et al. (Basel: Schwabe, 2001), 11:530–31. — *Trans.*

59 Leibniz, *Principles of Nature and Grace Based on Reason*, trans. Jonathan Bennett, 3; http://www.earlymoderntexts.com/assets/pdfs/leibniz1714a.pdf (accessed August 8, 2019). I have replaced "awareness" with "apperception" and "=" with "is" to reflect features of the Russian translation used by Bulgakov. — *Trans.*

60 Ibid., 4.

61 "The word *person*," says Leibniz, "stands for a thinking intelligent being, that has reason and reflection, and can consider itself as the same thinking thing in different times and places; which it does only by the sense that it has of its own actions. And this knowledge always accompanies our present sensations and perceptions — when they are sufficiently distinct, as I have remarked more than once already — and by this every one is to himself, that which he calls *self*: it not being considered in this case, whether the same self be continued in the same, or divers substances. For since consciousness always accompanies thinking, and 'tis that, that makes every one to be, what he calls *self*;

one considers more deeply this doctrine of Leibniz's about the law of universal analogy and the continuity of all being, one has to recognize that, for him, there is no such thing as a metaphysically self-sufficient *hypostasis*—a hypostasis which, precisely by being an interruption, would tear open the fabric of the philosophy of substance and would introduce a new principle into that philosophy. The same must be said of the logos, the ideal self-determination of substance. Leibniz knows only the psychological person in his or her development; he explains being from genesis, and wishes to understand essence from origin. For this reason, then, it is possible to say that there is no such thing as hypostatic personhood in Leibniz's theory, nor is there any place for it.

The difference between the fundamental projects of Leibniz and Spinoza lies in Leibniz's introducing into his conception an idea of God the Creator, who brought this world into being, and who can exist without it, whilst Spinoza openly asserts *substantia sive Deus*, that is, he proclaims an atheistic cosmism (pantheism) or an acosmic (or even an anti-cosmic) deism. Yet it is precisely at this point that Leibniz's system reveals its vacillation and contradictoriness. On the one hand, God in an indefinite way converges with the world, as its highest stage or as a monad of monads, the monads' universal center, a *centre par tout* [a center which is everywhere], the world-soul, and then Leibniz's thought inevitably becomes a pluralistic Spinozism, that is, a pantheism; but on the other, God is defined as "the basic unitary thing, the original simple substance" and "[a]ll created or derivative monads are produced by him. They are generated by the continual flashes of silent lightning (so to speak) that God gives off from moment to moment"—that is, by means of some sort of process of emanation.[62] At this point Leibniz, in his aporias, comes close to his ancient ancestor, the father of the theory of monadic entelechies, Aristotle, who, along with

---

and thereby distinguishes himself from all other thinking things, in this alone consists personal identity, i.e. a rational being: and as far as this consciousness can be extended backwards to any past action or thought, so far reaches the identity of that person; it is the same self now it was then." G. W. Leibniz, *New Essays on Human Understanding*, trans. and ed. Peter Remnant and Jonathan Bennett (Cambridge: Cambridge University Press, 1996), 235. (Strictly speaking, the words quoted are spoken as part of a dialogue by "Philalethes" ["lover of truth"]. — *Trans*.)

62 G. W. Leibniz, "The Principles of Philosophy Known as Monadology," trans. Jonathan Bennett, 7, §47 (http://www.earlymoderntexts.com/assets/pdfs/leibniz1714b.pdf, accessed at 28. viii. 19).

a monadologically organized and animated world, postulated a God who was the first cause or mover (and who is also characterized as a νόησις νοήσεως [noēsis noēseōs], pure self-thinking thought). The ambiguity and unclarity of this doctrine of God, according to which He on the one hand vaguely blends into the cosmos, whilst, on the other, He remains transcendent to it, indelibly marks both Aristotle's and Leibniz's philosophies. This aspect of Leibniz's thought, which is historically significant, does not, however, affect the question with which we are occupied here, since it sheds no light on the problem of the hypostaticity of the spirit.[63]

The nineteenth-century inheritor and descendant of Spinoza's and Leibniz's work in philosophy is Schelling, in his *Naturphilosophie* [philosophy of nature] and his philosophy of identity. In Schelling this problematic finds its consummate and fully developed form, as was natural for a thinker working after Kant and Fichte and alongside Hegel. The latter caustically mocked an absolute identity in which "all cats were grey" (although Hegel's work suffered no less from absolute identity than did Schelling's, and Hegel's work was directly dependent on Schelling's). Working in different directions at different periods of his life, Schelling expresses one and the same unvarying thought in many different forms. In the early phase of his philosophical activity, when still under the influence of Fichte, Schelling sought an escape from the contradiction between the subjective and the objective principle ("dogmatism" and "criticism") in the concept of the absolute I, which, by virtue of its pre-conscious or unconscious activity, reminiscent of the Schopenhauerian Will, posits an object or Nature. The same problem later appeared in Schelling as an explanation for the emergence of consciousness from the unconscious or from Nature, as Nature's path to life and to consciousness, and in the *Naturphilosophie*'s theory of the unity of Nature and of the world soul (Schelling's work in the philosophy of nature belongs here).[64] If Schelling

---

63 A series of weighty judgements on this question are met with in Leibniz's work, but they remain only partially developed. Here, for example: "Souls in general are living mirrors or images of the universe of created things, but minds are also images of the Divinity himself, i.e. of God, the author of Nature. They are capable of knowing the system of the universe, and of imitating aspects of it through sketchy constructions of their own, each mind being like a little divinity within its own sphere." *Monadology*, trans. Bennett, 12, §83 (accessed 29. viii. 19).

64 I examine Schelling's ideas on the philosophy of nature in detail in my *Philosophy of Economy*, whose problematic comes close to Schelling's.

travels in this way a path which leads from objectivity to subjectivity, in his *System of Transcendental Idealism* he already travels the opposite path from subjectivity to objectivity, with his doctrine that intellectual intuition is a way of perceiving that which lies beyond the distinction between subject and object, a way of perceiving absolute identity. The problem, which had already confronted Fichte and then Hegel in all its gravity, the problem, that is, of how to understand subject and object not in their difference from each other (as in Kant) but in their unity—in other words the problem of the I-ness of the cosmos and the cosmic character of the I (Fichte's I and not-I)—presents itself to Schelling too. Instead of drowning the object in the absolute I, like Fichte, or dissolving the subject-object relation into the logical predicate alone, without a subject, Schelling, coming close to Schopenhauer here, immerses them both in the dusk of an unconscious absolute identity, in which there is at first no bifurcation between subject and object. These last appear as identity's actions, stages, or potencies, possessing, evidently, no greater ontological force than Spinoza's modes. There are two series of potencies disposed in polar opposition to each other, series which are characterized by the gradually intensifying predominance of the subjective and objective moments respectively, and which reveal the eternal ideas of the absolute. In the concepts of the ideas or monads or potencies, which are united in absolute identity, Leibniz's monadology is seasoned with Platonism and is combined with the purest Spinozism. It is clear that, given such conceptions, the ontological rights of personhood, of the individual spirit, the hypostasis, will be overthrown, to the greater glory of the single, impersonal or supra-personal—and, for this reason, also natureless—absolute identity. One could think that here we are either entering the mystical night of contemplative immersion, or approaching the gates of paradise guarded by the flaming sword of the cherubim, that is, approaching the *not* of "negative" theology. Yet Schelling does not give us any grounds to think so, because his mission is the construction of a perfectly rational system of philosophy; he works in the noonday of rationalism, and with its sun over his head. Although intellectual intuition, like Spinoza's "cognition of the third kind," the *amor Dei intellectualis*, leads, as an already fully determinate mystical epistemology, beyond the limits of rationalism, this does not prevent either Schelling or Spinoza from remaining rationalists in the development and execution of their systems, even if their mystical roots reach down into the nocturnal darkness of the Absolute. It is evident, however, that it is impossible to say anything in the language of *ratio* about this midnight land of absolute undifferentiation, and every series of potencies, whether subjective or objective, issues from a logically empty place, and remains, thereafter, impossible to "deduce" or to demonstrate. It remains, in such a case, to impart to this whole conception a new, religious sense, to transpose it into religious symbolism, and, in this way, to turn one's back on rationalism. Schelling does precisely this in his *Philosophy of Revelation*, although he nevertheless does not manage to break completely with rationalism or to put an end to deductions of what cannot be deduced, so that his philosophical work retains to the end a certain aroma of rationalism. None the less, Schelling, submitting to the logic of his own ideas, is already moving from critical idealism and *Naturphilosophie* to theology, and the problem of deducing the absolute identity of subject and object already leads to the question of God's creation of the world, or, more precisely, of the world's coming-to-be in God. Although Schelling transfers the problem to the philosophy of religion, it retains the same content. His doctrine here is a philosophy of identity, but now applied to God himself, and in this respect it is already an authentic Christian heresy in the proper sense, a Sabellianism of a gnostic kind. Here, however, Schelling is merely giving a philosophical transcription of Jakob Böhme's theory, which he knew, it seems, through Baader.[65] The question of how a bifurcation of subject and object can arise out of identity proper turns into the question of the origination of something relative from what is absolute or within what is absolute, that is, the question of how the world comes to be. According to Schelling's doctrine, the world originates from God's nature or ground [*Grund*], which it is necessary to distinguish, within God, from God himself. This dark primal ground forms, so to speak, the material for the origination of God (in a similar way to that in which the chain of the dialectic of the concept in Hegel is material for the origination of the Logos or Concept itself). This absolute nature, as something dark and not yet clarified, harbours within itself the possibility of self-will, of falling, and also, through this, of individuation, and consequently of

---

65 Franz von Baader (1765–1841), Bavarian Catholic theologian, philosopher, and mystic. — *Trans.*

bifurcation into subject and object. Yet through this fall, being strives to illuminate and to actualize itself, to become a mirror-image of the Deity, endowed with reason. In this way, the light of the Son, the power of reason, is born within the dark primal ground of the Father, and the kingdom of the Spirit comes into being through the overcoming of chaos.

The world, therefore, is God's becoming. From the *deus implicitus* comes forth the *deus explicitus*. Schelling, imagining that he is just furnishing an authentic, well-grounded thesis, wants to fence himself off from pantheism. The primal identity is a dark, Schopenhauerian will, subsisting within Divinity as a *prius* of God himself, and which, in its disintegration and its fall away from Divinity, gives rise to the world, but, at the same time, to God. In his last treatises, beginning with the *Inquiries into Human Freedom*, Schelling developed this model with a different degree of depth, seriousness, and completeness, particularly in the *Philosophy of Revelation*.

There are many varieties of the philosophy of substance, and this is understandable, because it has to do with concrete reality, whose depth is the depth of life, and whose richness is the richness of life. There is not such a limited range of possibilities as exists in the philosophy of hypostaticity or the philosophy of purely logical form, the philosophy of the subject or of the predicate. Accordingly, just in as much as the depth and variety of experience is unfathomable, so the possibilities of orientation within it are inexhaustible, being distinguished by the character of one's susceptibility or of a particular focus of attention, or by a certain way in which one's philosophical "wonder" is excited. What appears decisive here, alongside the general direction taken, is the more particular philosophical choice of a motif, the "heresy" in that "heresy" which every system of substantiality which reduces the many to the one, or the complex to the simple, inevitably and by its nature appears as.[66] A natural variety of colours and shapes is proper to philosophies of substance, and it is quite mistaken to believe that "progress" in thought might change this fact by bringing them into unity or agreement. "Progress" in thought (to the extent that it exists or is possible at all) manifests itself only in what makes certain directions of thought impossible to go on with in their crude form — as, for example, vulgar materialism is impossible for

---

66 Bulgakov is playing here on the sense of Greek *hairesis* as "choice." — *Trans.*

serious philosophy (a materialism which has, however, precisely found unprecedented "democratic" success on the street, thanks to the zeal of enlightened educators, so that in this sense one must speak not of progress, but rather of decline), although this does not prevent it from arising again in a more refined form. Just as the sea of experience is inexhaustible, and just as the ocean of reality is unfathomable, so the possibilities of the philosophy of substantiality wax unlimited at the same time as and in connection with the successes of the empirical sciences. Antiquity already displayed these possibilities in the naive form of a cosmological wisdom-philosophy, first in the Milesian school and then in the work of all the other pre-Socratics, and the modern age has in no way diminished their number. For this reason it is necessary to renounce the hope of characterizing them exhaustively in detail, and to limit oneself to merely general indications relating to their structure. The fundamental task, and the fundamental difficulty, which arises here, consists above all in deducing a subject from an object, in connecting consciousness and being, and in explaining how intelligible and connected forms are possible in the dark mass of being. In essence, the first problem, the deduction of consciousness from non-consciousness, of a subject from an object, is incomparably more difficult to solve than the opposite one—to comprehend the not-I from the I. For the world is indeed a not-I, even though this relationship to the I does not exhaust its metaphysical nature. But it is in no way possible to understand the I as a not-not-I, deducing it from the indifference of identity or of the object. And deductions of this kind, whether scientific or metaphysical, are either evasions of the problem by means of cloudy phrases, or are simple dogmatism and self-deception. Here we see the position which inevitably comes about when a *third* definition of substance, the third hypostasis, is declared to be the first and only one. Philosophically, this is simply to walk on one's head, in Hegel's well-known saying—that is, to invert the natural order of things. At the same time the temptation offered by this path, the temptation to repeat the same experiment over and over again, is too great, for here thought evidently gives itself over to the domain of reality, wanting to know what reality is before thought and without the I, what is in the room when we are not there, what the world is like without a subject—and, indeed, in essence, without an object—transformed into this colorless, shapeless *it*. And the *temptation of reality*, if it is possible to put it like this, has in recent times been an ever-increasing one. The external reason for this is the quantitative success of scientific knowledge, but the inner reason lies in a particular feeling about the world, in a universal cosmic tension. The world thirsts to be revealed as a new creation, but before this revelation, the striving towards it, the expectation of the Holy Spirit, expresses itself in the philosophical thought of paganism in baleful and wretched surrogates, in numberlessly divided heresies which are nothing other than varieties of the universal heresy, the philosophy of substantiality as unmoved or as a mover, as an abstract being withdrawn into itself, anhypostatic and alogical, yet nevertheless producing both hypostasis and logic. The power of this heresy, however, its truth and its fascination, lies precisely in the fact that it holds to reality and seems to control it; it wishes to lay bare the mysteries of life, and in this possession it cannot be defeated by any idealism which would sway the world only in printed format, in a "scientific speech," nor by a panlogism which prides itself on its own concreteness simply by virtue of knitting together and ramifying its own abstract diagrams.[67] In other words, the power and advantage of the philosophy of substance lies in its empiricism; it is connected to concretion, to the colors and sounds of life (which also corresponds to the character of the third hypostasis). Yet at the same time, the impossibility and impracticability of realism's task leads thought to return involuntarily to one and the same point of departure, and to begin its labor anew, which is why the history of realist philosophy, more than that of any other kind, resembles the history of a series of individual failures and disappointments. And if realism feels and knows its failure less keenly, this is to be explained not merely by the elusive insufflation of the *comforter*, the Holy Spirit, or by the fascination which reality exerts, but also by the dullness of philosophical cognition,

---

67 Bulgakov's "idealism" probably alludes to Fichte, whose *Sun-Clear Report* to the public on his philosophy appeared in 1801 and whose *Speeches to the German Nation* in 1808. Khoruzhij suggests that there is, specifically, an allusion to the mockery of Fichte in *Nachtwachen* or "Night Watches," a novel of 1805 published under the pseudonym "Bonaventura" and now thought by many scholars to have been the work of E. F. A. Klingemann (1777–1831); Khoruzhij, citing an article by A. V. Gulyga, believes the work to have been written by Schelling (cf. Bulgakov, *Sochineniya v dvukh tomakh*, vol. 1, 549, 576). In *Nachtwachen* the hero meets a crazed "world-creator" who "has just as consistent a system as Fichte" and who "squeezes everything into, as it were, a pocket edition of a little I which every tiny little boy can shout out." "Monolog des Wahnsinnigen Weltschöpfers" in *Nachtwachen* (Stuttgart: Philipp Reclam, Jr., 1974), 80–86. — *Trans.*

by a certain lowering of level, in accordance with the alogical nature of reality, which, nevertheless, still has to be handled logically. What, then, is the result of this survey of philosophical heresiology? All turn out to be wrong, to suffer collapse and defeat—to the glory of a toothless skepticism's surreptitious laughter, of this philosophical *ramollissement* [softening, slackening]—but, at the same time, all are correct, and not one is able to abandon its position, or to renounce its own fundamental motif, its philosophical acquisitions—a paradoxical and difficult conclusion which compels thought in some way simultaneously to accept all three possibilities for thought, and, at the same time, obviously, compels thought to negate each of them in their isolatedness. The catharsis of thought, which is obtained as the result of this tragedy of philosophy, leads to thought's renewal through the deepening of its self-knowledge, its knowledge both of its strengths and limitations and of its nature. And the fundamental conclusion which follows will be that a thought which expresses substance will inevitably contain antinomies within itself: the single principle is fulfilled in triadicity, and thought turns out to be fated to this deliberate self-sacrifice. And the living truth of the gospel is laid bare anew: if the grain does not die, it cannot come back to life and cannot bear fruit.

> Und so lang du das nicht hast,
> Dieses: *Stirb und werde!*
> Bist du nur ein trüber Gast
> Auf der dunklen Erde.[68]
> (Goethe)

The way out of contradiction does not lie in eclecticism, which wishes to accept and to combine everything, blunting the cutting edge of the thoughts, and not resolving or not possessing the character to choose a "heresy"; nor does the way out lie in "dialectic," which, jingling the spurs of its "contradictions," strives, in reality, to understand and to explain

---

68 "And for so long as you lack it,/ This 'die, and become!'/ You are only a sad guest/ on this dark earth." A quotation from Goethe's "Selige Sehnsucht" ("Blessed Longing"), in his *West-östlicher Diwan: Gedichte*, 172. Bulgakov's quotation contains a number of small inaccuracies, so we can be sure that the quotation was important enough to Bulgakov for him to have memorized or to (mis-)remember it.—*Trans.*

everything, so that all genuine contradiction—that is, all antinomism—might be definitively banished from thought and from being. The way out lies in seeing the true structure of thought and in recognizing that substance does not, as in the monistic project, coincide with thought, and that is why, when substance is thought about, it leads to contradictions and antinomies within thought, antinomies which are necessary and insuperable, even if they are unbearable, for thought itself. Nevertheless, this recognition in no way despairs of thought. On the contrary, it testifies instead to thought's maturity; it can appear, therefore, only in an age of marked historical maturity, when philosophy has travelled a protracted, and, to a certain degree, a completed, path. Our time is indisputably such an age. It can also spring up from a soil which is not philosophical, but supra-philosophical—that is, from the soil of religious contemplation, of myth and contemplation, of dogma, from the soil of revelation, and, consequently, of a philosophy of revelation: this must become the most radical philosophical rallying-cry of our times, one which, in modern history, was first proclaimed by Schelling, in the ripest maturity of his working life. The complacency and narrow-mindedness of philosophical thought, to which the consciousness of tragedy is alien, led philosophy, as we know, to a conception of itself as standing higher than religion, as constituting the truth of religion, and as being able, finally, to explain religion. In reality the matter stands exactly the other way round: philosophy issues from and returns to religion, and, precisely, to religious myth and dogma, and this fact, rather than thought itself, specifies both philosophy's problem and the way out of that problem. And religious mystery is guarded by the flaming sword of the cherubim, whose name in the language of philosophy is *antinomy*. How can the three points, which have become separated from each other, be combined so as to obtain a triangle; can they, indeed, at all be so combined? There can evidently be only one honest answer to this question: either philosophy is impossible, and it will remain its lot repeatedly to walk along the same old paths which it has already traversed, like a squirrel on a wheel—*da capo* forever—or philosophy is possible, if it is grounded in the antinomies and is religiously, that is, dogmatically, conditional. And this is not a diminution of philosophy, but its higher calling—to be the *ancilla* not *theologiae*, but *religionis*, the handmaiden, not of theology, but of religion itself, to become a revealed and conscious (and in this sense, a critical) religious empiricism.

II

Philosophy of Triadicity

1
The Philosophical Meaning of Triadicity

MAN WAS CREATED IN THE IMAGE AND LIKENESS OF God. This means that the image of the Holy Trinity is imprinted upon every part of his spiritual nature. *Let us make man in our image, after our likeness* (Gen. 1:26). So says the word of God, precisely pointing, by means of this plural number, to the trihypostaticity of the Divinity and the triunity of the image of God—which, after all, is also the human image. It is wholly natural, therefore, that the literature of the church should be full of attempts to find this image of triunity in the human being, and that the fathers of the church should have seen it in one or another of the lineaments of the human spirit.[1]

---

[1] They pointed, for example, to the sun, to the sun's light, and its ray, which form a unity and yet are different; to the root, trunk, and fruit of a single tree; to the spring, source, and stream, continuously brought together in a unity, and yet distinct; to three candles which may be burning in a certain place, and which give out a single inseparable light; to a fire, the shining of its flames, and its heat, representing triadicity within unity; or to three different faculties within one and the same human being—mind, will, and memory, or consciousness, cognition, and desire (see Tertullian, *Against Praxeas*, chapter 8; Athanasius, *Fourth Discourse Against the Arians*; Gregory Nazianzen, *Fifth Theological Oration*, Gregory of Nyssa, *Against Eunomius*, book 1; Augustine, *Treatise on Faith and the Creed*, chapter 9, section 17; *On the Trinity*, book 9, section 18). Dimitry of Rostov, *Inquiry concerning the Schismatics*: "The spirit is the image of God, for it possesses threefold powers, but a single essence. The powers of the human spirit are the following: memory, reason, will. The memory resembles God the Father, the reason God the Son, and the will God the Holy Spirit. But just as in the Holy Trinity there are three persons, yet there are not three gods, but one God: so in the human spirit there are three spiritual powers, yet there are not three spirits, but a single spirit..." (*Rozysk o raskol'nicheskoj brynskoj vere* [Moscow, 1855], 292). To these similitudes it is without doubt possible to add certain others from the physical and spiritual worlds: just as, in the physical world, all bodies necessarily possess three dimensions, length, breadth and depth, so the space in which those bodies are situated also possesses the same dimensions; time, in which bodies develop and change, is also formed of three parts, past, present, and future; in the world of the spirit, every truth necessarily includes three conditions: the representation, the object of the representation, and the harmony between the representation and the object; every virtue is also threefold: the free action, the law, and the harmony between the free action and the law (Metropolitan Makarius of Moscow, *Pravoslavno-dogmaticheskoe bogoslovie* [*Orthodox Dogmatic Theology*], 2 vols. (Saint Petersburg, 1856–57), 1:208–9).

The Tragedy of Philosophy

Nevertheless, it is in its way surprising to have to seek for something which could not in any way be avoided, and without which a holistic perception of the human spirit is quite impossible. If the human being really is the image of God, then this image also *defines* the essence of the human being; the human being's whole nature points to its prototype, has its necessary and inevitable prerequisite in that prototype, and can be understood only in relation to it. If God is a Trinity, with one indivisible being, then the human spirit, although it is not a trinity, possesses, nevertheless, the form of a triunity, and necessarily derives its intellect from the Prototype. The triune nature of the human spirit is living proof of the Holy Trinity; equally, the revelation of the Trinity, the church's dogma about it, is the sole satisfactory postulate of thought by means of which the human spirit can be comprehended. Here is a position which is axiomatic for thinking, as is demonstrated by the whole of history, and the whole tragedy of philosophy as monism. If certain fathers of the church, with justice, depreciate the value of the likenesses or comparisons which reason uses to comprehend the Trinity, then this depreciation, it goes without saying, is not directed at that likeness which God himself instilled in the human spirit.[2] This likeness leaves an ever deeper and

---

2 "I have very carefully considered this matter in my own mind," says Gregory Nazianzen, "and have looked at it in every point of view, in order to find some illustration of this most important subject; but I have been unable to discover anything on earth with which to compare the divine nature. Even if I did discover some tiny likeness, what was most important [about God] eluded me and left me still here below with my example. As others have done before, I have imagined a source, a fountain, and a river, to see if the first might be analogous to the Father, the second to the Son, and the third to the Holy Spirit. For in these there is no distinction in time, nor are they separated from one another with respect to continuity, though each of the three seem to be distinguished in some way by its proper characteristics. But I was afraid in the first place that, by this analogy, I might be suggesting some sort of flow in the divine nature, which would exclude stability. Secondly, I was afraid that this image would introduce a numerical unity [of person]. For the source and the spring and the river are only one thing, though they take different forms.

"Again, I thought of the sun, a ray, and light. But here once more there was a danger that people might imagine a certain compound in the nature which is uncompounded, such as there is in the sun and what belongs to it. In the second place, there is the risk that we should assign the essence to the Father but deny any distinctive existence to the others, and thus make them only powers of God, existing in Him without being hypostases. But it is not possible for me to make use even of this analogy; because it is quite clear what gives the ray its motion. But there is nothing prior to God which could set Him in motion; for He is Himself the cause of all things, and He has no prior cause. And secondly, this analogy will not do because here also there is a suggestion of

more pronounced mark as humanity comes to historical maturity; it is the supreme and ultimate revelation about the human being, the truth about the human being.

a) *Judgement*. It is a fundamental and indisputable fact of consciousness that human beings think *in judgements*. This, however, is not enough. It is also necessary to say that the human being, in a certain sense, *is* a judgement, and that the life of the human spirit is a continuously self-developing and self-accomplishing judgement: I am something, a certain A. More precisely, it is necessary to express the sequence of judgements thus: *I* am something, *I—am—A*; the empirical forms of the judgement can always be fulfilled and unfolded in a tripartite formula: (1) *I am* signifies, essentially, the indefiniteness of the predicate: I am something, or, I am (potentially) everything; (2) *I am A*, I am something, in an obvious way signifies that **I** realizes its being in this A, that **I** am this something. Impersonal expressions have, essentially, a similar meaning, only with a different form: it is getting light, it is getting dark, it is boring, it is annoying, and so on; they imply a cognitive or grammatical subject, relative to which they function as a predicate: it is getting light for me, I watch the dawn, it is boring for me, I am getting bored, and so on. It cannot be assumed that the complete judgement arose by a differentiating development from this rudiment of judgement, as is sometimes suggested. Even if it were possible to establish such a case linguistically, in the history of language, the logical and ontological whole always exists before the parts. Just as the hand or the foot could not be understood without their link to the body, even if they might happen to be found in separation from it, so elliptical judgements do not give a full conception of the judgement, and must of their nature lead back to the form of the latter. Each new judgement consists of a subject, a predicate, and a copula.

---

such things as composition, diffusion, and an unsettled and unstable nature — none of which we can suppose in the divine nature. In a word, there is no fixed point for my mind in these illustrations from which to consider the Object which I am trying to represent to myself, unless one shrewdly accepts one point of the image while rejecting the others. Finally, it seems best to me to let the images and the shadows go, as being deceitful and falling very far short of the truth..." (Gregory of Nazianzus, *Fifth Theological Oration*, "On the Holy Spirit," from Gregory, *Five Theological Orations*, trans. Stephen Reynolds [2011], 97–123, 122–23, https://tspace.library.utoronto.ca/bitstream/1807/36303/1/Gregory%20of%20Nazianzus%20Theological%20Orations.pdf, accessed 2. ix. 2019).

The judgement is a grammatical proposition; its ontological first principle can always be reduced to the type: *I am something*. The object, as a noun, is only a mirror-image of the I, the first person pronoun, and that is why every individual judgement is a variant of the primary judgement, of the ontological judgement *I am something*, to which the individual judgement leads and on the basis of which it must be understood. It can be considered, if you like, not as a judgement about objectivity itself, but as an expanded predicate of the I, so that an I is always implied in or admixed with the individual judgement.

The I, as the kernel of the human spirit, is that which truly exists [*sushchee*] but is not an existing thing [*sushchestvuyushchee*], just as the center of a circle is not a point on the surface plane of the circle, as it is usually and conventionally represented by geometry. A point does not occupy space, and, moreover, only when connected to another point can it yield a particular direction, a straight line. The center, as a point, does not itself possess such a second point, although any of the points on the curve can serve this purpose. This means that the center exists only as a direction, as a connection, a force, and the curve is in this sense a function or a phenomenon of the center. The I is not in and of itself, it does not *exist*, but it *possesses existence*, it *receives being* from another, which is its predicate and which is different from the I. This is why the I can never be defined, but only specified, and the whole of life is nothing other than this specification. It can also be said that the I is not, but *super*-is, or *truly exists* [*est' sushchee*]. This in no way means that the *I* is merely a function, an *als ob* [as if], as Kant essentially thinks and as, following Kant, some modern epistemologists also think. Of course, the *I* is *also* a function, but functioning, action, requires someone who is acting and functioning. As non-*existent*, the *I* can also not be expressed by any kind of *concept* [*poniatie*], since a concept is an image of existence, its *conception* [*poiatie*]; the concept, therefore, wholly belongs to the realm of being, to which the *I* does not belong. None the less, the word *I* is a verbal and mystical gesture which everyone understands. It points to an ineffable and unutterable depth, to a darkness which is constantly being torn apart by the light into a chiaroscuro, to an underground spring which is continually welling forth at the surface. If we did not ourselves have the *I*, we could not know it by experience or from life, for no amount of verbal or conceptual effort would be capable of expressing or showing the *I*, or of demonstrating it or describing it, since the *I* is transcendent and absolute. Yet since we ourselves do have the *I*, there is no need for any sort of deliberate introspection in order to understand it, for it is given to us in an immediate, mystical and intuitive act. A different kind of clarity and distinctness is possible in the self-consciousness of the *I*, for this very self-consciousness is given in a completely easy and natural way, is given completely intuitively.

The real difficulty arises not in the original self-consciousness of the *I*, but in distinguishing between the many different coverings which clothe it, and, in a closely-related way, in distinguishing the subject from subjectivity. The *I*, as subject, is the subject of every predicate, whether this is heaven or hell, minerals or the passions. In practical terms, however, there is a very great difference between a realm which is found in the world outside us and our own subjectivity, which, usually, is precisely the field identified with the *I*, whilst everything remaining is considered as the *not-I*. Yet the *I*, as a *psychological* subject, that is, as a ceaselessly moving and varying ocean of states, of experiences, of emotions, and of passions, is, to the extent that all these are an external world for the noumenal, hypostatic *I* itself, a *predicate* of the hypostatic *I*. Both the psychological subject, as a complex of states which is eternally changing, and also the epistemological *I*, the totality of cognitive forms, schemas, and categories, are predicates with respect to the noumenal *I*; they are the most refined of the noumenal *I*'s forms, cast in the image and likeness of the noumenal *I*. Both Kant's philosophy and that of the epistemological movement which follows him suffer from an insufficiently distinct understanding of this truth. Nor is it possible to equate the *I* as an absolute subject, the absolute *I*, with the *I* of volition. Volition, too, is itself only a shell of the *I*, a manifestation of the *I* within being, for the powerful, self-sufficient will introduced by the metaphysics of Schopenhauerian voluntarism is merely a hypostatized psychologism. Volition is a predicate of the *I*, which is what truly wills, yet which is also just as much what thinks, recognizes, feels. In relation to this absolute *I*, pure hypostaticity, the will too is merely a form of existence: will exists in the one who wills, and not the other way round; the one who wills is above any particular volition, and a subjectless or pre-subjective will is merely a spectral nightmare of the philosophy of pessimism, which wishes to extinguish the light of day and submerge itself in the kingdom of darkness. If it is necessary to distinguish the hypostatic *I*, the absolute subject, from the epistemological and psychological *I*, it is still more necessary to separate the hypostatic *I* from the *body* as a unity of psycho-physical organization, as a sentient being. The body is our *cosmic I*, the whole ensemble of organs, by means of which we find ourselves in relation with the entire universe; at the same time, the universe is our peripheral and potential body (cf. my *Philosophy of Economy*). Our whole life takes place in, with, and by means of the body; the body is a laboratory for the spirit, where spirit develops itself in its functions. The question of the significance of natural and bodily life, and of the meaning of embodiment as such, can be particularly clearly seen here when we consider that our body, however close or intimate we might be to or with it, is not the *I*; it is not the *I* to the same degree and in the same sense that the psychological and the epistemological *I* are not the *I*. And our body, in relation to the *I*, is a *predicate*, a real, living predicate, in which and by means of which the *I* lives, that is, by means of which the *I* realizes its constant predicativeness. And if it is impossible to equate our bodies with the *I* (this would be materialism, which is a metaphysics which deduces the *I* from the *not-I*, as was shown earlier), it is even less sound to equate the *I* with the whole of the natural world, to dissolve the *I* into the cosmos. Although our *I* is a cosmic *I* to which *everything* belongs as a predicate, in so far as it beholds itself in the cosmos, it nevertheless — and this is the mystery and the wonder of the *I* — cannot be dissolved into the cosmos, nor is it amalgamated with the cosmos, since, not being of this world, it does not occupy any sort of point in it. In the last analysis, the *I* must be defined antinomically, on the model of "negative theology." On one hand, the *I* is completely and decisively *not* in relation to any definition, for it *is not* as such; yet that is why it cannot be treated as a zero, as a vacuum, simply as non-being, for to it belongs super-being [*sverkhbytie*]. On the other hand, the I is *everything* which forms a predicate for it, from the most intimate subjectivity to the most rigidified objectivity.

The *I* can never, even for a single moment, become a zero, because it is inseparably linked to its predicate, and in, through, and with the predicate the *I is*, comes to being. The existent [*sushchestvuyushchee*] is posited, the indeterminate determined, by what truly exists [*sushchim*] — not from without, but from within. This bond is unbreakable: an *I* without a predicate is a "what-less" *I*, relating to nothing at all; a predicate without an *I* is a "who-less" predicate, relating to no one at all. Predication, the capacity for predication, is nothing other than the disclosure within spirit of its own proper nature and depth, an act of self-definition and self-realization. The predicate does not come from outside, as might appear, but is born in the spirit. In the predicate, the hypostatic spirit recognizes its own self; through the predicate are disclosed the spirit's own nature and its inexhaustible riches. This sounds paradoxical: is it really the case that everything which is continually given to me, unknown to my will or even despite it, and not in the least in accordance with it, is my own self-realization, my own nature? Can it be that the *I*, which is manifestly and without doubt only a something, an insignificant little particle of the universe, possesses *everything* within itself, is the creator of the world, and the world its result? Here we come up against the question which turned out to be a "curse," to be insuperable, for monistic philosophy, and which, as the general problem of identity, presented itself to monism over and over again in different forms: how can a bridge be thrown from the subject to the object, from the subject to the predicate? How can a judgement whose form is quite clearly inherent in substance itself be realized? Even if this bridge itself has not been discovered, the conditions which any solution must satisfy have nevertheless become completely clear, even though these conditions of themselves lead to antinomies. On the one hand, for the predicate to be a predicate, to pertain to the *I*, the predicate itself must be in a certain sense an *I*, must possess *I*-ness; yet at the same time it must also separate itself, must be an *other* in relation to the *I*—that is, it must be a *not-I*. Predication is grounded in a violation of both of the fundamental laws of logic: the law of identity, and the law of contradiction. For predication testifies to the fact that the *I* is *both not I, and, at the same time, I*, simultaneously and at once. If the *I* were merely repeated, throwing off, in its predicates, reflections of itself—*I* is *I*, is *I*, is *I*—it would be a squirrel running on a wheel, an insatiable thirst for a predicate, but not the predicate itself, an unceasing craving for any kind of content or determinacy. Separated from any existence, deprived of any predicate, the *I* would be in spasms of torment over being, would be convulsed in its impotence to give birth to the absolute. (Is not this that inextinguishable fire of final *separation*, lacking all predicates, an immortality without the capacity for life, which awaits in the fiery Gehenna? And is not every death, in a certain provisional and temporary sense, also the separation of the subject from the predicate, or at least the paralysis of the connection between them?) Conversely, if the *I* were completely to step over into the *not-I* and to immerse itself in it, it would lose the force and sharpness of life, its sunlikeness; it would fall into the swoon of pre-being or post-being (death also appears as the latter, death which abandons the *I* to its craving and to the desert, and which leaves the *not-I*, the potential predicate, in a swoon of unconsciousness which can be overcome only by the resurrection). This domain of predication, which is simultaneously *I* and *not-I*, must be understood and interpreted as the *not-I* within the *I*—that is, as something which, being an *I*, nevertheless still remains unilluminated by the light of the *I*, that is to say, something which is not taken cognizance of, something like a twilight of the *I*, or an un- (or pre-, or sub-) conscious *I*. Such a definition sounds like a simple *contradictio in adjecto*, a contradiction (which, it goes without saying, is to be strictly distinguished from an antinomy). However, this contradiction is removed when it is added that unconsciousness here does not mean anti-consciousness, that is, the absence of consciousness in the sense of the impossibility of consciousness (the introduction of such an assumption would indeed be contradictory, and, therefore, inadmissible) but signifies simply its absence, as a state of consciousness's potentiality. *I* and *not-I* are distinguished from each other as consciousness *in actu* [in actuality] and *in potentia* [in potentiality], and the *I* is to be thought of as a source of the continual actualization of potential. The nature of the spirit is infinite, and the depth of the *I*—which, in accordance with Fichtean terminology, is also a *not-I*—is fathomless, as befits an immortal and eternal spirit.

Fichte came up against this difficulty, and was compelled to recognize an *unconscious* creative activity in the *I*, an activity by means of which arise the forms of the *not-I*, a *produktive Anschauungskraft* [productive power of intuition]. He comes close to the truth here in a matter of exceptional importance, and is deflected from it only thanks to a starting-point which is mistaken in the force of its one-sidedness. The philosophy of the abstract *I*, isolated from substance, can only be rescued either by ambiguities—such as those in the concepts of the absolute *I* and the pure *I*—or by the direct violence of a "deduction." Such a violence is seen in Fichte's leap into the domain of practical reason for the purpose of deducing the *not-I* as a "limit," whereas the *not-I* is not a "limit," but is, above all, a predicate of the I itself. In any case, in Fichte's problematic a genuine discovery which possessed permanent significance for philosophy was made, in that Fichte posed the question of the nature of *the not-I in the I*. Schelling, in his work *On the Essence of Human Freedom*, and also in his *Philosophy of Mythology and Revelation*, answers this question through his doctrine of the *nature in God*, which can be universalized into a doctrine of the nature of spirit, of the *I*. The nature or primal ground of God, according to Schelling, is that dark and unconscious principle by overcoming which God emerges as a personal principle. In connection with the question which interests us here, it is possible to say that here the *not-I* constitutes the nature of the *I*, that it is a φύσις [*phusis*] with respect to the hypostasis. Schelling's heresy and error (the reverse of Fichte's) lies in his putting the nature of the hypostasis *before* the hypostasis, and *deducing* the hypostasis from that nature. In other words, he takes the predicate, understood as a dark potentiality, *apart from* and *before* the subject, and forces it to engender its own hypostasis from out of itself. And this misshapen alignment, which Schelling inherits from Böhme through Baader, distorts and falsifies Schelling's whole conception. Schelling does not merely distinguish God's nature from God himself, but directly opposes the two: the world emerges from this nature as if arbitrarily, and then evil comes into being of its own accord, an evil which, in essence, turns out to be identical with individuation, that is, with the origin of a hypostatic form of being. With this there is accomplished here the severing of the indivisible Trinity, and the divine hypostasis is thought in isolation from the divine nature, even though it is depicted as having its origin in the divine nature, as a result of that nature's development. Leaving to one side for a while this dogmatic side of the question, we see in Schelling's doctrine of the nature of God an attempt to link God's hypostasis with his nature, to link subject with object, subject with predicate. Although as this thought develops it turns out to be a heretical distortion, the question was, nevertheless, correctly posed. But in consequence of the fact that nature, the predicate, was posited by Schelling before the subject, what eventuated, in the spirit of the philosophy of identity, was an unconscious primal origin, from which consciousness too originates. This is a radical lie, since spirit by its own nature cannot be unconscious or non-conscious; this would signify its being anhypostatic, whereas spirit is above all hypostasis, which is its alpha and omega, its source and destination. All its riches are expended in the light of hypostatic consciousness; the *I* may not be unconscious, since it is consciousness. And this intellectual sun cannot be explained as originating in darkness; consciousness, or the *I*, cannot be generated from anything else.

Yet consciousness cannot exist without something of which it is conscious, nor can a hypostasis exist without its content. Just as day presupposes its hidden foundation in night, and just as light presupposes what it reveals and presupposes the darkness which it disperses, so too consciousness always possesses its own depths, from which its objects originate. A hypostasis possesses that of which it is the hypostasis; a hypostasis is inseparable from its nature, is hypostatic with respect to its nature. Nature is the foundation or the predicative character for the subject which reveals and calls this predicate into being. What does this foundation conceal within itself? What does it contain, this predicative character of the subject? This question must be answered with a question: what does it not contain? In other words, it contains everything potential and everything which is actualized. The predicate speaks of everything; it is the universal word, the logos of the world. This logos rises from the depths of nature, from the depths of the hypostasis, which, through the logos, recognizes its own nature and its resources, since it turns out that, to adopt the expression of our popular mystic Syutaev, an expression repeated in chorus by all mystics of all ages and of all peoples, "all is within thee," and thou art within all; the whole world is the property of the I, and nature is the depth of my own spirit, which flings open its treasure before me.[3] And this character of spirit's, this pairing of the hypostasis with its nature, is revealed in and leaves its mark upon spirit's every movement, in its every act, and most distinctly of all, as we saw, in the act of thinking self-consciousness, in the judgement. The judgement, which is concerned with the subject-object pair, is living proof of the bi-unity of substance, that is, of spirit as hypostasis and nature.

Yet this bi-unity does not come to a halt in duality, but leads to a triunity. The predicate is not exhausted in a single grammatical object, but is filled, is linked with the subject by the *copula*, by *being*. And the subject, the hypostasis, never limits itself to seeing its predicate as its ideal reflection, but rather recognizes reality—both its own and the

---

3   Vasilij Kirillovich Syutaev (1819–1892). — *Trans.*

predicate's—or rather, which is the same thing, it feels *the force of being* proceeding from itself and returning to itself, and this "life-giving" force is also, properly speaking, existence "in the living soul," is life, reality, being. Reality, it would seem, does not possess its own voice or image; it is only the *how* of a *what*, is as it were its *modus*. More precisely, it is necessary to say that the predicate has the same identity as reality: *everything* which came into being as the universal logos is also reality's proper all. At the same time, too, the reality which the hypostasis receives, and which is realized in the hypostasis's own nature, is the same reality as the predicate's. It turns out that reality exists only *in the relation* between a hypostasis and its nature, in the movement from one to the other, which, it goes without saying, must be understood purely ideally, as the realization of the relation between moments in the life of spirit. This, however, is not enough, and reality cannot be reduced to a single relationship or a single movement; reality *is present in everything*, and everything, or the world, "becomes a living soul" (Gen. 2.7), becomes *being*—which the philosophy of identity, abstracting from its pan-unity and universality, then selects as the sole principle of the world. Philosophical cosmism orientates itself towards being as towards universal reality. We already know of the insuperable difficulties into which cosmism, or the philosophy of identity, falls. Reality as such, taken without its bond to hypostatic consciousness, to the subject, and to the universal logos or predicate, is colourless and mute, lacking consciousness or meaning, which is why abstract realism, too, is meaningless and impossible. Being is thinkable only as the copula, that is, only in the light of the hypostatic logos and in connection with it. Being is not just being, devoid of predicates and equivalent to nothing (as Hegel liked to suggest, and needed to suggest for the sake of his subsequent dialectical tricks—see the excursus on him); rather, being is always *someone's* (is hypostatic), and is always *something*. Its *modus* embraces all the Aristotelian categories[4] (apart from οὐσια [*ousia*] or essence, it goes without saying, which was counted amongst the Aristotelian categories by mistake or as a result of a misunderstanding). This colourful diversity of categories, however, belongs

---

4 The categories in Aristotle, besides οὐσια [ousia], are the following: ἢ πόσον, ἢ ποιὸν, ἢ πρός τι, ἢ ποῦ, ἢ ποτὲ, ἢ κεῖσθαι, ἢ ἔχειν, ἢ ποιεῖν, ἢ πάσχειν [ē poson, ē poion, ē pros ti, ē pou, ē pote, ē keisthai, ē ekhein, ē poiein, ē paskhein] (quantity, quality, relation, place, time, position, possession, activity, passivity).

only to a transient image of the world, and not to being itself, which is the unmoved and non-categorial foundation of all the categories. One of the greatest falsehoods of epistemological idealism, particularly in its most extreme tendencies (the Marburg school), after Hegel, lies in the fact that it treats being (as reality) as one of the categories, and declares it to be a category *of thought*; reality is only conceivability. This philosophical "defamation of the Holy Spirit" doubtless signifies an acosmism, or even an anti-cosmism, since the logos makes the cosmos only by virtue of reality. Being in and of itself belongs neither to the hypostasis as such—for the hypostasis, that which truly exists, is above being, and, consequently, is also outside of it—nor to the logos, the predicate, as a "representation" or as an ideal image which arises only in the bosom of being. By virtue of the fact that it is a life-giving power of being which allows *everything*, in one way or another, to participate in reality, the hypostasis descends to the realm of being, and being becomes accessible to the hypostasis. The realm of being already *is* something, and the predicate is not simply a word, but a word *about* something, or, more correctly, *from* something (for the true nature of the word lies in the fact that words are spoken by the objects themselves, that words already presuppose concretion, reality). To convert the force of being, reality, into the logical category of "givenness" or "being" means to dissolve the third moment of triune judgement and of tri-hypostatic substance into the second moment, so that—it goes without saying—this third moment can then be managed as one likes, and one can construct "the natural-scientific world" in one's own image and likeness, which is what Hegel and Cohen and company are each in his own way busy doing. Logic cannot do anything with being, but nor can it manage without it. Being is alogical, and yet is permeated through and through by the logos, which, however, is impotent without being. This is why a logic which has pretensions to deduce the being of the universe also comes to a halt before being in embarrassed helplessness.

EXCURSUS ON KANT

THE QUESTION OF BEING OR OF EXISTENCE IN KANT'S theory remains very unclear, whereas it should have received particularly careful explanation given the difficulties for idealism which it brings with it. Kant counts reality among the categories, under the rubric of *quality*, along with negation and limitation, and places existence under the rubric of *modality*, along with possibility and impossibility, but he does not provide particular applications of most of the categories, with the exception of causation, and the categories of reality and existence are not even subjected to any particular examination, but are considered only as modalities of the predicate, rather than in themselves (CPR, 113 [A 80/B106]). "The postulate bearing on the knowledge of things as actual," says Kant (CPR, 242–43 [A225/B272]), "does not, indeed, demand immediate perception (and, therefore, sensation of which we are conscious) of the object [?—S.B.] whose existence is to be known. What we do, however, require is the connection of the object with some actual perception, in accordance with the analogies of experience... In the mere concept of a thing no mark of its existence is to be found. For though it may be so complete that nothing which is required for thinking the thing with all its inner determinations is lacking to it, yet existence has nothing to do with all this, but only with the question whether such a thing be so given us that *the perception of it can, if need be, precede the concept.*" The italicized words introduce some kind of *givenness of things*, for which there is no place at all in Kant's general epistemology, where the thing or object is a categorial synthesis of perceptions. This is why the question of "givenness" in Kant's system has acquired such sharpness and significance. Kant deliberately comes to a halt before this question in the section on "the impossibility of an ontological proof of the existence of God." "'Being,'" Kant reasons here, "is obviously not a real predicate; that is, it is not a concept of something which could be added to the concept of a thing. *It is merely the positing of a thing, or of certain determinations, as existing in themselves.* [Nothing can be more ill-defined or more contradictory than such a definition of the main question.—S.B.] Logically, it is merely the copula of a judgement. The proposition, 'God is omnipotent', contains two concepts, each of which has its object—God and omnipotence. The small word 'is' adds no new predicate, but only serves to posit the predicate in its relation to the subject. If, now, we take the subject (God) with all its predicates (among which is omnipotence), and say 'God is', or 'There is a God,' we attach no new predicate to the concept of God, but only posit the subject in itself with all its predicates, and indeed posit it as being an object that stands in relation to my concept. The content of both must be one and the same; nothing can have been added to the concept, which expresses merely what is possible, by my thinking its object (through the expression 'it is') as given absolutely. Otherwise stated, the real contains no more than the merely possible. A hundred real thalers do not contain the least coin more than a hundred possible thalers. For as the latter signify the concept, and the former the object and the positing of the object, should the former contain more than the latter, my concept would not, in that case, express the whole object, and would not therefore be an adequate concept of it. My financial position is, however, affected very differently by a hundred real thalers than it is by the mere concept of them (that is, of their possibility). For the object, as it actually exists, is not analytically contained in my concept, but is added to my concept (which is a determination of my state) synthetically; and yet the conceived hundred thalers are not themselves in the least increased through thus acquiring existence outside my concept... Whatever, therefore, and however much, our concept of an object may contain, we must go outside it, if we are to ascribe existence to the object. In the case of objects of the senses, this takes place through their connection with some one of our perceptions, in accordance with empirical laws. But in dealing with objects of pure thought [*it is the idea of God in particular which is being discussed here—S.B.*] we have no means whatever of knowing their existence" (CPR, 504–5, 506 [A 598–601/B 626–29]).

The passage given here from Kant, together with the notorious example of the hundred thalers, is justly considered as one of the most vulnerable points of his account. All the Königsberg Copernicus's arguments, in fact, were directed towards absorbing all the energy of being into the subject, into thought, and towards presenting the object as a categorial synthesis. In reality, however, thinking turns out not to have the object, but only the *concept* of the object, at its command; being has to be added to this concept by an act of synthesis, not on the basis of speculative reflection, but by relying on some sort of intuitive and mystical givenness of the object (although this is shamefacedly disguised by an ill-defined reference to the "connection with some one of our perceptions, in accordance with empirical laws"). The distinction between the concept of the hundred thalers and the actual sum (setting to one side the unfortunate mercantile associations of this example) is not only hard to grasp from a logical point of view but is also epistemologically unintelligible.

The Philosophical Meaning of Triadicity

A mystical empiricism breaks out within Kant's epistemological idealism. And although Kant supposes himself to be celebrating his victory over the ontological proof of God, he reveals, in reality, the groundlessness and unsustainability of his idealism, since the latter lacks any foundation in being, and, at the last, becomes a certain synthetic $=x$. Nowhere in the whole span of the *Critique of Pure Reason* is the question of reality posed in any other way than in the sense of its being a formal and logical property of judgement. In the first lines of section 1 it is suggested that "intuition" — *Anschauung* — "takes place only in so far as the object is given to us. This again is only possible, to man at least, in so far as the mind is affected in a certain way. The capacity (receptivity) for receiving representations through the mode in which we are affected by objects, is entitled *sensibility*. Objects are given to us by means of sensibility, and it alone yields us intuitions; they are thought through the understanding, and from the understanding arise concepts" (CPR, 65 [B 33/A 19]). Kant begins his *Critique* with a completely dogmatic declaration which is in no way argued for, that in intuitions *objects are given*, objects which also act on us; consequently, at the basis of all cognition, as its precondition, lies the reality of the object, a reality given, according to Kant, only through sensibility, but not through thought (and his critique of the ontological proof of God relies on this). But this initial Kantian realism is of course not further developed or corroborated in what follows, since it turns out that objects are categorial syntheses, and that the *res* proper retreats into the realm of noumena, of which we can know nothing. Yet at the same time such a realism proves to be essential, so that we can distinguish between the real and the imaginary thaler. Kant's relation to the copula "is" is characteristic of his thought. In the copula he sees an expression of the "relation" between subject [*sub"ekt*] and predicate, but he neither explains nor even asks about the nature of this relationship. Kant does not go beyond a formally grammatical and formally logical approach to this question, even though in this form it possesses only a wholly derivative significance, and even though it is necessary first to understand the nature of the copula — that is, of being — ontologically, in order then to move on to its logical reflection in the copula. In any event, it is not enough to say that the copula is merely the relation between a subject and a predicate without asking oneself what kind of relationship this might be. For this reason it will not do to refer to the idea that being is *only* the copula and does not add any new predicate, because here something unknown is defined by something unknown, or at least by something undefined. The broader meaning of Kant's epistemology is that only the sensible elements of reality — *Anschauungen* — are given. These undergo the active influence of the epistemological subject, as a result of which is obtained experience, as the sole form of reality, and as something accessible; but when discussion turns to the power of concepts, Kant refers to the reality of the object itself, and with this introduces a special source of cognition — *the sense of reality* — whose testimony is synthetically added to the judgement.

It is wholly natural that Kant should pay so little attention to the third moment of the judgement, to the copula, that is, to the question of being or of reality. Kant's philosophy, as we saw, is a subjective idealism, in which the concept of the subject from which Kant starts is not even taken in its authentic form, as a hypostasis, but is treated as an epistemological casing stripped off from the predicate. This is a philosophy of the predicate mistaken for a subject. But with neither definition of the concept does Kant get as far as the third moment, as far as being; he lingers on the second moment, and the illumination of the problem of being in his work remains wholly inadequate. The problem is wrapped up in the theory of noumena and phenomena, which is itself problematic. This is why Kant's idealism proves to have so many different meanings, which it takes in different, and even in mutually incompatible, directions. (Hegel also considers Kant's example of the real and the imaginary hundred thalers in his *Logic*, in connection with his own theory of the identity of being and nothing. "[T]he abstractions of being and nothing both cease to be abstractions if they acquire a determinate content... *Determinate being* is the first category to contain the real difference of being and nothing."[5] On the whole, Hegel's discussion, which is necessary only to the development of his own point of view, adds nothing essential to the question.)

* * *

Being, therefore — "*is*" — is not merely a "copula." More precisely, it is necessary seriously to ask oneself what precisely this copula signifies, and whence it springs. And it at once becomes evident that its formal

---

5 SL, 87, 88. (Miller's "*[d]eterminate being*" translates *Dasein*, "existence" or, in the Russian version quoted by Bulgakov, *sushchestvovanie*. — Trans.)

logical function is only a reflection of an ontological givenness. The copula connects [*sviazka sviazyvaet*] and unites subject and object, which, if taken separately from each other, are antinomically correlated. There is no bridge between them. The subject has all the force of being, but it does not have the shape [*obraz*] of being; it remains transcendent. The object, the predicate, has all the fullness of being, but lacks its force. What is needed is a special mediating power which could connect subject and object in the act of being. Being is the unity of the hypostasis with its nature. There is no such thing as that being in general which was propounded by Parmenides or Spinoza in all their thinking about oneness. Being is always concrete and definite. That is why being cannot be grasped or understood without reference to the relationship of the subject of being to the object. It occupies a definite third place in the structure of substance, but also in that of the logic and grammar of the judgement, and the place of the category of being in this hierarchy can neither be changed nor abolished. Moreover, this third moment of substance has a definite relationship to its two predecessors, and the relationship is not in each case identical: being begins with the hypostasis, with the subject, *he is*, but it makes towards the predicate, towards *something that* he is. It can be said, to use theological language, that the third shape [*obraz*] of substance, the force of being, proceeds from the subject, as its first shape, and unites the first shape to the second in such a way that between the first and the second a new unity is established ("And all mine are thine, and thine are mine," John 17:10): the shape of being, the logos of the world, the predicate, is inseparable from being, for the predicate proceeds from the subject to the object. The subject cannot, in and of itself, color being with qualities; only the force of being belongs to the subject. From this results the property of the predicate, when compared with the subject, that the predicate always has a *general* character, that it expresses a concept or an idea, a certain property or qualitative feature of being—being which, in and of itself, without this property, would lack its own face; all individuality, all participation in a particular hypostasis, conversely, is proper to the subject, which, in this sense, is not a concept, but a name (a "proper name"). From this follows a conclusion which is, formally and logically, of paramount importance, namely that *one and the same predicate may characterize a whole series of subjects*. True, the subject may also have a series of predicates, and it would seem in this way not to differ from the predicate, but this sameness is only apparent. The point is that the predicate as such never possesses an exhaustive, complete nature. It is always an undefined plurality: A is B and B1 and B2...and Bn and Bn+1, etc. ..., which concludes in an ellipsis. The integral of this series, the sole universal (although also potential) predicate, is the *all* or the world. For this reason the domain of being, that is, of the predicate, is *one* and is common to many subjects, while these latter, conversely, are *many* and *non-recurring*, for they cannot recur in the absence of a content of being; they remain above being and have contact with it only through the predicate. In this way we have a unified world, the universal and most general predicate, the domain of being, and a multiplicity of hypostatic centres. The problem of the *universal* (τὸ καθ' ὅλου [*to kath' holou*]), the nature of the concept, which stands before us as it has done since antiquity and through all the subsequent centuries down to our time, comes down, that is, to the concept's relationship to the subject, which is never universal and which is not even a concept, but which is always a *non-concept*, a hypostasis which exists immediately in a personal name. The real nature of the question is obscured by the fact that the first person pronoun only acts as the grammatical subject in exceptional cases. As a rule, grammatical subjects are concepts (or "common" nouns, in distinction from "proper" names) or simply words, whereas a hypostasis as such is not even a word and cannot, of its nature, be expressed by a word, which is why it needs a predicate for its own sake. These particular forms of judgement, however, exist only by virtue of the general, ontological judgement of the type *I am something, such-and-such a person is A*, and so on. The subject, by virtue of its function, ceases itself to be a concept, and becomes, as it were, a proper name, and, for this reason, also requires a predicate of its own. As we showed earlier, all judgements come down to the hypostatic type, and presuppose the latter as their self-evident precondition. "The table has a black surface" signifies, in reality: I think, I see, that the table, etc.; that is, I am the one who thinks that the table, and so on. The other source of obscurity about the real state of affairs is the fact that in the judgement, as it is executed in our thinking, is manifested all the inconstant nature of thought, its untruthfulness. Hence the "modality" of judgement, its "problematic," apodictic or assertoric form (according to Kant) concerns not its ontological basis, but, so to speak, its logical

The Philosophical Meaning of Triadicity

technique, its way of conducting the search for a true judgement.[6] All these aspects of the categories are modifications of judgement as it is executed logically and grammatically, as thought, but *judgement*—and this is the very essence of our point of view—*is not thought*, or, rather, *is not only thought*, but is a fundamental fact of the self-determination of spirit. *Judgement expresses the nature of substance*. And here, when judgement is taken in this ontological sense, it follows that the subject is always in the singular number, that it is a self-enclosed monad, whereas the predicate is universal, is a concept expressing the nature of a being, to whomsoever that being might belong.

But here we find ourselves face to face with the most burning and most difficult of problems: the problem of the *multi-hypostaticity of being*, the oneness of the predicate and the multiplicity of subjects, unity in plurality and plurality in unity. The one world has an undefined plurality of sovereigns, of hypostases; the one nature of the spirit which is revealed in the world has many faces.

And, above all, whence come *we*? How does each *I*, enclosed within itself, and involuntarily imagining itself to be an absolute I, know another I? Where and how is the transition to the *thou* brought about, how do *we* come to be? This question appears equally urgent and fateful for Kant and for Fichte, but neither noticed it; they bypassed it instead. Their whole projects would have foundered upon it. Kant defines objective judgement as universally significant, that is, as binding for every mind, or for every *I*; his whole epistemological account of the *I* as a logical function, as transcendental apperception, would need revision in the light of the fact of the epistemological (and thus necessarily also of the ontological) existence of *thou* and *we*. An even greater difficulty for Fichte, who, no less than Kant, takes the presence of a plurality of individuals for granted, is how to make the other *I* part of his schema of *I* and *not-I*, for the *thou* is neither one nor the other, and the whole of the *Science of Knowledge* would have to be completely revised and re-organized in the light of the *thou*.

The main difficulty here consists in the fact that *thou*, the other *I*, is never in any sense a predicate, a form of being for the *I*, for the hypostatic

---

6   CPR, 107 (B 95/A 70). Here belong, too, all the other aspects of judgement which Kant distinguishes from each other in the categories of quantity (unity, plurality, totality), of quality (reality, negation, limitation) or of relation (of inherence and subsistence, of causality and dependence, of community).

subject [*podlezhashchee*], yet at the same time it is a *not-I*, an object. Every *I* naturally makes of itself something absolute and unique, and Stirner, in his philosophical pamphlet, only laid bare this egoistic nature of the *I* (although even in Stirner, unexpectedly and inconsequently, the "egoists" appear in the plural number, and even form a "union").⁷ The transition from the singular number to the dual, or, equally, to the plural number is not so easy and so readily intelligible as it might appear on the table of grammatical declensions. It is in its way no less mysterious and primordial than the transition from the subject to the predicate, which also takes place in the trivial and as if clear—yet, in fact, deeply mysterious—workings of the judgement. How can the *I* see and observe the *we*, that is, its own likeness and repetition, a *we* which is not a predicate, but a grammatical co-subject, not an object, but a cognitive co-subject? This act is so primordial and miraculous that there is not, nor can there be, an explanation for it; it is possible only to ascertain it, and then to take the proper notice and make the proper appraisal of it. The whole question has nothing to do with a psychological study of the other *I*, nor even with epistemological "introjection" (although this word, an invention of Avenarius's, says more or less nothing here) but concerns, rather, ontological contact with the other *I*, the comprehension of the other *I* as truly existing.⁸ We can show where the *task* lies for the other *I*, for the *thou* and for the *we*: it lies in the nature of the predicate as a universal, or a being, which has lost the exclusive link with its individual shape. Although the **I** is indeed *der Einzige* [the unique individual], the world which, as a predicate, is governed by the **I**, is not experienced by that **I** as *sein Eigenthum* [his property], or, at least, not *only* as "his property." On the contrary, even though the predicate is joined to the cognitive subject by the copula of being, the world, despite this, *does not belong to anyone, that is, it is common to all*, and judgement, precisely in its nature as universal and universally signifying, is a silent yet expressive enough gesture towards the *we*, is the site of the *we*. When the nature of the Subject, of the hypostasis, is scrutinized, we see with surprise that

---

7   Max Stirner (Johann Caspar Schmidt) (1806–1856), author of *Der Einzige und sein Eigentum* [*The Unique Individual and Its Property*] (1844). — *Trans.*

8   Richard Avenarius (1843–96), a "neutral monist" who held that the intrinsic nature of ultimate reality was neither physical nor mental; author of a *Kritik der reiner Erfahrung* [*Critique of Pure Experience*] (1888–90). — *Trans.*

although the I is an isolated, repelling centre, there is also present in it, as in the force of gravity, a power of attraction. In other words, the *non-uniqueness of the I*, the presupposition of other *I*s, inheres in the very nature of the *I*. As soon as we attempt to think or to perceive the *I* as a unity, without any *thou* (since *we* is also unable to meet such a demand), the *I* becomes unintelligible, loses its elasticity, and collapses. Without the *thou*, the *I* too loses its colour and fades. How this comes about is impossible to say or to explain, but it is so: the *I* implies not only a *not-I* (in the Fichtean sense, that is, a predicate), but also a *thou*, and a *we* or a *co-I*. The *I* also, in fact, experiences itself as the *singular number* of the plural *we*, and as the *first* person in relation to a *second — we* and *you plural —* and a *third — he, they*. And if this were not the case, neither *thou* nor *we* would be possible, nor would they exist. Consequently, the very nature of the *I* includes plurality. Hypostaticity does not presuppose mono-hypostaticity, but multi-hypostaticity, many *I*s in the presence of a single *not-I*, or predicate, or world. This is what Fichte, following Kant, bypassed, not having grappled with the problem of the *I* for longer than was necessary for the deduction of the *not-I*.

The plurality of the *I* is a fundamental axiom of thought and life. It must be shown, yet it cannot be seen; moreover, it is impossible and unnecessary to prove it. The impossibility of a proof is evident enough from the fact that the *I* as the truly existing [*sushchee*] lies *outside* the world of being, and, consequently, cannot be examined or demonstrated using its logic. Only apodictic judgements are possible in respect of the *I*, only axioms possessing the significance of the establishment of a fact. The I is not conscious of itself as unique; on the contrary, it presupposes an indefinite plurality of other hypostases. Its φύσις, the nature of the predicate, is not only reconciled to this, but also presupposes and even demands such a plurality. The predicate possesses a universal character; it is, logically speaking, always a general concept. Let us say it openly: the world is the common sphere of being for the plurality of hypostases. Hence, from one aspect, plurality is *Allheit* [all-ness], but from another it is universality — *Allgemeinheit*. Both commonalities close in a circle of universal pan-human judgement: *all know all, all are all*.

The *I* is thus something completely singular. On one hand, every *I —* or, more precisely, my own *I —* is unique, and in this sense is absolutely individual; yet at the same time it turns out to be a certain *genus* or species, since the *thou* and the *we* are given just as immediately as the *I*, and part of the consciousness of the *I* is consciousness of itself as a member of the *we*. There is no kind of logical or epistemological path from *I* to *thou* or *we*; not even Fichte, who deduces everything, undertook this deduction. It is possible, if one wishes, to arrange the triunity of *I — thou — we* according to the Hegelian triad, by representing *thou* as the antithesis of *I*, and *we* as a synthesis of the thesis, *I*, and the antithesis, *thou*. This innocent Hegelian game of triads only circumvents the difficulty, however, and blunts the sharp, thorny antinomy of the *I* by a happy recourse to Hegel's non-contradictory contradictions. I is *I*, and this *I* in its turn is *I*, and so on. Each *I* is self-enclosed and singular; like the Leibnizian monad, each *I* is windowless. And this very *I* knows not only a *not-I* (by means of which Fichte believed he could limit and exhaust the knowledge of the I) but knows also other *Is*. It knows *thous* and *wes*, and, consequently, knows itself also as a *thou* and a *we*, and knows the other *I* within itself. *By means of one and the same act* in which the I recognizes, or, in Fichtean terms, "posits" itself as a unique *I*, it knows or "posits" itself as generic, as co-hypostatic. Thus the hypostasis is simultaneously unique and non-unique, and this antinomy cannot be domesticated by breaking off its sharp end and turning it into an innocent Hegelian contradiction. It turns out that just what is most certain in us and for us, just that in which Descartes thought to find a ποῦ στῶ [*pou stō*, a place in which to stand], a support against or a calmative for doubt, an intelligible and reliable principle, contains within itself a gaping abyss.

> A splendoured firmament of burning stars
>   Mysterious shines from high
> On us who swim, by an abyss
>   Surrounded on all sides.[9]

Thus there is nothing which is intelligible in and of itself or without remainder. The intelligible is expelled from its last refuge, the

---

9 Bulgakov quotes the last quatrain of Fyodor Tyutchev's poem *Kak okean ob"emlet shar zemnoj*. Khoruzhij (ed. cit., 578n.) points out that Bulgakov (quoting from memory, perhaps) slightly misquotes the quatrain. A closer prose translation might be: "[t]he heavenly arch with burning starry glory mysteriously looks from the heights, and we swim, surrounded on all sides by a blazing abyss." — *Trans*.

self-consciousness of the *I*, and proves to be mysterious and unintelligible. The tragedy of reason has come to fruition; reason has been tormented and sacrificed on sharp antinomies. Yet catharsis is already beginning here. In the depths of hell, in ordeal by fire, the human being's own lineaments and their meaning are revealed to him. He appears before himself in the form of triadicity. The formula of the ecclesiastical dogma, which had up until now sounded alien, dead, paradoxical and absurd to reason, appears before him as the only answer to his perplexity, as the *truth* about his own nature, and, as lightning pierces the darkness, so the dogma fills everything with meaning. But more of this later; let us now resume our interrupted train of thought.

The question of the plural unity of the *I* repeatedly arose in philosophy, either in its essence or in a formally and epistemologically foreshortened form. The plural unity of the subject with a shared predicate signifies nothing other than a single shared nature in many hypostases, a unity of the predicate in many propositional subjects, of which each possesses it as if his own. Here lie the roots of the objectivity of judgement, the *I*'s testing of itself against every other *I*, *Allgemeingültigkeit* [universal validity]. Kant's epistemology, and epistemology after Kant, considers *universality*, bindingness for every thinking human being, as a formal mark of the truthfulness of a judgement. Positivists of Feuerbach's type speak openly of the species-character of truth, to such an extent that they identify this formal mark with the essence of truth: truth, for them, is an idea of the species', whilst error is an idea of the individual's. (A similar idea, but with a point of view further colored by utilitarianism and Darwinism, is put forward by Nietzsche, who equates truth with usefulness, and, moreover, with what is useful for the species.) Auguste Comte and the positivists expressed this idea in a religious and dogmatic form in the doctrine of humanity as a single being, a *Grand-être* [Great-being]. In essence, both Kant and Comte, the first in a carefully epistemological form, and the second in a crudely dogmatic one, recapitulate—in an extremely incomplete way, of course—the Christian doctrine of human nature, of the *one Adam* as all of humanity.

The problem of the *I as a plural unity* should have arisen for philosophers long ago, as also, above all, the question of how the alien *I* is to be understood both in its strangeness to and in its affinity with my own *I*. The singularity of this question lies in the fact that the alien *I* cannot be understood as lying within the domain of the *not-I* or predicate; it is not a predicate. Yet at the same time predication is the only domain of cognition and self-cognition, the domain in which the *I* knows its own nature. It is necessary, therefore, to say that we do not and cannot know the alien *I* as an object or as its own proper domain and nature. There is a special way for the subject to know a subject, but not an object: this way out of one's self is *not* through one's own nature, but from self to self, that is, to the *thou*. And the only organ of such cognition, a cognition not accountable to Kantian epistemology, is this exit from the self through which I know myself as another. This is love, the oneness of many, the knowledge of oneself outside oneself. "Love thy neighbor as thyself"—this commandment of both the Old and the New Testaments possesses, as do all the commandments, an ontological basis in the nature of things. It suggests above all that my neighbor, *thou*, is thy *I*, and by virtue of that love with which thou lovest, thou naturally affirmest thy own *I* as the unshakeable foundation of existence, but thou also affirmest the other *I*, must affirm it; and with this thou fulfillest the law of thine own existence, thou realizest thine own *I* in its true plenitude. This very thought also provides a guiding thread to the assessments of the question of *conciliarity* [*sobor'nost*] with which contemporary consciousness is preoccupied. The essence of conciliarity is sought on the basis of unity of object, of predicate, of love for one and the same thing. In this way, the essence of conciliarity is understood as believing *the same*, feeling *the same*, thinking *the same*—as agreement in opinions. It can be said, however, that all this is not enough, for all these are only derivative signs, and are not what is meant when the dogma of the one conciliar church is proclaimed, in which *conciliarity* does not bring us together into a mere sameness, but into a *unity*. Sameness of opinions is what unites a sect, a school, or a party, which can be cohesive and disciplined and yet can still prove to be as far removed from conciliarity as a body of soldiers which can be governed by one authority and one will. Conciliarity consists, above all, and in its original foundation, in a unity *in the subject*, in hypostaticity, which can be for each human being as though it is his or her own *I*, and love is also this ability of the *I* to identify itself with the other *I*, to love another as itself. And this is why conciliarity is in fact a *unity* and at the same time a *plurality*; this is why, too, all enter the church, yet at the same time the church is one; everyone who is truly in

The Philosophical Meaning of Triadicity

the church has everyone within himself, is himself the whole church, and, at the same time, everyone has him. This is why it is not possible to say that the church is an association, for an association is only an external expression for the church, a schema or an image of it; the church is more correctly defined as a uniplural being, which contains everyone within itself, and in this sense the church is the mother of all, who at the same time gives to each person a place within herself and pours herself into each person. Needless to say, in the present age barely a trace of conciliarity is detectible, since egoism, the antithesis of conciliarity, is the law of our life. Nevertheless, conciliarity is the abiding foundation of our existence, and if our life were freed from its burdensome and denatured veil, people would see their own wealth in love: "the things which are impossible with men are possible with God" (Luke 18:27). Let us, though, keep here to the epistemological and metaphysical aspect of the question alone, without digressing towards this incidental theologoumenon. Here it is necessary to show that real conciliarity is at the same time that catholicity and universal bindingness, *Allgemeingültigkeit* [universal validity], which is also so sought after by epistemology. To free oneself from subjectivity—this means to be a conciliar (that is, a true) *I*, to be in the truth, and therefore to know it. This means to be a true subject, who does not deface his or her own predicate, but leaves it free to reveal itself. In other words, this predicate must serve for each *I* and for the subject in general; there is in it no sort of partiality, no moment of heresy, that is, of selection.[10] Objectivity and catholicity of understanding cannot, then, be sought only beyond the subject, in the object, where the latter is usually sought and found in the properties of judgement, and in the observance of epistemological principles and the like. For none of this formal irreproachability in any way guarantees that the truth will actually be grasped. It is impossible to reduce all cognition to a matter of form, as some recent epistemologists do. Cognition is creation, that is, action, although within determinate forms, beyond which stands the one who is acting. With regard to "practical reason," that is, the domain of moral action, the active significance of the subject here is self-evident. It was clear to Kant, too, whose maxim of practical

---

10 As often in this text, Bulgakov is playing on the sense of Greek *hairesis* as "choice." — *Trans.*

reason runs: act in such a way as any other would have to act in your place, so that it is as if not you alone, but humanity itself, were acting in your person. Do not act as the egoistic *I*, but as the true, the conciliar *I*. The restriction or denial of the conciliarity of the *I* is that which in the language of contemporary philosophy is called, in a pejorative sense, *psychologism*, and the pursuit of life "to the lees" — in which life's pure essence is putatively fermented or crystallized — is such a psychologism. Psychologism is something which is given for the sake of its overcoming by the self-creation of Spirit. Spirit cannot be a given [*dannym*], like a thing; it is a task [*zadannym*]. Spirit is created in the image of God, that is, not in thing-like necessity, but in freedom, and for this reason it must know itself through its own self-creation.

We said that the comprehension of conciliarity in the *I* was accomplished through love and in love, and the epistemology of the subject is comprised of its opposite, self-love, which has many manifestations, from coldness to hostility and hatred. In so far as truthfulness is defined from the side of the subject, arriving at truthfulness depends precisely on this condition of the hypostasis, on whether it is withdrawn into egotistic mono-hypostaticity or is, instead, expanded in a conciliar fashion, impelled by love towards the truth as a hypostatic plural unity. This is why Satan, that pure monohypostaticity, that metaphysical egotism, is also the murderer of humanity and the father of lies, and why his children, the children of egotism incarnate, are also the progeny of lies.[11] For the negation of conciliarity is *in actu* [in actuality] a self-asserting egotism — an egotism which is not a weakness or a condition, as in psychologism, but which is a matter of fundamental self-definition, a noumenal egotism; it is a defamation of God's creation, a defamation of the *I*, which is not egotistical, but conciliar in its nature; egotism is a malicious incapacity for love and a complete abuse of the Holy Spirit. And this is a lie, the origin of lies, for all knowledge and all life flows from the subject, and clean and clear water cannot flow from this poisoned source. The wondrous hymn of love sung by the apostle Paul in the first letter to the Corinthians derives its metaphysical meaning from

---

11 "Ye are of your father the devil, and the lusts of your father ye will do. He was a murderer from the beginning, and abode not in the truth, because there is no truth in him. When he speaketh a lie, he speaketh of his own: for he is a liar, and the father of it" (John 8:44). — *Trans.*

this. "Though I have the gift of prophecy, and understand all mysteries and all knowledge; and though I have all faith, so that I could remove mountains, and have not charity, I am nothing" (1 Cor. 13:2). Consequently, along with the exceptional fullness of self-consciousness on the side of the content (of the predicate, or the object), a particular *quality* of this cognition proceeds from the subject, from the subject's health or sickness, which devalues and weakens this knowledge, and from which such cognition receives a negative coefficient. And this quality is a lack of conciliar self-consciousness, a denial of love. And knowing the truth, as the being of all within one, is replaced, in the world's cold expression for it, by *possessing* the truth—which, in reality, we do not, not at all.

In this way the subject, the hypostasis, is not an empty place, a transcendental point, lacking all colour. On the contrary, it is possible, instead, with Kant and Schopenhauer, to conceive of it as the noumenal character which underlies all empirical self-determinations, that is, which underlies factual knowledge and reality. We are not conscious of the intelligible character—that is, of the nature of the hypostasis in relation to conciliarity, its position and self-perception within the unity of everything, as an atemporal act lying at the very limit of creation—as an *act* of freedom; yet at the same time we experience it as a *deed* of our freedom, for which we are answerable (as Schopenhauer convincingly showed). This deed is in no way *in* being, but *before* being—that is, it is in the subject, and not in the predicate, or even before the predicate, but is rather the origin of the predicate. Does this mean that the deed of the intelligible self-definition of the subject is definitive and inalterable, that this deed is the subject's fate, a predestination, as Schopenhauer taught, and, before him, Calvin? Such it would be, if time were only a phenomenal appearance of timelessness, and did not itself belong to eternity in the form of temporality, if time were metaphysically void, inert and meaningless. But this is not the case. Time has roots in eternity; it, too, is eternity, although in the form of temporality, and fatalism is so much the more without foundation. It is possible to work on one's self over time, and such work can have significance in eternity; in this consists both the meaning of temporal life, and in this alone consists the metaphysical possibility of the Day of Judgement with its sentence for eternity. It is entirely correct that pre-temporal self-definition constitutes a givenness for the subject, some sort of fate for it, its own kind of metaphysical

The Tragedy of Philosophy

karma, and that the tree of life does not grow from a void. But the subject's life, its action in the predicate, as action, cannot be understood as a mechanism, but presupposes the presence of freedom, for action is freedom, but within necessity.

It has already fallen to me to show elsewhere (in *Unfading Light* and the *Philosophy of Economy*) that freedom and necessity are correlated concepts, and that both the one and the other are antinomically combined in the life of Spirit. Spirit is the eternally living and eternally acting origin; this is why freedom is its nature and its element. However, this freedom is freedom of action, and, therefore, of self-consciousness, but not the freedom of absolute creation or of omnipotence, which has nothing outside itself and which knows no limit. This creaturely freedom becomes aware of itself through its limits, and it perceives itself thanks to them (like the Fichtean practical I which, incessantly striving to overcome the *Schranke* [limit] of the *not-I*, at the same time needs this limit in order to overcome it). The antinomy of freedom and necessity unfolds simultaneously in two directions: in the subject itself; and in its relationship to the object, in the entirety of the judgement, in life. In the subject, in the self-consciousness of the hypostasis, which, however, is for the hypostasis also a predicate, there collide and wrestle with each other the subject's noumenal nature as givenness and its noumenal freedom as creativity—which latter cannot be reconciled with givenness, but which wants always to originate everything from out of itself—and the result turns out to be *work* on our own nature, an integral which we cannot see for so long as our eyes are closed by time. The relation between subject and object, subject and predicate—that is, being, life—is also an uninterruptibly continuing antinomy. The *I* is of its own nature always inclined to throw its weight about in a Fichtean manner, pretending to absoluteness and consequently to omnipotence. But its object, nature, the predicate, is *given* to it, is in actual fact its limit, as well as being at the same time its nature. Outside this nature and without it the subject is condemned to the wilderness of non-being, which is separation from nature and the dissolution of subject from predicate. The destruction of the copula is death, a dead faint of the subject, but also a dead faint of nature, which cannot exist without the subject either, so that both descend to a state of potentiality. In this way, the *I* requires necessity, which belongs to the predicate, just as the latter exists only on the presupposition of that freedom which is proper to the subject. Life can never be purely passive, remaining under the sway of necessity. This combination of a creative freedom with a necessity on the basis of which it acts, and a necessity which constitutes the foundation of temporal existence, is the life of this world.

Multi-hypostaticity remains a characteristic property of being. On the one hand, being is an ocean into which all rivers flow, the single moveless substance which absorbs everything into itself. On the other hand, being is proper to every hypostasis, and the hypostasis possesses being for itself and in itself. The hypostasis infuses its own actuality and freedom into being, and being is not one and immutable, but multiple and unstable, is becoming—so that Parmenides and Heraclitus were equally correct about it. The combination of both forms of being—of subject with object—corresponds to a unity of necessity with freedom, and forms the foundation of the two faces of being, which last is a combination of subject and object, a continually self-accomplishing "copula." The immovability and the unity of being is necessity, as is shown with full clarity in Spinoza's metaphysical determinism and in Hegel's dialectical parallel to Spinoza's doctrine. Multiplicity, creative work, fluidity (*évolution créatrice*) is linked, conversely, to a comprehension of the world in the categories of freedom, of personalism, as for J.G. Fichte, Renouvier, and the pragmatists.[12] Both sides are correct, not in an eclectic way, but antinomically. This is also the antinomy of subject and predicate, an antinomy which is both posited and sublated by being, by the copula.

Thus the triune image of substance is imprinted in the judgement, and the name of this image is *the human being*. Substance is the human being. The human being is a hypostasis who truly is, who has his or her being in the world, a subject who receives its predicate from, and is bound to the predicate by, the copula. The human being is a living judgement or, more precisely, is alive in the judgement, which is an archetype and a fundamental cognitive act containing the schema of substance and imaging forth its structure, for each judgement is a living act within substance, that is, within the human being. Of whatever

---

12 Charles Bernard Renouvier (1815–1903), neo-Kantian French philosopher who influenced, amongst others, Émile Durkheim. *L'Évolution Créatrice* is a work published in 1907 by the French philosopher Henri Bergson (1859–1941).— *Trans.*

kind a judgement is, whether it be a judgement of cognition or of the will, whether it be contemplative or active, it reproduces the triune countenance of being.

We are aware that the imprecision of our terminology here must long since have aroused the ire of logicians. What are the judgements in question about, and in what sense are they spoken? Judgements of course differ "by quantity, by quality, and by relation and modality," are *a priori* or *a posteriori*, analytic or synthetic and so on, as is usually set out in the chapter on judgements in a formal logic, and also in epistemology. But all these forms [*vidy*] of judgement, closer consideration of which falls completely outside the scope of our enquiry, are only *images* [*obrazy*] *of judgement*, judgement's embodiment, its psychological and logical faces. They derive from, and are to be understood from the point of view of, the nature of judgement as such, from the tripartite formula of its triunity. The logical images [*obrazy*] of judgement, and even judgement's epistemological meaning, rely on the ontological givenness of judgement. And the highest meaning of judgement, the mystery of judgement, must, of course, be sought not in logic, but in metaphysics, which, it goes without saying, finds expression in religion and flows from religion. In all forms of judgement, not only in its personal forms but also in its impersonal ones, we find only innumerable forms of a single judgement, which has for its subject the hypostasis or *I*, and has for its object any content whatever, or everything: *I* am everything or the world. Only this kernel of judgement interests us here. In the same sense, we are not in the least concerned with logic, with the study of its forms or with questions of its realization, nor even with epistemology, which examines these elements in dismantled form, as "categories." What is expressed in judgement is the nature of spirit, that is, of substance. And this philosophical view at once sheds light on the most involved and troubling questions in the metaphysics of that which truly exists [*sushchego*] and being, revealing their true meaning, in place of the significance of the separate philosophical schools or "tendencies" (whose meaning is a philosophical transcription of the word "heresy" in the neutral sense already explained, of the *selection* of one separate aspect as a guiding light). But what is much more important is that in the judgement the depths of our spirit, and, consequently, the nature of the human being, are illuminated as by a flash of lightning. For let us repeat: the human being is a living judgement or proposition, and life is the process of this proposition's articulation in time. The problem of judgement develops into an anthropological problem—the problem of the human being as substance. For the only knowledge of substance and about substance for the human being is the human being itself, or that which is human in the human being. "Human" by no means signifies something subjective and psychological, in need of being cleaned up by an application of epistemology; what is "human" is also substantial. In other words, we have access to substance and know it solely in and through ourselves. Even if we ourselves in our being are not yet substance, our only window into substance is this "we." For this reason the theory of substance necessarily becomes a philosophical anthropology, and substance—directly or obliquely, immediately or mediately—is we ourselves. Thus, in essence, did the matter already stand for Spinoza, for whom even though the human being is only a mode of substance, he or she may, through love for God, be immersed in substance, merge with it, dissolve into it, may, that is, become substance, and only through this becoming is it possible for the human being to have knowledge of substance. In Plotinus's account, where substance—the One—is much more transcendent than in Spinoza's, the situation is the same, because here too the human being, going beyond himself in a state of ecstasy and mingling identically with the One, makes himself substance at that moment, and it is only on this basis that he is able to know the One. On the whole, there can be no disputing the fact that the human being is substance in one sense or another. It is only a question of how his participation in substance is accomplished, and of what kind this participation might be. For my part, I see judgement as the hieroglyph of substantiality, the seal of the mystery of the human spirit; I am attempting, here, to open this seal, to decipher this hieroglyph.

2

From Image to Archetype

THE HUMAN SPIRIT POSSESSES A HYPOSTATIC nature—not uni-hypostatic, but multi-hypostatic—in which is revealed its content, and in which its being achieves reality. The hypostatic spirit has, in its self-consciousness and self-determination, a triune shape, but the many hypostases in which the human spirit exists possess a single common nature. The one is threefold in the form [*obraz*] of its existence [*sushchestvovaniya*] and the many is unified in the nature of its essence [*sushchestva*]. The analysis of the spirit undertaken above leads us, in this way, to a double paradox: a threefold unity and a unified multiple. It seems as if this paradox exhaustively describes the fundamental existence of the human spirit, yet thought can by no means satisfy itself with this, nor may it come to a halt here. The human spirit cannot comprehend itself; it demands an explanation for itself. It is self-evident that such an explanation, if it cannot be given by the human spirit to itself, must be sought outside it and above it, that is, in the Divine Spirit. As spirit, the human spirit cannot differ from Divine or Absolute Spirit so widely that it would be impossible for the human spirit to compare itself in any respect to It, or to comprehend It on the basis of this comparison. As human, that is, as non-absolute, spirit, it at the same time differs from Absolute Spirit in such a way that it is possible for it to comprehend the latter in this very difference. One thing cannot be doubted: the human spirit, as created and relative, cannot be understood *from out of itself*. It bears within itself, in its own contradictions, both the imprint of its own limitedness, and, at the same time, its own archetype, as a task. Absolute, Divine Spirit, the archetype of human existence, is neither an arbitrary assumption nor an auxiliary hypothesis, but is an internal postulate of human spirit itself. Whether God at all is, and what He is like in His own nature, cannot be ascertained by any human hypostasis; it can be ascertained only by God's revelation of Himself to human beings, religion. But without such a revelation it remains an unfulfilled *postulate* of the essence of the human spirit—the evidence of its image, which speaks of an archetype and which necessarily requires that archetype. The correspondence between image and archetype is reciprocal.

Man creates God in his own human image, just as Feuerbach and other atheists of his kind say, but does so precisely because in the image of his own spirit he also knows his own archetype, at least as an ontological postulate; that is, he knows Absolute and Divine Spirit, he comprehends God through his own self or in his own self. He knows that he is created in the image of God, and that his spirit is an icon of the Divine Being. Divine revelation is an objective process which does not depend on human beings; it is God's descent. Yet comprehension of the dogmas of revelation is itself connected to immanent human self-determination, to the nature of human spirit, which cannot comprehend itself or rest content if it does not ascend from itself to its Archetype, and remains instead within its own limits. This situation becomes clearer when the antinomies of the human spirit, the *I* and the *not-I*, have been revealed to be subject and predicate. Hitherto we have attended mainly to the fact that the *not-I*, which is the *I*'s predicate, reveals the *I* to itself. An *I* without a predicate is impotent and void; the *I* requires self-reflection, which it can receive only from the *not-I*. But the predicate, the *not-I*, also at the same time limits the *I* (Fichte's *Schranke*) and negates the *I*, so that Spinoza's *omnis definitio est negatio* turns out, in this sense, to be correct. The *I*, meanwhile, is, according to its own formal estimate of itself, absolute. It is the I, which, as such, sees no limits to itself and hence knows no difference between the created, human *I* and the Divine *I* (whence the Luciferian temptation: "ye shall be as gods," Gen. 3:5). In a certain sense, it is possible to say that nothing can be added to the human *I*, to its hypostasis, just as it is impossible to subtract anything from it: it is one and absolute, not having parts, and knowing no before or after, greater or lesser, or the like. Yet so much the more strikingly does it manifest its limitedness within itself: it is powerless to disclose its own nature or to cope with its own substance, which turns out to be given from without, as its *fatum*, necessity and limit. And the I must choose either a void which lacks predicates, but which protects its absoluteness (one of the faces of Lucifer, that of the self-isolated egoist) or to seek predicatedness and embodiment (another of the faces of Lucifer, namely, that of Satan, who works in the world, as "the prince of this world," to steal the Creator's creation from him).

But every predicate is discursive; it is something, is an indeterminate manifold—which can in no way be absolute. For this reason the absolute **I** in its I-ness is not absolute in any of its acts of predication. It is exhausted by its powerlessness to reveal its own absolute countenance. At the same time it may not renounce this countenance, for this absoluteness is its own essence. And the result is the "bad infinity" of temporal life, an eternal marking of time, powerlessness to digest the absolute, a bad infinity which Fichte was content to extol by elevating it into an *ewiges Streben* [eternal striving]. Fichte first introduced this striving into philosophy, and the powerlessness of the *I* to realize its own absoluteness, and its attempts to do so, resulting in this bad infinity, are depicted by philosophers as something absolute or "eternal": the world as *ewige Aufgabe* [eternal task] in Cohen, as an "absolute ought" in Rickert, and the like. This imaginary *Ewigkeit* [eternity] is in fact interrupted by an ellipsis—our own death. And for this reason the formally absolute *I* may not take its own predicate *as an absolute*—a predicate which for this reason begins and ends with an ellipsis.

Such is the antinomy of the hypostasis, of the *first* moment of the triunity. But there is also another way in which contradictions wrestle with each other within the *I*, lacerating it in their strife. The *I*, single and absolute, at the same time knows itself as a *genus*, as a species-*I*. It is unable, in its own self-isolated absoluteness, to exit from itself; yet at the same time it is conscious of itself as one of a number of *co-Is*, as a solidary [*sobornoye*] *I*. This question cannot be settled simply by crossing over from the *I* into an indefinite quantity of other *Is*. The *I* is solidary in its nature and is isolated by its "individuality." Individualism is a sickness of the *I* no less than is depersonalization, the loss or weakening of individuality. The unification of the solidary and the individual characters of the *I* sounds like a postulate which cannot be met, and the task of moving towards this unification, which is grounded in the *I* itself, tears the *I* apart with antinomies. For the *I* must go out into the *we*, whilst remaining the *I*. This antinomical task makes the *I* into a riddle for itself, into an insoluble charade. That which sometimes appeared in philosophy—in Descartes, and particularly in the *Ich-Philosoph* [philosopher of the "I"] Fichte—to be the most reliable and most self-evident Archimedean ποῦ στῶ [*pou stō*, fulcrum] turns out to be situated at the point of an antinomical knife, to be a living paradox, which, obviously, cannot be understood from out of itself. The *I* is compelled to look for the key to its own riddle outside itself, so that it may decode its own cipher.

The Tragedy of Philosophy

In this way the subject, the hypostasis, the first limb of the proposition or judgement, the *I*, suffers from antinomies and is unintelligible to itself; it points to a path out of itself and above itself. In other words, the image urgently speaks of an Archetype. The nature of the created *I* can only be understood from the nature of the Divine *I*; the human hypostasis is only an image of the Divine hypostasis. If we are able to learn anything reliable about the latter, then we will be able to comprehend the former. The path of speculation leads us to the fire-breathing Sinai of revelation.

The second limb of the proposition or judgement, the predicate, conceals within itself no less acute difficulties than does the first. The predicate is also absolute, as a predicate, *in respect of its own task*. The predicate must reveal the nature of the hypostasis, its *all*, which is also the *all* of the world, since, as we have already seen, the true predicate is the whole of the cosmos as an idea, as its *logos*. The predicate is the *logos* of the world, nothing more — for what could be a greater predicate? — yet also nothing less — for what else can each word be but the Word, or, more correctly, a ray, a point, an energy of the Word? Thus the predicate is a word about the Word by whom all things were made, and without whom was not anything made that was made (John 1:3). One can say still more concisely and more decisively that the word or predicate is also the *Word*, not in the sense that it is completely identical with it, but in the sense of a unity of the nature of the Word and of words, in the sense that every word is from the Word. Each word is as it were a letter or a sound of the one absolute Word. Every word which is cut off from this, its primal source, ceases to be a word; it is like an extinguished illumination, like the carcass or husk of a word. Words live in the meaning of the Word; ideas are connected and filled with meaning by the Idea of Ideas; an intellectual sun lights all earthly torches from its own fire and light. Such is the nature of the word as an incarnate idea, nor can it be otherwise.

But it seems to follow from this ontological definition of the predicate-word that every predicate-word expresses *everything*, as though each predicate expressed the whole world. And this inference about the universality and ubiquitous applicability of the predicate also follows quite indisputably from its nature. The predicate is indeed *everything* in its own essence. But at this turning Hegel awaits to announce triumphantly that although "being" in an indeterminate form is "nothing," it nevertheless, once we have travelled the whole path of logical determinations and have completed the task required by dialectical method, becomes *everything*, that is, becomes the Logos, the Idea. The whole of Hegel's philosophy issues from this thought: that every definition, every predicate is the Logos, since each, entering as a link into the dialectical chain, is necessarily bound up with the whole of this whole, that is, with the world-Logos, the Absolute Idea. Every idea and every predicate is, when taken in its essence, the absolute Word—this is a concise statement of the meaning of Hegel's philosophy as a philosophy of predication.

Yet at the same time every judgement is discursive, whilst every predicate is fragmentary and empirically limited. The predicate is always a *something* and only a something; it repels, excludes, and protects itself from the *all*. *Omnis definitio est negatio*: once again we recall this unhappy, and, unfortunately, correct formulation. The predicate can be *deployed* only as a partial definition, as a *something*, not as *everything*. Nevertheless, no predicate can remain within itself; each, necessarily, strives to go beyond itself, and Hegel, correctly, perceived this. There is in the predicate an eternal unrest, a disequilibrium, a busyness and a striving. The predicate strives to accumulate, on every side, every *And*; it proliferates upwards and downwards, it contains endless movement within itself. For thought—and the predicate is, precisely, thought—knows no resting place. This craving for the absolute Logos, by which thought was set alight and towards which it is directed, is its inner strength and energy. Yet at the same time this craving is its fate, its impotence. For eternal hunger and craving, the eternal staff of Ahasuerus, is also a powerlessness. It is a bad infinity, whose nature was so penetratingly explored by Hegel; it is an eternally revolving wheel of fire. It is correctness instead of the Truth, a correctness which assumes ever new faces, each alluring us with the image of the truth which shines through them, but which cannot be taken hold of. The task of the absolute with respect to the relative, or of the relative in the light of the absolute, is the unification at once of the absolute and the relative, of the immanent and the transcendent—such is the nature of the predicate. The relative-absolute or absolute-relative predicate is an antinomy which reason finds intolerable, and from which it can be rescued only by endless movement, by discursive thought, so that it should not explode from within, as forces which meet each other at a right angle yield a diagonal movement which prevents a conflict, but which does not mean that the forces do not meet. In this way, the predicate too turns out to be a paradox, and reason becomes a riddle for reason. The predicate, just like the subject, cannot be understood from out of itself. It becomes divided in its givenness [*dannost'*], for on one hand it is given [*dano*], while on the other it is a prescription [*zadano*]. It also points *beyond* itself, because it is unintelligible *from* itself. Its riddle is insoluble in the human world, that is, within absolute-relative existence. Either it remains insoluble as such, and then the human being himself is unintelligible and a riddle to himself (like the impossible Delphic instruction, γνῶθι σε αὐτόν [*gnōthi se auton*, know thyself], or the insoluble riddle set to Oedipus); or the human being, as the image of the Divine, is intelligible from his own Archetype. And the mystery of the human being must be sought in God; the riddle of the predicate finds its solution in the Divine Logos. *Such a postulate*, necessary and inevitable, is the only one possible, and follows directly from an examination of the nature of the predicate: either unintelligibility, the paradox of thought's despair with respect to itself, or the vision of one's self in God, an understanding of one's self and one's own nature from the nature of Divinity, as the image is understood from its Archetype.

The third moment of the judgement or the proposition — the copula — expresses being, substantiality, participation in essence. The copula connects both the first two limbs of the judgement, and already bears their stamp upon itself. Being, as we know, possesses neither its own hypostasis nor its own logical face in the judgement. Being establishes existence, in which the subject's act of self-determination receives living reality in the predicate; and in which substantiality reveals itself in such a way that both subject and predicate are only moments of being. Being, which thus has the force of a ground or background, is not susceptible of a self-sufficient definition, yet, nevertheless, it is possible to discover in being, too, the diremption and the antinomicality which characterize the subject and the predicate. *Being is one and indivisible*, as Parmenides taught; it is as much one and indivisible as the world-Logos, the world's *all*. This *all* consists of a single absolute act, which possesses the single, indivisible force of being. Being is of its nature one and absolute; this is its axiom, which, in various ways, is asserted by the philosophy of the identity of substantiality. It is not susceptible to being divided in any way, and there is in it no plurality of any kind; one might suppose that there is no content of any kind in it (Hegel's "nothing") or even that there is no being in general. Yet thought cannot think this without falling into contradiction, since this *no* is only the negative form of *is*, and the negation of being is at the same time its affirmation. To say *not being* is to say *being is not*, and this *not* either deletes and completely annihilates the very judgement, making it impossible and contentless, or it can be understood only as a *limitation* of being with respect to being itself, and, consequently, in no way as an elimination or denial of being. Much more correct is the other side of the Parmenidean definition—namely that only being is, and that non-being is not—in as much as non-being is only a variant of being.

Nevertheless, this one, immobile, absolute being, multiplies in the copula; it breaks apart into moments of happening, becoming, coming-to-be. It is torn into parts and multiplied in the multiplicity of the predicate. The Heraclitean πάντα ῥεῖ [*panta rhei*, everything flows], as well as all the evolutionisms of every epoch (evolutionisms not as scientific theory, but as metaphysics) are a negation of the absoluteness of being in the name of the relativity of becoming. Yet being's very nature does not permit us to understand it as a becoming without remainder, as a *Werden* [becoming], as can be perceived most clearly of all in the most extreme, and, one can say, the most audacious instance of evolutionism, the philosophy of Bergson. Movement is unthinkable without the immoveable; there is no such thing as an absolute movement or an absolute becoming, just as there is no river without banks, and no time without the hours (to express the matter through a paradox). Movement is possible only upon condition that there be a state of rest, just as becoming is symptomatic of being. Yet at the same time movement, like every process of any kind, evolution, temporality (in opposition to "eternal life"), is also being's impotence, its limitedness. The fate of being here is inseparably shared with that of the Logos of being, as the copula is inseparable from the predicate: the copula is relative-absolute to just the same extent as the subject, since the copula unites what truly exists, the hypostasis, with its ideal image of existence. That which truly exists [*sushchee*] posits that which exists [*sushchestvuyushchee*] in the copula, and this copula is just as dirempted and antinomical as the logos. The copula is both one and many, immovable and yet comprised of movement; it is being and process, relative and absolute. It is just as unintelligible in itself, just as much of a riddle, as the first two limbs of the proposition. It leads beyond itself just as they do, and can be understood and interpreted only from out of its Archetype, from out of the absolute. The copula, for its part, postulates an interpretation from without. Human-cosmic being must be understood from the being of the Divinity.

Thus the image testifies to the Archetype, and postulates the Archetype as the principle from which it can be expounded.[1]

---

1 In the work of St. Basil the Great we find the following interesting judgement about the Image of God: "The Image of God is not like an image made by man; He is alive, and, being a true, image-creating image, everything which participates in Him is an image of God. The Image of God is Christ, who, as it is written (Col. 1:15), is the image of the Invisible God" ("Adversus Eunomium," in J.P. Migne, *Patrologia Graeca*, vol. 29, col. 724). The "image-creating" power of the Image of God, that is, His ontological actuality, is precisely what defines the existence of man. To see the Image of God only in Christ, of Whom it is said that He is the image of the Invisible Father, scarcely corresponds to the direct testimony of Holy Scripture, which connects this Image to the Holy Trinity: "in *our* image, after *our* likeness" (Gen. 1:26).

3
The Postulate of Triadicity and Its Dogma

THE DOGMA OF TRIADICITY IS A DIVINE MYSTERY to which human beings can have access only by means of divine revelation, and which is apprehended by means of faith. Since it bears witness to something incomprehensible to us, the dogma is not so much a formula for knowledge or consciousness as an indication of the path, of the truth, and of the whole of the religious life. The religious life *habituates itself* to dogma, and life in the church is nothing other than this self-habituation to its dogmas, a participation in the mysteries of the divine life, in its plenitude: "if a man love me, he will keep my words: and my Father will love him, and we will come unto him, and make our abode with him" (John 14:23). The human being's contact with the divine frees him or her from the limits of reason, goes beyond reason, so that the supra-rationality [*sverkhrazumnost'*] of dogma is no longer an obstacle. Nevertheless, even as addressed to human consciousness—that is, to the face of reason—the dogma contains within itself a definite idea which has the significance of being a guiding thread for reason, either as a task for reason, as one of its axioms, or as both task and axiom at once. Dogma has a *philosophical meaning*. The efforts of philosophical (speculative) dogmatics are devoted to the discovery of this meaning, and, to this extent, dogmatics is also universal metaphysics. In undertaking an analysis of substance, we have come right up against the postulate of triadicity. The question stands thus: if the Absolute is Threefold Substance, the Absolute's own spiritual nature becomes intelligible for human beings through this Threefold Substance. Reason itself cannot say whether this Threefold Substance at all is, and must accept the answer of faith; yet reason looks for this answer, and the essence of the human being, which would otherwise be an inextricable paradox, demands it. Philosophy comprehends only that which it asks about, or which causes it to "wonder." The content of philosophy and its criteria are determined by the way in which it frames its problems. Philosophy's capacity to take on the meaning of the dogma of Triadicity, therefore, is determined by the extent to which the *problem* of triadicity arises for philosophy itself internally, at least as a postulate—or, more correctly, precisely as a postulate. For if the dogma in its full content were to enter into philosophy, if it were fully immanent to philosophy, as a philosophical theorem, then it would lose its religious nature, not only as an idea or as a concept, but also as a "myth," i.e., as the evidence of things not seen. (See the introduction to *Unfading Light*.) A dogma cannot be immanent to reason, just as it may not be transcendent to it; in the latter case, it would be nonsensical, absurd, and incapable of being conceptually expressed. Dogma, even though it is incomprehensible, is none of these. Reason affords a logical projection of dogma, like a shadow; but in order even to do this much, reason must find in its own structure, in the schema of its own problems, a way of approaching dogma. To reveal this problematic of reason, to show the full lawlikeness and necessity of dogma for reason, is to reveal the philosophical meaning of dogma. Dogma is an essential exit for reason, is rescue from reason's antinomies and aporias. At the same time, dogma is not a reply to reason itself; any such reply would be immanent to reason, would be a result of reason. Dogma is given to reason transcendentally, that is, by means of revelation, although it can be assimilated by reason or at least given reason's blessing. In the creed which takes the name of St. Athanasius of Alexandria, we read "And the Catholic Faith is this: That we worship one God in Trinity, and Trinity in Unity; neither confounding the Persons: nor dividing the Substance. For there is one Person of the Father, another of the Son: and another of the Holy Ghost. But the Divinity of the Father, of the Son, and of the Holy Ghost, is all one: the Glory equal, the Majesty co-eternal. Such as the Father is, such is the Son: and such is the Holy Ghost.... So the Father is God, the Son is God: and the Holy Ghost is God. And yet they are not three Gods: but one God.... And in this Trinity none is afore, or after other: none is greater, or less than another; but the whole three Persons are co-eternal together: and co-equal."[1]

The absoluteness of substance in the moment of hypostaticity, in the first of its definitions, as *I*, suffers from the fact that in the disclosure of

---

1   I have quoted the text from the Athanasian Creed in the *Book of Common Prayer*. — Trans.

The Postulate of Triadicity and Its Dogma

its own nature, of its own content, of its own logos, it comes up against the *not-I* as its own limit, and reflects upon itself from this *not-I*. The *I* depends upon a *not-I* which confronts the *I* as givenness. Therefore the *I* cannot be absolute, even though it wishes, and cannot even not wish, to be absolute.

The *I* would remain an *I* even in the *not-I*, in its predicate, if it were possible to possess the *not-I* as an *I* which would *at the same time* be a *not-I*. Such a task was precisely what Fichte's thought demanded, and he sought an exit from it with the help of the distinction between the absolute **I** and the relative *I* which emerges from it and which is connected to the *not-I*. Nevertheless, given the monohypostaticity within which Fichte's philosophy always remained strangely imprisoned, there is no way out of this difficulty. The way out is shown only by the Christian dogma of the Father, the everlasting begetter of the Son who is the Second Hypostasis of the Divinity.

The *not-I* ceases to limit the absoluteness of the substance of the *I* only if it is also an *I* which remains at the same time a *not-I*—if, that is, it has within itself some new element which reveals the hypostasis. Can there be such a relation, in which the *not-I*, the predicate, the Logos, would be at the same time *I* and *not-I*, would reveal an *I* which it does not limit, which would dwell in the father's bosom, whilst at the same time being a manifestation and image of his Hypostasis? Might the Logos of the **I**, His predicate, possess such characteristics? In other words, might the Logos of the Divinity, His Matter [*Soderzhanie*], His Word be such an **I** and *not-I*, both remaining within the **I** and being an **I** for itself, being not merely its own reflection in a mirror, a bad infinity of self-reflection, **I** = **I** = **I** = **I**, but something unconditionally new for the first **I**? This could not come about through the simple *positing* of a *not-I* within the **I**, for the *not-I* is limitation at the same time as being expression, but it can come about as a *spiritual begetting*. This is the mystery of the Hypostases of the Father and of the Son.

What is this *begetting*? It is clear that it cannot be exhaustively defined in the language of concepts, but can only be described, for it is a living act which is in its essence something not susceptible of being investigated. What is more, we are speaking here not of begettings or of begottennesses, but of *begetting itself*, of the Father from whom all fatherhood began. (Spiritual) begetting is an act in which the one begotten, the Son, is not separated from the Father, but remains in the bosom of the Father and, at the same time, reveals to the Father the Father's own self. "I and my Father are one" (John 10:30); "no man knoweth the Son, but the Father; neither knoweth any man the Father, but the Son" (Mt. 11:27); "If ye had known me, ye should have known my Father also" (John 14:7). Between the Father and the Son a complete identity is established, yet their hypostases are at the same time distinct. By his own act of begetting, the Father reveals Himself; yet he accomplishes this by begetting his Beloved Son. Father and Son are united in a single Divinity, and Love unites Them hypostatically. The Father loves the Son and renders everything unto Him, and the Son loves the Father and creates nothing in which he does not see the creating Father. The Son is begotten out of the essence of the Father, but in such a way that the Father suffers no detriment of any kind to his own absoluteness, for this begetting is an eternal begetting, which must be understood not as having been accomplished and concluded on some particular occasion, but as an act which is continually being accomplished and which exists in all its moments: as Augustine says, *semper gignit Pater, et semper nascitur Filius* [the Father is always begetting, and the Son is always being born]; He is born, and, at the same time, is not separated, but dwells inseparably (ἀδιαστάτως [*adiastatōs*]) in the bosom of the Father. The Father, everlastingly, has the blessedness of begetting the Son, the Son the blessedness of the Father's love. In the creaturely world we have only the body of the begetting, its schema, and this is also why the *meaning* of this begetting is in its essence hidden from us here.

In order that the **I** can have itself as its own predicate, and can overcome the *not-I* in this predicate, as a limit to its own absoluteness, this *not-I* must therefore also be an **I**; that is, the predicate must also be a hypostasis, and must have *its own* proper subject, while this subject must also be *the same and not the same* as the first, true, subject: it must be everlastingly *begotten* in the act of the Father's and the Son's love. Everything which the Father has or "knows," he knows and loves in the Son, and everything which the Son knows and loves, He knows and loves in the Father. The indivisibility, but also the immiscibility, is a unity; but a distinction between the two hypostases is also necessarily presupposed by this relationship—by the revelation of the Father in the Son and the Son's knowledge of the Father. The distinction, moreover, remains irreducible; it is connected, so to speak, to the metaphysical place of each of the hypostases. It is the attribute of the Father to be unbegotten (ἀγεννησία [*agennēsia*]): the beginning was from Him and He Himself without beginning (ἄναρχος [*anarchos*]) and without cause (ἀναίτιος [*avaitios*]). In this sense the Father is sometimes called God of himself, αὐτόθεος [*autotheos*], first God, πρῶτος Θεός [*prōtos Theos*], *Deus princeps*. This is why the image of the Father in us is our hypostatic I, which is self-sufficient and without beginning, which begins from itself and which issues from itself in all its self-determinations, the *noumenon* of human nature.

The personal attribute of the Son, by contrast, is in His being a begotten, beloved Son: "For the Father loveth the Son, and sheweth him all things that himself doeth" (John 5:20). He is the Only-begotten Son, who dwells in the bosom of the Father, the true Son. The personal attribute of the Son is begottenness — γέννησις [*gennēsis*], *generatio* (but sometimes it is also expressed with more general appellations, illustrating the way in which the Son proceeds from the Father: προβολή [*probolē*], *prolatio*, *processio*, *derivatio*, ἀπορροία [*aporroia*], *signatura* and with the verbs προπηδᾶν, ἐκλάμπειν, ἀναλάμπειν [*propēdan, eklampein, analampein*] and the like). God the Father and God the Son are completely equal and one as regards the Divine nature, and in this sense the Son is just as truly God as the Father, and they are one God, not two; but this does not prevent them from being distinct hypostases, of begetting and begottenness. On this relationship are founded the inseparability and immiscibility of both hypostases: fatherhood is inseparable from sonhood, but at the same time cannot be identified or confused with it: here is the unity of two, a dyad, ἕν διὰ δυοῖν [*hen dia duoin*], and such is every substance, as a unity of its own subject and predicate.

Here then is the only way in which the absoluteness, self-sufficiency, and unlimitedness of substance as hypostasis can be conserved: to overcome the *not-I* by means of a begetting does not mean to *find* or to "posit" the *not-I* as one's own predicate or definition, but to *beget* it in and out of oneself, as one's own proper second hypostasis. This is the only way to get out of the closed, burning hot circle of the I, whilst conserving its freedom and absoluteness: to become (for the time being) dihypostatic, to double the I. But the creaturely, monohypostatic *I* cannot think of itself in any other way than in the *singular* number. It does not know or permit of any doubling, and it pays for this with the tragedy of the powerlessness of its absoluteness, for, whilst conscious of itself as absolute and limitless, it turns out in each of its acts of self-definition to be relative. This second, doubled I, the I-*not-I*, is the Son, who reveals the Father to Himself and is the Father's own predicate.

The postulate of fatherhood and sonhood leads beyond the circle of the logic of the I. It breaks that circle, and the circle cannot accommodate this postulate. Yet at the same time, it is sufficiently evident to reason (even if reason has not fully understood it) that *if* such a begetting were at all possible and had taken place, then it, and only it, would settle the difficulty. Reason can tell us nothing about whether such a begetting is possible or whether it exists—even though reason comes up against the antinomy of the absoluteness and relativity of the I, and reason itself points *beyond* itself towards the plenitude of Divine existence, towards the Archetype. The predicate, the word of every *I* about itself, points to the hypostatic predicate, the Word, which "was with God and was God" (John 1:1). The Son reveals the Father to Himself, is His own Word, and the Father loves the Son and what is revealed by Him and in Him—that is, *everything*, for "all things were made by him; and without him was not any thing made that was made" (John 1:3), "all mine are thine, and all thine are mine" (John 17:10). The Son reveals what He sees in the Father, His wisdom, goodness, power, and glory.

Is the mystery of the divine begetting of the Son by the Father thus comprehensible to us? Not at all. May its philosophical meaning, however, be brought closer to reason? May this meaning be penetrated by that light by means of which this mystery can illuminate its own problem? Yes, absolutely. Philosophy, of course, sought only to comprehend the identity of subject and object, to remove the everlasting contradiction and discord between them. And the philosophy of identity can find its true path only in the dogma of the Father and the Son. The philosophers of identity sought identity by *cancelling* contradiction, by immersing contradiction in the twilight of the absolute. But the only identity which is not an indistinguishable void, but is instead a unity in difference and in concretion, is a spiritual begetting, Father-Son.

We, earthly fathers and children, have only that light which is reflected to us from true and archetypal fatherhood and sonhood. Spiritual begetting is inaccessible to us,[2] although everything in our own earthly, human fatherhood brings us closer towards it. If, however, we bring together all our own spiritual forces in the apotheosis of fatherhood and sonhood, we are able to perceive all the uniqueness and specificity of this relationship, which differs both from creation and from making things in one's own image. In begetting there is the joy of finding another and yet also a kindred I, the father in the son and the son in the father; of coming out of one's own *I* not into a *not-I*, but into an *I*, an act of substantial love. In this sense, the features of the image of God are traced in human fatherhood and sonhood, although the image is obscured by earthly begetting.

Let us then repeat: the begetting of the second *I*, instead of being the "positing" of the *not-I*, the living predicate, the Son, is an answer to the question of the synthesis of the *I* and the *not-I* which is completely unforeseeable by the logic of the separate, solitary, mono-hypostatic *I*, for there is nothing but the *not-I* outside this solitary *I*. Nevertheless, this answer does not contradict the nature of the *I*, which, as we know, is both individual and collective [*individual'no-soborno*] and to which is given consciousness of the other *I*, together with its own self-consciousness and simultaneously with it. In revealing its own predicate and in laying bare its own nature, the *I* at the same time reveals its own breadth and depth, which is why, at the same time as the *not-I*-predicate, there also appears an *I*-predicate, that is, a son.

There is nothing extraordinary or abnormal for reason here in the fact that the act of the begetting of the Son is not in and of itself intelligible to reason. Every concrete, individual *fact* is, thanks be to God, in this sense unintelligible to reason, without its thereby becoming irrational or anti-rational. It does not belong to reason to "posit," by means of its own "deduction," whatever is beyond the limits of purely logical postulation or deduction; so that reason judges of the fact *post factum*, not *ante factum*.

---

2 "Thou hearest of begetting; do not seek to know what sort of begetting" (Gregory Nazianzen, Oration 20); "thou desirest an explanation of how there is begetting. The begetting Father and the begotten Son know this" (Nazianzen); "God, because he is non-temporal, without beginning, impassible, inexhaustible, incorporeal, unique and without end, begets in a non-temporal way, without a beginning, without passion, without copulation, and his incomprehensible begetting has neither beginning nor ending" (Jean Damascène, *La Foi Orthodoxe*, ed. B. Kotter et al., 2 vols. [Paris: Éditions du Cerf, 2010] [Sources Chrétiennes, 535, 540], 1:170 [i. 8]).

And only Kant could be so deranged as to ascribe to the schemas of reason a power to prohibit—and consequently, by means of the law of causality, to abolish—the possibility of any new event in the chain of causes, having ruled out on this basis any new act of creation and any miracle. The fabric of causality is much more elastic than it appeared to Kant to be. And only the power of Hegel's delusions about reason's grandeur could have permitted him to take it into his head to declare that everything actual is rational, in so far as it is a self-determination of reason. Reason does not come first, but second; it defines and registers being, but does not confer power upon it. Hence reason cannot say anything either for or against the begetting of the Son out of the bosom of the Father, but it can accept and interpret this begetting as a *fact*, in so far as this fact is testified to by faith and is proclaimed by religious dogma.

The Dyad, however, does not exhaust Substance, which determines itself as triune. The subject is connected to the predicate by the copula; the predicate possesses only the form [obraz] of being, not the force of being, not being itself. To absolute substance must belong absolute being, and (it goes without saying) in absolute unity, plenitude, and force, distinct from any relative being or becoming. And is it necessary to add that if the predicate is itself the hypostatic, divine Word, then to Him must also belong absoluteness of being, life, sentience, power, whereas none of this can be conferred by a relative form of being? At the same time it is clear that if the predicate, the Word, is hypostatic, then the third determination of Divine substance, *Being*, cannot be impersonal and passive either. If the Son is hypostatic, His Being must be hypostatic too. Here too, of course, it is not a matter of "deducing" or of "positing," but of dogmatic givenness. Yet this givenness is quite easy and natural; it enters into thought as if with logical obligatoriness and as if thought were compelled to accept it. For with the begetting of the Son, the procession of the hypostatic Holy Spirit is already given. In the hypostatic form [obraz] of the second moment of substantiality is foreordained the hypostaticity of the third as well. Being is able to absolutize itself and to integrate its own endless succession only in the absolute form of the hypostasis, by becoming an I. It is the ontological place of the hypostasis of being to be the third hypostasis. The third hypostasis closes the circle, unifying the first two hypostases by giving the domain of being to the first and the force of being to the second. The definition of substance can by no means be exhausted by two hypostases and their reciprocal relationship, since the whole form of being is proper to begetting, but not being itself in its force. The words "[a]ll things were made by him, and without him was not anything made that was made" (John 1:3), or, in the corresponding words of the creed, "by whom all things were made," signify that every *form* [*obraz*] of being was determined by Him, and that without Him and in His absence nothing exists; He is not, however, being itself, although He also *has* being in the trihypostatic unity of the Divinity. Together with the divine bliss of the *begetting* of the Son, the Father also knows the divine bliss of the *being* of the Son, of His coming to life. But this Being is also determined by an absolute hypostatic act, which the Church's dogma calls the procession of the Holy Spirit from the Father to the Son or through the Son.

The procession of the third Hypostasis from the Father is just as much of a mystery of the life of the Divinity as is the begetting of the Son. The very fact of this procession cannot be explored by man; it is hidden in the depths of the divine life. But the philosophical meaning of this fact is open to reason. Hypostaticity confers absoluteness on being to just the extent that it also confers absoluteness on the predicate. Only such a hypostatic being can correspond to the absolute, hypostatic form of the Word. The nature of substance, which is revealed in *all being*, in the Being of the universal Logos, in the unity of the logical and the alogical principle, the ideal and the real principle, the intellectual and the aesthetic principle, is exhausted in the three hypostatic definitions.

The hypostatic procession of the Holy Spirit, which is the "life-giving" force of being, originates together with the hypostatic begetting of the Son. The begetting of the Son is bound up with the procession of the Holy Spirit (in a way similar to that in which a predicate, a word, an idea necessarily implies a copula, being). This procession *is an act which in its essence is implied by the begetting of the Word*. Just as a logical predicate is indivisible from the copula, so that only when taken together do they disclose the subject, so the begetting of the second and the procession of the third hypostasis are inseparably bound up with each other.

Reason, naturally, has nothing to say about *how* one ought to understand the distinction between begetting and procession, for here it is not a question of "deducing" or of co-ordinating concepts, but of symbolic signs of the primordial givenness of the Divine life. What is more, we have some basis on which we can comprehend begetting, sonhood and fatherhood from our own human nature. When it comes to the procession of the Spirit this basis is lacking, since we who are clothed in flesh are completely without any absolute force of being proceeding from us; we know it as givenness, that is, as that which has already proceeded into the world and which is perceived by us through this world.³

Orthodox dogma speaks of the procession of the Holy Spirit from the Father. The Father is, as Dionysius the Areopagite puts it, the origin of Divinity (μόνη δὲ πηγὴ τῆσ ὑπερουσίου Θεότητος [*monē de pēgē tēs huperousiou theotētos*, the sole source of super-essential divinity]).⁴ God the Father is the cause, αἰτία [*aitia*], *causa*, ἀρχή [*archē*], *principium*, *auctor*, in which is grounded the *single* principle of Divinity, the divine μοναρχία [*monarkhia*, monarchy]. In *this* sense, and only in this sense, it can be said that the Paternal Hypostasis is the first hypostasis, the image of which is our noumenal *I*, which is revealed in the predicate. The procession of the Holy Spirit (ἐκπόρευσις, ἐκπόρευμα [*ekporeusis, ekporeuma*], *processio*, πρόροδος, προβολή, πρόβλημα—ἐκπορεύεσθαι, προσελθεῖν, προιέναι [*prorodos, probolē, problema—ekporeuesthai, proselthein, proienai*]) proceeds from the Father for the same reason as the begetting of the Son; for the Father is the source of Divinity, and from the God who begets the Son proceeds also His life-giving Spirit, which lives, and which gives being. And in this relationship the Son and the Spirit proceed equally from the Father, although in different ways. The

---

3 "Quid inter nasci et procedere intersit...explicare quis potest?... Haec scio: distinguere autem inter illam generationem et hanc processionem nescio, non valeo, non sufficio" [Who can explain the difference between being born and proceeding? This I know: I do not know how to distinguish between being begotten, on the one hand, and proceeding, on the other; I am not adequate to the task] (Augustine, *Contra Maximinum Haereticum Arianorum Episcopum*, ii.14, in J.P. Migne, *Patrologia Latina*, vol. 42, col. 743–814, col. 770). "If the Holy Spirit also proceeds from the Father, it does so not by being begotten, but by procession [ἐκπορευτῶσ (*ekporeutōs*)]. This other modality of existence is incomprehensible and unknowable, just like the begetting of the Son. We do not at all know in what this distinction consists, nor what the begetting of the Son or the procession of the Holy Spirit might be." (Damascène, *La Foi Orthodoxe*, ed. Kotter, 172; the final sentence is, however, translated from the Russian quotation given by Bulgakov, as no precise equivalent to it is found at this place in the Greek text.)

4 Pseudo-Denys, *Les Noms Divins*, ed. B.R. Suchla, 2 vols. (Paris: Éditions du Cerf, 2016 [Sources Chrétiennes, 578–79], 1:382 [ii. 5]).

The Postulate of Triadicity and Its Dogma

first hypostasis is in the position of the subject by which the predicate is disclosed, is That which truly exists [*Sushchee*] which generates that which is existing [*sushchestvuyushchee*] and which in its turn is revealed through two moments: the predicate and the copula, the Word and the Spirit. In this way, if the Paternal and Filial hypostases, the Father and Son, compose between themselves a Dyad, in the sense that they are reciprocally turned towards each other, a bi-unity of begetter and begotten, then the Son and the Spirit compose another dyad, making up the bi-unity of the predicate which reveals the nature of the Father—as Gregory of Nazianzen says, "it is common to the Son and to the Holy Spirit that they are from the Father"—and, in this sense, they stand contrasted with the Transcendent, with the Father. The Son and the Spirit are alike linked to each other through their common procession from the Father (although the manner of this procession is not the same in each case), for which reason They are dyadically unified. Between the First and the Third hypostases there also exists their own dyadic unity of procession, from the Father to the Holy Spirit. In other words, along with an essential unity and parity of divine rank[5] in the relations between the hypostases, there is also a definite sequence or distinction. Triunity does not consist of three unities indistinct from each other, as if they were numerical atoms arranged arbitrarily, but of concrete, living hypostases, which stand in a specific relationship to each other. Why, and in what sense, then, is the third Hypostasis the third, rather than a variant of the second, since both the second and the third proceed together from the essence of the Father? Here begins the Catholic divergence in the dogma of the Holy Spirit, which gives rise to the question as to the precise sense in which the character of the third Hypostasis is to be understood. This question can even be expressed as follows: is the relationship between the Father and the Holy Spirit also dyadic, similar to (although not identical with) the dyad of the Father and the Son, or is it, on the contrary, triadic, in the sense that in the place of the first limb of the Father-Son dyad, the Father, it is necessary to set a dyad: the Father and the Son *together*,

---

5 "Divinity is the infinite shared nature of Three infinites, where each considered in itself is God, as Father, Son, and Holy Ghost, each conserving its own personal properties, and the Three considered together are also God, the former on the grounds of a unity of essence, the latter on the grounds of a unity of origin." Gregory of Nazianzen, Oration 31, in J.P. Migne, *Patrologia Graeca*, vol. 36, col. 133–71.

filioque [and the Son]?⁶ This question can itself also be put as follows: is the First Hypostasis *paternal* (not in the sense that it begets, but in another sense not accessible to human reason)? Is the Father the origin both of the Son and of the Holy Spirit, or does the Third Hypostasis, instead of possessing only a single origin, proceed from both?⁷ The whole doctrine of the Holy Spirit, in the reciprocal relations of its hypostases, hangs in the balance in this question. For the procession of the Holy Spirit, although not identical with begetting, is nevertheless connected to paternity, as to its origin. Since the source of the Holy Spirit's procession has also been extended to the Son, this procession as it were also transfers to Him a paternity, and makes of Father and Son co-originators, if not simply co-fathers of the Third Hypostasis. It goes without saying that the mysteries of intra-divine life cannot be fathomed by our propositional definitions; here, however, there is a direct contradiction of the dogma of the sempiternal begetting of the Son from the Father. If the Father is the originator of the Son through an everlasting begetting, and if He is the primordial originator of the Holy Spirit, as even the Catholics acknowledge, how is it possible to consider the First Originator as insufficient for the procession of the Holy Spirit, and to add to this act the further participation of one Begotten by this Originator?⁸

---

6   Bulgakov alludes to the *filioque* clause which was added to the Nicene Creed at the Third Council of Toledo (589) to specify that the Holy Spirit proceeds both from the Father and from the Son. The clause was the subject of a medieval dispute between the Roman and Orthodox churches, and is often thought of as the central doctrinal difference between the two. Bulgakov argues in his study of the Holy Spirit, *The Comforter*, that the difference between the churches over the *filioque* is by no means insuperable and that the precise nature of its significance has been misstated. See Bulgakov, *The Comforter*. — Trans.

7   It is true that Catholic theology introduces a distinction between the part played by the Father and that played by the Son in the procession of the Holy Spirit: "the Father is the uncaused origin or originator of the Holy Spirit who does not Himself have an originator (*causa improducta*), the origin who does not Himself have an origin (*principium inprincipiatum*), the primordial (*principalis*) source; but the Son is the origin of the Holy Spirit, an origin which is not *lacking an origin* (*causa ex causa*), an origin which depends upon the fundamental origin, the Father" (Makarij [Bulgakov], *Dogmaticheskoe Bogoslovie* [Dogmatic Theology] 1:319). However, this distinction introduces only details which do not affect the fundamental thought, which is precisely that the Father and the Son in their dyadic combination give rise to the Holy Spirit, which without doubt also contravenes the dogma of the Holy Trinity in its pure form, for on this view the Holy Trinity is also understood not as a triunity of equal individual hypostases, but as a complex, dyadic dyad.

8   The ideas of Catholic theology on this question are quite unconvincing and even strange. "If the Holy Spirit did not proceed from the Son, the Spirit could not really be

In a word, there is no kind of internal basis for the peremptory requirements of the Catholic dogma of the Holy Spirit. On the contrary, it brings only confusion and a contravention of the dogma of the Holy Trinity. The order or structure of the divine Monarchy determines the begetting of the Son and the procession of the Holy Spirit from the Father, the First Originator. From the Father who sempiternally begets the Son, the Holy Spirit too proceeds. Having revealed by means of His own Word the mystery of His Nature, the Divine All, the Father proceeds into the Spirit as life-giving force, which confers life on *everything*. The Logos is the Reason of Being, His Word; the Spirit is the Force of Being, is Life, Love, the Blessedness of Divine Being. The Father loves the Son and gives Him all that is His own, upon which the Son answers Him with an act of reciprocal love, with a recognition that "all that is Mine is Thine," and this Love becomes life, the original force of being in the Holy Spirit. It is not of course appropriate to speak of temporal succession in Divinity, in the Absolute, yet, conversely, it is quite in order to speak of an ideal succession and correlation. And the fact that the Holy Spirit is the Third Hypostasis means that Its place in the Holy Trinity is defined with reference to the already existing relationship between Father and Son; the procession of the Holy Spirit is connected to the begetting of the Son, since the Holy Spirit (as Augustine and Ambrose, for example, sometimes define it) is the Hypostatic Love of the Father for his Only-Begotten.

---

distinguished from Him, for the Persons of the Holy Trinity, the Father, the Son, and the Holy Spirit, in whom all are One, are distinct from each other only in their oppositional relation. If the Holy Spirit did not proceed from the Son, there would be no sort of oppositional relation among them; they would not be opposed, but completely separate (*essent non oppositae, sed disparatae relationes*)" (*Theologiae cursus completus* [Paris, 1841], 8:642). This naïve argument is sufficiently refuted by the suggestion of Metropolitan Makarij (*Dogmatischeskoe Bogoslovie*, 1:345): "[t]he Church has from time immemorial distinguished the Divine Persons not through this or that relation of opposition among them, but through the belief that the Father is unbegotten, the Son begotten of the Father, and that the Holy Spirit proceeds from the Father." Even more naive is an idea such as this: "[i]f the Holy Spirit did not proceed from the Son as well as from the Father, this would mean that the Father would be distinct from the Son in two ways, that is, first by the Son's being begotten by the Father, and second by the Holy Spirit's proceeding from the Father. But we can accept only one difference, only one peculiarity in each of the persons of the Divinity, for Its perfection consists in their having amongst them the greatest possible unity and the least possible distinction, and, consequently, in none of the Persons' having more than one distinguishing personal mark" (cited in ibid.). We cannot, however, give a full discussion of the question of the *filioque* here.

This is a correct remark, but it has been incorrectly understood, and for that reason a distorted interpretation of it was received by scholastic theology, a circumstance which led to the question whether the Holy Spirit might proceed not from one, but from two, hypostases. This question cannot, indeed, arise in relation to the second Hypostasis, who is immediately begotten from the depths of the Father and who has nothing between Himself and His Begetter. But it naturally and even inevitably arises in relation to the Third Hypostasis, precisely in so far as It is the Third, and, consequently, is to be understood with reference to the relationship between the First Two. The Holy Spirit proceeds from the Father in His movement to beget the Son; it is the Fatherly embrace of the Son. And this participation of the Son, through whom the Father as it were offers or occasions Himself to send the Holy Spirit, cannot be denied; on the contrary, this is precisely the meaning of the orthodox dogma of the Holy Spirit as the *Third* Hypostasis. As was explained earlier, being does not exist separately from one who exists, separately from the subject or separately from the subject's specificity, from the object. Being, on the contrary, is always concrete, is the being of something for someone, the copula. The Holy Spirit, who is the life-giver, proceeds from Him Who Exists, from the Father, in reply to the Word begotten and uttered by Him about Himself. It is the Hypostatic Being of the Father in the Son and of the Son in the Father. But Spirit's ascription jointly to the Father and to the Son, which makes it the Third Hypostasis, by no means, nevertheless, presupposes Its procession from both the Father and the Son, as the interpretation given by Catholic theology holds. The latter is right to indicate that the Hypostasis of the Holy Spirit comes third, but at the same time it also over-emphasizes the joint participation of both the first hypostases, the dyad of Father and Son, in the procession of the Holy Spirit. This must be understood not as a simple and crude combination of the two (*una spiratione*), but in a more subtle and more complex sense. It is well known that many fathers of the church refer to the procession of the Holy Spirit jointly from the Father and the Son; at such points the ambiguity of the conjunction "and" is most often replaced by a thought which, if insufficiently definite, nevertheless also introduces a descriptive expression with the requisite nuance of thought by using the preposition *chrez* [through], διά [*dia*], *per*: who proceeds from the

Father through the Son,[9] or this is replaced by yet another descriptive expression: who proceeds from the Father, but who is also "proper" (ἴδιος [*idios*]) to the Son (Athanasius).

The fathers' indefinite references to the Holy Spirit's proceeding both from the Father and from the Son have to be understood in the light of these definitions and of the meaning of the theological thought harbored in them. The theological thought here is that the Holy Spirit proceeds from the Father, but towards the Son, and, in this sense, also through the Son; or it can also be expressed by saying, albeit with great imprecision and ambiguity, that the Spirit proceeds from Both, without, however, by any means forgetting the distinction between the parts played by the First and the Second Hypostases. It is impossible completely to deny the role and significance of the Second Hypostasis in the procession of the Holy Spirit, for the reason that He would otherwise not be the Third Hypostasis, but (as has already been shown) only a variant of the second, which would form, with the Father, a second independent dyad.

---

9   In St. Basil the Great, for example: "The Spirit appeared from God through the Son (δι' υἱοῦ πεφεγμέναι [*di' huiou pephegmenai*])"; in Gregory of Nyssa, "shining through Him (the Son), but having the cause of its being from the light of the archetype (δι' αὐτοῦ ἐκλάμπων [*di' autou eklampōn*])"; in St. Cyril of Alexandria, in whose work, in a way typical of him, both formulas are combined, and the first is understood by means of the second: "The Spirit, which has its existence from both, that is, proceeds from the Father through the Son (or is shared with the faithful) is the Spirit of God the Father and at the same time of the Son"; in St. Maximus the Confessor: "The Latins by no means recognize the Son as the cause (αἰτίαν [*aitian*]) of the Spirit, because they know that the *sole* cause of the Son and the Spirit is the Father, the first by begetting, the second by procession, and they affirm only that the Spirit was sent through the Son — δι αὐτοῦ προιέναι [*di' autou proienai*]"; and in St. John Damascene: "The Holy Spirit is not the Son of the Father, but the Spirit of the Father, and proceeds from the Father. He is also the Spirit of the Son, but not because he is from Him, but because he proceeds through Him from the Father, for there is one Cause — the Father." For many testimonies from the fathers of the church, with varying shades of meaning, see Metropolitan Makarii's *Dogmaticheskoe Bogoslovie*, 1:302 ff.; B. Silvestre's *Dogmaticheskoe Bogoslovie*, vol. 2; the Catholic *Theologiae cursus completus*, vol. 8 (*de Trinitate*); and the works of Zernikav on the procession of the Holy Spirit from the Father, etc. Compare also the well-known essay of Prof. V. V. Bolotov.

Translator's note: Khoruzhij, ed. cit., 579, gives further details of some of these sources: Bishop Silvestr (Malevanskij), *Opyt pravoslavnogo dogmaticheskogo bogosloviya s istoricheskim izlozheniem dogmatov* [Attempt at an orthodox dogmatic theology, with a historical exposition of the dogmas], 5 vols. (Kiev, 1878-91); Adam Zernikav, *Ob iskozhdenii Sv. Dukha* [On the Procession of the Holy Spirit] (Königsberg, 1774-76); V. V. Bolotov, *Uchenie Origena o Sv. Troitse* [Origen's Doctrine of the Holy Trinity] (Saint Petersburg, 1879).

In such a case it would, strictly speaking, be impossible even to speak of the Holy Trinity, since the circle of Triadicity would not close; instead it would be necessary to speak of a bi-unity of Dyads, each possessing a common member, of a right angle—

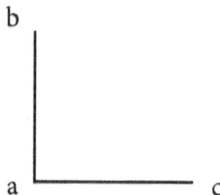

—but not of a triangle:

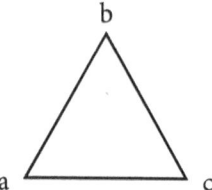

This is why, when we speak of the presence of two dyads in the Holy Trinity, the first of the Father and the Son, and the second of the Son and the Holy Spirit, this needs to be understood not in the sense of a new division of the indivisible Trinity, but only in the sense of a distinction amongst the hypostases in their reciprocal relations. The relation of the Father to the Holy Spirit who proceeds from the Father and has in the Father his Primordial Origin is to be understood dyadically only in a provisional sense, in contrast to the relationship between the Father and the Son, for the Father is related to the Holy Spirit which proceeds from Him in the Son or through the Son, and in this consists, although obscured and distorted, the thought of the Catholic dogma. In other words, the dogmatic consciousness of the universal Church did not yet display such sharp contours on the question of the Holy Spirit as took shape with regard to Christological questions, as a consequence of the acute sharpening of the latter in the age of the ecumenical councils; this is a task for the future (although the theological polemics of the twelfth to the fourteenth centuries already discussed these questions with great precision).

In this way, to return to the problem with which we began, the problem of the riddle of human consciousness, we may find its solution only in the Archetype—in the Triunity of tri-hypostatic Divinity, which has a single essence, for all three hypostases reveal the divine nature, and each hypostasis, while original as a hypostasis, is, as a hypostatic moment of the one Divine self-determination, inseparable from the other hypostases.[10] Or, as Gregory Nazianzen says, "the infinite conjunction of Three Infinite Ones, Each God when considered in Himself; as the Father so the Son, as the Son so the Holy Ghost; the Three One God when contemplated together; Each God because Consubstantial; One God because of the Monarchia."[11] The triplicity of the image of God is familiar and intelligible to us through the triune substantiality of our spirit. The mystery and the incomprehensibility of Absolute Substance consists not in its triunity, but in its trihypostaticity, and, by virtue of this, in the hypostatization of the three moments of indivisible Substance, and also in the origination of the hypostases through begetting and procession. As we saw previously, however, we have in this respect too an indication and a likeness in the nature of our own hypostaticity, since our *I* too is conscious of itself as an inseparable, but also immiscible moment of a certain *we*, and consequently, the *I* knows that it is not monohypostatic. This *non*-monohypostaticity of our *I*—while we can as yet say nothing more of this astonishing characteristic of our spirit—is also a *we*, and the *we* is in truth a great miracle in the *I*. The *we* awakens genuine philosophical wonder in the reason which attempts to conceive it. However, this characteristic in the *I*'s own nature cannot be understood from the *I* itself, but only by its going *beyond* and *above* itself towards the Archetype. The Most Holy Trinity is one in three and three in one. In

---

10 "God the Father, God the Son, and God the Holy Spirit," says Ambrose, "yet not three gods, but one God who has three Persons, as there is the soul as intellect, the soul as will, and the soul as memory, yet not three souls in one body but one soul which has three powers [*dignitates*], and in these three powers our inner human being reflects the Image of God in an astonishing way." "Even as God is in three persons," argues Dimitrij Rostovskij, "so the human soul is in three powers—intellect, word, and spirit. And even as the word is from the intellect and the spirit is from the intellect, so the Son and the Holy Spirit are from the Father. And even as there cannot be intellect without the word and the spirit, so the Father is never without the Son and the Holy Spirit, and could never be without them. And even as intellect, word, and spirit are three powers of the soul, yet a single soul not three souls: so Father, Son, and Holy Spirit are three Persons of God, yet not three Gods, but one God."

11 Gregory Nazianzen, Oration 40 on Holy Baptism, at www.newadvent.org/fathers/310240.htm (accessed 1. xii. 2019).

Its hypostaticity, the Trinity is **I** in each of Its three hypostases, each of which exists inseparably from the **I** of the other two hypostases, and at the same time the Trinity is a *We*, the mysterious oneness of many, the oneness of several, that is, of three, hypostases. The word of God itself witnesses to this, when God in the Most Holy Trinity speaks of Himself in the first person plural, that is, as a *We*.[12] I = We, Three = One: such determinations as these contradict the rational law of identity. The plural number *We* is by its nature not limited, unlike the dual number which exists in various languages for the expression of a dyadic relationship, but is open to an indefinite, unlimited plurality, a "bad infinity." At the same time, however, it is, in any given complement [*sostave*], closed within itself, since all its members are reciprocally linked by being turned towards each other in a *we*. The *we* is a ring, a circle, which, although it is of variable and undefined diameter, is completely closed, rather than being a straight line which can be broken off at any point. The question is: how many *Is* make a *we*? By its own existence, the *we* evidences the way in which the *I* goes out of itself into another *I*, and consequently this second *I*, at least, is necessary for there to be a *we*: the genius of language already expresses both *I* and *thou* in *we*. In certain languages, however (Greek, Church Slavonic), that genius singles out duality, distinguishing a dyad from a plurality by means of the dual number, as opposed to the plural. By doing this, it testifies to the fact that the dual number is not a full plural; *I* and *thou* and *thou* and *I* are not yet a fully closed *we*, but are only a preliminary step towards it. The *thou* is a path towards the *we*, the origin of the *we*, but it is not yet the *we* itself. A full *we* is something more than *I* and *thou* or than *I* in *thou*, and is also more than *thou* in *I*; it is at least three *Is*, which make up by themselves a full plural number. "For where two or three of you are gathered together in my name, there am I in the midst of them" (Mt. 18:20), declares the Lord.

---

12 "And God said, Let us make man in our image, after our likeness" (Gen. 1:26); "And the Lord God said, Behold, the man is become as one of us" (Gen. 3:22); "Go to, let us go down, and there confound their language" (Gen. 11:7). The same thing was shown in incarnate form in the appearance of the three strangers to Abraham, the Divine *We*. *We* as a dual number is found in the New Testament: "I and my Father are one" (John 10:30); "that they may be one, even as we are one" (John 17:22); and as a plural number, with reference to the Holy Trinity, in the Savior's promise: "If a man love me, he will keep my words: and my Father will love him, and we will come unto him, and make our abode with him" (John 14:23).

The Postulate of Triadicity and Its Dogma

This "two or three" is, of course, not accidental in defining the power and essence of the church, that living plurality, that blessed human *we*. In accordance with the meaning of the whole of the eighteenth chapter of Matthew's Gospel, it is the Church that is being discussed here, and this passage defines the quantitative minimum for this *we*. First, the Lord distinguishes *two or three*, not, it goes without saying, in the sense of a tautological identity, so to speak, as an example, as if one were going to continue "or four or five," and so on, but in the sense of degrees of the *we*, of the basic *we* and the full *we*. Secondly, the first *we*, which is not a full *we*—*two*—becomes a full triunity, since the Lord himself is the *Third* (such is marriage, which is concluded "in Christ and in the Church," and which already establishes a small church; such, too, is friendship). The second *we*, *three*, is already a full *we*, human society, which, although it can also grow and increase, already contains within it the fullness of the triple number, is already the Church. In this way, *three* is the basis (and hence also the minimum) for a *we*, or, as Pythagoras, the ancient promulgator of the mystery of number, taught, "each and every thing can be defined by means of three,"[13] for *three* includes within itself the whole power of number. However, the problem of hypostaticity remains alien to Pythagoras himself, as to the whole of ancient thought, and so does any application of an interpretation of number to its solution.

In the Divine triunity of the Holy Trinity is given the full *We*, complete and enclosed within itself. This is by no means yet the case with the dyad, the even number, which the Pythagoreans correctly judged as an undefined, feminine, and unstable number, standing in need of an uneven number for its completion and consummation. This is correct also in relation to the question which interests us: the diremption of *I* and *we* without doubt destroys the enclosedness, the abstractedness, and the isolation of the I, and also destroys the impotence and

---

13 Aristotle, *On the Heavens*, I, 1: καθάπερ γάρ φασι καὶ οἱ Πυθαγόρειοι, τὸ πᾶν καὶ τὰ πάντα τοῖς τρισὶν ὥρισα. τελευτὴ γὰρ καὶ μέσον καὶ ἀρχὴ τὸν ἀριθμὸν ἔχει τὸν τοῦ παντός, ταῦτα δὲ τὸν τῆς τριάδος [*kathaper gar phasi kai hoi Puthagoreioi, to pan kai ta panta tois trisin hōrisa. teleutē gar kai meson kai arkhē ton arithmon hekhei ton tou pantos, taura de ton tēs triados*]. "For, as the Pythagoreans say, the universe and all that is in it is determined by the number three, since beginning and middle and end give the number of the universe, and the number they give is the triad." Aristotle, *On the Heavens*, in *The Complete Works of Aristotle: The Revised Oxford Translation*, 2 vols., ed. Jonathan Barnes (Princeton, NJ: Princeton University Press, 1995), 1:447–511; 447.

incompleteness of the *I* which are linked to these, for *I* is an *I* only in, with, and through the *we*, and *vice versa*. The *Thou* is the *I*'s window on to another monad, a window which Leibniz failed to notice; it is this which reveals the embrace of two in one. But unity still predominates too strongly here. The *I* looks at itself in the *thou*, but sees in it only another *I*, its own mirror; it can come to a halt as it were in mid-step before this mirror-like bi-unity, and the *we* simply remains incompletely revealed, half-accomplished. What is needed is a simple *I* which carries this transition through to its conclusion, which leads the *I* into the *we* by standing face to face not only with a solitary *thou* but also with the *Thou* as such, for a second iteration of the *thou* also destroys this solitariness. The *I* and the *thou* constitute an incomplete, restricted *we*, in which the nature of the *we* has not been fully accomplished. The *I* sees itself in the *thou*, as in its own mirror, and to a certain extent it is still aware of the *thou* only as itself, but as appearing outside itself. In a certain sense, the *I* posits the *thou* for itself, as its own *not-I*, appearing on this particular occasion as a *thou*. Here the *I* has thus not yet completely emerged from itself, since the dyad *I-thou* is merely the first and most basic form of the overcoming of the *I* and of a progression *beyond* and *out of* the I—family and friendship. However, if this emerging comes to a stop, and if the *I* hardens within this dyad, then what results is an egoism *à deux*, and the *I*'s emergence from itself through the *thou* to the *we* does not take place. For this reason, the *I-thou* dyad finds its own justification and meaning only in a further development *beyond* the dyad—in other words, as a link in the plural chain of the *we*. The third *I*, or the second *thou*, already removes the possibility of a *mirror-like* relationship between the *thou* and the *I*, of a dyadic egoism. Besides the *thou*, which is *immediately* correlated with the *I*, appears the *we*, which already subsists *outside of* this direct and to some extent mirror-like correlation, yet at the same time *enters into* this correlation, unifying the *I* and the *thou* and at the same time maintaining their distinctness and removing any mirror-like quality. The second *thou*, or the third *I*, brings the *we* to completion. All further *thou*s present the possibility, but not the necessity, of a *we*, and this plurality is of a triune kind, introducing no new elements into the structure of the *we*. This is why the plurality of human hypostases, the *we*, is simply an image of Divine triunity come true: three *I*s in a *We*.

The Postulate of Triadicity and Its Dogma

The peculiarity of the third *I* in relation to the first and the second lies in the fact that it completes their coupling; it opens up the fullness of *we* for the *I* and the *thou*. If, in the dyad, the *I* exists only for the *thou*, and the *thou* for the *I*, here an *I* appears which is a *thou-too* (and indeed an *I-too*), an Also as such in relation to these *two*. By moving the point from which it starts, the triad (or plurality) can possess each *I* as an *I-too* or as an *I-thou*, that is, as a *co-I* or a *co-thou*. In grammatical terms, this situation is expressed by the *third* person pronoun, *he*, which also has a plural number, *they*; to it answers the *we*, that is, many *co-Is*, or *you (plural)*, that is, many *co-thous*. (The third person, of course, also has a dual number in some languages.) In grammar, the third person, generally speaking, is ambiguous, and, for this reason, it harbours the danger of subreptions; Adam's fall into sin weighs the third person down. In its genuine, personal sense, it can signify only *thou-too*, as a further possibility of the *I-too*. True, it leaves the *thou-too* half-shadowed, half-realized, as if waiting for its turn, and hence tarrying in a certain incompleteness in the accomplishment of personhood, yet at the same time it is the necessary background for a full and definitive realization of the *I* and the *thou*, which, in bringing themselves into being, bring the third person into being too. In a word, the third person really is the *third* person, which necessarily presupposes *before* itself and *with* itself the first and the second persons, and which, at the same time, harbours within itself the possibility of realizing the first and the second persons, and, in this way, contains them. The *he* is, in this sense, a mystical gesture which expresses a *third I*, that is, the fulfilment of the solidary [*sobornoj*] nature of the *I*, of its pluri-unity. And only in this sense is *he* a personal pronoun. Yet in the *he* a certain catastrophe is also taking place, a fall from the proper sphere: the personal pronoun is diremted, and acquires an impersonal significance, an a-personal, demonstrative, relative significance. Grammatically and logically, this is only a development of the personal pronoun, but ontologically what is happening here is a leap from persons to *things*, from the personal to the thing-like. The person is objectified; the subject becomes an object; a living, hypostatic relationship of person to person, which, interiorly and essentially, is love, becomes a relationship of a person to an object; the hypostasis freezes into the hardened form of the *he*, into a cold non-love instead of a hypostatic relationship. It can be said that the whole life of that which is evil in the world is built according to the categories of the *I*'s self-love, an *I* rent asunder from the *we* and knowing the *thou* only as its own mirror, and of a demonstrative, objectifying *he*, which is mingled with the objects of the world as the *not-I* (the position of Fichte's science of knowledge). In truth this is a monstrous abuse, which is the consequence of a universal unfeelingness, and of the scarcity of love in the sinful human being. To a living and loving understanding of the *we*, there are no dead, but only the living; there is no *he*, which could never go together with a *thou* and which could never, as a *he*, enter into a *we*. In this lies the fundamental difference between the *Church* and every human association (we find the extremest expression of this objectification of the hypostasis in the way in which the very problem of personhood is altogether absent from the radical sociological determinism seen in Owen, Marx, and the like).

The Divine Triplicity is determined by the internal life of the Divinity, which reveals itself tri-hypostatically in the begetting of the Son by the Father and in the procession of the Holy Spirit from the Father to the Son. Yet at the same time this triplicity also reveals with exhaustive completeness the nature of hypostaticity, **I** as **We**, in so far as three **I**'s are already a complete **We**, and no more is required for the sake of its plenitude. The image of God shines forth not only in the nature of the human being, but also in the human being's hypostaticity, in the solidarity [*sobornost'*] and catholicity of the nature of our **I**, which of its own nature always requires a collective [*derzhat' sobor*]. And in this sense it can be said that the Holy Trinity furnishes the Archetype not only of the nature of an individual human being, but also of human community, that is, of the human *we*. Man exists in many individuals, who possess not merely a similar, but actually a single, common, nature. Man is a single Adam, even though the children of Adam have many faces. In this sense medieval realism (which is essentially only a repetition of the substance of the Platonic theory of ideas) is the truth itself: general concepts possess reality as universal predicates (ideas) of multiple subjects, and man, humanity, is the common predicate for all human hypostases or subjects. Adam (the old Adam) is the universal human being or humanity as such, and the new Adam, Christ, is truly the Man, who, by becoming incarnate, took on human nature. This renovated nature was as it were a new shared predicate for human hypostases. In human beings, however, the image of Divine hypostaticity appears only to the extent that humanity's human, creaturely nature can contain it. In place of tri-hypostaticity, without separation and without confusion, what inheres in man is mono-hypostaticity, which isolates and surrounds itself with the line of the *not-I*, and if it goes beyond this line, it arrives in the plural infinity of society, the human *we*.

For the Divine Trinity, the *I* and the *We*, which possesses in Itself a consummate plenitude of hypostaticity, the creation of new *Is*, of human hypostases, in whom God desires to have for Himself *other* selves in his likeness, is purely and entirely an act of munificence towards and love for humanity, a gift given by Divine Love, and by It alone. It is by no means an act of metaphysical necessity or of some kind of divine fate, which *modi* adhering to substance would, say, bring about *more geometrico*. Each new hypostasis who emerges beyond the Divine Plenitude could in a certain sense *not have been*; there is in them as such no ontological necessity for their being. They are *created* by Divine love and omnipotence (which, as such, is situated *beyond* any antithesis between freedom and necessity), for the Wisdom of God's "delights were with the sons of men" (Proverbs 8:31); "God reposes in His saints."[14] The God of Love was willing, of His ineffable love and kindness, to light from His Light innumerable myriads of spiritual suns or stars, that is, hypostases, not only in the human world, but also in the angelic world — "in the beginning God created the heaven and the earth" (Gen. 1:1). Angels do not possess in themselves, in its fullness, the tri-hypostatic image of God which the human being possesses, but they possess within themselves the image of Divine hypostaticity; they are hypostases. And hypostatic being is also given to the human being, a god "by the grace of God." The one trihypostatic God begot Divine sons, multiplied Himself in them, became a *We* with them, and received them into His Divine *We*. This was accomplished both through the original begetting of the human spirit from out of God's essence ("and man became a living soul," Gen. 2:7), and through the introduction of Humanity into the Divine Trinity in the hypostasis of the Son, who indeed became man and rose in the flesh from earth

---

14   Khoruzhij (ed. cit., p. 579) notes here an allusion to the Church Slavonic text of Isaiah 57:15 ("For thus saith the high and lofty One that inhabiteth eternity, whose name is Holy; I dwell in the high and holy place, with him also that is of a contrite and humble spirit, to revive the spirit of the humble, and to revive the heart of the contrite ones").

to heaven. "That they may all be one; as thou, Father, art in me, and I in thee" (John 17:21). The ineffability of the Divine love and kindness, which appears in the creation of new hypostases, created gods, in this venturing beyond the bounds of His own trihypostaticity, sequestered and absolute within itself, exceeds all thought: it is from this amazing miracle of God's love that all the other miracles of His omnipotence derive their significance. The Lord can by His word create worlds, yet the human soul, the hypostasis, is better than the whole world, and, in order that it might be saved, the Good Shepherd leaves heaven and its glory and takes upon himself the form of a servant (Phil. 2:7). And the fact that God says *thou* to human beings, that He by His Word acknowledges, and, consequently, creates the human being's personhood, and the fact that He gives to the human being, to a created being, the power to approach God as *Thou* (by teaching him to pray to Him as a Father: "Our Father, who *art* in heaven"), that is, He accepts a creature into the Divine *We*, this is a miracle of God's charity, a miracle more stupendous than all the starry worlds and abysses of the universe. And this new, created *we*, the heavenly host of angelic hypostases together with humankind in all its peoples, forms an ontologically singular multi-hypostatic *unity*, which overcomes the many-facedness of the one human nature, and reveals this unity as the *Church*.

The Most Holy Trinity proceeds from the absoluteness of triunity to the multiplicity of hypostases, which is unified in the Church. If God begets, in and through the Church, innumerable hypostases, the Lord himself has the Church not as Divine, but also not as extra-Divine (or created); not as Absolute, yet also not as relative. The essence of the Church lies on the very border between absoluteness and non-absoluteness, between Divinity and creatureliness. This is the Divine Sophia, the Wisdom of God, the intellectual world, the object of the trihypostatic Love of God, the Divine *All*, as an intellectual organism of Divine ideas, the heaven of heavens. That which the Son reveals in God the Father as His might and His word, and that to which the Holy Spirit gives life, this *All*, being, on the one hand, the revelation of the nature of Divinity, is also at the same time the Glory of the Lord, in whose light His own inaccessible Divinity is clad, a Glory which is at one and the same time shut up in His temple and apparent in His miracles. This glory of God, which exists for God as His radiance and emanation, can be hypostatized in created hypostases, without being itself a hypostasis (and no "fourth hypostasis" is therefore introduced into the Divinity).[15] But these created hypostases already go beyond the bounds of the plenitude of the Divine triplicity, of the Divine *I-We*, being in a certain sense, from the point of view of Divine absoluteness, surplus to it. Such is the property of *created* [*tvarnykh*] hypostases:[16] they are *created*; they are images, and, as it were, iterations. Their foundation is not in themselves, but outside and above them — in the Archetype.

15 See my essay "Hypostasis and hypostaticity" in the collection in honor of P. B. Struve. (And see, now, Anastassy Brandon Gallaher and Irina Kuklota, ed. and trans., "Protopresbyter Sergii Bulgakov: Hypostasis and hypostaticity: scholia to *The Unfading Light*," *St. Vladimir's Theological Quarterly* 49:1-2 [2005]: 5-46. — *Trans*.)

16 A strikingly clear intimation of the meaning of the triad and the tetrad is found amongst the Pythagoreans, who saw in the tetrad something like a compressed created ALL. The tetrad contains within itself the plenitude of number, its life, its mysterious source and root; the tetrad harbors within itself a whole decade (1 + 2 + 3 + 4 = 10). The first square and the first complex number, the tetrad is neither a product nor a sum; it contains within itself the positive strength of begetting, the reproduction of number. The corners of the square quadrilateral were consecrated to the great mother-goddesses: Rhea, Demeter, Aphrodite, Hera, Hestia. Four is the first positively feminine number. The triad is the radical origin of disclosure, the number of showing, while four is the origin not of outer appearance alone, but itself signifies the essence in appearances. See Prince S. Trubetskoj, *Metafisika v drevnej Grezii* [*Metaphysics in ancient Greece*] (Moscow, 1890), 201-2.

Excurses

I
Excursus on Kant

ON TRANSCENDENTAL APPERCEPTION IN KANT

KANT'S EPISTEMOLOGY CONSIDERS AND TREATS THE predicate separately from the subject, extra-hypostatically. Hypostaticity, however, exerts a determining influence on his epistemology, especially in the doctrine of transcendental apperception, which occupies the most central place of all in Kant's whole architectonic. It is remarkable that this doctrine is completely absent from the transcendental aesthetic—absent that is, from the key, decisive position of the critique. The I, as a supra-temporal principle which is therefore capable of contemplating time and of being conscious of temporality, and as a supra-spatial principle which is for just this reason capable of contemplating space, is completely absent here, which makes of the transcendental aesthetic an edifice built on sand. As a consequence, Kant ends up with a distorted doctrine of space and time as empty, abstract forms for all possible intuition and as insuperable barriers separating the thing in itself from appearances, whereas in the hypostatic nature of every act of cognition there is established a living, indestructible bridge between essence and appearance, in so far as temporality and spatiality can be conceived only by means of the non-temporality and non-spatiality of the *I*. This *I* is unconsciously presupposed by Kant in his whole analysis: the ambiguous and opaque concept of the subject continually creeps into that analysis, and in order to attach the forms of the transcendental aesthetic to this concept, Kant continually speaks of them as *subjective* forms of intuition, or conditions of sensibility which alone make possible for us visual representations of an external kind. "Since, then, the receptivity of the subject [*which one?—S.B.*], its capacity to be affected by objects, [*?—S.B.*] must necessarily precede all intuitions of these objects, it can be readily understood [*!—S.B.*] how the form of all appearances can be given prior to all actual perceptions, and so exist in the mind *a priori*. [. . .] It is, therefore, solely from the human standpoint [*what kind of definition is that?—S.B.*] that we [*which we?—S.B.*] can speak of space, of extended things, etc. If we depart from the subjective condition [*?—S.B.*]

under which alone we can have outer intuition (*Anschauung*), namely, liability to be affected by objects, the representation of space stands for nothing whatever."[1]

In the absolutely decisive passage of the critique there is a continuous contraband, opacity, and confusion: "subjective, we, human being" and similar expedients. The whole account of time and space, the decisive passage in the *Critique of Pure Reason*, is at the same time the shakiest and the least defensible. Even worse expounded is the doctrine of time, where the role of the *subject* stands out in a markedly evident way. Here we find dropped in passing such perfectly unclear remarks as the following: "Time is nothing but the form of inner sense, that is, of the intuition of ourselves and of our inner state. It cannot be a determination of outer appearances; it has to do neither with shape nor position, but with the relation of representations in our inner state" (CPR, 77 [A33/B49-50]). Clearer, more intelligible judgements are absent here.

The chief deficiency of this analysis, as of the whole plan of the *Critique*, with its reified approach to cognition and its philosophical cubism, lies precisely in the fact that the **I** is missing from it. The doctrine of pure transcendental apperception as the unity of experience should have begun not in the analytic, but here, in the aesthetic, as the overall basis of the *Critique*; even the formal doctrine of the unity of space and time as universal *a priori* forms, upon which the *a posteriori* supervenes, would require this unity of the I. But Kant was hypnotized by the fact of mathematical natural science, and he prioritized the grounding of this science.

To the second edition of the *Critique of Pure Reason*, in the "General Observations on the Transcendental Aesthetic" was added, incidentally, a section II which, in Kant's opinion, contained a "theory of the ideality of both inner and outer sense" (CPR, 87 [B66]), and which in fact contained a complete and utter muddle. We instance a passage about the subject, a passage which comes up against the problem of hypostaticity: "Now that which, as representation, can be antecedent to any and every act of thinking anything, is intuition; and if it contains nothing but relations, it is the form of intuition. Since this form does not represent anything save in so far as something is posited in the mind, it can be nothing but the

---

1 *Critique of Pure Reason*, in Lossky's translation, 46, from the first edition of the *Kritik der reinen Vernunft*, 42-46 (CPR, 71 [A 26/B 42-43]).

Excursus on Kant

mode in which the mind is affected through its own activity [?!—S.B.] (namely, through this positing of its representation), and so is affected by itself; in other words, it is nothing but an inner sense in respect of the form of that sense [*what is this ability of the mind to posit itself "in respect of its form"?*—S.B.]. Everything that is represented through a sense is so far always appearance, and consequently we must either refuse to admit that there is an inner sense, or we must recognize that the subject, which is the object of the sense, can be represented through it only as appearance, not as that subject would judge of itself if its intuition were self-activity only, that is, were intellectual [*this means that first of all a self-positing of forms is ascribed to the mind, and then by means of this self-positing the mind is shut out of itself by being converted into an appearance*—S.B.]. The whole difficulty is how a subject can inwardly intuit itself [*indeed!*—S.B.]; and this is a difficulty common to every theory. The consciousness of self (apperception) is the simple representation of the 'I' [?!—S.B.], and if all that is manifold in the subject were given by the *activity of the self*, the inner intuition would be intellectual. In man this consciousness demands inner perception of the manifold which is antecedently given in the subject, and the mode in which this manifold is given in the mind must, as non-spontaneous, be entitled sensibility [!!—S.B.]. If the faculty of coming to consciousness of oneself is to seek out (to apprehend) that which lies in the mind, it must affect the mind, and only in this way can it give rise to an intuition of itself. But the form of this intuition, which exists antecedently in the mind, determines, in the representation of time, the mode in which the manifold is together in the mind [*two storeys of the mind: abstracted form and content!*—S.B.] since it then intuits itself not as it would represent itself if immediately self-active, but as it is affected by itself, and therefore as it appear to itself, and not as it is" (CPR, 88–89 [B67–69]). A passage exemplary of the opacity and dogmatism of the most fundamental theses of the *Critique*!

It is in the anhypostaticity and inhumanity of Kant's account that the chief deficiency and the most unfounded aspect, as well as the contentlessness, of the transcendental aesthetic lies. True, one finds "consciousness," "we," and "soul" involuntarily popping up all the time, as we saw in the preceding extract, but all this is without foundation, is fleeting, inconsistent, and confused. On the contrary, the whole analytic is built on the presupposition of the *hypostatic* character of all cognition, to which

Kant gives the name *pure apperception*. Of course it proves fruitless here after it is removed from the aesthetic. The "transcendental deduction of the pure concepts of the understanding" (§§ 15–27, which exists in two different versions in the first and second editions) begins with the exposition of the doctrine of the possibility of synthesis as such. "[A]ll combination of a manifold is an act of the understanding, to which we assign the general title 'synthesis', which presupposes the synthesis of apperception (an overview and a gathering-together of the manifold), as well as its reproduction in the imagination and its identification by concepts."[2] At the basis of this whole synthesis lies transcendental apperception. "There can be in us no modes of knowledge, no connection or unity of one mode of knowledge with another, without that unity of consciousness which precedes all data of intuitions, and by relation to which representation of objects is alone possible. This pure original unchangeable consciousness I shall name *transcendental apperception*" (CPR, 136 [A 107]). In the second edition this thought is expounded thus: "It must be possible for the 'I think' to accompany all my representations; for otherwise something would be represented in me which could not be thought at all, and that is equivalent to saying that the representation would be impossible, or at least would be nothing to me. That representation which can be given prior to all thought is entitled intuition. All the manifold of intuition has, therefore, a necessary relation to the 'I think' in the same subject in which this manifold is found. But this representation is an act of *spontaneity*, that is, it cannot be regarded as belonging to sensibility. I call it *pure apperception*, to distinguish it from empirical apperception, or, again, *original apperception*, because it is that self-consciousness which, while generating the representation '*I think*' (a representation which must be capable of accompanying all other representations, and which in all consciousness is one and the same), cannot itself be accompanied by any further representation. The unity of this apperception I likewise entitle

---

2   I have been unable to identify a precisely continuous source in Kant's text for this quotation, and have therefore translated it here directly from the Russian; cf., however, CPR, 151–52 (B 130–31): "all combination—be we conscious of it or not, be it a combination of the manifold of intuition, empirical or non-empirical, or of various concepts—is an act of the understanding. To this act the general title 'synthesis' may be assigned, as indicating that we cannot represent to ourselves anything as combined in the object which we have not ourselves previously combined, and that of all representations *combination* is the only one which cannot be given through objects."—*Trans*.

the *transcendental* unity of self-consciousness, in order to indicate the possibility of *a priori* knowledge arising from it" (CPR, 152–53 [B 131–32]). The attachment of these various labels does not, however, diminish the fact of the discovery of the **I**, although later on, instead of being understood metaphysically, it is dogmatically concealed, in "critical" fashion, as a logical function, and only that (in which Kant falls back behind Descartes). Kant uses this discovery, which is forced upon him against his will, for the purposes of his own critical dogmatism alone. "Only in so far, therefore, as I can unite a manifold of given representations in one consciousness, is it possible for me to represent to myself the identity of the consciousness in [i.e., throughout] these representations. In other words, the analytic unity of apperception is possible only under the presupposition of a certain synthetic unity. The thought that the representations given in intuition one and all belong to me, is therefore equivalent to the thought that I unite them in one self-consciousness, or can at least so unite them; and although this thought is not itself the consciousness of the *synthesis* of the representations, it presupposes the possibility of that synthesis. In other words, only in so far as I can grasp the manifold of the representations in one consciousness, do I call them one and all *mine*. For otherwise I should have as many-colored and diverse a self as I have representations of which I am conscious to myself. Synthetic unity of the manifold of intuitions, as generated *a priori*, is thus the ground of the identity of apperception itself, which precedes *a priori* all my determinate thought. *Combination does not, however, lie in the objects, and cannot be borrowed from them, and so, through perception, first taken up into the understanding. On the contrary, it is an affair of the understanding alone* [cubism! — S. B.], which itself is nothing but the faculty of combining *a priori*, and of bringing the manifold of given representations under the unity of apperception. The principle of apperception is the highest principle in the whole sphere of human knowledge" (CPR, 153–54 [B 133–35]). Kant assiduously distinguishes the synthetic unity of apperception from an inner sense (distinguishes, in other words, the epistemological **I** from the psychological), while the chief instrument of the distinction proves all the same to be the form of appearance of outer sensation, that is, time and space. "On the other hand, in the transcendental synthesis of the manifold of representations in general, and therefore in the synthetic original unity of apperception,

I am conscious of myself, not as I appear to myself, nor as I am myself, but only that I am. This representation is a thought, not an intuition. Now in order to know ourselves, there is required in addition to the act of thought, which brings the manifold of every possible intuition to the unity of apperception, a determinate mode of intuition, whereby this manifold is given; it therefore follows that although my existence is not indeed appearance (still less mere illusion), the determination of my existence can take place only in conformity with the form of inner sense, according to the special mode in which the manifold, which I combine, is given in inner intuition. Accordingly I have no *knowledge* of myself as I am but merely as I appear to myself.... I exist as an intelligence which is conscious solely of its power of combination; but in respect of the manifold which it has to combine I am subjected to a limiting condition (entitled inner sense), namely, that this combination can be made intuitable only according to relations of time..." (CPR, 168–69 [B157-59]). In the note to this text we read: "The 'I think' expresses the act of determining my existence. Existence is already given thereby, but the mode in which I am to determine this existence, that is, the manifold belonging to it, is not thereby given. In order that it be given, self-intuition is required; and such intuition is conditioned by a given *a priori* form, namely, time, which is sensible and belongs to the receptivity of the determinable [in me]" (CPR, 169n. [B157n.]). This remarkable recognition of some sort of mysterious "existence" of the **I**, that is, of hypostaticity, is let fall here in passing without any explanation, although it constitutes a breach in the whole system (Fichte!). Here Kant cannot manage to keep up his epistemological formalism, precisely because the *I* is an absolute ontological point, and everything, here, pushes him up against the separation between noumenal and phenomenal, subject and predicate, hypostasis and nature, being and life. Kant does not remember this when it comes to his own psychological paralogisms, even though it would be entirely appropriate for him to do so.

In the first paralogism, of substantiality, Kant makes (in the first edition) the following judgement: "I can say of any and every thing that it is substance, in the sense that I distinguish it from mere predicates and determinations of things. Now in all our thought the 'I' is subject, in which thoughts inhere only as determinations; and this 'I' cannot be employed as the determination of another thing. Everyone must, therefore, necessarily regard himself as substance, and thought as [consisting] only [in] accidents of his being, determinations of his state. But what use am I to make of this concept of a substance? That I, as thinking being, *persist* for myself, and do not in any natural manner either *arise* or *perish*, can by no means be deduced from it. Yet there is no other use to which I can put the concept of the substantiality of my thinking subject, and apart from such use I could very well dispense with it" (CPR, 333–34 [A 349]).[3] Earlier, as we saw, Kant associated some sort of undefined existence with the **I**. In the second edition, this thought is expounded thus: "Consequently, I do not know myself through being conscious of myself as thinking, but only when I am conscious of the intuition of myself as determined with respect to the function of thought. *Modi* of self-consciousness in thought are not by themselves concepts of objects (categories) but are mere functions which do not give thought an object to be known, and accordingly do not give even myself as object. The object is not the consciousness of the *determining* self, but only that of the *determinable* self, that is, of my inner intuition..." (CPR, 368 [B 406–7]). This reduction of the I to a logical function is, in the first place, incompatible with the admission that the I has some sort of "existence," and is moreover, of course, false, because the function is epistemologically hypostatized by being torn away from what is functioning, that is, the concrete, living, substantial I. Yet the very concept of substance, as it is developed by Kant, that is, of stability amid fluctuation, essentially comes down to supra-temporality; true substance, that is, always remains bound only to the I. "[O]nly in the permanent are relations of time possible. In other words, the permanent is the *substratum* of the empirical representation of time itself; in it alone is any determination of time possible," for "time cannot be perceived in itself" (CPR, 214 [B 226]).

"[T]he permanent in the appearances is therefore the substratum of all determination of time, and, as likewise follows, is also the condition of the possibility of all synthetic unity of perceptions, that is, of experience. All existence and all change in time have thus to be viewed as simply a mode of the existence of that which remains and persists. In all appearances the permanent is the object itself, that is, substance as phenomenon; everything, on the other hand, which changes or can change belongs only to the way in which substance or substances exist, and therefore to their

---

3 The words in square brackets are Kemp Smith's. — *Trans.*

determinations" (CPR, 214 [B 226–27]). In this way it turns out here that time in itself, the stronghold of the transcendental aesthetic, cannot be perceived. Time turns out to be subordinated to substantiality, and the latter is declared to be a "category," to the greater glory of criticism. But in the paralogisms it is demonstrated that substantiality does not belong to the I, whilst only the I is stable in time. Kant announces, entirely dogmatically, "[t]hat the 'I' of apperception, and therefore the 'I' in every act of thought, is *one*, and cannot be resolved into a plurality of subjects, and consequently signifies a logically simple subject, is something already contained in the very concept of thought, and is therefore an analytic proposition. But this does not mean that the thinking 'I' is a simple *substance*. That proposition would be synthetic. The concept of substance always relates to intuitions which cannot in me be other than sensible, and which therefore lie entirely outside the field of the understanding and its thought" (CPR, 369 [B 408]). And further on there is the following astonishing notion: "It would, indeed, be surprising if what in other cases requires so much labour to determine—namely, what, of all that is presented in intuition, is substance, and further, whether this substance can be simple (e.g., in the parts of matter)—should thus be given me directly, as if by revelation, in the poorest of all representations" (ibid.) "The proposition"—Kant continues—"that in all the manifold of which I am conscious I am identical with myself, is likewise implied in the concepts themselves [?—S. B.] and is therefore an analytic proposition. But this identity of the subject, of which I can be conscious in all my representations, does not concern any intuition of the subject, whereby it is given as object, and cannot therefore signify the identity of the person, if by that is understood the consciousness of the identity of one's own substance, as a thinking being, in all change of its states" (ibid.). It is remarkable how weak is Kant's argumentation when, in the first edition of the *Critique*, he suddenly remembers the problem of the plurality of the *I*—a problem which should not exist at all for his cubist objectivism—and, without any elaboration, uses this problem as an argument against the personal character of the *I*. "[I]f I view myself from the standpoint of another person (as object of his outer intuition), it is this outer observer who first represents *me in time*, for in the apperception *time* is represented, strictly speaking, only *in me*. Although he admits, therefore, the 'I', which accompanies, and indeed with complete identity, all representations at all times in *my* consciousness, he will draw

Excursus on Kant

no inference from this to the objective permanence of myself. For just as the time in which the observer sets me is not the time of my own but of his sensibility, so the identity which is necessarily bound up with my consciousness is not therefore bound up with his, that is, with the consciousness which contains the outer intuition of my subject. [*Wherever did these different times in these different subjects come from?*—S.B.] The identity of the consciousness of myself at different times is therefore only a formal condition of my thoughts and their coherence, and in no way proves the numerical identity of my subject. Despite the logical identity of the 'I', such a change may have occurred in it as does not allow of the retention of its identity, and yet we may ascribe to it the same-sounding 'I', which in every different state, even in one involving change of the [thinking] subject, might still retain the thought of the preceding subject and so hand it over to the subsequent subject" (CPR, 341–42 [A 362–63]). In the last analysis, Kant concludes, "all that I really have in thought is simply the unity of consciousness, on which, as the mere form of knowledge, all determination is based" (CPR, 380 [B 427]).

Hegel attaches a very great importance to Kant's doctrine of transcendental apperception. "It is one of the profoundest and truest insights to be found in the *Critique of Pure Reason* that the unity which constitutes the nature of the concept is recognized as the original synthetic unity of apperception, as unity of the I think, or of self-consciousness. This proposition constitutes the so-called transcendental deduction of the categories; but this has always been regarded as one of the most difficult parts of the Kantian philosophy, doubtless for no other reason than that it demands that we should go beyond the mere representation of the relation in which the *I* stands to the understanding, or concepts stand to a thing and its properties and accidents, and advance to the thought of that relation. An object, says Kant, is that in the notion of which the manifold of a given intuition is unified. But all unifying of representations demands a unity of consciousness in the synthesis of them. Consequently it is this unity of consciousness which alone constitutes the connection of the representations with the object and therewith their objective validity and on which rests even the possibility of the understanding. Kant distinguishes this unity from the subjective unity of consciousness, the unity of representation whereby I am conscious of a manifold as either simultaneous or successive, this being dependent on empirical conditions. On the other hand, the principles of the objective determination of concepts are, he says, solely to be derived from the principle of the transcendental unity of apperception. Through the categories which are these objective determinations, the manifold of given representations is so determined as to be brought into the unity of consciousness. According to this exposition, the unity of the concept is that whereby something is not a mere mode of feeling, an intuition, or even a mere representation, but is an object, and this objective unity is the unity of the ego with itself. In point of fact, the comprehension of an object consists in nothing else than that the ego makes it its own, pervades and brings it into its own form, that is, into the universality that is immediately a determinateness, or a determinateness that is immediately universality. As intuited or even in ordinary conception, the object is still something external and alien. When it is comprehended, the being-in-and-for-self which it possesses in intuition and pictorial thought is transformed into a positedness; the I in thinking it pervades it. But it is only as it is in thought that the object is truly in and for itself; in intuition or ordinary conception it is only an appearance. Thought sublates the immediacy with which the object at first confronts us and thus converts the object into a positedness; but this its positedness is its being-in-and-for-itself, or its objectivity. The object therefore has its objectivity in the concept and this is the unity of self-consciousness into which it has been received; consequently its objectivity, or the concept, is itself none other than the nature of self-consciousness, has no other moments or determinations than the I itself" (SL, 584–85). (Compare the definition of the idea as subject in the *Encyclopaedia*, p. 31.)[4]

Hegel solves Kant's philosophical charade in his own way, in a spirit of logical identity, that is, of the penetration even of the alogical by the logical and the sublation of predicates—and, consequently, the sublation of the subject too.

Noumenon and phenomenon—this distinction, which has, in Kant, a formal and epistemological character, and which is given a distortedly cubist interpretation, is in fact meaningful only if it is accepted that the only noumenon is the hypostasis, a living, concrete *I*, and that the

---

4 "Hence thought, viewed as a subject, is what is expressed by the word 'I'; and since I am at the same time in all my sensations, conceptions, and states of consciousness, thought is everywhere present, and is a category that runs through all these modifications" (*Hegel's Logic*, trans. Wallace, 31). — *Trans.*

Excursus on Kant

phenomenon is everything of which the noumenon is aware, that is, its theoretical and practical and aesthetic capacity, as well as the whole world. Kant does not know what to make of the noumenon, and still less does neo-Kantianism know what to make of it. Here is part of his account of freedom as it relates to the noumenon in connection with the third cosmological antinomy: "If appearances are things in themselves, freedom cannot be upheld. Nature will then be the complete and sufficient determining cause of every event. The condition of the event will be such as can be found only in the series of appearances; both it and its effect will be necessary in accordance with the law of nature. If, on the other hand, appearances are not taken for more than they actually are; if they are viewed not as things in themselves, but merely as representations, connected according to empirical laws, they must themselves have grounds which are not appearances. The effects of such an intelligible cause appear, and accordingly can be determined through other appearances, but its causality is not so determined. While the effects are to be found in a series of empirical conditions, the intelligible cause, together with its causality [? — S. B.] is outside the series" (CPR, 466–67 [A536–37/B 564–65]). Kant remarks of the distinction between the "empirical" and the "intelligible" character that "this acting subject would not, in its intelligible character, stand under any conditions of time; time is only a condition of appearances, not of things in themselves. In this subject no *action* would *begin* or *cease*, and it would not, therefore, have to conform to the law of the determination of all that is alterable in time, namely, that everything *which happens* must have its cause in the *appearances* which precede it. [...] In its empirical character, therefore, this subject, as appearance, would have to conform to all the laws of causal determination. To this extent it could be nothing more than a part of the world of sense, and its effects, like all other appearances, must be the inevitable outcome of nature. In proportion as outer appearances are found to influence it, and in proportion as its empirical character, that is, the law of causality, becomes known through experience, all its actions must admit of explanation in accordance with the laws of nature. In other words, all that is required for their complete and necessary determination must be found in a possible experience. In its intelligible character (though we can only have a general concept of that character) this same subject must be considered to be free from all influence of sensibility and from all determination through appearances. Inasmuch as it is *noumenon*, nothing happens in it; there can be no change requiring dynamical determination in time, and therefore no causal dependence upon appearances. And consequently, since natural necessity is to be met with only in the sensible world, this active being must in its actions be independent of, and free from all such necessity" (CPR, 468–69 [A 540–41/B 568–69]). As is well known, this motif is given a special development in the *Critique of Practical Reason*. Here we find a very substantial item of contraband, a real *Ding an sich*, the *person* — under the cover, admittedly, of moral value. Kant does not provide even the possibility of a theory of the other person, of the *thou*. In the *Groundwork of the Metaphysics of Morals* this concept suddenly appears *ex abrupto* [without warning]: "man [where did Kant get him from?—S.B.] and in general [?—S.B.] every rational being, exists as an end in himself, not merely as a means for arbitrary use by this or that will: he must in all his actions, whether they are directed to himself or to other rational beings, always be viewed at the same time as an end. [...] Beings whose existence depends, not on our will, but on nature, have none the less, if they are non-rational beings, only a relative value as means and are consequently called things. Rational beings, on the other hand, are called *persons* because their nature already marks them out as ends in themselves — that is, as something which ought not to be used merely as a means — and consequently imposes to that extent a limit on all arbitrary treatment of them (and is an object of reverence). Persons, therefore, are not merely subjective ends whose existence as an object of our actions has value for us: they are objective ends — that is, things whose existence is in itself an end, and indeed an end such that in its place we can put no other end to which they should serve simply as means; for unless this is so, nothing at all of absolute value would be found anywhere. But if all value were conditioned — that is, contingent — then no supreme principle could be found for reason at all."[5]

Unexpectedly, *humanity* appears. The "practical imperative" will consist in the following: "act in such a way that you always treat humanity, whether in your own person or in the person of any other, never simply as a means, but always at the same time as an end."[6]

---

5 Kant, *Groundwork*, 95–96.
6 Ibid., 96.

II
Excursus on Hegel

1

HEGEL'S LOGIC IS AN ONTOLOGY AND A THEOLOGY

"THE OBJECTIVE LOGIC, THEN, TAKES THE PLACE rather of former metaphysics which was intended to be the scientific construction of the world in terms of thoughts alone. If we have regard to the final shape in the elaboration of this science, then it is first and immediately ontology whose place is taken by objective logic—that part of this metaphysics which was supposed to investigate the nature of *ens* in general; *ens* comprises both being and essence.... But further, objective logic also comprises the rest of metaphysics in so far as this attempted to comprehend with the forms of pure thought particular substrata taken primarily from figurate conception, namely the soul, the world, and God; and the determinations of thought constituted what was essential in the mode of consideration."[1] In this sense "[t]he system of logic is the realm of shadows, the world of simple essentialities freed from all concrete consciousness."[2] Pure science (that is, logic) is absolute knowledge. "Absolute knowing is the truth of every mode of consciousness because, as the course of the *Phenomenology* showed, it is only in absolute knowing that the separation of the object from the certainty of itself is completely eliminated: truth is now equated with certainty, and this certainty with truth. Thus pure science presupposes liberation from the opposition of consciousness. It constrains *thought in so far as this is just as much the object in its own self, or the object in its own self in so far as it is equally pure thought* [*words which are of the very greatest weight for understanding Hegel's doctrine as a philosophy of identity and, at the same time, a panlogism!—S. B.*]. As science, truth is pure self-consciousness in its self-development and *has the shape of itself* [??!!*—S. B.*], so that *the absolute truth of being is the known concept*

---

1 SL, 63–64.
2 SL, 58.

and the concept as such is the absolute truth of being. This objective thinking is the *content* of pure science. Consequently, far from it being formal, far from it standing in need of a matter to constitute an actual and true cognition, it is its content alone which has absolute truth, or, if one still wanted to employ the word matter, it is the veritable matter—but a matter which is not external to the form, since this matter is rather pure thought and hence the absolute form itself. Accordingly, logic is to be understood as the system of pure reason, as the realm of pure thought" (SL, 49–50). This realm of pure thought and of absolute knowledge is realized in the movement of the concept, in the dialectical method which is the life of this concept. At the end of the *Logic*, looking back and bringing everything together into a unity, Hegel says this. "The absolute idea alone is being, imperishable *life, self-knowing truth*, and is *all truth*.... [L]ogic exhibits the self-movement of the absolute idea only as the original *word*, which is an outwardizing or utterance [*Äusserung*], but an utterance that in being has immediately vanished again as something outer [*Äusseres*]; the Idea is, therefore, only in this self-determination of *apprehending itself*; it is in *pure thought*, in which difference is not yet *otherness*, but is and remains perfectly transparent to itself. Thus the logical idea has itself as the infinite form for its content—*form* which constitutes the opposite to *content* to this extent that the content is the form-determination withdrawn into itself and sublated in the identity in such a manner that this concrete identity stands opposed to the identity explicated as form; the content has the shape of an other and a datum as against the form which as such stands simply *in relation*, and its determinateness is at the same time posited as an illusory being [*Schein*]. More exactly, the absolute idea itself has for its content merely this, that the form of determination is its own completed totality, the pure concept. Now the determinateness of the idea and the entire course followed by this determinateness has constituted the subject matter of the science of logic, from which course the absolute idea itself has issued into an *existence of its own*; but the nature of this its existence has shown itself to be this, that determinateness does not have the shape of a *content*, but exists wholly as *form*, and that accordingly the idea is the absolutely *universal idea*.... [T]he universal aspect of its form ... is the *method*.... [T]he method has emerged as the *self-knowing concept that has itself*, as the absolute, both subjective and objective, *for its subject matter*, consequently as the pure correspondence of the concept and its reality, as a concrete existence that is the concept itself.... [M]ethod is [only] the movement of the *concept* itself, the nature of which movement has already been cognized; but first, there is now the added significance that the *concept is everything*, and its movement is the *universal absolute activity*, the self-determining and self-realizing movement. The method is therefore to be recognized as the unrestrictedly universal, internal and external mode; and as the absolutely infinite force, to which no object, presenting itself as something external, remote from and independent of reason, could offer resistance or be of a particular nature in opposition to it, or could not be penetrated by it. It is therefore *soul and substance*, and anything whatever is comprehended and known in its truth only when it is *completely subjugated to the method*; it is the method proper to every subject matter because its activity is the concept" (SL, 824–26). "By virtue of the nature of the method just indicated, the science exhibits itself as a *circle* returning upon itself, the end being wound back into the beginning, the simple ground, by the mediation; this circle is moreover a *circle of circles*, for each individual member as ensouled by the method is reflected into itself, so that in returning to the beginning it is at the same time the beginning of a new member" (SL, 842).

The absolute idea which is logic's object "is truth in itself and for itself—the absolute unity of the concept and objectivity. Its 'ideal' content is nothing but the concept in its detailed terms: its 'real' content is only the exhibition which the concept gives itself, while yet, by enclosing this shape in its ideality, it keeps it in its power, and so keeps itself in it."[3] The note on this passage reads: "The definition, which declares the absolute to be the idea, is itself absolute. All former definitions come back to this. The idea is the truth: for truth is the correspondence of objectivity with the concept—not of course the correspondence of external things with my conceptions, for these are the only correct conceptions held

---

3   *Hegel's Logic*, trans. Wallace, 274–75, §213. (I have replaced "notion" with "concept" and have removed extra capitalization. The quotation as reproduced in Russian by Bulgakov differs somewhat from the quotation given, and I translate it separately here, while keeping as close to Wallace's Hegel as possible. In Bulgakov's quotation we hear not of the "identity" but of the "idea" of concept and object; and Hegel's reference to "real" content goes missing. The absolute idea "is truth as it is in and for itself; it is the absolute idea of the concept and the object. Its ideal content is only its revelation of itself in the form of external existence, while yet, by enclosing this shape in its ideality, it keeps it in its own power, and in its own identity." —*Trans*.)

The Tragedy of Philosophy

by me, the individual person. In the idea we have nothing to do with the individual, nor with figurate conceptions, nor with external things. And yet, again, everything actual, in so far as it is true, is the idea, and has its truth by and in virtue of the idea alone. Every individual being is some one aspect of the idea: for which, therefore, other idealities are needed, which in their turn appear to have a self-subsistence of their own. It is only in them altogether and in their relation that the concept is realized. The individual by itself does not correspond to its concept. It is this limitation of its existence which constitutes the finitude and the ruin of the individual. The idea itself is not to be taken as an idea of *something or other*, any more than the concept is to be taken as merely a specific concept. The absolute is the universal and one idea, which, by an act of 'judgement', particularizes itself to the system of specific ideas; which after all are constrained by their nature to come back to the one idea where their truth lies. As issued out of this 'judgement' the idea is in the first place only the one universal substance: but its developed and genuine actuality is to be as a subject and in that way as mind."[4]

Hence the relationship between philosophy and religion is clear (compare the preface to the second edition of the *Encyclopaedia*). The opening words of the introduction (chapter 1, section 1, page 1) are as follows: "The objects of philosophy, it is true, are upon the whole the same as those of religion. In both the object is Truth, in that supreme sense in which God and God only is the Truth. Both in like manner go on to treat of the finite worlds of Nature and the human Mind, with their relation to each other and to their truth in God."[5] "Philosophy has the same content and the same end as art and religion; but it is the highest mode of apprehending the absolute idea, because its mode is the highest mode, the concept" (SL, 824). The same thought also appears in the *Phenomenology of Spirit*.

But this is not enough. From the definition of the content of logic it follows that it not only coincides with the content of religion, taken in the sense given above; it is, that is, not only the knowledge of God

---

4 *Hegel's Logic*, trans. Wallace, 275. (The quotation is not, in fact, part of a *Zusatz*, but of § 213 itself. — *Trans.*)

5 *Hegel's Logic*, trans. Wallace, 3. (Note that the words quoted are not the very first words of the "Introduction," but follow these sentences: "Philosophy misses an advantage enjoyed by the other sciences. It cannot like them rest the existence of its objects on the natural admissions of consciousness, nor can it assume that its method of cognition, either for starting or for continuing, is one already accepted." — *Trans.*)

[*bogopoznanie*] but is also the *consciousness* of God [*bogosoznanie*]; in other words, the idea is also God, at least in its logical nature, the Logos (although in Hegel's theology the logos turns out to be not the second, but the third hypostasis). True, Hegel states this only as if in passing, but it is no less significant for all that: logic is defined as "enclosed within pure thought, and is the science only of the *Divine concept*," and "in the idea it remains essentially and actually [*an und für sich*] the totality of the concept, and science in the relationship to nature of *divine cognition* [*that is, in the sense given by the context here, of* logic — S. B.]" (SL, 843).[6]

But this is also stated immediately, in words which are incredible in their audacity: "[d]ie Logik ist sonach als das System der reinen Vernunft, als das Reich, des reinen Gedankens zu fassen. *Dieses Reich ist die Wahrheit, wie sie ohne Hülle an und für sich selbst ist. Man kann sich deswegen ausdrücken, dass dieser Inhalt die Darstellung Gottes ist, wie er in seinem ewigen Wesen vor der Erschaffung der Natur und eines endliches Geistes sind* [logic is to be understood as the system of pure reason, as the realm of pure thought. *This realm is truth as it is without veil and in its own absolute nature. It can therefore be said that this content is the exposition of God as he is in his eternal essence before the creation of nature and a finite mind]*" (SL, 50).[7]

This claim, unique in the history of thought, is nothing else than a philosophical Khlystism, in which the mind of Hegel is immediately identified with the mind of Christ; it is more obnubilatedly expressed in the quotation from Aristotle in the *Encyclopaedia*: "Bisher haben wir die Idee der Entwicklung durch ihre verschiedene Stufen hindurch zu unserem Gegenstände gehabt, nunmehr aber ist die Idee für sich gegenständlich. Dies ist die νόησις νοήσεως [*noēsis noēseōs*], welche schon Aristoteles als die höchste Form der Idee bezeichnet hat. [Hitherto *we* have had the idea in development through its various grades as *our* object, but now the idea comes to be its *own object*. This is the νόησις νοήσεως [*noēsis noēseōs*] which Aristotle long ago termed the supreme form of the idea]."[8]

---

6 Bulgakov's quotation emphasizes the Russian equivalent of the whole of the phrase *divine concept*, but Miller's Hegel emphasizes only *concept* (*Notion* in Miller's version), and does not capitalize the word "divine." — *Trans.*
7 Bulgakov leaves Hegel's German untranslated in this instance. — *Trans.*
8 Bulgakov again leaves Hegel's German untranslated; an English translation is supplied here from *Hegel's Logic*, trans. Wallace (Oxford: Clarendon Press, 1975), 292 (§236, Zusatz). For the "Khlysty" ("whips") or "Khristoveroi," see p. 51, n. 24 above. — *Trans.*

The Tragedy of Philosophy

In book twelve of the *Metaphysics* (chapter nine), Aristotle discusses the Deity, which, as the most perfect of all beings, also possesses the most perfect activity, consisting in theoretical contemplation having itself for its object, namely the νόησις νοήσεωσ: "αὐτὸν ἄρα νοεῖ, εἴπερ ἐστὶ τὸ κράτιστον, καὶ ἔστιν ἡ νόησις νοήσεως νόησις ... οὕτως δ'ἔχει αὐτὴ αὑτῆσ ἡ νόησις τὸν ἅπαντα αἰῶνα" [*hauton ara noei, eiper esti to kratiston, kai estin hē noēsis noēseōs noēsis ... houtōs d'ekhei autē hautes hē noēsis ton hapanta aiōna*—therefore it must be itself that thought thinks (since it is the most excellent of things), and its thinking is a thinking on thinking ... so throughout eternity is the thought which has *itself* for object].[9] The meaning of this excerpt bears out the divine nature of the idea, that is, that logic is God's consciousness. It contains truth within itself: "being in truth," "coming to know oneself in truth," that is, in dialectical connection and movement, is a frequently reiterated motif in the *Logic*. Logic is the self-consciousness or self-unfolding of the Deity, which Deity also leads this self-consciousness to veracity. The latter is divided into three basic stages, to which moments correspond the three parts of the *Logic*. "Thus God, too, in his immediate concept is not spirit; spirit is not the immediate, that which is opposed to mediation, but on the contrary is the essence that eternally posits its immediacy and eternally returns out of it into itself. *Immediately*, therefore, God is *only* nature. Or, nature is only the inner God, not God actual as spirit, and therefore not truly God. Or, in our thinking, our *first* thinking, God is only pure being, or even essence, the abstract absolute, but not God as absolute spirit, which alone is the true nature of God" (SL, 527). But consequently (and in accordance with everything else in Hegel's theory), *Gott wird* [God becomes]; the self-consciousness of spirit only appears in history, in human being. "God is God only so far as he knows himself," such that "man's knowledge of God ... proceeds to man's self-knowledge *in* God."[10] For God works "in and through humanity," humanity alone is God's "medium."[11] "Faith in the divine is only possible if in the believer himself there is a divine element

---

9 Aristotle, *Metaphysics* 1074β–1075α, in *Complete Works of Aristotle*, 2:1698–99. (Bulgakov leaves Aristotle's Greek untranslated, but a translation is provided here from Barnes for the reader's convenience.—*Trans.*)

10 *Hegel's Philosophy of Mind: Part Three of the Encyclopaedia of the Philosophical Sciences (1830)*, trans. William Wallace (Oxford: Clarendon Press, 1971), 298 (§564).

11 G. W. F. Hegel, *Ästhetik*, 2 vols. (Stuttgart: Philipp Reclam Jr., 1971), 1:74, 75 (my translation—*Trans.*).

which rediscovers itself, its own nature, in that on which it believes."[12] The cosmic process has not come to an end, and that is why God has not yet come into being but is still coming into being; that is why we cannot avoid the question of how it is possible to describe God fully as He was even *before* the creation of the world. Thus the question inevitably arises as to *how Hegel is possible*, and hence *how it is possible for Hegel's Logic to be the self-consciousness of truth, to be itself the truth unveiled*? How is absolute philosophy possible, an absolute philosophy which is God's consciousness and is thus the creation of the world? Does the existence of such an absolute philosophy mean that the cosmic process has come to an end, and that there is nothing further for earthly humans to say, that their self-emancipation (in so far as "freedom is the knowledge of necessity") is already complete, and that the continued existence of all chairs and schools of philosophy is already a misunderstanding, just as the appearance of a second edition of (the first volume of) Hegel's *Logic* is a misunderstanding? Truth cannot be published in different editions; it exists only in a single edition. The *Logic* claims to be a divinely inspired book and the last word of revelation (and in this there is some basis for the ironical anecdote that Hegel applied to himself the words of Christ: "I am the way, the truth, and the life"). In the *Logic* an all-seeing eye looks upon us and upon itself, the Logos, which shines in the darkness, and the darkness comprehendeth it not. In consequence there arise, from Hegel, Feuerbach, Strauss, the man-god! Hegel and Feuerbach, who are philosophical antipodes in a religious and dogmatic sense, are, in essence, of one mind, as is the positivist A. Comte. There is something terrible and significant in the harping of such different minds upon a single note, in the sameness of religious motifs amongst such *different* philosophical systems; in it is heard the measured tread of "that which is written," which "shall come in its own name," which is announced by its precursors and prophets, and which is inspired by itself.... In this claim, of course, a verdict is already arrived at. Hegel, as he *nolens volens* [willy nilly] proclaimed himself to be in the *Logic*, is incapable *of being Hegel*; his claim is a misunderstanding, a misunderstanding unmasked by history and by the development of Hegel's own doctrine. The *Logic* is not a depiction of

---

12 G.W.F. Hegel, "The Spirit of Christianity and Its Fate," in *Early Theological Writings*, trans. T.M. Knox (Philadelphia: University of Pennsylvania Press, 1975), 182–301; 266.

The Tragedy of Philosophy

God in creation, but only an analysis of the philosophy of logic, which possesses its own dazzling discoveries and striking delusions.

Despite this, however, the whole interest, significance, and even the singularity and grandeur of Hegel's philosophical experiment is contained precisely in the *Logic*. It is only the *Logic* that makes Hegel Hegelian. If one sets aside his *Logic*, the whole of his system of natural philosophy and so on can be understood as a spiritualism, as a variant of the philosophy of identity, like Spinoza's and Schelling's, and readers are continually reminded of those thinkers by Hegel's proximities to them. This second system, although rich in valuable individual observations and insights, is not fundamentally original, and, in this sense, is not of interest. The whole meaning of Hegel's experiment and the whole interest in the foundation of his thought lies in the *transition* from the *Logic* to cosmology, in the deduction of the world from thinking. In this also consists its panlogism, or, more precisely, its monologism. The kingdom of the Father, of the Creator, and of the Almighty is in Hegel the realm of the Logos. *In Hegel the Second hypostasis is the First.* Thought, which engenders itself, and which develops itself out of itself, is the primal ground of the being of the world; the mystery of the universe becomes transparent to thought. The object of thought is completely immanent to thought, and in this consists the universal identity of opposites which was sought by the philosophy of identity, an identity which, however, thought considers as dialectical rather than as antinomical. Logic is ontology, and is also cosmology, anthropology, and so on; logic wishes to be the Word by which all things were made. Evidently, such a logic is not only mistaken, but is also philosophical blackmail, a stacking of the deck. At the same time, it is the only dialectical inquiry into the categories of thought since Plato's *Parmenides* and Zeno's paradoxes. This Hegel-Parmenides is an intellectual colossus who attacks the impermeable partitions between the categories with a battering ram and discovers that they are passable. Hegel's logic is a true and authentic "gnoseology"; it is a *dynamic* of thought, whereas Kant merely came to a stop with his static diagrams, taking them for reality. In this sense, Hegel is "the truth of" Kant, and is, at the same time, his supersession. Hegel showed the authentic creative strength of thought in which the categories originate. He showed the logicity of being, showed precisely how thought is thinkable, how it assimilates its object to itself. Yet here too his claim goes further; he wishes not only to offer a series of brilliant and deep analyses of the separate categories and of their universal correlations, of their mutual interpenetration, but also to establish the *path* of these categories' *ascent* towards increasing concreteness, so that the system of logic is not a "rhapsody" of categories (in Kant's expression) but a strictly measured and articulated scale, in which each successive step *presupposes and in a certain sense includes* within itself *all* the preceding steps. Hegel's logic, without doubt, fails convincingly to fulfil this aim. All that is needed is for there to be errors or strained interpretations in a single point of any kind, and all the water leaks out through that crack. Hardly anyone will claim to be infallible to this extent. At the same time it is clear that the whole edifice of the *Logic* is internally defined by a metaphysical problem, and is the revelation of a definite ontological plan. It aims to show the origin of the metaphysical concept, towards which the whole of the logic, in its tripartite division, is drawn: being, essence, concept; "objective" and "subjective" logic. The content of the logic is nothing other than the deduction of the Concept, its onto-genesis. If this metaphysical presupposition of Hegel's is rejected, the whole edifice becomes devalued, distorted, and violent. It disintegrates into what is simply a series of separate deep analyses, which are more valuable, the less any Hegelianism is detected in them: that is why the most valuable and remarkable part of the *Logic* is the doctrine of being, the first part, whilst the second section, on reflection or on essence, is a good deal worse and more scholastic, and the third, on essence, is a counterfeit, a scandalous violence upon thought. As Trendelenburg and others have already shown, Hegel, in his own putative *a priori* deduction, all the time presupposes that thoughts have being, and speaks, essentially, not of thought as a self-thinking, but of conceivability or of thoughts. That is why the most instructive and substantive part of his analysis is where, leaving the supposed realm of shadows, he concerns himself openly, rather than in a veiled manner, with concrete thoughts. Such, for example, are the doctrine of mathematical infinity, of bad infinity, of the nature of the Kantian antinomies, and so on. Here his dialectic is a work of genius. But where that dialectic loses the freedom of the *jeu divin* of the *Parmenides*,[13]

---

13 Not for nothing does Hegel, contrasting Plato's dialectic with his own conception of dialectical method, reproach it as follows: "[e]ven the *Platonic* dialectic, in the Parmenides itself and elsewhere even more directly, on the one hand, aims only at abolishing and refuting limited assertions through themselves, and, on the other hand, has for result simply nothingness" (SL, 55–56).

The Tragedy of Philosophy

and admits the necessity of a deduction of the concept, it is obtuse, obstinate, and mediocre.

Hegel's *Logic*, on the whole, still awaits both its interpreter, and a true evaluation (this gap, unfortunately, is not filled by Il'in's study, which dwells least of all on the *Logic* and which does not deal at all with Hegel's path of ascent and its critique).[14] The *Logic, and it alone* of all Hegel's works, indisputably deserves interpretation and evaluation. The philosophical blackmail which is "panlogism" consists in the fact that here, whether deliberately or not, there is all the time implied or presupposed "the world before its creation," yet in conscious aspiration to a *pure* thinking which possesses no other sort of object than itself, than the requirement for a pure thought which would unfold itself to embrace all the "categories" of the world and to create the world through logic. Empty, abstract, worldless, and pre-worldly categories become full of the being of the world. How can this happen?

To answer this question is to provide a physiognomy of the whole of Hegel's project. What is definitive and decisive for it, naturally, is the beginning and the end — the fixing of the end of the rope to the heavenly firmament, a rope from which depend the cosmos, the subject, and life. The *beginning* possesses a definitive significance, according to Hegel himself, the *reiner Ursprung* [pure origin] (Cohen). "It may seem as if philosophy, in order to start on its course, had, like the rest of the sciences, to begin with a subjective presupposition. The sciences postulate their respective objects, such as space, number, or whatever it be; and it might be supposed that philosophy had also to postulate the existence of thought. But the two cases are not exactly parallel. It is by the free act of thought that it occupies a point of view, in which it is for its own self, and thus gives itself an object of its own production. Nor is this all. The very point of view which originally is taken on its own evidence only, must in the course of the science be converted into a result — the ultimate result in which philosophy returns into itself and reaches the point with which it began. In this manner philosophy exhibits the appearance of a circle which closes with itself, and

---

14 Bulgakov has already referred to Ivan A. Il'in (1883–1954), "Uchenie Gegelia o svobodnoj vole" [Hegel's account of free will] in *Voprosy Filosofii i Psychologii* [Questions of philosophy and psychology], 137–38. As he indicates below, he did not yet, whilst writing the present excursus, know Il'in's 1918 monograph, *Filosofiia Gegelia kak uchenie o konkretnosti Boga i cheloveka* [The philosophy of Hegel as a doctrine of the concreteness of God and humanity]. The latter has been translated into English by Philip T. Grier, 2 vols. (Evanston, IL: Northwestern University Press, 2010). — *Trans.*

Excursus on Hegel

has no beginning in the same way as the other sciences have. To speak of a beginning of philosophy has a meaning only in relation to a person who proposes to commence the study, and not in relation to the science as science."[15] "[T]he idea turns out to be the thought which is completely identical with itself, and not identical simply in the abstract, but also in its action of setting itself over against itself, so as to gain a being of its own, and yet of being in full possession of itself *while it is in this other*."[16]

In other words, what is attributed to philosophical thinking is not an orientation in what exists or in reality, but self-engendering and self-legislation.

Rosenkranz, in his preface to Hegel's "Propaedeutic," says that "there has been much contention about the beginning of the system. It is always forgotten that the subjective, the objective, and the absolute must be distinguished. The absolute beginning of the system, in the sense [that] what is being sought is also the real principle of the world of appearances and the subject, is the concept, which also forms its end, the concept of spirit, for which the concept of being is only the lowest, most initial predicate. The objective beginning of the system is the concept of utterly immediate being, than which no simpler determination exists. The subjective beginning is the deed of the consciousness which raises itself to thinking, to positing this abstraction."[17] "[P]ure science presupposes liberation from the opposition of consciousness. It contains thought in so far as this is just as much the object in its own self, or the object in its own self in so far as this is equally pure thought" (SL, 49). "Logic was defined as the science of pure thought, the principle of which is *pure* knowing, the unity which is not abstract but a living, concrete unity [*sic!*—S.B.] in virtue of the fact that in it the opposition in consciousness between a self-determined entity, a subject, and a second such entity, an object, is known to be overcome; being is known to be the pure concept in its own self, and the pure concept to be the true being" (SL, 60).

This recalls the expression from the "Preface" to the *Phenomenology of Spirit*: *es kommt nach meiner Einsicht, welche sich nur durch die Darstellung des Systems selbst rechtfertigen muss, alles darauf an, das wahre nicht als Substanz, sondern ebensosehr als Subjekt aufzufassen und auszudrücken*

---

15   *Hegel's Logic*, trans. Wallace, 22–23 (§17).
16   Ibid., 23 (§18).
17   Karl Rosenkranz (1805–1879), "Vorrede" to G. W. F. Hegel, *Werke* (Berlin: Duncker and Humblot, 1840), 18: v–xxii, xviii–xix.

The Tragedy of Philosophy

[In my view, which can be justified only by the exposition of the system itself, everything turns on grasping and expressing the true, not only as *substance*, but equally as *subject*].[18] (Philosophy of identity!)

"The beginning is *logical* in that it is to be made in the element of thought that is free and for itself, in *pure knowing*. It is *mediated* because pure knowing is the ultimate, absolute truth of *consciousness*. [...] Logic, then, has for its presupposition the science of manifested spirit, which contains and demonstrates the necessity and so the truth, of the standpoint occupied by pure knowing and of its mediation" (SL, 68–69). "All that is present is simply the resolve, which can also be regarded as arbitrary, that we are to consider *thought as such*. Thus the beginning must be an absolute, or what is synonymous here, an abstract beginning; and so it *may not presuppose anything*, must not be mediated by anything nor have a ground; rather it is to be itself the ground of the entire science. Consequently, it must be purely and simply an immediacy, or rather merely *immediacy* itself. Just as it cannot possess any determination relatively to anything else, so too it cannot contain within itself any determination, any content; for any such would be a distinguishing and an interrelationship of distinct moments, and consequently a mediation. The beginning therefore is *pure being*" (SL, 70). "The advance [*of philosophizing*] is a *retreat into the ground*, to what is *primary* and *true*, on which depends and, in fact, from which originates, that with which the beginning is made. Thus consciousness on its onward path from the immediacy with which it began is led back to absolute knowledge as its innermost *truth*. This last, the ground, is then also that from which the first proceeds, that which at first appeared as an immediacy. This is true in still greater measure of absolute spirit which reveals itself as the concrete and final supreme truth of all being, and which at the end of the development is known as freely externalizing itself, abandoning itself to the shape of an immediate being—opening or unfolding itself into the creation of a world which contains all that fell into the development which preceded that result and which through this reversal of its position relatively to its beginning is transformed into something dependent on the result as principle. The essential requirement for the science of logic

---

18 Bulgakov gives the quotation in German; a translation is provided here from *Phenomenology of Spirit*, trans. Miller, 9–10. Miller's capitalizations have been removed. The quotation in the Russian text mistakenly gives *reiner* instead of *meiner*. — Trans.

is not so much that the beginning be a pure immediacy, but rather that the whole of the science be within itself a circle in which the first is also the last and the last is also the first" (SL, 71).

2

THE CONSTRUCTION OF THE *LOGIC*

SO HEGEL POSITS PURE BEING AS THIS IMMEDIATE beginning; pure being is thus the foundation of the whole system. There are two ways of understanding the project of the logic: either to see in it, with Caird (*Hegel* [1883], chapters 7–8), an investigation into the categories of thought as *implying* the objectivity of the categories, which, clearly enough, does not correspond to Hegel's project, since it clips that project's wings, and does not take into account the pretensions of panlogistic logic to ontology and metaphysics; or to see here an attempt at the logical deduction of the entire universe, both subject and object—in a word, following Hegel's own definition, the *logical creation* of the world in which we live.[19] It is, of course, a *second* creation, in which the role of the chaos or *meon*, out of which the world comes into being before our very eyes in the six days of logical creation, is taken by the category of being. This putative act of creation is, it goes without saying, a contraband and a prestidigitation. Hegel wishes to think away the world by means of a phenomenological ascent, or, more precisely, to think the world *without* and *before* the world, obeying only the requirements of pure thought. In reality, Hegel has the being of the world continually in mind. He presupposes it, so that, as a matter of fact, Caird, from whose point of view the difficulties of pan- or of monologism do not, for this reason, exist, is right; but in return for this the essential aroma of Hegel's thought disappears.

Thus the *beginning* must be, on the one hand, immediate, and, as a result, becomes universal mediation. "The essential requirement for the science of logic is not so much that the beginning be a pure immediacy, but rather that the whole of the science be within itself a circle in which the first is also the last and the last is also the first" (SL, 71). "Thus the

---

19 Bulgakov gives the date of publication of Caird's *Hegel* as 1898; Kresling gives it as 1888. — *Trans.*

ground, the reason why the beginning is made with pure being in the pure science is directly given in the science itself. This pure being is the unity into which pure knowing withdraws, or, if this itself is still to be distinguished as form from its unity, then being is also the content of pure knowing. It is when taken in this way that this *pure being*, this absolute immediacy has equally the character of something absolutely mediated. But it is equally essential that it be taken only in the one-sided character in which it is pure immediacy, precisely because here it is the beginning. If it were not this pure indeterminateness, if it were determinate, it would have been taken as something mediated, something already carried a stage further: what is determinate implies an other to a first. Therefore it lies in the *very nature of a beginning* that it must be being and nothing else. To enter into philosophy, therefore, calls for no other preparations, no further reflections or points of connection" (SL, 72). At the same time, the beginning must be completely abstract, completely general; it must be "wholly form without any content" (SL, 72). In the beginning this is "only an empty word and only being; this simple determination which has no other meaning of any kind, this emptiness, is therefore simply as such the beginning of philosophy" (SL, 78).

This combination of *two* of the beginning's properties—first, immediacy, and second, abstraction, in the sense of the absence of determinacy, already conceals within itself an ambiguity: abstraction cannot be immediate, because it presupposes something abstracted from, that is, concreteness, objectivity, which is precisely what Hegel wants to think away at this point. *What is abstract is not immediate.* Hegel himself understands that the beginning "cannot be made with anything concrete, anything containing a relation *within itself*. For such presupposes an internal process of mediation and transition of which the concrete, now become simple, would be the result. But the beginning ought not itself to be already a first and an other; for anything which is in its own self a first and an other implies that an advance has already been made. Consequently, that which constitutes the beginning, the beginning itself, is to be taken as something unanalysable, taken in its simple, unfilled immediacy, and therefore as being, as the completely empty being" (SL, 75).

"If being had a determinateness, then it would not be the absolute beginning at all; it would then depend on an other and would not be immediate, would not be the beginning. But if it is indeterminate and

Excursus on Hegel

hence a genuine beginning, then, too, it has nothing with which it could bridge the gap between itself and an other; it is at the same time the end" (SL, 72). On one hand, therefore, immediacy; on the other, abstraction, in the sense of indeterminacy. Does being satisfy these requirements? Is being such a beginning? On this question depends the fate of the whole of the logic. Is being the tail of the absolute serpent, which, twisted into an absolute coil, is seized by its own head or Concept?

It is not, and it cannot be. In being as the beginning is found self-deception and objective deception, panlogism's blackmailing.

The crucial point is that *there is no such thing as being as such.* There is no such thing as being, but there *is is*, an auxiliary verb, *the copula*, which, by a deceptive feature of language (and particularly of German: *seyn — das Seyn*), and thanks to the capacity for formal abstraction, turns into something autonomous and even (in Parmenides) absolute. A copula cannot be abstracted from what it links, nor a relation from what is related; being necessarily draws to itself that *of which* it is the being, that is, the form of this being — to express it logically and grammatically, being draws to itself the subject as well as the predicate. Being does not exist; it is inconceivable; it cannot be thought apart from this copula in any other way than by abstracting from it by means of the mind's activity, by thought's concentrating on being as a moment. That is why being is *not* immediate in the sense which Hegel requires. On the contrary, it is always mediation, and cannot be separated from what mediates it. If one does not wish to introduce these mediations into being surreptitiously, as contraband (which is what Hegel's *Logic* both wishes to do and does), it is impossible to begin with being. To take being as the beginning is to take the *all* and *totality* not in their logical definition (which is given later on in the *Logic*) but in their actual existence, which, at least to begin with, is alien to and impenetrable by logic, whereas panlogism amounts to a claim to eliminate every remnant not transparent to thought. Being is not even a category, precisely because a category is an expression, a specification, a mode of being; to speak figuratively, being is the raw material for the categories, or, if you like, their *mater*, their mother. To put it crudely, there is no such thing as being in general, nor, in a logical sense, can there be, because being is invariably the being of something in particular or of someone in particular in some particular way; it is the copula. Consequently, if it is possible to put the copula under the logical microscope, this can be done only by the force of abstraction, not in the sense of indeterminateness and emptiness, of a lack of determinacy, as Hegel requires of the *beginning*, but in the sense of the ratiocinative isolation of that which, in reality, exists only *in concreto*: it is necessary to take its veins between logical tweezers and to interrupt the blood supply in order to arrive at this logical preparation. In sum: to place the *neuter gender* and the *third person* at the beginning of that whose result is to be a first person can only testify to a pre-judgement.

For Hegel the matter stood thus: he needed to deduce *everything* out of nothing (in the sense of objective being), out of mere conceivability—to deduce it in logical silhouettes, certainly, yet nevertheless to do this so as to obtain "the world before its creation." The putative deduction is possible only on the condition that one begin by accepting a concept of such vagueness and ambiguity that in it, to use Hegel's own expression, all cats are grey. Hegel's "being" is in no way superior, in this respect, to Schelling's absolute indifference.

In vain does Hegel judge that in one respect (necessary to him) being is immediate, and that in another, equally necessary, it is abstract and empty, lacking any color. We have seen that *being* is never in any case immediate. So by beginning with being, Hegel silently brings in and puts aside in his box of magic tricks all the things which, when the moment comes, he will be able to pull out of it again. He converts the logical hypostatization of that which mediates and connects into immediacy itself; and with this, the impotence and failure of panlogism, and the impossibility of the panlogistic project, are also revealed. For either a real *all*, or a potential and hidden one, must already be present at the very beginning of the logic, or such a beginning simply does not exist, any more than does absolute philosophy (that is, panlogism), and any philosophy is only what it is—that is, philosophizing.

Not only is the immediacy of being thus in fact not immediate, but its abstractness or emptiness is not at all abstract. Being, as the copula, as a relation, is just nothing, and does not contain anything which could be abstracted from; it has no colors, for colors belong to the forms of being. Being just *is*, and there is nothing more to say about it, just as nothing can be said about the properties of a geometrical point. If Hegel also speaks, as regards being, of its abstractness, immediacy, and emptiness, then this is further needless evidence that he is presupposing both subjects and objects

Excursus on Hegel

here, that is, forms of being, and is therefore finding them. There can be no abstraction from being, because it is universal, but as such, it is of its own nature completely without content, because it is a copula, is a relation.

At the basis of the *Logic* there thus lies an *incorrect* application of the idea of *being*, by whose mediation there is squeezed into this idea the entire world of essences. In reality, *being* is not, as Hegel considers it, a logical idea or category.[20] What leads to the error here is the fact that the idea of being is expressed in a word, like everything, and can consequently be thought. Yet although everything can be thought, not everything is an idea. A preposition, a conjunction, an interjection: all these are expressed, are thought, and can be put under the microscope of thought and made into a *das* [that], into an object or into a category. It is impossible arbitrarily to make, out of each and every *das*, an idea or a category possessing immediacy. There is a class of words and ideas which may not be immediate, since they directly express mediation. For example, the preposition *v* [into, to, in] can be made into an object of thought, but it cannot be thought immediately: it exists only within a series of concepts, and in this sense it is impossible to begin with it; it carries with it a *pre*supposition (to use Hegel's own expression). One can begin only with an idea which possesses the immediacy and force of being, not with nothing, which is what a pure relation is.

Being is also just such a *relative* concept, and it is absolutely unfitted to be a beginning, because it leads *beyond* itself, contains presuppositions *before* itself, and leads of itself *not* to the Hegelian idea of universal dialectical correlation, no, but to another point already indicated by Hegel, that it is impossible to understand [*poniat'*] — to "I" [*po-iat'*] — the concept, to obtain it, without its context, without its (logical) past, present, and future. Being, in the sense of the Hegelian beginning of logic, does

---

20 In the *Encyclopaedia*, Hegel gives the following definition: "Pure Being makes the beginning: because it is on one hand pure thought [*tautology!* — S. B.] and on the other immediacy itself, simple and indeterminate [*!* — S.B.]; and the first beginning cannot be mediated by anything, or be further determined" (*Hegel's Logic*, trans. Wallace, 124 (§ 86). Further on a completely mistaken thought is expressed: "If we enunciate Being as a predicate of the Absolute, we get the first definition of the latter. *The Absolute is Being*. This is (in thought) the absolutely initial definition, the most abstract and stinted" (*Hegel's Logic*, trans. Wallace, 125 [§ 86]). This is completely false: the Absolute is *not* being in this sense; it brings being into being, and grounds it through itself, but it does not have being as one of its own determinations.

not exist. It is impossible to think pure being as Hegel wanted to think it; it is a non-thought, *non-sens*. The idea *of pure being* is a completely false idea, and Hegel purchases his whole *Logic* with this counterfeit coin.

Since the *Logic* is an ontogenesis (or, if you like, a logical autobiography) of the Absolute, the Absolute too is thus defined as being.

This is a movement of thought characteristic of immanentism and pantheism, in which it has already been determined in advance that being = the world = the Absolute = God, and in which the whole of evolutionistic philosophy is already present embryonically. But it goes without saying that the Absolute or God cannot in any way be defined by means of being, as the predicate of a created and relative existence.

It is telling that the father of the doctrine of the categories, Aristotle, does not include, amongst his ten categories (οὐσια or τί ἐστι, πόσον, ποιὸν, πρός τι, ποῦ, ποτὲ, κεῖσθαι, ἔχειν, ποιεῖν, πάσχειν) [*ousia* or *ti esti, poson, poion, pros ti, pou, pote, keisthai, ekhein, poiein, paskhein*], a category of being. For Aristotle, evidently, being is not a category, any more than it is for Kant, with whom Hegel argues over the "hundred thalers." Under the category of being, Hegel in reality takes hold, not of logical being, but of existence, that is, of every *what* that exists, either in the sense of a subject or in the sense of a predicate. In this way, a betrayal of pure panlogism is already happening at the "beginning," and indeed precisely in the "beginning." If one accepts this beginning, what comes afterwards—happily or unhappily—follows, and logic turns out to have been converted into ontology. The beginning, however, contains a trick, a hocus-pocus. And this ambiguity or polysemy of Hegel's "being" is already revealed in the first steps, in the doctrine of *nothing*.

It is already clear at first glance that being, *das Seyn*, is *not* the opposite of *Nichts* [nothing] but only of *nicht Seyn* [not being]. Hegel must be aware that the negation lacks any meaning, yet he leaves the significance of his own *not* completely unilluminated. It might be an ἀ *privativum* or an οὐ [*ou*] or a μή [*mē*].[21] The *not*, by which Hegel authorizes his own negation of the category of being, may, to begin with, be an ἀ *privativum*, that is, the factual *annihilation* of thought, or the unthinkable, and in a double sense: either as that which is not exhaustively thinkable

---

21 See chapter one of my *Unfading Light*. (See, in the Smith translation, especially 108–9. — *Trans.*)

Excursus on Hegel

[*nedomyslimost'*], as a limit to thinking, a *Ding an sich*; or as what is other to the nature of thought, as an alogism, as unthinkable. It is this unthinkability which characterizes being in its alogical essence. The sphere of the unthinkable is an extensive one, but it is precisely the negation of this sphere which is the essence of Hegel's thought: no kind of further dialectic, it goes without saying, can be obtained from such a negation. The *not* may be οὐκ — that is, the *logical* negation or crossing-out of a thought (for example: the circle *is* a square, the circle is *not* a square) and here too there is no kind of dialectic, for not every negation contains within itself a contradiction, that is, an op*position*, that is, an affirmative content, even if only with a different symbol. Not every negation is a minus sign which preserves the previous absolute magnitude; there can be a negation which annuls all content absolutely and which is completely non-dialectical. Such is negation in its pure form, the so-called infinite judgement in logic, of the type "A is not B, C, D...." This is a rag which wipes out an incorrect thought, which expunges the mistake, but which in the end eliminates the whole content of the thought. Finally, there is a third negation, μὴ [*mē*], which is, in essence, an *affirmation*, but one expressed as a correlation or non-correlation, and here the sting of a pure negation, a negation which annuls the content or which negates the conceivability of the content, is extracted in advance. Such a negation also forms the *basis of dialectic* and of dialectic's contradictions, which Hegel so vaunts. This contradiction is, in fact, not contradictory at all, just as this negation does not negate anything. It is simply *otherness*, another form of being, and so it is in no way dreadful for thought; all the contradictions are safely resolved, taken account of, and sublated, as lovers' quarrels are quelled by the wedding banquet. But we return to the fundamental contradiction — being: non-being.

This contradiction could possess an ontological meaning — but not a dialectical one — if it were taken in all its ontological seriousness and acuteness, as an antinomy of *createdness*: as being coming out of and into non-being, the creation of the world out of nothing, *the mystery of creation* (although Hegel remembers this only at the wrong moment, of which more below), but in that case this antinomy is not decidable by thought, and cannot be resolved, only registered. If this antinomy is blunted by stepping away from the brink of being, away from the logical precipice, and turning one's back on it to gaze over the domain

The Tragedy of Philosophy

of already existing being, then the dialectic has a happy ending: on the one hand, *omnis definitio*, that is, every delimitation, is a negation, a repulsion away from these limits; while on the other, every *what*, which is not presently determinately shaped, is, in this its indeterminacy, still *nothing*—that is, *something* (*Nichts* = *Etwas*). But once it has got this *was* [what] in its possession, dialectic has secured everything needful—that is, a springboard which it would be futile to seek in the pure logical definition of being. And then the performance can begin: the dialectical serpent reaches its target safely.

Hegel suffers, above all, from verbal untidiness and imprecision. There are pairs of assertions and negations which correspond to each other:

(I) *Seyn*—*nicht Sein*: being—non-being.

(II) *Etwas* (*Ichts* is the old word which one finds in Böhme)—*Nichts*.

In Hegel, by contrast: Seyn (I)—Nichts (II): being—nothing.[22] The first member of the comparison belongs to the first pair, the second to the second. The confusion here is not merely verbal, and is by no means innocent, because by its means a single meaning is selected in advance from among all the many meanings of the category of *being*, a single meaning which, to be sure, passes through wavering nuances and shades, but which, when all is said and done, switches Hegel's thought

---

22   Hegel apparently senses this himself, yet he disposes of his doubts with an argument of supreme imprecision. Here he is *verbatim*. "Nothing is usually opposed to something; but the being of something is already determinate and is distinguished from another something; and so therefore the nothing which is opposed to the something is also the nothing of a particular something, a determinate nothing. Here, however, nothing is to be taken in its indeterminate simplicity. Should it be held more correct to oppose to being, *non-being* instead of nothing, there would be no objection to this so far as the result is concerned, for in *non-being* the relation to *being* is contained: both being and its negation are enunciated in a single term, nothing, as it is in becoming. But we are concerned first of all not with the *form* of opposition (with the form, that is, also of relation) but with the abstract, immediate negation: nothing, purely on its own account, negation devoid of any relations—what could also be expressed if one so wished merely by 'not'" (SL, 83). And that is all. Hegel, with conspicuous blindness, walks straight past the essence of the question, seeing in it only a "form of opposition" rather than a substantive one, and blinded by a formulation which has already been anticipated and decided upon in advance. That is how it proves possible to make the judgement, astonishing in its frivolity (how strange such a word sounds in connection with Hegel), that "nothing" is an absolute negation, a simple *not* (simple in what *sense*, exactly?). *Not*, as the à *privativum*, simply annihilates a thought, and no kind of "formulation" results from it. The whole imprecise, unclear and incomplete passage is contained in Remark 1 (SL, 83–90). And only here does Hegel consider in detail, or utter a word about, a question which is of cardinal importance to him.

on to different rails, away from logical being and into the domain of reality, of existence. This switching of the points happens just here, in the movement *from being to nothing*, and it can already be seen in advance that the train, instead of running into an exitless siding and breaking up, will happily arrive at the station "becoming," *Werden*, and will continue on its journey. Let us inspect this cunning switching of the points with the most careful attention.

"Only in, and by virtue of, this mere generality is it [pure Being] Nothing, something *inexpressible*, whereof the distinction from Nothing is a mere intention or meaning."[23] All Hegel's exertions to bring this movement, from an "inexpressible" being to nothing, closer to thinking, testify to the two different ways in which that movement can be understood: either the "inexpressible" is a pure nullity for thought, in which case it is beyond its limits and cannot be the *beginning* of the logic, or the *inexpressible* in general is *not* a pure nullity for thinking, since thought as such *presupposes* something which is inexpressible, yet which is always to be expressed, and Hegel's concept of the "inexpressible" is in essence a synonym for that which has not *yet* been expressed. The first meaning, the panlogistic one, produces *non-sens*, but the second affords an exit from panlogism and a completely different understanding of the *Logic* (as in Caird: "The general argument of the Logic, when we pursue it through all these stages, therefore is this: that reality,—which at first is present to us as the Being of things which are regarded as standing each by itself, determined in quality and quantity, but as having no necessary relations to each other,—comes in the process of thought to be known as an endless aggregate of essentially related and transitory existences...").[24] If one already possesses the cosmos, then philosophizing *about* the cosmos is natural and intelligible, but to bring the cosmos into being is not.

Hegel compares being and nothing with each other as "indeterminacy"

---

23 *Hegel's Logic*, trans. Wallace, 127 (§ 87). Here too are found the following panlogistic remarks, very characteristic of Hegel: "[t]he reflection which finds a profounder connotation for Being and Nothing is nothing but logical thought, through which such a connotation is evolved, not, however, in an accidental, but a necessary way. Every signification, therefore, in which they afterwards appear, is only a more precise specification and truer definition of the Absolute" (ibid., 127–28). Thus being is here directly admitted to be a predicate of the absolute, which is thereby identified with the cosmos, that is, with being.

24 Edward Caird, *Hegel* (Edinburgh and Philadelphia: Blackwood and Sons and J.B. Lippincott, 1886), 165.

and "emptiness," without any further determination, and because of this "[p]ure being and pure nothing are, therefore, the same" (SL, 82). They are identical, yet at the same time different; "each immediately vanishes in its opposite. Their truth is, therefore, this *movement* of the immediate vanishing of one in the other: becoming..." (SL, 83). This can mean only one thing: pure being, that is the completely indeterminate *something* [*nechto*], is, in this its indeterminacy, still nothing, that is, a not-what [*ne-chto*], that which has not yet become itself, has not been determined as a *what*, in other words, *is not yet* anything. Pure being—*which, as such*, is pure nothing—is still not anything as such; in beginning to be determined as a *what*, which is at the same time *not-what or something* [*ne-chto*], *it becomes*, that is, it is determined: the starting-point for this determination is the indeterminate *what* ("being-nothing") and the movement tends towards the dissolution of being and nothing into coming-to-be.[25]

Dialectic can have no other meaning, and without it, dialectic is simply impossible (as was explained above).

What is more, Hegel never offers any kind of substantive explanation of this fundamental point. In the greater *Logic* there follow some further remarks about it (SL, 83–105), turning the question over from various points of view, but they do not in substance explain anything about the fundamental question of principle, but instead even in part confuse the matter further, because they show how far Hegel himself wavers between various nuances of these fundamental concepts. Here is the clearest and most substantively significant example: to begin with, Hegel recalls Parmenides's pure being and the nothing of Buddhism, and then at the end he recollects the eternally present becoming of Heraclitus. "But these expressions [that is, the oriental view of the passage from life to death—S. B.] have a substratum in which the transition takes place; being and nothing are held apart in time, are conceived as alternating in it, but are not thought in their abstraction, and consequently, too, so that they are in themselves absolutely the same" (SL, 84). But even the "realm of shadows" presupposes a "substrate," even if it does not come after that substrate temporally, for a shadow is a shadow *of something*—a

---

25 Bulgakov here plays on the Russian word for something (*nechto*), which, when split in the middle, becomes "not-what" (*ne-chto*). — Trans.

Excursus on Hegel

figure which contains within itself a self-critique on Hegel's part.

Further on there follows an even more important remark, and one which reveals much about Hegel.

"*Ex nihilo nihil fit* is one of those propositions to which great importance was ascribed in metaphysics. In it is to be seen either only the empty tautology: nothing is nothing; or, if becoming is supposed to possess an actual meaning in it, then, since from *nothing* only nothing becomes, the proposition does not in fact contain *becoming*, for in it nothing remains nothing. Becoming implies that nothing does *not* remain nothing but passes into its other, into being. Later, especially Christian, metaphysics whilst rejecting the proposition that out of nothing comes nothing, asserted a transition from nothing into being; although it understood this proposition synthetically or merely imaginatively, yet even in the most imperfect union there is contained a point in which being and nothing coincide and their distinguishedness vanishes. The proposition: out of nothing comes nothing, nothing is just nothing, owes its particular importance to its opposition *to becoming generally, and consequently also its opposition to the creation of the world from nothing*" (SL, 84). In this Hegel detects a "pantheism." There is a confusion here which is characteristic of panlogistic immanentism—characteristic, that is, precisely of Hegel's own pantheism. The Christian idea of the creation of the world out of nothing has nothing in common, even externally, with Hegel's logical *origination*, because here the movement is in the opposite direction, from nothing to being rather than from *being to nothing*. Most importantly, there is in the Christian idea a *creation*, rather than a logical, immanent, *origination*. In any case, instead of the Chinese "shadows" of logic, we have here a completely realized reality and completely concretized concretion, an origination of *everything* out of *nothing*, or even, potentially, an origination of chaos from nothing. Hegel continually cautions against confusing the abstract with the concrete, but here, by using the very first categories of the logic to depict creation, he himself brings this confusion about, and with this exposes the fact that his "being" and "nothing," although logically empty, already constitute in his own eyes a universal chaos, containing all possibilities, that being and nothing are *already* some universal *what*, or, rather *totality*, which has originated from chaos. The colossal and fundamental difference between Christian dogma and Hegel's teaching lies in the fact that the former contains within itself an *antinomy*. Christian dogma rends thought in two and is in this sense super-rational: it registers the *transcens* by means of the *oukon* (οὐκ ὄν), by means of absolute non-being, against (Hegel's) *meon*-being (μὴ ὄν [*mē on*]), and between these two beginnings there is no bridge of any kind. Reason cannot see the *transcens* and cannot look upon it, since here there is a beckoning from the hand of God, the Lord God's creative *Let there be,* and it is not given to the creature to *understand* its own creation, even though it can understand nothing if it will not take into account its own createdness. In this way, the Christian creation out of nothing is located beyond Hegel's dialectic. The creation is presupposed as already having taken place. The dialectic of being is already this side of creation, in being. And Hegel himself does not understand this; having dissolved creation and its antinomies into the dialectic of being, and then immediately passed on to the Divinity, Hegel is, of course, a pantheist. Nothing as *oukon* and Nothing as *meon* are not identical, but opposites, like *nothing* and *something*, nor can there even be any dialectical correlation among them. All this is quite impenetrable to the rationalistic mind; it is a *mystery*. But dialectic is the negation of mystery, the disclosure of mysteries as a matter of principle. The antinomies bring reason to the brink by showing forth the chasm in thought, whereas dialectic wants to put up bridges everywhere. Antinomy and Hegel's dialectical contradiction are different from each other, and, in their meaning, are even opposed to each other.

That Hegel understands being and nothing pantheistically, that is, cosmically, is emphasized by the remark on the same page to the effect that "nowhere on heaven or earth is there anything which does not contain within itself both being and nothing" (SL, 85).

In the same way, the analysis of the Kantian example of the "hundred thalers" (SL, 86–87) does not bring us any closer at all to an understanding of the question at issue; nor does any of the rest of the Remark.

We are not, therefore, after Hegel's founding initial thought about the identity of being and nothing, left either with antinomies or with a genuine dialectical contradiction. The relationship between being and non-being in *existence* was already shown by Plato and by the ancients in general, and Hegel added nothing to this. Yet his own application of these concepts is in fact *not* dialectical: being and nothing constitute an identity in the sense that they are a void, an indeterminacy, but they do *not* represent a dialectical contradiction, of the kind that Hegel assumes in his exposition in order to satisfy the requirements of dialectic: as Hegel writes, this is neither being nor non-being but merely *something*, indeterminacy. There is no dialectic here, nor can there be in a void, and consequently there is no becoming either, nor any beginning. Hegel's logic lacks a foundation, and so the whole edifice is a castle in the air. It is built on an ambiguity, and a *reiner Ursprung* [pure origin], of the kind which being-nothing is supposed to be, cannot work. Hegel nevertheless declares, with a feeling of relief: "Becoming is the first concrete [*sic!* — S. B.] thought, and therefore the first concept: whereas being and nothing are empty abstractions. The concept of being, therefore, of which we sometimes speak, must mean becoming, because it is the transition of being to empty nothing, and of nothing to empty being."[26] Becoming is a transition from nothing-as-*meon* to a thing ("being"), but not from being to nothing, and in this sense Hegel's dialectic is mistaken here. If one already seeks the beginning of becoming, one can find it with the *meon*, as in Cohen, but not the other way round. Of course, Hegel wishes, in beginning with being, to remain within the limits of the purely logical, of what is conceivable independently from and irrespective of any extra-logical *what*. In reality, however, he shows that a thought which has emptied itself of all content, and whose predicate has been reduced to zero — a being which in its emptiness is equal to nothing — is *not even a thought*, is not thinkable, even though it nevertheless *is not equal* to zero, to the complete emptiness of thought. Hegel himself testifies precisely to this: nothing still has being for thought as the possibility of possibilities. It is not a void, just as a zero is not a pure zero, not a zero as such, but only the absence of a concrete number, a placeholder for a number, as in, e.g., the numbers 10, 101, and so on. An absolute zero as such, by contrast, cannot be counted, and is not a number. And since Hegel's zero content of thought, the being-*nothing*, with which he begins the *Logic*, is not an absolute zero, which could not be thought and which would be the very absence of thinking — it is not an absolute, but

---

26 The beginning of this quotation is quoted from *Hegel's Logic*, trans. Wallace, 132 (Zusatz), except that Wallace's capitalizations have been removed, "notion" has been replaced by "concept" and "Nought" by "nothing," but the last two clauses ("because it is... empty being") have been translated directly from the Russian version given by Bulgakov, because they are so far from Wallace's version. — *Trans.*

a relative zero—this zero as the logical *meon* differs from non-thought, from the logical *oukon*, by being the possibility of thought, the logical *place* of thought.

This zero as the logical place of thought differs from the zero as non-thought not in its content but in its objectivity; it is a logical gesture towards the object which shows that the absence of logical content or of determinate being is not the absence of being—or, in other words, that what is revealed in thought has a non-logical, non-cogitative basis. In a word, the original deduction of the *beginning* testifies against absolute panlogism, and, consequently, against absolute philosophy; it speaks of the fact that the shadows in the shadow-realm are cast by an alogical reality. For this reason, concepts, too, are in their nature not merely logical, as Hegel represents them as being, but also symbolic. Concepts are not shadows of shadows, but symbols of reality; concepts are the very *realia* of logical being. But this symbolic realism is quite different from Hegel's panlogistic realism. According to the latter, concepts are reality, because reality itself is established only by thought, is only a category (of being, of existence, of reality, and so on), while everything else is beyond the concept; sensibility is, genetically or phenomenologically considered, a lower stage through which spirit has already passed, and ontologically considered it is illusion, that is, the being-other of the concept, which the concept takes as something to be overcome, so that ontologically what is apart from and outside the concept is nothing at all, is a pure zero, the void of the *ouk on*. Symbolic realism, Platonism, like medieval realism, affirms the reality of concepts as symbols, that is, as possessing within themselves the force of being of their own objects, which are immanent to thought in their own logical nature, but transcendent to it in their own alogical, ontic foundation. Concepts as symbols grow from this root: they may be subjective or mistaken, but they cannot be empty or groundless. Amongst these concept-symbols, these first principles, however, there are, by virtue of thought's capacity for abstraction, concepts which are generated by abstraction, superstructures which are not first principles but which are forms of verbal elaboration, not *idea-words* but *word-words*, and Hegel's realism, properly speaking, is concerned with these latter: such concepts are ontic zeros which are created to order for Hegel's dialectic. But these too, as has been shown, are only relative zeros. So for symbolic realism, concepts are the self-evidences of logical-alogical, supra-logical

Excursus on Hegel

essence; for panlogistic realism they are the self-engendering of thought in its dialectical movement, the self-engendering of the logical world, of Divinity, which also creates the extra-logical world. In the end, the ordinary logical point of view, the pragmatic point of view, consists in our *creating* concepts by means of abstraction following an "outline." This pragmatism, correct in its own way, speaks of the *how*, but not of the *what*.

Further analysis of Hegel's logic lies outside the limits of our enquiry, since it does not have foundational significance. Here there is much that is remarkable for its profundity and perspicacity, but there is as much which is remarkable for the stubborn pedantry with which, step by step, "absolute philosophy" is traced out: the further the deduction moves on, and the more concrete it becomes, the more these concepts come to savour of the earth. The logic becomes an abstract theory of the sciences, like Kant's aprioristic natural science. The wholeness and indivisibility of the system, it goes without saying, the "circle" of self-enclosing absolute philosophy, is an illusion; the system is a series of analyses, some valuable, others less so. The fundamental task of Hegel's logic is a *philosophy of identity*, or more precisely *of logical* identity. Instead of Schelling's Absolute, which unites in itself subject and object, nature and consciousness, the rational and the irrational, what is affirmed here is a rational identity of everything which is revealed by the dialectic of the concept: from the original indifference of being and nothing, before one's eyes, like links in a chain, there arise and emerge in an orderly fashion, each at the right moment, the subject or concept, life, and the Absolute, which, having been brought to light, is wholly logically transparent, is free from all mystery, and is the naked truth as found in G.W.F. Hegel himself. It goes without saying that these most difficult and most fundamental of deductions, and in particular the appearance of the subject and the transformation of the categories into the Concept, that is, into Spirit — to which there belongs, however, only a logical being, thinking without a thinker, being without anyone who is, spirithood without *a* spirit — are completely unconvincing and unsatisfactory. They are rapidly and verbally decreed, even though they constitute the task with which the logic is faced from the start, the goal of the entire enterprise. But they also cannot be followed with conviction, because the relationship between subject and object — that is, between essence and hypostasis — is not a logical, but an ontological one, which leads to antinomies rather than to felicitous dialectical contradictions.

A particularly flagrant and straightforwardly scandalous example of the misapplication of abstraction in the very worst sense is found in the way in which the "category" of Life appears in the *Science of Logic*. The very idea of turning the universal definition of the existence in which we live and move and breathe into *one* of the categories, to be placed at a particular point on the philosophical shelf, is, for the product of such a dialectical head, striking in its lack of discrimination, in its dull-wittedness and in its intellectual philistinism. The category of *life* appears in the "subjective" logic, where the *concept of the concept* is already under consideration, first as subjectivity (the concept as judgement and inference), then as objectivity (the concept as mechanism, as chemism, and as teleology), and, finally, as idea (the concept as life, as the idea of cognition, and as the Absolute idea). The further on the *Logic* goes, and the more its "Hegelianism" reveals itself not simply to be a dialectical enquiry, but the demonstration at all costs of a prejudiced, mistaken, and consciously metaphysical thesis, the weaker and more unconvincing Hegel's argumentation becomes, and its final pages, amongst which are those on Life, are the weakest and the most arbitrary. Hegel justifies introducing a consideration of the category of *life* into his logic with the argument that "the idea... is essentially the subject matter of logic; since it is at first to be considered in its immediacy, it must be apprehended and cognized in this determinateness in which it is *life*... [T]his is not the place, however, to concern ourselves with how life is treated in the unphilosophical sciences, but only with differentiating logical life as pure idea from natural life which is dealt with in the philosophy of nature, and from life in so far as it stands in connexion with spirit. The former of these, as the life of nature, is life as projected into the *externality of existence* and having its condition in inorganic nature, and where the moments of the idea are a multiplicity of actual formations. Life in the idea is without such *presuppositions* which are in the form of shapes of actuality..." (SL, 762).[27] "Life, considered... in its Idea, is in and for itself absolute universality; the objectivity that it possesses is permeated throughout by the concept and has the

---

27 Marks of elision are absent from Bulgakov's Russian quotation; I have removed Miller's capitalizations of "Idea." — *Trans.*

Excursus on Hegel

concept alone for substance... [T]he concept is the omnipresent soul in it, which remains simple self-relation and remains a one in the multiplicity belonging to objective being" (SL, 763). This pedantic nonsense induces such boredom that it is impossible to examine it further. It is, at the same time, a blasphemy against *Life* itself. The category of life is successfully dismembered into three pseudo-dialectical parts: the living individual, the life-process, and the genus (Hegel falls very rapidly into self-stylization and expounds matters "dialectically" even where dialectic is completely beside the point, like Marx in his ludicrous "value-form"). When all is said and done, "[l]ife is the immediate idea, or the idea as its *concept* not yet realized in its own self. In its *judgment* the idea is *cognition* in general" (SL, 775).

In the *Encylopaedia*, §216, we read that "[t]he immediate idea is *life*. As *soul*, the concept is realized in a body..."[28] Further on there is a deduction of death: "[i]n this way life is essentially something alive, and in point of its immediacy this individual living thing. It is characteristic of finitude in this sphere that, by reason of the immediacy of the idea, body and soul are separable. This constitutes the mortality of the living being."[29] "From the point of view of understanding, life is usually spoken of as a mystery, and in general as incomprehensible. By giving it such a name, however, the understanding only confesses its own finitude and nullity. So far is life from being incomprehensible, that in it the very concept is presented to us, or rather the immediate idea existing as a concept. And, having said this, we have indicated the defect of life. Its concept and reality do not thoroughly correspond to each other. The concept of life is the soul, and this concept has the body for its reality. The soul is, as it were, infused into its corporeity; and in that way it is at first sentient only, and not yet freely self-conscious."[30] "The defect of life lies in its being only the idea implicit or natural: whereas cognition is in an equally one-sided way the merely conscious idea, or the idea for itself. The unity and truth of these two is the absolute idea, which is both in itself and for itself."[31]

Hegel's doctrine is a typical Sabellianism in which a mono-hypostatic

---

28 *Hegel's Logic*, trans. Wallace, 279 (§216).
29 Ibid., 280.
30 Ibid., 280 (§216, Zusatz).
31 Ibid., 292 (§236, Zusatz).

Divinity possesses three modes; at the same time it is also a pantheism, as a doctrine of the continuous becoming of a God who has not yet definitively *become*: before Christ there was no second hypostasis, and now the third is bringing itself about, for which reason there is essentially no trinity here. In Hegel, the Logos, the hypostasis of the Son, plays the role of the Father, but everything is consequently turned upside down, everything comes out in reverse: instead of the Father's timelessly begetting the Son within His own bosom, revealing, through Him, His Divine All, uttering the Word by means of Which the world is created, we have a logical idea, devoid of any ontic kernel, which suddenly and apropos of nothing plunges into its own "being-other."[32] With this, panlogism essentially liquidates itself, because a transcendent Logos is installed at the beginning of logical being. This beginning, however, is constructed merely as an exercise for the logical idea, as a stimulant for its own needs, rather than as the abundant spirit of love in an omnipotent Divinity, since this latter has, in Hegel, no sort of extra-worldly, intra-divine life of its own. The kingdom of the Spirit, moreover, the kingdom of the Third Hypostasis, is introduced more in order to satisfy triadic schematism and Lutheran orthodoxy than out of actual logical necessity. There is not, and cannot be, a genuine place in Hegel for the Kingdom of the Spirit, because, having started from the logos, he prescribes it as necessary for the logos to realize itself through being-other and to return into itself. For this reason, religion *ist nicht bloss ein Verhalten des Geistes zum absoluten Geist sondern der absolute Geist ist das Sich-beziehende auf das, was wir als Unterschied auf die andere Seite gesetzt haben, und höher ist so die Religion die Idee des Geistes, der zu sich selbst verhält, das Selbstbewusstsein des absoluten Geistes* [is not merely a way in which spirit behaves towards absolute spirit, but absolute spirit is, instead, that which

---

32   There are some penetrating words in Hegel about the seriousness of the creation of the world, words which, however, do not contain a full answer to this question: the life of the Divinity, the life which reason anticipates and delights in when it ascends to the absolute unity of all things, can be depicted as the action of love within itself; but this idea becomes a banal commonplace or even a vulgarity when it does not include within itself, in their full force, the suffering, patience, work, of which the negative side of things consists, that is, it appears from this that God *needs* the world, that the world is a moment of God and in God. (Cf. *Phenomenology of Spirit*, trans. Miller, 11 [§19]: "Thus the life of God and divine cognition may well be spoken of as a disporting of Love with itself; but this idea sinks into mere edification, and even insipidity, if it lacks the seriousness, the suffering, the patience, and the labour of the negative." — *Trans*.)

relates itself to that which we have posited as a distinction on the other side, and in its higher form religion is therefore the idea of spirit which relates to itself, the self-consciousness of absolute spirit].[33]

Here Hegel comes close to the militant spiritualism of the pantheists Hartmann and Drews.[34]

The result of Hegel's religious philosophy is a pantheistic *man-god*, since spirit recognizes itself and comes into being in humanity, who is also the God which becomes, that is, which recognizes itself little by little as God. Here Hegel is of one mind not only with those who descended from him, like Feuerbach, Bruno Bauer, and even Marx, but also with Comte, irrespective of the metaphysical gulf which divides Hegel from Comte, and irrespective of the fact that neither suspected his proximity to the other. In this way, unexpectedly and uncoordinatedly, from different points of view, in different languages and with different approaches and systems, a philosophy of time which is in *all* respects different speaks of one and the same thing — of the future superman or usurper who will come *in his own name*; and henceforth is heard from all sides one and the same music of the Antichrist.

As immanentism and logical pantheism, Hegel's system, which begins with the abstraction of a faceless being, is also an *impersonalism*, coming close in this respect to Spinoza's pantheism. It is true that this contradicts the letter of Hegel's own statement, in which he contrasts his position with Spinozistic impersonalism, in which *das Selbstbewusstsein nur untergegangen, nicht erhalten ist* [self-consciousness was only submerged and not preserved],[35] and in which he defines his own task as *das Wahre nicht als Substanz, sondern ebenso sehr als Subjekt aufzufassen und auszudrücken* [expressing the true, not only as *substance*, but equally as *subject*].[36] But personhood, here, is a *result* of the development of the *whole*, as a moment of the whole, one of its self-determinations. Thus

---

33 Bulgakov quotes Hegel in German here from Kuno Fischer's *Geschichte der neuern Philosophie*; cf. Hegel, *Werke*, 20 vols. (Frankfurt am Main: Suhrkamp, 1986), vol. 16, *Vorlesung über die Philosophie der Religion I*, 197–98. — *Trans.*

34 For Hartmann, see p. 77, n. 53 above; Christian Heinrich Arthur Drews (1865–1935) was a follower of Hartmann and the author of *The Christ Myth* (1909). — *Trans.*

35 Bulgakov gives the quotation in German only; a translation is provided here from *Phenomenology*, trans. Miller, 10 (§17). — *Trans.*

36 Again the quotation is given in German and a translation provided from *Phenomenology*, trans. Miller, 10 (§17), but without Miller's capitalizations. — *Trans.*

the development of the *Logic* leads from an impersonal being through an impersonal substance to the concept, which is already defined by Hegel as subject (although completely arbitrarily and unconvincingly). Thus man too *für sich ist er nur als gebildete Vernunft, die sich zu dem gemacht hat, was sie an sich ist* [for itself... it only is as cultivated reason, which has *made* itself into what it is in itself].[37]

In a similar way, personhood appears, in the transition from the philosophy of nature to the anthropology, as consciousness and self-consciousness: *Das Für-sich-sein der freien Allgemeinheit ist das höhere Erwachen der Seele zum Ich* [the being-for-itself of free universality is the higher awakening of the soul to the I]. *In Ihr erfolgt ein Erwachen höherer Art, als das auf das blosse Empfinden des Einzelnen beschränkte natürliche Erwachen; denn das Ich ist der durch die Naturseele schlagende Blitz; in Ich wird daher die Idealität der Natürlichkeit, also das Wesen der Seele* [in the "I" a waking ensues of a higher kind than the natural waking which is confined to the mere sensation of single things; for the "I" is the lightning which pierces through the natural soul and consumes its natural being. In the "I", therefore, the ideality of natural being, and so the essence of the soul, becomes *for* the soul].[38]

Just as self-consciousness non-temporally appears only at a certain stage of the self-development of the concept, just as it is a moment, a determination of that self-development, so in the world, too, self-consciousness *comes into being* in man, forming the basis of "subjective spirit" in accordance with the science of *phenomenology*.

Thus in relation to personhood, the source of the hypostasis, Hegel's doctrine is a metaphysical evolutionism. The "spirit," the "concept," is, in Hegel, a certain faceless substance within which arises self-differentiation, subject-object, inside-outside, *an sich* and *für sich*, and so on; personhood, the hypostasis, is in Hegel's eyes only a "subject," that is, not an absolutely present point which cannot be deleted by speculation and *from* which this speculation comes into being, but only a moment in the self-positing

---

37 Bulgakov again gives Hegel's German untranslated; a translation is given from the *Phenomenology*, trans. Miller, 12 (§21). The subject of the sentence given only in part by Bulgakov is, in fact, the embryo: "Though the embryo is indeed *in itself* a human being, it is not so *for itself*: this it only is as cultivated reason, which has *made* itself into what it is in itself." — *Trans.*

38 Bulgakov quotes in German. A translation is provided here from Hegel, *Philosophy of Mind*, trans. Wallace and Miller, 151–52 (§412 and Zusatz). — *Trans.*

Excursus on Hegel

of a supra-conscious or unconscious origin—just as in Hartmann. But Spinozism and even materialism each explain personhood in their own way; it is only that they fail to recognize its absoluteness and self-evidence, as does all evolutionism, which, from Spinoza to Hegel, is always a philosophy of identity. And this philosophy of identity, which is thereby an evolutionistic pantheism of various kinds, is in contradiction with personalism, for which the hypostasis comes first among all determinations. And any being *an und für sich* is possible only upon the presupposition of a subject, *within* hypostatic being, as a being for the hypostasis and before its face, as *its* life and being, but not as any kind of *it* or faceless substance harboring pantheistic atheism and acosmism. Here lies the boundary within all modern philosophy. Even Vladimir Solovyov is, in his dictionary entry on Hegel, strangely tempted by Hegel's evolutionism, in contrast to Solovyov's own earlier, more correct point of view in which he found Hegelianism to be thinking without a thinker; here, however, by contrast, he says that "[i]t is unfair to reproach Hegel's dialectical process with in some way representing thinking without a thinker or anything thinkable. Hegel, of course, did not identify subject and object as two separate *things* externally distinct from one another, and he did well not to do so: the whole of the very origin of his philosophy is linked to the speculative necessity of definitively freeing oneself from the dualistic Cartesian opposition between thought and extended substance. For Hegel, substance becomes subject or spirit in the true process of being and thinking, and, if he gave particular emphasis to the term 'becoming,' it does not follow from this that he negated the two other terms: he only ascertained their distinctness [!?—S. B.]."[39] Solovyov later praises Hegel for his "decisive establishment for science and universal consciousness of the true and fruitful concepts of *progress, development,* and *history* as a true and consistent realization of ideal substance."[40]

In fact, this imaginary achievement belongs to Hegel (or not) only to the same extent as to Comte, Spencer, Marx, Haeckel and the whole evolutionary heresy, and it is taken by Hegel, as by all the others, in a pantheistic sense completely unacceptable to Solovyov.

That Hegel, having devoted his entire colossal power of thinking to

---

[39] V. S. Solov'ev, "Gegel'," entry from *Entsyklopedicheskij Slovar'*, 318; reproduced at http://odinblago.ru/soloviev_10/4_30 (accessed 12. x. 2019).

[40] Ibid.

the dialectic of being (or simply "evolution"), did *not* resolve, and could not resolve, this question for philosophy is just the point, because he was a pantheist, and, for a pantheist, the very question cannot even be correctly formulated. The question consists precisely in the *co*-positing of God and the world, and, in the world, of humanity, of the hypostasis and its essence, person, and nature—that is, the question concerns the true nature, meaning, and limits of evolutionism. And the most treacherous opacity of Hegelian thought (which Solovyov, strangely, failed to perceive) consists precisely in the fact that evolutionism is in his work combined with Christian speculation of a Sabellian kind—that is, Hegel's thought, like every pantheism and evolutionism, is a *Christian heresy.*

Postscript. That one of the fundamental characteristics of Hegelian thought is the anhypostaticity of the Absolute, an anhypostaticity which leads Hegel not to provide a metaphysical foundation for human individuality, is clearly demonstrated, with the close attention which the topic deserves, in Il'in's monograph on *The Philosophy of Hegel* (2 vols, Moscow, 1918), in which a separate chapter is devoted to the development of Hegel's theory of personhood. (I did not have access to a copy of this monograph when writing the present excursus.) It is a fact that although, in the practical application of his principles, especially in the philosophy of law, Hegel says a good deal about personhood, he nevertheless never provides any metaphysical grounding for it in his ontology—that is, in his logic—and the complete unfoundedness of this way of proceeding needs to be shown by a critique. For Hegel, personhood can be understood as a particular moment or form of absolute being, as a limit to the overcoming of this particularity, but it can by no means be understood as an unconditional, absolute center, indissoluble from and ineradicable from the life of substance itself. And this, for all his thick *impasto* of Hegel's words and expressions, Il'in fails to show (2:176–183ff.). Il'in's and Hegel's whole argument as to the importance of the principle of the individual, of course, is indisputable, but on one condition, binding for the rationalist and even for the panlogist: the question whether, ontologically, it exists. It must be shown to be there; without this, all such argumentation rests upon a *petitio principii.* On the whole, the merits of Il'in's book are indisputable. Hegel is subjected to an exposition which is quite astonishing in its industry and (if one excepts the excessive citation style already mentioned) in its skill alike; but the book is not so much a contribution to the research on Hegel and his theories as it is an exposition of Hegel, and one which is, it hardly needs to be said, not devoid of modernizations. As a contribution to research into the philosophy of Hegel, it has a most serious and incomprehensible deficiency: it lacks an exposition and critique of the *Science of Logic*, that is, of the very essence of Hegel's thought, and, in general, much more is said about the project and the aims of Hegel's philosophy than about the way in which these are carried out. The most valuable and perceptive remarks are in the critical discussion of the uneven quality of Hegel's cosmology (and I would add, of his anthropology), or "pantheism." In the rest of the book, nevertheless, the author seems to reconcile himself to this fact, and sets out Hegel's practical philosophy as if it were grounded in his theoretical philosophy. Despite this, the panlogism of the *Logic* and the spiritualism of the remainder of his philosophy are completely *different* systems, unconnected to each other, while only the former has any philosophical originality or significance.

III

Excursus on Fichte

I

EXPOSITION OF THE IDEA OF A SCIENCE OF KNOWLEDGE

IN THE *GRUNDLAGE DER GESAMTEN WISSENSCHAFTS-lehre* [foundation of the whole science of knowledge] Fichte sets out the basis of his doctrine of the I. He considers as the "first and completely unconditional foundation" not thought, but "an efficacious action"—a *Thathandlung* which does not and cannot appear among the empirical states of our consciousness, but rather lies at the basis of all consciousness and alone makes it possible.[1]

Fichte takes, as the basis for the reflection which establishes the presence of this action as a self-evident proposition, the proposition "A is A" (the same as A = A, since such is the meaning of the logical copula), which "is accepted by everyone and that without a moment's thought: it is admitted to be perfectly certain and established" (SK, 94). Needless to say, this self-evidence, and this equation of "A is A" with "A = A" are by no means indisputable; the form of judgement or "copula," which Fichte here abstracts, is not at all simple and perhaps contains the central problem, for which reason even to begin with it as if it were self-evident is an arbitrary act, and the rest of the edifice is built on sand. None the less, just this necessary link is also "*absolutely* certain, that is, without any other ground" (SK, 94); it is trustworthy even if A does not exist (a copula *before* and *without* anything which is coupled)! Then this world, this I, by means of two or three tricks, is attached to this imaginary foundation by a single thread. But precisely "X [*that is, the copula*—S.B.]

---

[1] The words from "which does not and cannot" to the end of the paragraph are a quotation from J.G. Fichte, "Foundations of the Entire Science of Knowledge (1794)" (quoted here from *The Science of Knowledge*, trans. Peter Heath and John Lachs [Cambridge: Cambridge University Press, 1982], 87–286, at 93), but are not placed between quotation marks in the Russian text. References to this work are given from this point forward as "SK." — *Trans.*

The Tragedy of Philosophy

is at least *in* the I, and posited *by* the I, for it is the I [*which one?* — S. B.] which judges in the above proposition, and indeed judges according to X, as a law; which law must therefore be given to the I, and since it is posited absolutely and without any other ground, must be given to the I by the I alone" (SK, 95).[2] Next, once he has (but whence and how?) posited the X in the **I**, he squeezes the A into it too, on the basis that "X is possible only in relation to an A; now X is really [? — S. B.] present in the I: and so A must also be present in the I, insofar as X is related to it" (SK, 95). In the next trick the subject and the predicate are extracted from the copula and seen to their places, and the triumphant conjuror announces: "the above proposition can also be expressed as follows: if A is posited *in the I*, it is thereby *posited*, or, it thereby *is*" (SK, 95). With this ludicrous and naive prestidigitation the "deduction" is concluded, and it is later solemnly announced that "[t]hus the I asserts, by means of X, that *A exists absolutely for the judging I, and that simply in virtue of its being posited in the I as such;* which is to say, it is asserted that within the I — whether it be specifically positing, or judging, or whatever it may be — there is something that is permanently uniform, forever one and the same; and hence the X that is absolutely posited can also be expressed as I = I; I am I" (SK, 95–96). Fichte proposes that "[b]y this operation we have already arrived unnoticed [*bravo!* — S. B.] at the proposition: *I am*" (SK, 95). This is, of course, doubly absurd: there is no deduction at all here, and the proposition I *am* I (which is in no way equivalent to the proposition I *am*) is meaningless, is an application of the copula or form of judgement to something to which it cannot be applied, that is, to the subject *alone* (which is always an I). To shut the **I** away in a room with mirrored walls, where it will gaze on repetitions multiplied to infinity, is to make the violent abstraction which lies at the basis of Fichte's entire system and which determines its inner task. That task is as follows: to *deduce* from the **I**, that is, from the propositional and philosophical subject, the predicate as a *not-I*, to absorb predication, along with all judgement and all self-determination; the essence of all Fichteanism lies in this mono-hypostaticity, and, at the same time, in this abstraction, an abstraction carried out by means of a misapplication of

---

2   Fichte's *Ich* is at this point translated by Heath and Lachs as "self." Bulgakov's interpolated question — "which one?" — is implicitly asking whether it is the "transcendental" or the "empirical" "I" which is "judging" in the proposition mentioned. — *Trans.*

the copula, taken *before* the completion of a judgement, and the introduction of the copula into the **I** as a mirror for the **I** and for a tautology which is therefore meaningless: I *am* I, to which is joined an **I** = **I** which is clearly false, since *am* is not at all the same thing as =. In this way is established the reliability of the proposition *I am*, and a path cleared to the *Ich-Philosophie*: "prior to all postulation in the I, the I itself is posited" (SK, 95).

"The I's own positing of itself is thus its own pure activity. The *I posits itself*, and by virtue of this mere self-assertion it *exists*; and conversely, the I *exists* and *posits* its own existence by virtue of merely existing. It is at once the agent and the product of action; the active, and what the activity brings about; action and deed are one and the same, and hence the 'I am' expresses an Act, and the only one possible" (SK, 97).

Now it is time to extract from the conjuror's hat—from the proposition I *am* I—that which had previously been put into it. To begin with, the "*absolutely posited*...I" (that is, the Subject) is distinguished from the I "which exists" (the predicate): "the *I* exists *because* it has posited itself" (SK, 97-98). "The I in the first sense, and that in the second, are supposed to be absolutely equivalent" (SK, 98). [*This assertion is, of course, the greatest nonsense: they are* not at all *the same, since* "is" *is not the same as* "=." *It is, in any case, superfluous, because the correctness of what follows is self-evident and does not stand in need of any sort of deduction.*—S.B.] "Hence one can also reverse the above proposition and say: the I posits itself simply *because* it exists. It *posits* itself by merely existing and *exists* by merely being posited" (SK, 98).

Then follows a definition of the I as the "absolute Subject": "*That whose being or essence consists simply in the fact that it posits itself as existing*, is the I as absolute subject. As it *posits* itself, so it is; and as it *is*, so it *posits* itself; and hence the I is absolute and necessary for the I. What does not exist for itself is not an I" (SK, 98). Here the self-groundedness, or self-positing, or absoluteness of the **I** is quite correctly shown, since it is the nature of the **I** to be self-grounded; the **I** is the really real act in which being and consciousness coincide in a single point. But it is completely unnecessary to provide a cumbersome, counterfeit deduction to show this, a deduction which only diminishes the absoluteness of the *I*. "You cannot think at all without subjoining in thought your I, as conscious of itself; from your self-consciousness you can never abstract" (SK, 98). "*To* *posit oneself* and *to be* are, as applied to the I, perfectly identical. Thus the proposition, 'I am, because I have posited myself' can also be stated as: '*I am absolutely, because I am*'. The Act now unfolded may be given immediate expression in the following formula: *I am absolutely*, i.e., *I am absolutely* because *I am; and am absolutely* what *I am; both* for the I.... *The I begins by an absolute positing of its own existence*" (SK, 99). In the notes there is the following eludication: "*the I* is a necessary identity of subject and object: a subject-object; and is so absolutely, without further mediation" (SK, 99n.). All this is correct in so far as it shows the self-groundedness of the **I**; it is incorrect and also fatal to the extent that it extends the principle of identity to the **I**, that it ascribes *being* to the **I**, when the **I** is *that which truly exists [sushchee]*, and more generally in its obscuring of the fact that the I without a predicate does not possess being.

"[W]e can point out something from which every category is itself derived: the I, as absolute subject. Of every other possible thing to which it may be applied, it has to be shown that reality is transferred to it *from the I*: — that it would have to exist, provided that the I exists" (SK, 100).

Fichte specifies his own relationship to Kant and Descartes in the following way. "That our proposition is the absolutely basic principle of all knowledge, was pointed out by *Kant*, in his deduction of the categories; but he never laid it down specifically *as* the basic principle. *Descartes*, before him, put forward a similar proposition: *cogito, ergo sum* [I think, therefore I am] — which need not have been merely the minor premise and conclusion of a syllogism, with the major premise: *quodcumque cogitat est* [whatsoever thinks is]; for he may very well have regarded it as an immediate datum of consciousness. It would then amount to *cogitans sum, ergo sum* [I am thinking, therefore I am] (or as we should say, *sum, ergo sum* [I am, therefore I am]). But in that case the addition of *cogitans* [thinking] is entirely superfluous; we do not necessarily think when we exist, but we necessarily exist whenever we think. Thinking is by no means the essence, but merely a specific determination of existence" (SK, 100).

On *Spinoza*: "For him the I (what he calls *his* I, or what I call *mine*) does not exist absolutely *because* it exists; but because *something else* exists. — The I is certainly an I *for* itself, in his theory, but he goes on to ask what it would be for something other than the I. Such an 'other' would equally be an I, of which the posited I (e.g., *mine*) and all other selves that might be posited would be modifications. He separates *pure* and *empirical* consciousness. The first he attributes to God, who is never conscious of himself, since pure consciousness never attains to consciousness; the second he locates in the specific modifications of the Deity. So established, his system is perfectly consistent and irrefutable, since he takes his stand in a territory where reason can no longer follow him; but it is also groundless; for what right did he have to go beyond the pure consciousness given in empirical consciousness?—I further observe, that if we go beyond the *I am*, we necessarily arrive at Spinozism (that, when fully thought out, the system of Leibniz is nothing other than Spinozism, is shown...by Solomon Maimon...) and that there are only two completely consistent systems: the *critical*, which recognizes this boundary, and the *Spinozistic*, which oversteps it" (SK, 101–2).

The *Not-I*. "Every opposite, in so far as it is so, is so absolutely, by virtue of an act of the I, and for no other reason" (SK, 103). "Nothing is posited to begin with, except the I; and this alone is asserted absolutely. Hence there can be an absolute opposition only to the I. But that which is opposed to the I = the *not-I*" (SK, 104). "As surely as the absolute certainty of the proposition '~A is not equal to A' is unconditionally admitted among the facts of empirical consciousness, so surely is a *Not-I* opposed absolutely to the I" (ibid.) Fichte explains, moreover, that "in order to set something up as an *object*, I have to know this[3] already; hence it must lie initially in myself, the presenter, in advance of any possible experience.—And this is an observation so striking, that anyone who fails to grasp it, and is not thereby uplifted into transcendental idealism, must unquestionably be suffering from mental blindness" (SK, 105).

"Insofar as the not-I is posited, the I is not posited, for the not-I completely nullifies the I. Now the not-I is posited in the I: for it is counterposited; but all such counterpositing presupposes the identity of the I, in which something is posited and then something set in opposition thereto. Thus the I is not posited in the I, insofar as the not-I is posited therein. But the not-I can be posited only insofar as an I *is* posited in the I (in the identical consciousness), to which it (the not-I) can be opposed. Now the not-I is to be posited in the identical consciousness.

---

3 Namely, "that everything, wherein this X may be, is not that which presents, but an item to be presented."—*Trans.*

Thus, insofar as the not-I is to be posited in this consciousness, the I must also be posited therein" (SK, 106). "Both I and not-I are alike products of original acts of the I, and consciousness itself is similarly a product of the I's first original act, its own positing of itself" (SK, 107). I and Not-I mutually limit each other, and thus is deduced the concept of the *divisibility* of the I: "*both the I and the not-I are absolutely posited as divisible*" (SK, 108).

"Only now, in virtue of the concept thus established, can it be said of both that they are *something*. The absolute I of the first principle is not *something* (it has, and can have, no predicate); it is simply *what* it is, and this can be explained no further. But now, by means of this concept, consciousness contains the *whole* of reality; and to the not-I is allotted that part of it which does not attach to the I, and *vice versa*. Both are something: the not-I is what the I is not, and *vice versa*. As opposed to the absolute I ... the not-I is *absolutely nothing*; as opposed to the limitable I it is a *negative quantity*" (SK, 109).

Thus in the depths of the absolute *I* arises the divisible **I**, a "something," which divides its own being with the *Not-I*, and which depends upon the *Not-I* for its own reflective definition. Without the *Not-I*, in essence, there is no **I** as consciousness or as subject, nor is there a world. The transition to the *Not-I* is managed in an opaque and ambiguous way, since for the sake of this transition the absolute **I** (which possesses no predicate at all—or rather no logos), preparing for a Hegelian *salto mortale* of the spirit into being-other or nature, disguises itself, in an absolutely illogical or extra-logical way, as a subject-**I**, and assumes a predicate, which, to begin with, consists only in opposition, in a simple *not* or a minus sign (-A). Yet this too is impossible with respect to the indeterminate and inexpressible logically transcendent **I**. **I** as a subject cannot arise through the absolute **I**, but only through the relative *I*, and no transition is possible from the **I** to the *I*;[4] there is a hiatus, as is finely and correctly remarked in *I. Il'in*'s excellent essay, "The Crisis of the Idea of the Subject in Fichte the Elder's *Science of Knowledge*" (*Voprosy*

---

4   It is relevant to remark that an ambiguity in the German language plays a role here, since in German *Ich* is always written with a capital letter, whereas in Fichte there are clearly *two*, if not *more Ich*s, and this should be signaled in the Russian translation. (Bulgakov's note is partially misleading; it is only when used as a substantive that (*das*) *Ich* must, in German, be written with a capital letter. — *Trans*.)

Excursus on Fichte

Filosofii i Psykhologii ["Problems in philosophy and psychology"], 1912, nn. 111–12): "Between the first real act of 'self-positing' and the second act of 'other-positing' there is just as great a distance as there is between God before the creation of the finite world and God after its creation.... The whole problem of the *Science of Knowledge* arises from the fact that alongside the Absolute 'I' there appears another 'I' which is *not absolute*, and the task of the whole work is to construct some kind of relationship between the Absolute 'I' and the relative 'I' which might be able to produce some sort of *unity* between the two. It will be remembered that, in fact, the *Absolute* 'I' cannot be equated with or opposed to anything at all, whilst the 'Not-I' arises as an opposite term to the 'I'. It is clear that the 'Not-I' is not opposed to *the same* 'I' as the one which was originally 'posited'" (*Voprosy Filosofii i Psykhologii*, no. 111:33). (The further question of the *divisible I* and of the definition of the relationship between "I" and "not-I," that is, between subject and predicate, is artificial and absurd, the πρῶτον ψεῦδος [*prōton pseudos*, original error] of Fichte's philosophy, but more of this below.)

Fichte himself says: "In the very act of opposing a not-I to it, the latter [*the I — S. B.*] is simultaneously equated thereto, but not, as with all other comparisons, in a *higher* concept (which would presuppose both contained in it, and a higher synthesis, or at least thesis), but rather in a *lower* one. The I as such is degraded into a lower concept, that of divisibility, so that it can be set equal to the not-I... Here, then, there is no sort of *up*grading, as in every other synthesis, but a *down*grading. I and not-I, as equated and opposed through the concept of their capacity for mutual limitation, are themselves both something (namely accidents) in the I as divisible substance; posited by the I, as absolute, illimitable subject, to which nothing is either equated or opposed" (SK, 116–17).

This mysterious "descent" or "lowering" to a lower concept in the absolute **I** is a metaphysical catastrophe which completely destroys the "system" on which Fichte so prides himself (SK, 113ff.). Fichte continues: "[n]ow the essence of the *critical* philosophy consists in this, that an absolute self is postulated as wholly unconditioned and incapable of determination by any higher thing... Any philosophy is, on the other hand, *dogmatic*, when it equates or opposes anything to the I as such; and this it does in appealing to the supposedly higher concept of the *thing* (*ens*) which is thus quite arbitrarily set up as the absolutely highest conception. In the critical system, a thing is what is posited in the I; in the dogmatic, it is that wherein the I is itself posited: critical philosophy is thus *immanent*, since it posits everything in the self; dogmatism is *transcendent*, since it goes on beyond the self" (SK, 117). "So far as dogmatism can be consistent, Spinozism is its most logical outcome" (ibid.)

From the divisibility of the **I** into **I** and **Not-I**, Fichte deduces the nature of synthetic judgements and the inseparability of thesis and antithesis, anticipating Hegel's "dialectical method." Quite rightly he establishes that the latter is completely innocuous, just in so far as "[t]here can be no antithesis without a synthesis; for antithesis consists merely in seeking out the point of opposition between things that are alike; but these things would not be alike if they had not first been equated in an act of synthesis... And conversely, too, there can be no synthesis without an antithesis. Things in opposition are to be united; but they would not be opposed if they had not been so by an act of the I ..." (SK, 112). (Hence, by the way, Fichte draws the conclusion that "pure analytic judgements do not exist.") But along with this he establishes a category of "thetic" judgements, that is, put simply, judgements in which is contained the kernel of an ontological and critical problem. "A thetic judgement, however, would be one in which something is asserted, not to be like anything else or opposed to anything else, but simply to be identical with itself" (SK, 114). All judgements of this kind are held to be grounded in the *I am*, "even if these judgements should not always happen to have the I for logical subject" (ibid.). This is a deep and characteristic error, for *I am* is not a judgement at all; the absolute **I** is devoid of predicates, and this approximation testifies once more to the unclarity of the bases on which Fichte proceeds.

Developing a further "synthesis" of the *I* and the *not-I*, Fichte indicates some of its features in the proposition that "the *I posits itself as determined by the not-I*," singling out two moments here: "the I posits itself as determined by the Not-I... the *Not-I determines... the I*," and, finally, "the *I posits itself* as determined, through an absolute activity" (SK, 123–24).

ON REALITY

"In saying that the I determines itself we ascribe to it an absolute totality of the real. The I can only determine itself as a reality, for it is posited as the absolutely real, and as containing no negation. Yet it was supposed to be determined by itself. This cannot mean that it abolishes some reality

Excursus on Fichte

in itself, for then it would at once be thrown into contradiction with itself. The meaning must be: the I determines reality and, by means of that, itself. It posits all reality, as an absolute quantity. Beyond this reality there is no other, and it is attributed to the I. Hence the I is determined, insofar as the reality is so" (SK, 125). "The not-I is opposed to the I; and it contains negation as the self contains reality. If an absolute totality of the real is posited in the I, there must necessarily be posited in the not-I an absolute totality of negation; and negation itself must be posited as an absolute totality" (ibid.). "However many portions of negation the I posits in itself, a corresponding number of parts of reality is posited in the not-I" (SK, 126).

"The source of all reality is the I, for this is what is immediately and absolutely posited. The concept of reality is first given with and by way of the I. But the I *exists* because it *posits itself,* and *posits itself* because it *exists.* Hence *self-positing* and *existence* are one and the same. But the concepts of *self-positing* and of *activity* in general are again one and the same. Hence, all reality is *active*; and everything *active* is reality. Activity is positive, absolute... *reality*" (SK, 129). "Passivity [*of the* I—*S. B.*] is *positive*, absolute negation, and to that extent is contrasted to merely *relative* negation" (SK, 130), and is a quantitative negation ("for mere negation of activity, without regard to its quantity = 0, would be rest" [ibid.]). "The *not-I*, as such, *has no reality of its own; but... it has reality insofar as the self is passive,*" that is "*to the extent that the self is affected*" (ibid.).

The following is characteristic: "Every possible predicate of the self denotes a limitation thereof. The subject (e.g., I present, I strive, etc.) confines this activity within a delimited sphere" (SK, 135).

Later there follows a very typical *Ich-Spinozismus* [Spinozism of the I]: "Insofar as the I is regarded as embracing the whole absolutely determined realm of all realities, it is *substance*. So far as it is posited within a not absolutely determined area of this realm... to that extent it is *accidental*, or *has an accident within it*" (SK, 136). "No substance is conceivable without relation to an accident: for only by positing possible areas within the absolute realm does the I become a substance; only through possible accidents are *realities* engendered, for otherwise all reality would be absolutely one" (SK, 136). "Substance is *conceived of as all change in general*: accident is a *determinate that interchanges with some other changing thing*. There is initially only one substance, the I; within this one substance, all possible accidents, and so all possible realities, are posited" (ibid.). Fichte envisages the emergence of further, as it were derivative, substances from accidents, but he places a single substance at the foundation—the **I**. Moreover, it remains of course completely undecided whether this substance is a singular, individual **I**, in which case the question arises of how it is related to the plurality of *Is*, or whether the universal **I** is to be understood here, in which case we may ask how we are to understand the relationship between the particular *Is* and the universal **I**? No reply is forthcoming, for it is impossible to count as a reply the short and dense remark in the lecture "Concerning Human Dignity": "All individuals are included in the one great unity of pure spirit,"[5] or *Das ist mir, der ich Ich bin, jeder, der Ich ist* ["I am an I, and this is what everyone who is an I is to me"].[6] But the *I* has the property of thinking and perceiving itself in the singular number—not simply in the first person, but in the first person singular—and to write itself with a capital letter, like Fichte's **I**, and from such an *I* to someone else's *I* or to a *thou* there is no logical transition.

The following further judgement is of interest: "We have left untouched and in total obscurity, first, that activity of the I whereby it distinguishes and compares itself as substance and accident; and second, what it is that leads the I to engage in such an act. The latter . . . could well be an effect of the not-I. . . . The truly supreme problem which embraces all others is, how can the I operate directly on the not-I, or the not-I on the I, when both are held to be utterly opposed to each other?" (SK, 136–37). Ever new intermediaries are interposed between them, and yet there always remains a point "at which I and not-I are in immediate contact" (SK, 137). "We may view the matter from still another angle.—Insofar as the I is restricted by the not-I, it is finite; in itself, however, as posited through its own infinite activity, it is infinite. These two, its infinity and its finitude, are to be reconciled. But such a unification is intrinsically impossible" (ibid.).

"[T]he contradiction [*between light and darkness*—S. B.] is soluble in no other way than this: light and darkness are not opposed in principle, but differ only in degree. Darkness is simply a very minute amount of light.—That is precisely how things stand between the I and the not-I" (SK, 138).

---

5 Fichte, "Concerning Human Dignity," in *Early Philosophical Writings*, trans. and ed. Daniel Breazale (Ithaca, NY: Cornell University Press, 1988), 83–86, 86.
6 Ibid., 85.

Excursus on Fichte

In exploring further "syntheses" of the **I** and the Not-I, of their "independent activity" (a verbose and obscure formulation), Fichte again returns to the question of the point of immediate contiguity between the I and the Not-I. "[I]nsofar as the I is not to posit something in itself, it is itself not-I. Yet since it must, after all, exist, it must posit: and since it is not to posit in the I, it must do so in the not-I" (SK, 161). "That the not-I *does not* posit something in the I, or negates it, means that, for the I, the not-I does not posit at all, but merely annuls; to that extent, therefore, it is *qualitatively* opposed to the I, and is the *real ground* of a determination of the latter. — But that the I does not posit something in the I does not mean that the I does not posit at all; it certainly posits, in that it does not posit something, or posits it as negation; what the proposition means, rather, is that the I does not posit only *in part*. Hence the I is not *qualitatively* opposed to itself, but only *quantitatively*; it is thus merely the *ideal ground* of a determination in itself.... What is now merely posited *idealiter* [ideally] in the not-I must become *realiter* [really] the ground of a passivity in the self; the ideal ground must become a real one..." (SK, 161). The question "[h]ow... the real ground is to become an ideal one... presupposes" for its solution "the direct encounter of I and not-I" and is answered "by means of our synthesis" [*sic!* — S. B.], which means the following: "[i]*n the concept of efficacy... ideal and real ground are one and the same*" (SK, 161–62). Then follows an explanation: "[i]n things-in-themselves there must be something independent of our presentation, whereby they intrude upon one another without intervention on our part; but that *we* relate them together must have its ground in ourselves, for instance, in sensation. So then we also posit our I outside us, who are *doing the positing*, as a *I-in-itself*, as a thing existing without our co-operation, and who knows how; and now, without any co-operation from us, some other thing is supposed to act upon it, as the magnet does on a piece of iron" (SK, 162). (It goes without saying that this obscure and contradictory idea about the positing of an "I in itself" in the form of a thing is an inadmissible yet indispensable item of contraband for *Ich-Philosophie*.) "But the I is nothing outside the I, for it is simply the I. Now if the nature of the I consists simply and solely in the fact that it posits itself, then for it *self-positing* and *existence* are one and the same. Real and ideal ground are here at one. — Conversely, *non-self-positing* and *nonexistence* are equally one, for the I..." (SK, 163).

"[T]hat there has to be a not-I for the I, can only mean that the I has to posit reality in the not-I; for there is and can be no other reality for the I, save one that is posited thereby" (ibid.) "That the activity of the I and not-I are one and the same, means that the I can only *not* posit something in itself by positing it in the not-I; ... Posit in general it must, so long as it is an I; but it need not posit in *itself*. — Passivity of the I, and of the not-I are also one and the same. That the I posits something not in itself, means that the same is posited in the not-I. Activity and passivity of the not-I are one and the same. Insofar as the not-I is to operate on the I, to annul something therein, the same is posited in the not-I by the I.... Hence the question, what is the ground of passivity in the I? is in general without an answer, and is least of all to be answered by presupposing an activity of the not-I, as a thing-in-itself; for there is no mere passivity in the I" (SK, 163–64). This question cannot be solved by a theoretical science of knowledge, but only by a practical one. Fichte opposes his system of "critical idealism" to one of "dogmatic idealism" and realism, since "neither does the mere activity of the I provide the ground of the reality of the not-I, nor the mere activity of the not-I provide the ground of passivity in the I" (SK, 164).

Thus arises the opposition between subject and object, between the *I* and the Not-*I*, while in the *I* there arises a representation of the reality of the Not-*I*. Although the Not-*I* is not in fact the real basis of the suffering posited in the I—otherwise it would be a thing in itself—it must nevertheless be represented as such. This "wonderful power... without which nothing at all in the human mind is capable of explanation" (SK, 188) is *produktive Einbildungskraft* [productive imagination]. Of this it is said that "all reality—*for us* being understood, as it cannot otherwise be understood in a system of transcendental philosophy—is brought forth solely by the imagination" (SK, 202). Self-consciousness, too, is brought into being by means of this self-hypnosis. So what is referred to here is a certain activity of the *I* which extends beyond the limits of consciousness and comes before all consciousness, since consciousness is grounded in it. K. Fischer correctly identifies this remark as referring to a *bewusstlose Produktion* [unconscious production] as the basis of consciousness.[7] The

---

7 Kuno Fischer (1824–1907), a German neo-Kantian philosopher and historian of philosophy. — *Trans.*

question which inevitably arises is this: how is it possible to ascertain this *pre*-conscious function of the *I*? With what (epistemological) justification does Fichte himself speak of it? Does not the same question which arises with respect to Hegel's philosophy also necessarily arise in relation to Fichte's: *how is Fichteanism possible* as absolute philosophy? How can the *I*-subject ascend above its fatal coincidence with the Not-*I*, and cognize every act in the Not-*I* as an *I*? How can it observe itself from one side, or look at the world with the eyes of a creator even *before* his creation? There is no answer. Fichte himself refers to Salomon Maimon, who had called this a *deception* by the imagination.[8] And all Fichte can put forward to defend himself from this illusion is the suggestion that "to every deception a truth must be opposed, and there must be a means of escaping it" (ibid.). There cannot be a deception here, "unless we are to abstract from the I; which is a contradiction, since it is impossible that what does the abstracting should abstract from itself. Hence the act is not a deception, but gives us truth, and the only possible truth. To suppose that it deceived us would be to institute a skepticism that told us to doubt our own existence" (ibid.).

The reference to the naturalness or inevitability of illusion, however, is a psychological argument rather than an epistemological one. And as soon as the power of imagination which produces the illusion of reality is revealed, there also inevitably appears either a skepticism or a Berkeleianism.

Fichte himself makes the following remark: "[f]or the deity, that is for a consciousness in which everything would be posited by the mere fact of the I having been posited (though for us the concept of such a consciousness is unthinkable) our Science of Knowledge would have no content, since in such a consciousness there could be no other positing whatever, save that of the I; but even for God [*sic!*—S.B.] the science would have formal correctness, since its form is the form of pure reason itself" (SK, 224).

The **I** which represents, the theoretical **I**, is an *intelligence* and "is by no means one and the same with the absolute, unconditionally self-posited I" (SK, 219). "[W]e could in no way think of presentation in general as

---

8 Salomon Maimon (1753–1800), a Lithuanian-Jewish philosopher who published in 1790 an *Essay on the Transcendental Philosophy* containing significant objections to Kant. — *Trans.*

possible, save on the assumption of a check occurring to the infinitely and indeterminately outreaching activity of the I. Thus, as *intelligence in general*, the self is *dependent* on an undetermined and so far quite indeterminable not-I; and only through and by means of such a not-I does it come to be an intelligence. But the I, in all its determinations, must be absolutely posited by itself, and must therefore be wholly independent of any possible not-I. Hence the absolute self and the intelligent self... are not one and the same, but are opposed to each other; which contradicts the absolute identity of the self" (SK, 220).

A contradiction arises in the I between the I as absolute and unlimited and the I as intelligence, which is linked to the object. The contradiction is solved in the *practical* science of knowledge by the I's simultaneously combining (in different relations, and therefore non-contradictorily) an absolute I without limit and an intelligent I. In overcoming the Not-*I*, the limit of the **I**, the I at the same time pushes on beyond this limit, and this infinite striving, the ideal I, expresses the infinite nature of the I; reflection on this limit or object produces the theoretical or intelligent I. "The absolute I must therefore be *cause* of the not-I, insofar as the latter is the ultimate ground of all presentation" (SK, 221). "Insofar as the self is absolute, *it is infinite and unbounded*. Everything that exists it posits; and what it does not posit, does not exist... But everything it posits is posited as I; and the I posits it as everything that it posits. *From this point of view, therefore, the I includes everything*, that is, an infinite, unbounded reality" (SK, 225).

"[T]he pure self-reverting activity of the I is a *striving*; and... an *infinite striving* at that. This boundless striving, carried to infinity, is the *condition of the possibility of any object whatsoever*: no striving, no object" (SK, 231). The **I**, unconditionally positing itself, finds no distinction of any kind within itself, and such a distinction can be introduced only by a Not-I; the possibility of this "alien influence," however, must be grounded in the I itself, since "[i]f it lay *outside the I*, it would be nothing for the I" (SK, 240). "The I posits itself absolutely, and is thereby complete in itself and closed to any impression from without. But if it is to be an I, it must also posit itself as self-posited; and by this new positing, relative to an original positing, it opens itself, if I may so put it, to external influence; simply by this reiteration of positing, it concedes the possibility that there might also be something within it that is not actually posited

Excursus on Fichte

by itself. Both types of positing are conditions for an operation of the not-I; without the first, there would be no activity of the I to undergo limitation; without the second, this activity would not be limited for the I, and the latter would be unable to posit itself as limited. Thus the self, as such, is initially in a state of reciprocity with itself, and only so does an external influence upon it become possible. By this, too, we have at last discovered the point of union we were seeking between the absolute, the practical and the intellectual characters of the self. — *The self demands that it encompass all reality and exhaust the finite.* This demand of necessity rests on the idea of the absolutely posited, infinite self; and this is the *absolute* self, of which we have been talking. Here the meaning of the principle, *the self posits itself absolutely*, first becomes wholly clear. There is no reference at all therein to the self given in actual consciousness; for the latter is never absolute, its state being invariably based, either mediately or immediately, upon something outside the self. We are speaking, rather, of an *idea* of the self which must necessarily underlie its infinite practical demand, though it is inaccessible to our consciousness, and so can never appear immediately therein (though it may, of course, mediately, in philosophical reflection)" (SK, 243–44). "It is equally implicit in the concept of the I, that it must reflect about itself, whether it really includes all reality within itself. It bases this reflection on the foregoing idea, and thus carries the latter out to infinity, and is to that extent *practical*: not absolute, since it actually goes forth from itself, through the tendency to reflection; and yet not theoretical either, since its reflection rests on nothing save this idea deriving from the I as such, and is wholly oblivious of the possibility of a check, so that no real reflection is present. — Hence arises the series of those things that *ought* to be, and are given through the self alone; in short, the series of the *ideal*. If reflection addresses itself to this check, and the self thus regards its outgoing as restricted, we obtain thereby a quite different series, that of the *real*, which is determined by something other than the mere self. — And to that extent the self is *theoretical*, or an *intelligence*."

Fichte posits a distinction between the *absolute being* of the **I** and its *actual existence*, which arises only in the process of the Not-I (278; there is an interesting note on stoicism on the same page).

"[T]*he principle of life and consciousness, the ground of its possibility* — *is admittedly contained in the I; but this gives rise to no genuine life, no empirical existence in time; and any other kind, for us, is absolutely unthinkable. If such a genuine life is to be possible, we need for the purpose another and special sort of check to the I on the part of a not-I. . . . [T]he ultimate ground of all reality for the I is an original interaction between the self and some other thing outside it, of which nothing more can be said, save that it must be utterly opposed to the I. In the course of this interaction, nothing is brought into the I, nothing alien is imported; everything that develops therein, even out to infinity, develops solely from itself, in accordance with its own laws; the self is merely set in motion by this opponent, in order that it may act; without such an external prime mover it would never have acted, and since its existence consists solely in acting, it would never have existed either. But this mover has no other attribute than that of being a mover, an opposing force, and is in fact only felt to be such. Thus, in respect of its existence the self is dependent; but in the determinations of this its existence it is absolutely independent* [italics mine—S.B.]. *In virtue of its absolute being, it contains a law of these determinations, valid to infinity, and an intermediary power of determining its empirical existence according to this law. The point at which we find ourselves, when we first set this intermediary power of freedom in play, is not dependent on us; considered in its full extension, the series that from this point on we shall traverse to all eternity, is wholly dependent on ourselves. The Science of Knowledge is therefore* realistic. *It shows that the consciousness of finite creatures is utterly inexplicable, save on the presumption of a force operating independently of them, and wholly opposed to them, on which they are dependent in respect of their empirical existence. Nor does it assert anything beyond this opposing force, which the finite being feels, merely, but does not apprehend. All possible determinations of this force, or not-I, which may emerge to infinity in our consciousness, the Science of Knowledge undertakes to derive from the determinant power of the self . . ."* [italics mine—S.B.] (SK, 246).

"In respect of their ideality, all things depend upon the I; but in regard to its reality, the I is also dependent; yet nothing is real for the I, unless it is also ideal" (SK, 247). The science of knowledge, for this reason, is defined as a critical idealism, or a real-idealism (ibid.).

"[T]here is something *in us* that can be fully accounted for only by something *outside us*. We know that we think it, and think it according to the laws of our mind; and hence that we can never escape from ourselves,

Excursus on Fichte

never speak of the existence of an object without a subject" (SK, 252).

* * *

Precisely in its treatment of its central concept, that of the I, the *Science of Knowledge* suffers from a lack of clarity (as is made quite clear in the study by Il'in which has already been quoted). The Fichtean subject, or I, is, in the first place, that which truly exists [*sushchee*] to which, as absolute efficacity, all reality belongs, yet to which consciousness does not (there is a curious proximity between Fichte's *Ich-Philosophie* and the philosophy of unconscious spirit in Hartmann and Drews); secondly, the Fichtean subject is a pure absolute striving, an idea, a requirement, a bad infinity of the practical I; and, thirdly, it is an intelligence which arises in the absolute I by means of the Not-I and which explains the empirical subject, the real hero of the *Science of Knowledge*. The correlation of these subjects produces a whole series of obscurities and problems, but we will set these aside, since here we are not concerned with an immanent self-examination and self-critique of Fichteanism so much as with its fundamental themes and its religio-philosophical meaning. (Fichteanism's man-god-like character is shown to a certain extent by Il'in, who draws attention to the anthropological side of the question, but not in any real depth.)

II

CRITIQUE OF FICHTE'S THEORY

1. ICH-PHILOSOPHIE

Fichte's early system (the 1794 *Science of Knowledge*) represents an attempt, unique in the history of philosophy, at a radical *Ich-Philosophie*; and it is in this sense a philosophical experiment of cardinal importance and significance. In its scope and aim it is closest of all to the Spinozism to which it finds itself in polar opposition: the Spinozistic philosophy of the absolute object, *substantia sive Deus* [substance or God] and the Fichtean philosophy of the absolute subject, *substantia sive Ego* [substance or I] are absolute opposites, and yet at the same time are also identical as resolute implementations of the principles of identity or monism, the elimination either of the subject for the sake of the object, or, conversely, of the object for the sake of the subject, in a doctrine either of pure anhypostaticity or of pure hypostaticity, of pure objecthood or of pure objectlessness.

The depth, strength, and positive significance of Fichteanism lies in the fact that in it, uniquely, the problem of hypostaticity is put in first place, and an attempt is made to understand all being and the whole world through and in the light of this principle. Moreover, although the *Science of Knowledge* is misshapen by the burden of its deductions (see first of all the deduction of the empirical *I*), what is shown here with complete clarity and in full force is the *absolute* nature of the I-I, an absoluteness which is expressed in its positing itself as existing, and whose starting-point, instead of being taken from naive contemplation, is an efficacious act — the *Thathandlung* [active deed] of self-positing, in which the I-I comes into being at once really and ideally. This I-I, as atemporal and unconditional, exceeds all definition; it bears upon itself the stamp of the divine tetragrammaton of Yahweh, *I am that I am*, the Absolute Hypostaticity which God reveals Himself to be in the Old Testament. Fichte's theory is a theology of the Old Testament *I am that I am*, Yahweh. Fichte's philosophical discovery, which, however, had already been established in religion at least as early as the Old Testament, is that thought inevitably begins with the *I* and that the *I* not only cannot in any way be thought away from thought, but that it inevitably thinks *everything in the light of* the *I*, which is always and everywhere thought along with everything which it thinks. In this sense, everything is in the *I* and for the *I*, and must be expressed in terms of the *I*, understood in the illumination which the I sheds upon it. To this extent Fichte's thought about the inevitable correlation between the *I* and the *Not-I*, about the correlatedness of the object and the subject in the I, about the I-ness of the world, is indisputably correct.

Indeed, if this I-ness is rejected, how is it possible to comprehend subjectivity? What remains once the *I* has been liquidated is to plunge being into the unconscious with the flickering glimmers of Spinoza's modes.

The hypostasis is a primordial givenness, *from* which it is necessary to proceed and to which it is necessary to return: it is both the center and any given point on the circumference, because consciousness (in principle) penetrates everywhere, and, consequently, all things become determinations of consciousness, are emanations of the *I*, whilst, at the same time, everything enters into consciousness.

At the same time Fichte quite correctly notices that because consciousness has broken out in the *I*, because the *I* has emerged into being, or, as Fichte puts it, has become *something*, or has received actual existence, a *Not-I*, a "stimulus," an object of contemplation is needed for the theoretical *I*, for the intelligence; a limit is needed which can be overcome by the striving of the practical *I*. That Fichte so insistently contrasts his own philosophy, as "transcendental," with the doctrine of a transcendent thing in itself, is not only the result of a Kantian contagion, but is also the entirely justified thought that *I* and *world*, subject and predicate, are inwardly connected with each other, are identical in their own development, and are correlated in their own attributes and in the ways in which they can be expressed.

2. THE NOT-I AND NATURE

Hypostaticity is the primary and inalienable form of all being, the subject of every predicate, the universal propositional *subject* as such. Yet it does not exist, it is unthinkable, without a predicate, in which it is revealed. And this predicate is the *nature* of the spirit and the nature of the world. The **I**, the sole noumenality, is disclosed in phenomenality — not in a bad, Kantian sense (in which the phenomenon is an illusion or a condition) — but in the genuine sense of self-disclosure and self-revelation. If the hypostasis is called substance, then this substance will, with Fichte, be the accident produced by the hypostasis; if, conversely, substance is taken for the inexhaustible depth of being, then the *I* will, as Spinoza held, appear as merely phenomenal, or as a *modus*, in relation to it. In reality it is neither one nor the other, or rather both one and the other: *substance is hypostatic being* — and this essential relationship, as an inseparable and inconfusible archetype, *cannot*, therefore, be subject to *any sort of deduction* or be given any kind of explanation. It is necessary and possible only to become aware of it and to confirm it. And then problems about the deduction of the **I** *from* the Not-I, or from nature, or of nature *from the* **I**, problems of the kind with which the philosophy of false monism and imaginary identity is preoccupied, fall away of themselves, because such problems are impossible and unnecessary. Yet the usual path of such a philosophy runs from the Not-I to the **I**, and *only in Fichte* is this path the other way round: from the **I** to the Not-I. This path cannot be followed, and therefore necessitates diversions, but it is instructive as an experiment.

The **I** stands in need of the Not-I, according to Fichte, not as it might stand in need of its own nature, the possibility of its own life, or self-consciousness, or self-realization, but above all as a *mirror*, in which it can be reflected or "reflect itself," and can see and know itself, because otherwise, as we already know, the absolute, self-sufficient **I** remains on the threshold of actual existence or being. The absolute **I** does not exist, is not, for only the relative *I* which stands in relation to the *Not-I* is—although this only as the countenance of the absolute **I**. How does this catastrophe, the emergence of the (relative) *I* and the *Not-I*—which Fichte himself defines as a "reduction to a lower concept," to "the concept of divisibility," or as a degradation of the **I**, how does this happen?

Nothing, of course, can be opposed to the **I**, nor limit it, since to it and to it alone belongs all reality (see above). How does there spring up, in the depths of the essential, absolute **I** which is higher than being [*sverkhbitijnoe*], the existing **I** which is linked to the Not-I? How does that which truly exists give rise to existence, how does that which is higher than being give rise to being? It would seem to be impossible to deduce this catastrophic act, in which the causal and logical series is severed, and in which, in place of a continuity, there arises a discontinuity; yet Fichte deduces it, and is forced to deduce it, as a consequence of his *Ich-Philosophie*. For this reason, nature—both the nature of spirit and the nature of the world—is given only the most meagre definition in his work: *Not-I*. It is necessary to say at once that this "*Not-I*" is ambiguous and has a number of different meanings, and doubly so: it is not only ambiguous and polysemous in consequence of the many meanings of *not*, but also in consequence of the specific character of this combination, Not-I. Yet Fichte himself does not notice this plurality of meanings, and never devotes a single word to settling the meaning, even though, nevertheless, "Not-I," like *I*, plays with various shades of meaning. What can Not-I signify? In the first place, if the **I** is everything, and if there is nothing, only "outer darkness," without the **I**, the first meaning of the *Not-I* is an absolute metaphysical *void*. And the question arises: can the **I** so far extinguish itself as to obtain a Not-I in a precise sense, an ἀ *privativum*? Such an extinction could be thought of only as absolute death, but death, like time, is transcendent to the **I**. The **I** is *without* and *above* time, but for this reason it does not know death, any more than, in fact, it knows life. The absolute **I** is Divinity itself. It is clear

Excursus on Fichte

that to qualify the Absolute with an ἀ *privativum* is absurd nonsense. Fichte himself does not explore this possibility, although he should have begun with it: is it possible to limit or to negate the Absolute? If the **I** is Absolute, can a *Not-I* be possible, be conceivable, or be deduced? In religious terms, this means: if there is a God, God is everything; is the idea of *not-God* then possible or conceivable? In a certain sense *not-God* is nothing—οὐκ ὄν—"outer darkness," or that which *absolutely is not*. Then being, even in the combination "not-being" (which is always as such only a form) will already be presupposed as unthinkable in the bare form *not*, as the completely contentless other of thought, as an *after-image* of thought. At best this will be an "infinite judgement" in logic: not-table, not-elephant, not-apple, and so on, an infinite series of *nots* which can never be brought to a close, a negative *shadow* of being, which thought torments itself with trying to cut off and make into something on its own account, like the shadow in Andersen's tale.[9] In a second, positive sense, *not-God* signifies *world*, but then *not* already receives a different meaning, not an ἀ *privativum*, but a μή: that is, *not yet* God, or a world becoming God, becoming, that is, in some sense God—who will one day also be all in all.[10] It is impossible to understand the *Not-I* as an unconditional negation and *elimination* of the **I** as such; in this Fichte is quite right. The **I**, as a hypostasis, is *absolute*, is everything (although in a different and more precise and correct sense than in Fichte), but the *Not*-**I** is completely transcendent to thought and to consciousness. It can be said that the *Not*-**I** is also in this sense both unthinkable and non-existent: there is only the **I**, and not the *Not*-**I**. (Parmenides was therefore right, not in relation to being and becoming, but in relation to the **I** as subject: there is no predicate and no thought without a subject, and to think the *Not-I* is really to attempt to manage without a subject, to manage without oneself, which is impossible.) Thus the admission of a *Not-I*, the introduction of a *Not-I* as a category of thought in *this* sense is either nonsense or it is a concealed abandonment of the principle of

---

9 In Hans Christian Andersen's story, "The Shadow," a man's shadow separates itself from him, usurps his social position, and arranges for him to be put to death. "The Shadow," in *Andersen's Fairy Tales* (London and Glasgow: Collins, 1954), 267–80.

10 Bulgakov alludes to 1 Corinthians 15:28: "And when all things shall be subdued unto him, then shall the Son also himself be subject unto him that puts all things under him, that God may be all in all."—*Trans.*

the *Ich-Philosophie*, an abandonment which should also be disclosed and admitted to. I repeat that Fichte does not take account of this impossibility of comprehending the NOT-I, although he ought to have taken account of it right at the start.

There is a second meaning of the *Not-I*: οὐκ ἔγω [not-I] can have the purely logical significance of the *opposition* of one content of thought to another, of a negative judgement, which has an affirmative meaning only when it relates to something positive and which is negative only in its form. The negative judgement is in this sense inseparable from a positive judgement and has a positive judgement as its basis; it exists only within the fabric of thought, within thought's dialectic (as an "antithesis"). Yet the **I** does not permit of any dialectic with itself, nor of any negation nor diminution: it is obstinate and can neither be prevailed upon nor diminished. And this is understandable, because the **I** is never a predicate, but only a subject, and a relation, including a relation of negation, can exist only in a predicate. Fichte fabricated the tautology **I** is **I**, or **I** equals **I**, and used it to turn *I* from a subject into a predicate; or, more precisely, he held up a mirror and so merely duplicated an image.

In this sense, the *Not-I* is also an impossible and contentless thought, and this becomes clear if, as *subject*, we replace I with *Not-I*, on an equal footing with I: *Not-I* speak, *Not-I* think, and so on.

There remains a *third*, and, in practical terms, the most important meaning of *Not-I*, in the sense of μή. Μή signifies a direct and affirmative relation; it is not a negation, but an affirmation. The Not-I is merely a mode of the **I**; it is the **I**'s *meon*. It can be the *I* which is coming into being, which is emerging within nature and from out of nature, and then we have various forms of naturalism and evolutionism, from the materialists to Schelling; it can be "the being-other of spirit," spirit's loss of consciousness, as in Hegel. The obscurity of Fichte's thought—and, in a certain way, its cunning—consists in his taking the *Not-I* primarily in this sense, with a view to loading all sorts of contraband, i.e., nature, into the *Ich-Philosophie* under the flag of μή, whilst grounding or "deducing" the *Not-I* by pure reflection out of the *I*. The *Not-I*, in Fichte, turns out, on the one hand, to be the unconscious creation of the *I*, to be an act which the *I* does not remember, but which it can only infer, by comprehending everything which is outside the *I* as being in fact the *I*'s own result, as being within the *I*; in this way there is revealed in the *I*, on a

Excursus on Fichte

lower level, the inexhaustible wealth realized in the "astonishing powers" of the *produktive Einbildungskraft* [productive imagination]. On the other hand, however, the *Not-I* is posited within the *I* as a limit, as a stimulus, as its necessary mirror. Finally, Fichte comes to the *I in itself*, which is at the same time everything which is outside us. Here a universal "positing" is at Fichte's service: the *I* begins by "positing" itself, and it can do this because the essence of the *I* consists in self-consciousness or self-positing, and, as Fichte, interpreting Descartes's thought correctly, rightly shows, positing and being are identical in the *I*.

But the realm of positing is limited to this self-asserting I-ness, whilst later Fichte makes the *I* "posit" the *not-I*, whereas in the genuine *not-I*, that is, in its own nature, the predicate, the *I*, does not "posit," but *is*, lives, unfolds for itself, rather than positing itself. As a consequence of this "positing" of the *not-I* in the *I* there appears one of the features which disfigures his whole system, and which inevitably creates a rupture in it, at the same time as it constitutes one of its inalienable characteristics: the *quantitative* specification of the relation between the *I* and the *not-I*. Having opposed the *I* and the *not-I*, Fichte then had to put them together, to combine them. As a consequence of the poverty of the fundamental principles of the system, that is, of the solitary *I*, Fichte was forced to interpret the *not-I* not as *nature for the I*, but as a *minus sign* in the *I*, a *not-I*, and only the **I** remained as an absolute quantity. The **I** is not yet personhood. The personal principle in its plenitude is an *I* which realizes itself in nature. A bare *I* is not yet a person: personhood is expressed in a subject and a predicate and in their being for one another. This is not what happens in Fichte: on his account the **I** is person, absolute, and world at once, and everything, for this reason, is expressed in terms of the *I*, in terms of the quantities of *I*. How does an *Ich-Philosophie* arrive at this outlandish idea of a quantity of *I*? Yet this is what none the less had to be resorted to in the end, in order to satisfy the pedantic frenzy of the unyielding system on just this point, and the *not-I* turned out to be *a quantity of I*. But in order that it should be possible to measure this quantity, a surface area is needed in which the absolute **I** should appear; within it, as within a larger circle, there should be two reciprocally varying smaller circles, the *I* and the *not-I*. But then what is this larger **I**? Is it an absolute **I** which is nevertheless present in every further *I*, or a Divinity—as Fichte more than once declares? But how many such absolutes are there? How many such gods are there, and how is their unity to be combined with their plurality? (Cf. Il'in, *op. cit.*) In any case, it ought to be established as a fact that this new *I*, which, strictly speaking, is also the only real *I* known to us, has nothing in common with the absolute **I** in which both the *I* and the *not-I* originate. Here there is a sheer *transcens*, a logical leap or miracle, beyond the comprehension of the all-seeing absolute "system." Fichte's philosophy breaks its promises: having started out from the *I*, it encroaches beyond its limits, because it presupposes an **I** which is not an *I*, presupposes an unconscious or supra-conscious Absolute **I**, about which he, Fichte, narrates and postulates, and so on, without any (epistemological) warrant, being himself only a little *I*, and knowing only this little *I*. In German every I is written with a capital letter, and this conceals the ambiguity with whose help the empirical *I* is substituted for the unique absolute **I**.[11] At the very center of Fichte's system there is a hiatus, and the system ceases, in reality, to be an *Ich-Philosophie*. The fundamental conception of the project founders, and all the further lucubrations concerning the *I* and the *not-I* which then follow lack interest.

Finally, the *third* meaning of the *Not-I*, upon which Fichte does not dwell at all—and here lies the main defect of his system—is not a *not-I* posited by the *I* at all, but another *I*, a *thou*. Fichte's **I**, like a Leibnizian monad, is windowless; it is impenetrably locked. True, Fichte speaks with pathos of the dignity of each human individual as one who can say, of himself or herself, *I am*; but this flight of eloquence from the speech "Concerning Human Dignity" lacks any support in Fichte's philosophical work, and this thought nowhere receives serious discussion in the *Science of Knowledge*.[12] Above all, Fichte's *I* has no means of comprehending the *thou*. For the absolute **I**, which also constitutes the only source of reality, **I** as substance in the *singular*, permits only the positing of a *not-I* and the positing of an *I*, whilst the positing of a *we*—that is, the

---

11   This sentence is omitted from Kresling's German translation. The German noun, *das Ich*, meaning "the I" or "the self," is written beginning with a capital letter, but the pronoun "ich," meaning "I," can begin with a lower case letter. — *Trans.*

12   See, for example, the following passage. "This is man. This is everyone who can say to himself, 'I am a man.' Should he not stand in sacred awe of himself? Should he not tremble and quake before his own majesty? This is everyone who can say to me 'I am.'" Fichte, "Concerning Human Dignity," in Breazale, ed., *Early Philosophical Writings*, 83–86; at 85. — *Trans.*

positing of another *I* which is, at the same time, its own *not-I*—remains impossible and self-contradictory. The *Ich-Philosophie* founders, in fact, on the problem of the *thou*. Although it is necessary to Fichte's practical philosophy, and especially to his philosophy of law, that the **I** should be multi-hypostatic, there is no place for any such multi-hypostaticity in the *Science of Knowledge*. The singular THOU as *I* and *not-I* necessitates a different way out from the *I* than its merely being posited in the *not-I*, because the *thou* is as much *positing* as *posited* in the other *I*. The *thou* makes no appearance in the natureless *Ich-Philosophie*, for which the world is merely a *not-I* or a *Schranke* [limit], is material upon which the *I*, the "practical *I*," can exercise its infinite striving.

This particular case illustrates a general deficiency of the *Ich-Philosophie*, which possesses, apart from the *I*, only one determination, and that purely negative: the *not-I*. In the latter all cats are, as the saying goes, grey, and, above all, there is no distinction between *nature* as a universal predicate and the other *I*, that is, the *thou*. Both have an identical significance: both are a *Schranke* [limit] or *Anstoss* [push, impetus] in relation to the *I*, an awakening of I-ness within the *I*, a release from its loss of consciousness. The categories are deduced from the *I*, "sensation" and the "push" are deduced from the *I*, every possibility of the not-*I* as such is derived from the *I*, but, it goes without saying, without any *specificity* which might possess a breath of life. Not even the most insignificant bedbug, nor a withered blade of grass, can be deduced from the *not-I*. Nor is this all. Although Fichte more than once mentions the Deity in passing, characterizing him as an absolute **I** without any *not-I* (and for this reason not in need of a science of knowledge, which exists only for the relative *I*), these references are always only logical illustrations of the arguments of the *Science of Knowledge*, nothing more. It is left completely open how the Deity is to be understood, and how the Deity can reveal himself in the **I** without the **I**'s knowing anything at all apart from itself, except itself in the *not-I*. Even the Deity, if indeed he is intelligible, is, here, also only a *not-I* (or, in an early argument from the time of the *Atheismusstreit* [the atheism controversy] a moral guarantee, an ethical order—but in the *Science of Knowledge*, the Deity is not even that).[13]

---

13   Fichte was accused of atheism in 1798 and was forced to surrender his post in Jena as a result. See Dan Breazale, "Fichte," in the *Stanford Encyclopedia of Philosophy*, at https://plato.stanford.edu/entries/johann-fichte/ (accessed 22. x. 2019).—*Trans.*

In sum, Fichte's *I* proves, against his own intention, to be a Stirnerian *Einzige* [individual], and the *not-I* this individual's *Eigentum* [property]; the *I* exists only in the singular number and has no second nor third person pronoun. Neither *thou, he, we,* nor *you plural* can fit into its inflexible and obstinate self-assertion. This is disguised, psychologically, by the fact that Fichte talks of human nature, and appears to be thinking anthropologically. This, however, is without foundation, and for this reason is only a caprice, extraneous to the system's underlying character, whilst the essence of the system is expressed in the Luciferian, closed, atheistical, acosmist, inhuman, overweening *I*, which reflects its own self, which pursues itself (in the *theoretical I*) and is pursued by itself (in the *practical I*). The science of knowledge is by no means the anthropology for which it might be taken as a result of some of the expressions it uses; it is not only a theory of knowledge, but also a theology and an ontology. The border between the **I** as an absolute subject, which creates all reality by its own activity, and which spins out of itself the world as the mirage of the not-I created out of nothing, and, on the other hand, as the human, individual *I* is completely elusive, since each human *I* writes itself as an absolute *I*, with a capital letter, according to the usage of Fichte's native tongue.[14] In theological terms, the boundary between the image and the Archetype, between the created and the Creator, is here so far effaced that the human being appears in his own consciousness to be the equal of God—a purely Luciferian self-consciousness. For this reason the difference between God and his image and likeness is interpreted in a characteristic fashion (Fichte himself does not touch on this question directly, but in essence he is also talking about this): this is the relationship between the absolute **I** and the *I* which is linked to the *not-I*: the empirical *I* chases and is chased by the specter of the absolute **I**, like a serpent biting its own tail, lacking all eternal rest. This indefatigable striving of the *I* beyond the *I* and towards the **I** is the practical *I* as eternal task, as idea, as obligation. Considered from various points of view, therefore, Fichte's system is a *self-deification*, in so far as it is a *deification of man* caught between Feuerbach and Stirner, caught, that is, between the universal apotheosis of the human species in the former,

---

14   See p. 212, n. 4 above. Kresling again omits the last part of this sentence, with its claim about capitalization in German. — *Trans.*

and that of the human individual in the latter. Fichte boarded up all the windows and left no exit of any kind from the I. How can one speak of humanity without speaking of the nature proper to this humanity? How can one speak of the Deity when every path to heaven has been blocked? It goes without saying that Fichte does not even mention revealed Christianity and the dogma of the Trinity. There is no room at all in Fichte's doctrine for the Christian teaching of the Holy Trinity, which combines a triad of hypostases with a unity of their nature, for in Fichte there is no nature at all but only a *not-I*, and no place for a triad of hypostases, for there is only the *I*.

Fichte's doctrine is the philosophical negation of tri-hypostaticity, and to this extent it must be defined as a unitarianism, a mono-hypostaticity, an idealist Islam. "There is no God but the I-God, and I, Fichte, am its prophet." Any discussion of either human beings or nature in the *Science of Knowledge* is of course so completely absent that here there can arise neither the question of the problem of human history nor that of the redemption of the human race, neither the question of God's incarnation nor that of His becoming-human (and would it not, in any case, be nonsensical to speak of the incarnation of the *I* in the *not-I*?). If one were to seek a theological diagnosis for Fichte's erroneous doctrine, his unitarianism would seem to be a variant of Sabellianism, in the sense that he recognizes only the *first* hypostasis as an absolute I, which, by virtue of its "positings" or self-definitions, establishes the *not-I* as a mirror of the *I*, but also to a certain extent as its self-revelation, and which, moreover, also co-ordinates the theoretical *I* and the practical *I* as a continual striving, the fire of life. Everything is in the *I*, by the *I*, through the *I*. As was shown above, this is a philosophy of the *I am that I am*, a philosophical Yahwism (and for this reason Fichte's impoverished "Johannine Christianity" is a complete misunderstanding).[15] The absence of nature and of humanity from Fichte's system is combined, moreover, with a Luciferian man-god in whom is deified the philosophical and propositional *subject*, the *I*, in contrast to the Feuerbachian man-god of the deified *predicate*, human nature (the latter is at least less impious than the former). The sum total of Fichte's earlier *Science of Knowledge*

---

15 Bulgakov may here be playing on the proximity between the Russian for "I"—*Ia*—and that for Yahwism, *Iagvizm*.—*Trans.*

is a radical, if to a certain extent deranged, attempt to invest all substantiality in the *I*, and to make manifest the uttermost possibilities of the *I*. The chief significance of this manifestation of the *I* consists in Fichte's attempt to "walk on his head" and to observe the world from this position. In this manifestation of the *I* also consists the *truth* of Fichte's system as a philosophy of pure—although also, unfortunately abstract—hypostaticity. It is impossible to escape Fichte or for philosophy to forget him, because he added something genuinely new to the history of philosophy. Hegel's thought is also a doctrine of monohypostaticity; it is also, however, considered as a whole system, a complicated delusion, because it takes the second hypostasis for the first, confusing the *order* of the hypostases. Fichte's thought, by contrast, can be retained, but only in combination with its negation, with a naturalism, whether in a Spinozistic or in some other form. *Fichte plus Spinoza*—this is the task. Just as true as the thought that all nature is in a certain sense a *not-I*, that all nature exists or is posited within the *I*, is the thought that the *I* exists *in nature*. Fichte, it need not be said, was unable to keep up his own "transcendentalism" to the end, however highly he prized it, and even with his fear of the *Ding an sich* he postulated the most fundamental acts of the *I*, and, in particular, the positing of the *not-I*, as unconscious. He admitted, that is, a *transcendence* within the *I*, turning the *I* into a *Ding an sich* for itself; the absolute **I**, in which originate the *I* and the *not-I*, proved to be transcendent to the *I* of consciousness. Fichte did not want to permit a nature which would exist in itself, a *Ding an sich*, but absorbed it into the *I*. What resulted was a distortion: the **I**, the true noumenon, the *Ding an sich*, which is at once transcendent, in its own essence, and immanent, in its own self-disclosure, in its nature, was to find its character in hypostaticity alone, instead of expressing it in the fullness of substance, that is, in a real connection to the **I**'s predicate, the world.

3. FICHTE AND HEGEL

The two thinkers suggest themselves for comparison and contrast. For Fichte *Ich = Alles*, just as *Alles = Ich*; for Hegel the same role is played by pure thinking, νόησις νοήσεως [*noēsis noēseōs*]. Fichte "deduces" from the **I** not only the forms of thought, the categories, but also the forms of being, time and space; in Hegel, by contrast, the **I** itself is deduced from the categories, or, more precisely, the **I** exists only as a fleeting moment of the dialectic of the concept. Thus the path which leads from the **I** to thinking and back leads in opposite directions in each thinker. It should be noted that in Hegel thinking and the forms of thought are necessarily linked to the *not-I*, since without the *not-I* neither consciousness nor difference can arise within the *I*, so that the *I* itself, strictly speaking, is seen from the perspective of the *not-I*. It is both an epistemological peculiarity and also a weakness of Fichte's system that it cannot give an account of its own origin. More than once Fichte himself admits that any observer who could describe what goes on inside the *I* would themselves remain outside it, but this is just what the *Science of Knowledge* is: it tells of mysteries of the spirit at which the human being himself was never in attendance, of unconscious or preconscious acts in the *I* which are, nevertheless, not merely postulated or imagined, but even described. The author of the *Science of Knowledge*, that is, of the "pragmatic history of spirit," must himself be an external, transcendent observer to whom all mysteries are known; in other words, he lays claim to the omniscience of God, to whom every creature is revealed.[16]

For this reason — and for this reason alone — Fichte's system claims to be an absolute philosophy, without being at the same time a philosophy of revelation. He tells a story of the **I** before the creation of the world — that is, before the *not-I*. We saw that similar features also characterize Hegel's philosophy, which also imagines itself an absolute system and lays claim to a godlike reason. Fichte's system, issuing from the *pre*-logical or *meta*-logical **I**, nevertheless remains completely within logic, is a rationalistic philosophy; Hegel's system, issuing from absolute anhypostaticity, endeavors to squeeze hypostaticity into itself by making the idea into a subject, an **I**. In *this* sense, and only in this sense, both absolute systems are forms of the philosophy of identity, which is characterized just by its suspension of the radical and primordial distinction between hypostasis and essence, person and nature, subject and predicate,

---

16 "We are not the legislators of the human mind, but rather its historians. We are not, of course, journalists, but rather writers of pragmatic history." J.G. Fichte, "Concerning the Concept of the *Wissenschaftslehre*," in Breazale, ed., *Early Philosophical Writings*, 94–135; 131. Breazale, 131n., quotes Kant's *Foundations of the Metaphysics of Morals*: "A history is pragmatically composed when it teaches prudence, i.e., instructs the world better than, or at least as well as, has been done in the past." — *Trans.*

and which sees these as modes of a universal substantial potentiality which is neither one nor the other, but which "posits" both as it needs to, for itself and in itself. In this sense, both Fichte's and Hegel's work belong to a single uninterrupted series of ancient and modern philosophical systems, a series of Christian heresies, in so far as they claim for their own rationalism, for their own monism, the power to bring everything together with a single rational connecting principle which is free from antinomies and which lies at the basis of all being. Whilst every philosophy, and every religion, includes a moment of the identity or of the unity of all things, each at the same time remains dual or plural by virtue of the elements from which it begins: not an identity, but a monodualism, a monopluralism, a trihypostaticity. And the most fundamental, most primary concept, that of *substance*, is in the philosophy of identity deployed in a knowingly incorrect and simplified monistic fashion which already condemns the system to falsify and violate reality. Substance is a *living proposition* consisting of a subject, a predicate, and a copula.

INDEX OF AUTHORS NAMED

Ambrose, 143
Andersen, Hans Christian, 227 n.9
Andronikov, Constantin, xl n.14, 7 n.4
Aquinas, Thomas, xxviii
Archimedes, 125
Aristotle, xxii, l, 80–81, 101, 149 n.13, 176, 188
Athanasius, lxi, 91 n.1, 145
Augustine of Hippo, xxxi–xxxii, 91 n.1, 140 n.3
Avenarius, Richard, 110

Balthasar, Hans Urs von, xlii n.19
Barnes, Jonathan, 176 n.9
Barth, Karl, xxviii
Basil the Great, 130 n.1, 145 n.9
Benjamin, Walter, lvi
Bennett, Jonathan, 78 n.55, 80 nn.61–62
Bergson, Henri, xxx, lv, 119n., 129
Berillus, 23 n.1
Berkeley, George, Bishop of Cloyne, xvi, 26–27
Baader, Franz von, 83, 99
Bauer, Bruno, 201
Böhme, Jakob, x, xx, 68, 70, 83, 99
Bolotov, V. V., 145 n.9
Bolzano, Bernard, xxii n.10
Breazale, Daniel, 216 n.5, 231 n.13, 235, n.16
Buber, Martin, lvi
Bulgakov, Mikhail, x

Caird, Edward, 59, 183, 191
Calvin, John, 117
Caygill, Howard, lvi
Coda, Piero, xlii n.19
Cohen, Hermann, 41–42, 53, 102, 125, 180
Collier, Arthur, 26
Comte, Auguste, 113, 177, 201, 203

Cottingham, John, 28 n.7
Cusanus, Nicholas, 70
Cyril of Alexandria, 145 n.9

Darwin, Charles, and Darwinism, 113
Dawkins, Richard, xxxvii
Democritus, 70
Denzinger, Heinrich, xliv n.20
Descartes, René, xiv–xvi, xxi, xxxi–xxxii, 20, 28–29, 31, 34, 112, 125, 210, 229
Destivelle, Hyacinthe, xxxvi n.4
Diels, Hermann, 25 n. 3, 69 n.43
Dionysius the Areopagite, xxvi, 140
Dmitry of Rostov, 91 n.1
Dostoyevsky, Fyodor, xli
Drews, C. H. A., 201, 223

Eckhart, Meister, x–xi, 68, 70
Empedocles, 66
Eriugena, John Scotus, xi
Evtuhov, Catherine, xxxvi n.4, xxxix n.13, xl

Fastiggi, Robert, xliv n.20
Feuerbach, Ludwig, 113, 124, 201, 232
Fichte, J. G., ix, xi–xxv, xxviii–xxix, xxxiii, xli, l–li, lv–lvi, lviii, 16, 30, 36–39, 42, 44–51, 53, 57 n.27, 59, 62–63, 81–82, 86 n.67, 98–99, 109, 112, 118, 124–25, 133
Fischer, Kuno, 79 n.57, 201 n.33, 218 n.7
Florensky, Pavel, xl–xli
Florovsky, Georges, xlviii n.27
Franks, Paul W., xviii n.6
Frege, Gottlob, xxii n.10, xxxiii

Gallaher, Brandon, 155 n.16, xlii n.18
Gavrilyuk, Paul, xlii n.18, xlviii n.27
Gerber, Gustav, xlv

237

Goethe, J.W. von, 25 n.4, 62 n.33, 87
Gregory Nazianzen, 91 n.1, 92 n.2, 137 n.2, 141, 147
Gregory of Nyssa, xxvii, 91 n.1, 145 n.9
Grier, Philip T., 180 n.14
Gulyga, A.G., 86 n.67

Haeckel, Ernst, 73, 203
Haldane, E.S.B., 73 n.49
Hallensleben, Barbara, xlii nn.18–19
Hamann, J.G., xi, xxii, xxvii, xxxiii
Harnack, Adolf von, lii
Hart, David Bentley, xlii n.19
Hartmann, Eduard von, 77, 201, 223
Hartmann, Nicolai, 53
Hatfield, Gary, 39 n.16
Heath, Peter, 207 n.1, 208 n.2
Hegel, G.W.F., ix, xi–xii, xvii, xix–xxii, xxv, xli, xliv, l, liii–lvi, lviii, lxi, 4–7, 15, 20–21, 28 n.8, 30, 36, 39, 47, 51–64, 81–82, 85, 101–102, 106, 112, 119, 126–29, 138, 167–68, 171–205, 228, 234–35
Heidegger, Martin, xvii, lv–lvi
Hemmerle, Klaus, xlii n.19
Heraclitus, 5, 66, 69–70, 119, 129, 192
Herder, J.G., xi, xxii, xxxiii
Hoping, Helmut, xliv n.20
Humboldt, Wilhelm von, xi, xxii
Hume, David, 29
Hünemann, Peter, xliv n.20
Husserl, Edmund, xvi, xviii, lv–lvi

Iamblichus, xxvi
Il'in, Ivan A., 180 n.14, 204–5, 212–13, 229
Irenaeus, lxi

Jacobi, F.H., xi, xviii–xxi
Jakim, Boris, xl n.14, xlix n.30, li n.34, lvii
James, William, xxxviii
John Damascene, 137 n.2, 140 n.3, 145 n.9

Kant, Immanuel, ix, xiii–xviii, xx–xxii, xxxi–xxxiii, xli, l, liii, lv–lvi, lviii, 5–6, 8, 10–12, 15, 27, 29–42, 45, 48–50, 82, 94, 102–21, 138, 159–70, 178–79, 188, 210, 225, 235 n.16
Kemp Smith, Norman, 6 n.3, 165 n.3
Khoruzhij, Sergij, xl n.14, lvii, 86 n.67, 145 n.9, 153 n.14
Kierkegaard, Søren, xxxi
Kirk, G.S., 19 n.11, 67 n.35, 68 n.38, 69 n.43
Kisner, Mathew J., 71 n.48
Klingemann, E.F.A., 86 n.67
Kranz, Walther, 25 n.3, 69 n.43
Kresling, Alexander, xl, lvii, 183 n.19, 230 n.11, 232 n.14
Kripke, Saul, xxiv
Kuklota, Irina, 155 n.15

Lacan, Jacques, xxiii
Lachs, John, 207 n.1, 208 n.2
Larkin, Peter, xlviii
Leibniz, G.W., 77–82, 112, 150, 211
Leucippus, 70
Lossky, N.O., 29 n.9, 160 n.1
Louth, Andrew, xlii n.18
Luther, Martin, x

MacIntyre, Alasdair, xxi
Maimon, Salomon, 211, 219
Makarius of Moscow, Metropolitan, 91 n.1, 142 nn.7-8, 145 n.9
Malevanskij, Silvestr, 145 n.9
Martin, Jennifer Newsome, xlii n.19
Marx, Karl, and Marxism, xxxvi, 60, 152, 199, 201, 203
Maximus the Confessor, xxvi, 145 n.9
Milbank, John, xliii nn.18–19, xlviii, lv n.38

Index of Authors Named

Miller, A. V., 15 n.9, 61 n.32, 106 n.5, 198 n.27
Miller, Michael, xl n.15
Moore, G. E., xxxii
Moshenska, Joe, xxxv n.2
Murdoch, Dugald, 28 n.7

Nash, Anne Englund, xliv n.20
Newton, Sir Isaac, xiv
Natorp, Paul, 53
Nichols, Aidan, xlii n.18
Nietzsche, Friedrich, 51, 113
Noetus, 23 n.1
Novalis, xi, xxiii, xxv

O'Regan, Cyril, xlii n.19
Owen, Robert, 152

Pabst, Adrian, xlii n.18
Parmenides, 19, 66–71, 107, 119, 128, 178, 185, 192, 227
Paton, H. J., 39 n.15
S. Paul the Apostle, 64, 117–18
Paul of Samosata, 23 n.1
Plato, xxvii, xxviii, l, lii, 5, 40, 52–53, 66, 70, 78, 178, 179 n.13, 194, 196
Plotinus, xxvi, 46, 121
Potebnya, Alexander, xlv
Praxeas, 23 n.1
Pythagoras, 66, 149

Rasputin, xxvi
Raven, J. E., 19 n.11, 35 n.35, 68 n.38, 69 n.43
Remnant, Peter, 80 n.61
Renouvier, Charles Bernard, 119
Ricoeur, Paul, xxi
Rickert, Heinrich, 42, 125
Rose, Gillian, xix
Rosenkranz, Karl, 181 n.17

Rosenzweig, Franz, lvi
Rosmini, Antonio, *Teosofia*, xxviii

Sabellius, 23 n.1
Schelling, F. W. J., ix, xi–xii, xvii, xix–xxi, xxv, lv–lvi, 44 n.23, 47, 81–88, 99, 186, 197, 228
Schlegel, Friedrich, xi, xxiii, xxv
Schneider, Christopher, xlii n.18
Schofield, M., 19 n.11, 67 n.35, 68 n.38, 69 n.43
Schopenhauer, Artur, 4, 24, 42–45, 60, 77, 81, 95, 117
Schuppe, Wilhelm, 41
Silverthorne, Michael, 71 n.48
Simson, Frances H., 73 n.49
Slesinski, Robert, xlii n.19
Smith, S. A., xxxv n.1
Smith, Thomas Allan, xlviii, 188 n.21
Socrates, xxxi, lii n.36, 66
Solovyov, Vladimir, xxxviii, xli, liv, 3 n.1, 59 n.30, 203
Spencer, Herbert, 203
Spinoza, Baruch, xvi, xviii, lvi, 46, 71–78, 80–82, 107, 119, 121, 201, 203, 210–11, 214–15, 223–24
Stoothoff, Robert, 28 n.7
Struve, P. B., 155 n.15
Swift, Jonathan, xi, liv, 20 n12
Stirner, Max, 110, 231–32
Syutaev, Vasilij Kirillovich, 100

Tannery, Paul, 68 n.37
Tarski, Alfred, xxii n.10
Tertullian, 91 n.1
Thales of Miletus, 69 n.47
Tolz, Vera, lvii
Trubetskoj, S. N., 59 n.30, 68 n.37, 155 n.16
Turner, Nicholas, xliv n.20
Tyutchev, Fyodor, 112

Vallière, Paul, xlii n.18

Wagner, Richard, x
Walker, Nicholas, lvii
Wallace, William, 28 n.8, 195 n.26
Walsh, Marcus, 20 n.12
Whitehead, A. N., xxxii
Whitton, Mike, xl n.15

Williams, Rowan, xlii n.19, xlix
Windelband, Wilhelm, 42
Wittgenstein, Ludwig, xxxiii

Zeno of Elea, 178
Zernikav, Adam, 145 n.9
Zwahlen, Regula, xlii n.18

www.ingramcontent.com/pod-product-compliance
Lightning Source LLC
Chambersburg PA
CBHW020325170426
43200CB00006B/272